DATE DUE

MY 2 2 08		

DEMCO 38-296

Men and Women Adrift

Men and Women Adrift

The YMCA and the YWCA
in the City

EDITED BY

Nina Mjagkij and Margaret Spratt

New York University Press

NEW YORK AND LONDON

NEW YORK UNIVERSITY PRESS
New York and London

© 1997 by New York University
All rights reserved

Library of Congress Cataloging-in-Publication Data
Men and women adrift: the YMCA and the YMCA in the city /
    edited by Nina Mjagkij and Margaret Spratt.
    p. cm.
Includes bibliographical references and index.
ISBN 0-8147-5541-0 (clothbound: alk. paper).—ISBN 0-8147-5542-
    9 (paperbound: alk. paper)
    1. YMCA of the USA—History. 2. Young Women's Christian
    Association of the U.S.A.—History. 3. Young Men's Christian
    associations—United States—History. 4. Young Men's Christian
    associations—Membership. 5. Young Women's Christian associa-
    tions—United States—History. I. Mjagkij, Nina, 1961- . II.
    Spratt, Margaret, 1955- .
BV1040.M46 1997
267'.3973—dc21   97-4666
                    CIP

New York University Press books are printed on acid-free paper,
and their binding materials are chosen for strength and durability.

Manufactured in the United States of America

10 9 8 7 6 5 4 3 2 1

Contents

Illustrations

Contributors

Michelle Busby is a doctoral candidate in the history department of the University of Florida.

Jessica Elfenbein is an assistant professor of history and Public History Program Coordinator at the University of Baltimore.

Sarah Heath is a doctoral candidate in the history department of the University of Cincinnati. She teaches at Northern Kentucky University and at the University of Cincinnati's University College.

Adrienne Lash Jones is Associate Professor and former Chair of the Department of African American Studies at Oberlin College. She is the author of *Jane Edna Hunter: A Case Study of Black Leadership, 1910–1950* and several articles on African American women's history. She is currently writing the history of African American women in the YWCA.

Paula Lupkin is a visiting assistant professor of art at Denison University.

Nina Mjagkij is Associate Professor of History at Ball State University and author of *Light in the Darkness: African Americans and the YMCA, 1852–1946.*

Raymond A. Mohl is Professor and Chair of the department of history at the University of Alabama at Birmingham. His most recent books are *Urban Policy in Twentieth-Century America*, coedited with Arnold R. Hirsch, and *The New African American Urban History*, coedited with Kenneth W. Goings. He is currently working on a history of racial and ethnic relations in Miami, Florida.

Elizabeth Norris has held a number of positions with the YWCA over the years, including archivist and librarian, and is currently the historian of the organization. Most recently, she spearheaded the effort to create a photographic exhibition chronicling the first 135 years of the YWCA of the U.S.A.

Clifford Putney teaches history at Emerson and Bentley colleges and is the library coordinator for the Boston Theological Institute.

Nancy Robertson is completing her dissertation, "Deeper Even Than Race?: White Women and the Politics of Christian Sisterhood in the YWCA, 1906–1949," at New York University. In addition to teaching at New York University and Hofstra University, she has worked as an archivist and researcher.

Margaret Spratt is Associate Professor of History at California University of Pennsylvania and Research Associate Professor at the University of Pittsburgh.

Thomas Winter is an adjunct assistant professor of history at the University of Cincinnati.

John D. Wrathall received his Ph.D. in American history from the University of Minnesota. He is the author of *Take the Young Stranger by the Hand: Male Homoeroticism and the YMCA in America*.

Preface

Joanne Meyerowitz

In the late nineteenth century, a host of local YWCAs and YMCAs opened their doors to young Protestant women and men alone in the cities. With missionary zeal, YWCA and YMCA leaders worked to protect their charges from the perceived temptations of dance halls, cheap theaters, brothels, and saloons. In the late twentieth century, hundreds of local YWCAs and YMCAs maintain physical fitness facilities in suburbs as well as cities. The evangelical religious fervor has all but disappeared, and the overriding concern with morality has gradually succumbed to an emphasis on social service and health. Along the way, local branches have provided training grounds for generations of social reformers, classrooms for workers and immigrants, laboratories for experiments in interracial cooperation, and social spaces for friendship and homoerotic encounter. Through more than a century of growth, the YWCA and the YMCA seem to disprove those sociological theories in which ossified institutions, burdened by bureaucracy, lose the resilience to respond to social and cultural change.

In fact, the YWCA and the YMCA stand with only a handful of American reform organizations that originated in the nineteenth century and continue to flourish as the twentieth century draws to a close. The topography of this history reveals the benchmarks of recent social trends. The secularization of the YWCA and the YMCA provides a window into the decline of religious influence in mainstream civic culture. The professionalization of their staffs parallels the rise of social work and the fall of voluntarism in American society. The corporate sponsorship of their programs reflects the cultural clout of big business, and the changing location of some local branches mirrors the demographic shift from city to suburb.

Most striking, the shifting concerns with gender, class, and race illuminate the central social conflicts of modern American life. In this volume, Nina Mjagkij and Margaret Spratt have skillfully edited essays that highlight these social relations. In the late nineteenth century, YWCA and YMCA officials promoted bourgeois versions of womanhood and manhood. Maternal supervision and manly character would shield young migrants from the predations of city life. Adhering to a doctrine of "separate spheres," they trained their leaders separately and housed their residents in sex-segregated homes. The YWCA, in particular, used its separate institutions to protect unmarried women from the perceived sexual dangers of unchaperoned mingling with men. But their educational and recreational programs competed in an increasingly heterosexual and homophobic culture. YWCA leaders soon invited men to join in certain supervised activities, while YMCA leaders worried that sex segregation promoted homosexual cruising. At the end of the twentieth century, the YWCA and the YMCA continue as separate organizations, but women and men participate jointly in many of their programs.

At the turn of the century, as immigrants streamed to American cities, the native-born middle-class leaders of both the YWCA and the YMCA displayed heightened interest in educating the foreign-born and spreading their programs to workers. The class conflict they hoped to ameliorate emerged again within the local branches themselves. Workers, both women and men, spoke their minds when they detected condescending attempts at social control or unabashed support for the labor policies of their employers. And they pushed the organizations to change: From attendance at English classes to participation in sports to demands to evict strikebreakers, they shaped YWCA and YMCA programs to reflect their own needs for education, leisure, and solidarity.

In a racially segregated social world, middle-class African Americans carved out a niche for separate (but not equal) programs and used their YWCA and YMCA branches to train their own leaders and help their own kind. In both organizations, a policy of racial segregation gave way to one of integration, with continuing struggles for racial equity in programs, facilities, and representation. Ironically, the principled move on the national level to discard segregation led on the local level to the dismantling of African American community centers.

Taken together, the essays in this volume invite readers to compare and contrast the YWCA and the YMCA. The striking parallels in the histories are undeniable, but the hints of difference are equally intriguing. Through its sustained efforts to train women for positions of leadership, the YWCA challenged patriarchal prerogatives in ways the YMCA did not. With its own separate institutions, the YWCA had the resources to push for gender equity on a variety of fronts. YWCA leaders worked, for example, for women's suffrage, higher pay for women workers, women's education, and an end to domestic violence. Their commitment to improving conditions for women gave the YWCA a reformist agenda that the YMCA sometimes lacked.

This reformist mindset, it seems, informed other YWCA programs as well. YWCA leaders, imbued with the spirit of progressive reform, took the more activist role on issues of class, ethnicity, and race. The YWCA supported labor unions more directly than did the YMCA, which more frequently backed its industrial sponsors. In its International Institutes, the YWCA pioneered in the kind of multicultural education that celebrates ethnic diversity, and through concerted efforts at interracial cooperation, African American women in the YWCA played a vanguard role in fighting for racial justice.

Throughout the essays, the authors remind us that institutional change moves slowly through detours and dead ends. By twists and turns, readers will travel down some of the less well known byroads of YWCA and YMCA history. They will learn, for example, that the YWCA sponsored missions in China, a home in Hollywood for aspiring actresses, and programs for Japanese Americans incarcerated during World War II. And that the YMCA established a News Boys' home for male orphans, billiard parlors for railroad workers, and a Family Communications Skills Center. The sheer variety of programs suggests, once again, that these national federations stood then, and still stand today, at the forefront of American social service.

Preface: Towards a Future History of the YMCA

Clyde Griffen

This collection views the YMCA as an urban institution which provided a supportive environment and services for a constituency which changed over time, as did the purposes of the institution itself. The essays suggest how much the YMCA was reshaped by the very expansion of its services and by the effort to satisfy simultaneously the interests of donors and of clients. They move us closer to an integration of social and institutional history, adding to the strong foundation laid by C. Howard Hopkins' 1950 *History of the Y.M.C.A. in North America*. Perhaps the essays' greatest contribution is to encourage further investigation of the interaction between donors, YMCA board members, professionals, other employees, YMCA members, and non-member users of YMCA dormitories and athletic and other facilities. The collection suggests, more broadly, the usefulness of this focus on interaction in studying the institutional evolution of other large charitable and philanthropic organizations.

Some essays already begin to show how local associations dealt with the aims of different groups which conflicted with official YMCA aims. Sometimes secretaries responded with reluctant but overt accommodation, as they did to the railroad workers' push for billiards for recreation, and sometimes they turned a blind eye to activities which they officially abhorred, such as homosexual cruising in Association dormitories. Through oral history, Wrathall's essay shows how fragmented behavior could become at different levels of the employee hierarchies of huge inner-city Association residences like Manhattan's Sloane House. Gay desk clerks could make homosexual encounters

easier by room assignments, while secretaries denied to their boards
that sexual activity was a problem at the YMCA. The ironic result until
the late 1960s was a "Christian" haven, safe from police harassment,
for gay men and for others experimenting with sexual identity or "let-
ting off steam."

The increase in scale which facilitated this institutional fragmentation
owed much—as Elfenbein's case study of the Baltimore branch indicates—to the YMCA's successful quest during the late nineteenth century
for a legitimacy independent of support from the evangelical churches.
After a varied religious and humanitarian journey which at times reached
out to women and children, too, the YMCA chose to focus on bringing
young men to Jesus, improving their character, and increasing social
order. Its nondenominational character and lay leadership became widely
admired as a model of Protestant outreach that was more inclusive than
the churches. Not surprisingly, increasing membership reinforced YMCA
leaders' sense of occupying a moral high ground within the world of
Protestant evangelism and service.

As Lupkin's essay emphasizes, the YMCA model proved so appealing
to corporate leaders and other businessmen that by the 1890s they
became active campaigners for YMCA buildings as expressions of civic
virtue and moral outreach. The institutional momentum generated after
the 1880s by the resulting new dormitories and athletic facilities in turn
favored resort to professional leadership for local Associations, making
the national network of YMCAs a world unto itself. By the mid-1880s
two training colleges had been launched, by 1924 national certification
had been mandated for YMCA secretaries, and by the mid-1930s the secretaries had come to think of themselves as professionals.

But the businessmen who dominated the boards of local associations
as well as the national YMCA expected, and for many years largely
received, secretarial support for their notions of political economy. In the
special case of YMCAs created for railroad workers, railroad companies
saw them as a way of "producing more loyal servants of the corporation." Correspondingly, conflict between the interests of employers on
Association boards and employees using their facilities and services
posed difficult choices for secretaries. As Winter's essay indicates, they
occasionally supported striking railroad workers in defiance of employers or else found striking clients challenging company control of the
YMCAs. Secretaries of nonrailroad YMCA branches did not face so
obvious a conflict of interest, but they still had to try to satisfy both their
boards and donors and their members and users.

Charting YMCA branches' relaxation of moralistic regulations and abandonment of missionary activities also illustrates how users of YMCA facilities helped reshape the institution. Winter notes that one railroad branch quit religious work as early as 1899 and that in 1913 religious "interviews" at another branch produced no converts, while 1,600 workers played pool during that year. A probable part of the explanation which Winter does not address is the fact that Roman Catholics—who could become nonvoting associate members after the 1870s—were more numerous by the 1890s in railroad branches than members of any other church. Future investigators need to ask how much changes in YMCA policies and activities owed to this large nonvoting constituency and to the changing situation of professional staff. For example, did income-producing activities like rental of the dormitories make YMCAs less dependent on their boards and donors and more receptive to residents' interests and desires, including Roman Catholics uninterested in Protestant evangelism?

Equally important for future research is investigation of shifts in the YMCA's membership and clientele since the 1920s, when a few Roman Catholics became leaders in local Associations and a growing number of Associations reported participation of women in clubs, physical work, informal opportunities, and some joint programs with YWCAs. Some of the essays on the YWCA in this collection note specific forms of cooperation with YMCAs early in the twentieth century, such as YWCA women taking courses at the YMCA Commercial School in Cincinnati. But the essays on the YMCA do not show how women participated or when. Nor do they indicate whether the YMCA's perspective on ethnic pluralism and on labor relations changed as early as the YWCAs did—through the work of its International Institutes and Industrial Department during the 1920s.

By 1937 women comprised 6 percent of the total membership of the YMCA, and by 1951 Roman Catholics and Jews comprised two-fifths of the total. How does this shift in membership contribute to the new era in relations between the YMCA and the churches in the 1950s, to the burst of reform in the 1960s, and to the increasing secularization thereafter which Putney's essay describes? And how does the changing mix in users of YMCA facilities and services affect the attitudes of professional staff and board members, especially after the early 1930s, when the national organization abandoned any doctrinal identification? For example, did the probable dwindling of rural and small-town Protestant newcomers among inner-city dormitory and gymnasium users discourage moral as well as religious outreach programs? Did the huge influx of GIs during World War II contribute to a perception of YMCAs as conveniences, to be used for what clients desired regardless of official YMCA aims? This kind of investigation should help in interpreting the YMCA's increasingly secular approach in the late twentieth century to providing athletic and other services for local residents.

Both the YMCA and the YWCA maintained segregated branches for apparently largely middle-class African American members until the mid-1940s; both organizations soon found their inner-city branches resegregated with lower-income blacks as white members moved to suburbia. The response of African American YWCA members to the newcomers seems to have varied, some reaching out, some not. Whether the middle-class black men who had found the old segregated YMCA branches a useful haven—where they could build their self-esteem while simultaneously pursuing a conservative masculine ideal toward an assimilationist goal—reached out in turn to the new inner-city influx of poor Southern blacks is yet to be determined since Mjagkij ends her essay on "racial advancement" through the YMCA in 1930. Putney's essay suggests that the presumably largely white staffs of inner-city YMCAs responded with campaigns for social justice, but only temporarily.

The 1960s, as Putney says, confronted the old WASP and business-dominated YMCA boards with a whole new phalanx of difficult social issues. The new religious, racial, and gender mix in membership within YMCA branches now predominantly familial and suburban in orientation furthered a shift in emphasis long underway toward the athletic and other services the YMCAs provided. But we will not know whether the result has been a relatively uniform and complete secularization of this formerly evangelical Protestant institution until we have case studies of local Associations in various settings during the late twentieth century. The local diversity Hopkins shows before 1950 suggests that future research may find after 1950 important echoes of the social gospel in some YMCA branches and of the more distant evangelical past in others.

Clyde Griffen
Professor Emeritus of History
Vassar College

Men and Women Adrift

Introduction

Nina Mjagkij and Margaret Spratt

Since the mid-nineteenth century, the Young Men's Christian Association (YMCA) and the Young Women's Christian Association (YWCA) have provided America's urban population with a variety of services and programs. Initially the associations, although motivated by religious concerns, differed little from the numerous voluntary and mutual aid societies that surfaced in American cities during the last century. Yet, unlike many other short-lived urban associations, the YMCA and the YWCA withstood the test of time and continue to flourish more than a century after their emergence. The YMCA and the YWCA established a physical presence in large and small cities by constructing buildings used for lodging, education, and recreation, and today both organizations continue to cater to millions of Americans regardless of race, age, class, or religious affiliation. However, despite their popularity, scholars have neglected to write a comprehensive history of either association.[1] The essays in this volume document the influential role the YMCA and the YWCA came to play in America's cities. They trace the emergence and growth of both organizations, the expansion of services and programs, the role of the organizations in the emerging profession of social work, and the interaction between the associations' leadership and membership. More important, the essays explore how both associations helped to shape the gender, class, racial, ethnic, and religious identities of America's urban communities.

The YWCA and the YMCA emerged in the mid-nineteenth century in response to a massive population shift that brought large numbers of native-born rural white migrants and immigrants from Europe to American cities. The resulting population increase affected not only the cities' physical environment and spatial dimensions but also their social structure. Members of the emerging Protestant middle class were concerned about the moral welfare of the growing number of city-bound single young men and women, as well as their potentially disruptive impact on the urban landscape. In the eyes of these middle-class reformers, cities were corrupt and bound to ruin the pure and innocent youth from America's unspoiled countryside. They feared that the men and women adrift in the cities were particularly vulnerable to urban temptations because they lacked the moral support and proper supervision of their families. Yet, members of the urban middle class were not only distressed by the prospect of the migrants' fall from grace. They also feared that the moral debasement of these men and women would corrupt other segments of the urban population. Determined to safeguard the souls of the migrants and to preserve the established urban order, Protestant middle-class reformers launched the YWCA and the YMCA as agents of Christian morality and traditional values.

Although separate organizations with distinct structures, funding, and leadership, the YMCA and the YWCA shared similar objectives during the early years. Afraid that disreputable boarding houses and immoral landlords, as well as taverns, dance halls, and other places of vile entertainment, would destroy the moral fiber of the migrants, YMCA and YWCA advocates tried to create alternative living and leisure spaces designed to promote wholesome activities and respectable behavior. YMCA and YWCA leaders envisioned the associations as homes away from home, providing young men and women with a structured refuge from the demoralizing forces of urban life. However, while many YMCA and YWCA leaders regarded the associations as a means of molding the cities' newcomers in their own middle-class image, the young migrants were not acquiescent subjects. They may have embraced some of the ideals fostered by the YMCA and YWCA leadership, but for them the associations also provided spaces in the urban landscape that allowed them to explore and define their own identities. In the process, the young men and women adrift in the cities shaped the associations to suit their own needs.

The YMCA was the first of the two associations to take root in the United States. Founded in London on June 6, 1844, by George Williams and a group of young merchants, the association was initially little more than a prayer group that offered Christian fellowship to single young men who came to the city during the Industrial Revolution. Yet, the association movement grew quickly among the merchant class, which was concerned about safeguarding young respectable men from the perils of urban vice and debauchery. By 1851 sixteen cities in Great Britain had formed associations, and four years later YMCA delegates from other countries gathered in Paris to establish an international alliance. By 1905 the YMCA recorded 5,000 associations in twenty-four countries.

Americans first became acquainted with the YMCA during the 1851 World's Fair in London. Several American men who had attended the fair visited the city's YMCA and on their return to the United States organized associations in Boston and New York City in 1852. Other American and Canadian cities quickly followed suit, and in 1854 delegates from thirty-two associations in Canada and the United States gathered to establish the Confederation of North American YMCAs. The Confederation, a loose alliance of autonomous associations, was mainly responsible for organizing annual conventions which served as public forums for the YMCA during the 1850s. In the years prior to the Civil War, the association movement spread rapidly across the United States, flourishing particularly in the cities of the North.

Throughout the 1850s, the YMCA's tremendous popularity in the United States was directly linked to the nation's increasing urbanization. Members of the Protestant middle class feared that the churches were not equipped to cope with the problem of single young men flocking to the cities and embraced the YMCA in an attempt to help the migrants adapt to urban life. Yet, while the laymen who launched the YMCA movement believed that the churches were largely failing to protect the young men from the demoralizing forces of the city, they initially solicited the support of the clergy.

As Jessica Elfenbein's case study of the Baltimore YMCA shows, association leaders sought the endorsement and support of Protestant churches in an attempt to establish the YMCA's credibility and legitimacy. Working through the churches not only gave the nascent YMCA an air of respectability but also provided it with access to a network of socially responsible men. Many ministers welcomed and supported the YMCA as long as the association's services and programs did not conflict or compete with the work of the churches. YMCA leaders were aware that their organization was still in its infancy and tried to avoid alienating potential supporters among the clergy. They repeatedly assured ministers that the association had no denominational ties and was dedicated to the moral and spiritual salvation of those men who remained outside the influence of the city's Protestant churches. Despite this assurance many ministers remained skeptical of the YMCA, fearing the association as a competitor for souls and financial contributors. Clergymen became particularly wary of the association when its leaders aggressively recruited an ever-growing number of young men, who found the Christian fellowship of the YMCA more appealing than the work of the churches. Despite its ambiguous relationship with the Protestant churches, however, the association movement successfully took root in America's cities and more than 200 YMCAs were operating in the United States by the end of the 1850s.

The outbreak of the Civil War put a temporary halt to the further expansion of the youthful association movement. Less than a decade old when hostilities erupted, the YMCA had been plagued by sectional tensions since its inception. Throughout the 1850s, the debate over slavery had divided the membership of associations in the North and the South. YMCA leaders tried to avoid the politicization of their organization and agreed to ban any political discussions; however, sectional allegiances persisted. When the Civil War started, members of the association affiliated with the Union or the Confederacy and the first Confederation of North American YMCAs disintegrated. The war reduced the membership and number of American associations as many men left the cities to join the armies of the North and the South. By the end of the war, sixty American associations were still in operation; of these, only two were located in the South.

While the Civil War took a heavy toll on the YMCA, the wartime experience also strengthened the association and established its legitimacy. During the war, many associations discontinued their regular services for single men in the cities and instead followed their constituents to the battlefields. In November 1861, northern YMCAs organized the U.S. Christian Commission to provide for the religious and humanitarian needs of soldiers and sailors, and numerous associations formed army committees to assist the commission. The relief work of the U.S. Christian Commission helped garner much public support for the YMCA, allowing the association to evolve into an independent force that no longer required the endorsement of the Protestant churches. Although the YMCA adopted an "Evangelical Test" in 1869, stipulating that active association members had to be members of a Protestant congregation, the YMCA ceased to portray itself as an auxiliary of the churches.

Following the Civil War, the YMCA not only became an institution independent of the churches but also began to occupy an important place in the spatial structure of America's urban landscape. The YMCA increasingly embraced secular programs, launching recreational, social, educational, and athletic activities in an attempt to compete with the cities' commercial leisure-time facilities. Broadening its appeal, the YMCA attracted not only an ever-increasing number of migrants but also the support of the urban commercial elite. Prominent businessmen assumed leadership positions in the YMCA and transformed the association from a loose alliance into a more centralized organization "that resembled the corporations they owned or dominated."[2] The cities' commercial elites not only helped to create the YMCA's institutional structure but also extended their financial support to assist associations in the acquisition of permanent homes. Prior to the war, when the YMCA was still in its infancy and ill-funded, most associations operated out of rented rooms. However, this situation changed when members of the mercantile class started to take an interest in the work of the YMCA in the years following the Civil War.

Paula Lupkin demonstrates that the cities' commercial elites often financed the construction of YMCA buildings in an attempt to regulate the business practices of the mercantile community. Traditionally, they had relied on the apprenticeship system to initiate new generations of men into the community of merchants. However, during the late nineteenth century this system, which allowed for the close personal supervision and discipline of an apprentice, was replaced by the complex and often impersonal structure of the corporation. The older generation of urban merchants concerned about ensuring the survival of their values in this new corporate age turned to the YMCA. The association represented an ideal partner because it fostered proper business ethics through the promotion of Protestant virtues such as thrift, honesty, temperance, industriousness, and benevolence. With the financial assistance of urban merchants, the YMCA created a network of "manhood factories" designed to socialize young men new to the cities.

With the construction of buildings, the YMCA moved beyond its original purpose of providing young single men with wholesome religious fellowship aimed at spiritual and moral salvation. Attempting to lure men away from commercial leisure-time facilities, association leaders utilized the buildings to expand their services. YMCAs started to house libraries, gymnasiums, bowling alleys, swimming pools, classrooms and reading rooms, employment bureaus, cafeterias, and dormitories. Soon the buildings' social, educational, athletic, and recreational functions started to overshadow the YMCA's religious work. Moreover, conducting the growing number of programs and operating the association buildings became a time-consuming task that increasingly overwhelmed those who had organized association work during their spare time. The new programs and buildings required the attention of full-time personnel and resulted in the professionalization of YMCA work. Local associations started to hire "secretaries" to manage the buildings, administer funds, and supervise the programs. The acquisition of buildings and the introduction of the professional YMCA secretary transformed the association from a religious organization to a semipublic civic institution with the distinct secular mission of promoting middle-class values.

Like the YMCA, the YWCA emerged in England in the mid-nineteenth century. In 1855 a group of middle-class Christian women founded a Prayer Union to provide charity to less fortunate women, and by 1859 it was known as the Young Women's Christian Association. The association movement found a receptive audience among middle-class Christian women in America, partially because of the religious revival sweeping through the eastern portion of the country during 1857 and 1858. This revival helped to legitimize nondenominational Christianity and encouraged the impulse to "save" those in moral danger. For urban women, involvement in religious outreach activities provided an opportunity to expand the boundaries of their domestic sphere. As the historian Anne Firor Scott has observed, women could "grapple with social and political issues that could have seemed alarmingly radical in a secular political setting." Thus, when Mrs. Marshall Roberts formed the Union Prayer Circle in New York City in 1858, she did not challenge Victorian notions of separate gender spheres. The group of thirty-five members, which changed its name to the Ladies' Christian Union in 1866, pledged to "labor for the temporal, moral, and religious welfare of young women who are dependent on their own exertions for support." Within a few years, the group reorganized as the Young Ladies' Christian Association and rented and equipped rooms in a warehouse in midtown Manhattan for recreational use by working women. Thus, the YWCA of New York City was born.[3]

Another American city also lays claim to the first YWCA. In 1866, a group of middle- and upper-class women in Boston organized the first association to use the name "Young Women's Christian Association." They sought to protect young female migrants from the evils of the city by providing a supervised boarding home. Within two years YWCAs sprang up in other industrial centers, including Hartford, Pittsburgh, Cincinnati, Cleveland, and St. Louis. By 1875, women in twenty-eight cities had established associations, eighteen of which provided boarding facilities.[4]

Throughout the last decades of the nineteenth century, groups of women in American cities and on college campuses continued to organize new YWCAs. However, there was very little coordination between associations and virtually no consistent training or standards for their employed administrators, known as "secretaries." Local associations could join one of two different oversight committees, the American Committee or the International Board. Both groups claimed to be the true YWCA. As might be expected, this dispute caused great confusion on the local level. Finally, after much negotiation by the leadership of both groups, the two united in 1906. The 608 existing associations joined to form the Young Women's Christian Association of the United States of America, elected a National Board, and made Grace Dodge, a New York philanthropist, their president. The YWCA opened its national offices in New York City, and the board employed a staff to oversee the implementation of policy formulated at national conventions. These staff members, called "national secretaries," often traveled to local associations, gave advice, gathered data, prepared informational materials for the membership, and organized regional meetings and national conventions. Thus, the YWCA was composed of volunteers, some of whom served on local, regional, and national boards, and paid professionals who filled the ranks of the burgeoning social work profession. The two groups often worked together in harmony; however, occasionally, controversial issues, such as the right of workers to unionize, created conflict between various constituencies of the organization.[5]

Plagued by low wages, dangerous working conditions, and occupational segregation, women workers looked to the YWCA to provide employment bureaus and vocational training classes. Membership in the YWCA was extended to any woman who belonged to a Protestant church and could pay the modest membership fee. From its beginning, the organization reached across class lines to include working women as voting members and to involve them in the process of determining the association's policy and programs.[6] In the 1870s, YWCA volunteers and staff members began to visit the industrial districts of the cities and persuaded factory owners to furnish space for lunch hour Bible classes. In the following years the YWCA expanded its "industrial extension" work to include vocational classes, low-cost lunchrooms, and social events. By 1904 industrial work had become an essential part of the association's program, and the National Board hired a prominent leader in the labor movement, Florence Simms, as National Industrial Secretary. Simms brought together a progressive and persuasive group of staff members who visited cities to help local associations conduct surveys of working conditions and organize industrial girls' clubs. Moreover, Simms' staff mobilized the wives and daughters of industrialists and managers who dominated the leadership ranks of local YWCAs but were often reluctant to support the YWCA's labor agenda. By 1918 Simms' Industrial Department had helped to form more than 800 industrial clubs, with a membership exceeding 30,000. In 1920, when YWCA delegates gathered for their national convention, the association's working-class membership demonstrated its strength not only in numbers but in purpose. At that convention, the industrial club members convinced the majority of middle-class members of the YWCA to support a broad program of labor reform, including collective bargaining.[7]

The YMCA also started to take an interest in the working class in the second half of the nineteenth century. Concerned about the workers' propensity for political radicalism and industrial unrest, the YMCA established an Industrial Department to thwart union activities among the cities' working poor. But the association's push to create a content, reliable, and pacified workforce was often undermined by its working-class constituents. In 1877 the YMCA launched its first industrial program, creating a Railroad Department to introduce workers to the association's middle-class standards of respectability, gentility, and masculinity. Railroad companies often supported the efforts of the YMCA, hoping that the association's programs would prevent workers from attending union meetings or spending time in taverns.

Yet, as Thomas Winter demonstrates, the railroad workers who visited YMCAs challenged the association's attempt to mold them into content, morally reformed workers, and pious Christian men. They boycotted the association's Bible study and gospel meetings and defied the YMCA's notion of respectable middle-class behavior by stealing supplies or spitting on the associations' floors. Other railroad workers attended meetings intoxicated, started fist fights, or disregarded the YMCA's ban on morally corrupting games such as billiards. The workers' attempt to exercise control over the associations manifested itself particularly during labor conflicts. Workers sometimes withdrew from the YMCA or resorted to violent retaliation when the secretaries of railroad associations collaborated with company strike breakers.

The interaction between railroad workers and association leaders illustrates that the relationship between the YMCA and its working-class members was characterized by a constant struggle for power. While the workers made use of the association's facilities and programs, they challenged the middle-class standards of behavior and ideals of masculinity propagated by YMCA leaders. The workers refused to be patronized and demanded at least some control. Initially the association dismissed such working-class claims, but over time some YMCA leaders started to support the workers' demands for industrial and social reform, forging close ties between the associations' middle-class staffs and their working-class constituents.

Just as the YMCA fostered a middle-class code of behavior among railroad workers, middle-class YWCA volunteers and staff attempted to impose their own values on working-class women. From its inception, one of the YWCA's priorities was to provide an environment of moral respectability for young wage-earning women. In many cities, the YWCA supported the efforts of the Traveler's Aid Society and stationed matrons at local train stations. These women directed female travelers to proper lodging and social service agencies in an attempt to surround the young migrants with the association's middle-class values from the moment they arrived in the cities. As Sarah Heath documents, the YWCA assumed that women's low wages created a difficult moral situation, forcing women to supplement their incomes by granting employers and other men sexual favors in order to survive in the city. In an attempt to erect a barrier against the temptation of casual prostitution, the YWCA tried to convey a middle-class code of morality to women workers. The association created a Christian, homelike atmosphere in its boarding facilities, helped the young women find respectable employment, and further promoted middle-class ideals of virtuous behavior and hard work through its educational and leisure-time programs. In many ways, the YWCA helped working women deal with the harsh reality of their lives, but it failed to shape them into the traditional ideal of Victorian womanhood. Although the young migrants who roomed at the YWCA often seemed to adopt its middle-class values, many women also challenged the association's strict rules and social constraints. Working-class women lobbied for increased physical recreation, less rigid residence regulations, and varied entertainment, forcing association leaders to reexamine the YWCA's standard of acceptable female behavior.

The association's working-class constituents also altered the YWCA's involvement in industrial relations. Initially association leaders took little interest in improving the working conditions of wage-earning women because they regarded them as temporary members of the labor force who worked until marriage and motherhood took them into the proper domestic sphere. However, when working-class members of the YWCA participated in strikes and boycotts, the association was forced to take a stand. Although the YWCA discouraged militant labor disputes, staff members often supported the demands of women workers. As a result, the association gradually retreated from its program of moral uplift and started to advocate social reform.

Through their involvement with working-class women, YWCA volunteers and staff members also came in contact with immigrant women, who made up a large proportion of the female workforce in America's cities. By 1910 more than 40 percent of the urban population was foreign born, and the large-scale influx of non-Protestant immigrant women had created a more heterogeneous urban population that changed the cities' landscape and placed new demands on the YWCA. The organization, concerned about the protection and welfare of immigrant girls, began its work with foreign-born women in 1910. Raymond Mohl traces the development of the International Institute movement and shows how the YWCA retreated from its initial goal of "liberal assimilation" to embrace an ideology of ethnic and cultural pluralism during the 1920s.

The foremost advocate of International Institutes was Edith Bremer, a young settlement and social welfare worker. Bremer rejected the prevailing belief that work with immigrants should consist of meeting them at Ellis Island or Angel Island and teaching them English. She conceived of International Institutes as agencies which would protect immigrant women and help them adjust to life in America. Thus, the YWCA established centers in immigrant neighborhoods which offered recreational activities and housing and employment bureaus, as well as English classes. The movement grew quickly and by the mid-1920s, fifty-five International Institutes were operating under the auspices of local YWCAs in ethnic neighborhoods in cities throughout the nation.

Unlike settlement houses, International Institutes utilized foreign-born women and daughters of immigrants as case workers. These "nationality workers" could reach the immigrants more successfully than native-born white charity or settlement workers because they knew the language and the ethnic culture of the immigrants they were assigned to aid. They were not only able to help immigrant women obtain the knowledge they needed to survive in urban America, but they also sought to foster pride in the immigrants' heritage by encouraging the retention of their languages and traditions. Few other agencies were as successful as the International Institutes in promoting cultural pluralism.

While the International Institutes advocated pluralism in their work with ethnic minorities, YMCAs and YWCAs displayed less tolerance in their interaction with African Americans. Both associations served the black population, however, in separate facilities. Although segregated black YMCAs and YWCAs were the product of racism and discrimination, they also provided African Americans with community institutions that were funded, staffed, and operated in large part by the black community. Under the guidance of the fledgling black middle class, YMCAs and YWCAs offered African American men and women the opportunity to exercise their leadership skills.

The YMCA had started to encourage African Americans to establish separate associations and join the Christian brotherhood on separate but equal terms following the Civil War. However, it was not until the late nineteenth century that black urban professional men and businessmen started to embrace YMCA work despite the association's segregation policy. The growth of black association work was largely a response to the needs of the increasing number of African Americans who left the plantations and moved to the cities of the North and South. The fledgling black urban middle class, alarmed by the influx of rural African Americans into their communities, perceived the lower-class migrants as a destabilizing force. The population increase, they feared, would contribute to the physical decay of black neighborhoods, overburden existing recreational facilities, and increase crime rates. Moreover, black elites were concerned that the careless appearance and disreputable public behavior of the rural migrants would result in the decline of their own social status and heighten discrimination against all members of the race. In an attempt to discipline the rural migrants and to lessen the disruptive impact of their influx on black urban communities, African American elites created a network of black YMCAs.

Yet, middle-class African Americans did not establish YMCAs only to regulate the behavior of the black masses. Nina Mjagkij demonstrates that members of the educated and professional black elite enthusiastically supported YMCA work in the hope of providing African American men with the opportunity to build their manhood. Through the manifestation of their masculinity, black YMCA supporters tried to prove to white men that African American men were indeed men and deserved to be treated as such. They were convinced that once black men displayed all of the characteristics of gentlemen, they would earn the respect and esteem of white men. Large numbers of African Americans took advantage of the opportunity to assert and affirm their masculinity. They welcomed the YMCA's mission to develop "the whole man—body, mind, and spirit," particularly at a time when white society refused to recognize black men fully as men. Faced with emasculation through lynchings, disfranchisement, race, riots, and Jim Crow laws, African American men flocked to the YMCA.

Although the YMCA maintained segregated branches until 1946, the association furnished important services to black urban communities and played a crucial role in the struggle for racial advancement. Black YMCA leaders launched programs that fostered self-respect and self-reliance and tried to provide young men with proper role models and male companionship. Moreover, black-controlled YMCAs shielded African American men from racial humiliation, enabling them to display their masculinity without losing their dignity and self-esteem. Thus, black YMCAs served as sanctuaries which preserved African American masculinity and prepared black men and boys for their leadership role in the struggle for equality that lay ahead.

Similarly, the YWCA attempted to deal with the complexities of race as the association expanded its services to include black college campuses and neighborhoods. In 1870 African American women established the first black city association in Philadelphia, and soon other cities followed suit. The African American–funded and –staffed associations had complete autonomy until the establishment of the National Board in 1906. Adrienne Lash Jones traces the development of the early independent black associations and the National Board's decision to include some and exclude others from the newly created YWCA of the U.S.A. African American reformers such as Addie Hunton, wife of a YMCA official and special consultant to the YWCA National Board, stressed the importance of racial autonomy, claiming that "the special needs of black women could best be managed from within the community." However, she also realized the advantages of being affiliated with an organization that could provide recruitment and training for African American women as professional YWCA workers, thereby creating an avenue for African American women to enter the new profession of social work.

In 1907, the National Board responded to the recommendations of a group of southern white members and decided that only one association was to exist in any city. Henceforth, the white YWCA was to serve as the city's central association, while the black association became its branch. In cities with no white association in place, the black association was to affiliate directly with the National Board until white women established a YWCA in their city. African American women resented this policy because it empowered the central association to appoint a white woman as chairperson of the black branch but did not provide for the representation of black women on the board of the city association. Despite these serious objections black branches continued to grow, and in 1913 the National Board hired Eva Bowles, a black social worker from Ohio, to head the YWCA's Colored City Work Division.

Although many Protestant church women and single female workers had been familiar with the YWCA since the late nineteenth century, it was not until World War I that the majority of Americans became acquainted with the association. During the war, the federal government asked the National Board to oversee recreational work for the troops. The National Board raised hundreds of thousands of dollars, established the War Work Council to supervise its work, and allocated $200,000 of its $1,000,000 budget to Eva Bowles and her staff to provide services to black soldiers and sailors and their families. Present in virtually every military camp at home and abroad, the segregated YWCA "Hostess Houses" attracted thousands of black and white servicemen. As a result of this infusion of money and attention, the YWCA emerged from the war years with a strong staff and a varied program which reached myriad groups. For Bowles and other African American women of the YWCA, wartime activities attracted thousands of new members, requiring an increase in the "colored division" staff. The presence of a large number of African American women at national staff meetings brought an exchange of ideas and new perspectives, which were quickly visible in National Board publications. With the support of nationally prominent African American women, YWCA women challenged the National Board's racial policy and struck a compromise in 1920. That year, the National Board decided to grant branch members limited representation on central association boards and committees.

While African American women served an all-black constituency on the local level, their membership in a national organization composed of both races also provided them with a forum to communicate with white women. In the years following World War I, black women increasingly used the YWCA as a national arena to advocate interracial relations based on mutual respect. Margaret Spratt explores the dynamics of interracial work in Pittsburgh and Cleveland between 1920 and the end of World War II. Both northern industrial centers attracted thousands of southern migrants escaping the poverty and terrorism of a Jim Crow South. Overcrowded living conditions, occupational segregation, and low wages greeted the cities' newest inhabitants. The majority of black female migrants had no choice but to enter domestic service, often working in the homes of middle-class white YWCA members. Pittsburgh's and Cleveland's large and influential African American middle class responded differently to the influx of these young single women. The black and white communities of Cleveland chose to support the efforts of Jane Edna Hunter, who established an all-black working girls' home. Although approached several times by YWCA national staff, Hunter refused to affiliate with the YWCA and maintained a separate organization throughout the 1940s. The Pittsburgh YWCA, however, followed the more traditional path, established a black branch in the Hill District, and eventually engaged in interracial work, culminating in a complete reorganization of the local association in the 1950s.

The histories of the Pittsburgh and Cleveland YWCAs illustrate two very different patterns of race relations. Both are important in providing insight into the YWCA's increased emphasis on social justice and racial equality between the wars. Motivated by a progressive national staff, many local associations began to examine their programs and policies regarding the place of white and African American members within their structure. The YWCA's efforts to advance racial equality culminated in the adoption of the 1946 Interracial Charter, which called for the desegregation of all local associations "and the inclusion of Negro women and girls in the main stream of Association life."⁸

The struggle to implement desegregation continued to haunt the YMCA and YWCA in the years following World War II. When large numbers of white Americans left the cities for the suburbs, many associations found themselves once more catering to a racially exclusive membership. While suburban YMCAs and YWCAs attracted a growing number of white middle-class families, inner-city associations served a predominantly black underclass. Both groups of constituents left their mark on the associations, forcing them to address issues of social and economic reform as well as sexual orientation.

Michelle Busby discusses the process of desegregation of a large association in a New South city. The Charlotte, North Carolina, YWCA, like many southern associations, refused to implement the recommendations of the *Interracial Charter* until the local board, faced with the specter of urban renewal and suburban white flight, began to make plans for a new, expensive building. The city association's planning committee requested the help of a national staff member to organize a building campaign. Mildred Esgar traveled to Charlotte, observed the situation, and submitted a report that was much broader than the local white leadership had anticipated. Instead of suggesting a strategy for the construction of a modern whites-only facility, Esgar recommended an overall plan for future development which included the needs of the African American community and the eventual integration of all facilities and services of the Charlotte YWCA.

White association leaders, rather than adopting the Esgar Plan, dismantled it. Nevertheless, the issue of integration had been raised in Charlotte and over the next few years, the number of black women on the board and committees increased. However, the white majority was reluctant to tackle the problem of integrating facilities. In light of urban renewal in Charlotte's downtown area, many white YWCA members wanted to locate the new $2,000,000 building close to the white middle-class suburbs, whereas black members wanted it near their communities. After a number of meetings, the white majority of the central board voted to locate the new building in a white suburb. Aware that few, if any, African American women would use the new building, the white board members voted to integrate the facility in 1963. On paper, the Charlotte YWCA had implemented the *Interracial Charter*; however, the association's white majority had managed to maintain de facto segregation.

The post–World War II suburbanization of American society also transformed the YMCA. Cliff Putney documents how the demographic shifts of the 1950s and 1960s affected the YMCA's constituency, as well as its mission. In the 1950s, large numbers of white Americans left the cities for the suburbs, propelling many associations to open suburban branches. Increased leisure time and a lack of recreational facilities made these new YMCAs popular destinations for many suburbanites. With older married men, women, and children flocking to its doors, the YMCA lost much of its concern for young, single men and began focusing on families. Moreover, YMCA membership ceased to be exclusively Protestant. Many of the families who joined the suburban associations were Catholic and Jewish. This influx of non-Protestants was caused in part by the association's response to the cold war. In an attempt to stem the spread of communism and promote worldwide democracy, the YMCA advocated producing world citizens rather than Christian individuals, a policy which increasingly attracted members of other faiths. Catering to the leisure-time needs of a more diverse suburban constituency, the YMCA retreated from its traditional mission of building character in Protestant young men and started to focus on secular, family-oriented programs.

The YMCA's traditional commitment to character building was further undermined by the association's changing inner-city constituency. The flight of white middle-class Americans to the suburbs and the dwindling number of city-bound Protestant farm boys brought the YMCA into direct contact with the urban underclass. Exposed to urban poverty and ghetto riots, YMCA leaders supported civil rights, assisted underprivileged youth, aided handicapped children, and launched other programs designed to ease the conditions of the urban poor. In 1972, the YMCA's longtime emphasis on Christian character building finally ended when the association, instead of pledging to convert young men, proposed to organize in support of social justice and global democracy and in opposition to racism, poverty, crime, delinquency, and social alienation.[9]

The YMCA's dedication to social causes, however, was short-lived. In the aftermath of the Vietnam War and the Watergate scandal, the association stopped advocating social reforms. Disillusioned by political upheavals and exhausted by protest, YMCA leaders instead encouraged individuals to focus on themselves in order to develop their full mental and physical potential. As a result, fitness programs designed to enhance personal health spread throughout the associations, and body building replaced the YMCA's traditional character-building programs.

The increasing number of families who joined the YMCA during the postwar decades not only changed the association's mission and programs but also affected the organization's attitude toward its large gay constituency. Gay men had discovered associations as safe places for homoerotic encounters in the late nineteenth century. The YMCA's single-sex ambience made the associations inadvertently one of the primary means by which many men were first introduced to an emerging urban gay sexual subculture. Single young men could share a dormitory room without arousing much suspicion, and the association's devotion to physical culture provided a homoerotic element. By the early twentieth century, YMCAs were attracting a growing number of young men who were interested in exploring their sexual identities, experimenting with new relationships, or meeting sexual partners. During World War I and World War II, YMCA cruising further intensified as a result of the association's work with soldiers, sailors, transient military personnel, and defense industry workers. Cruising in the YMCA peaked between 1940 and 1960. By then, associations had gained a reputation as safe havens for possible sexual encounters, and gay guidebooks started to list and describe them.

Ironically, the emergence of a militant gay rights movement in the late 1960s signaled the end of the golden era of YMCA cruising. The early successes of the gay rights activists made coming out less dangerous, and participation in gay community institutions became more attractive to those who had embraced a gay identity. YMCA cruising continued to be an important field of erotic interaction, particularly for men who feared to come out or who denied their gay identity. The gay rights movement, however, made the YMCA less safe for homosexual interaction as public awareness of cruising in the association increased. In particular, the influx of families during the 1950s and 1960s had made YMCA staff more sensitive to its homosexual constituents, and associations started to curtail the activities of gay men in the 1970s. The YMCA abolished its long-standing policy of nude bathing, and some associations began to consider the use of closed-circuit television monitoring to put an end to cruising.

John D. Wrathall demonstrates that for nearly a century the YMCA provided an ideal place for cruising, not in spite of its Christian reputation but because of it. Cruising thrived in the association because men's intentions could remain ambiguous. Unlike going to a gay bar, a park, or a house of male prostitution, men could visit the YMCA and experiment sexually without having to embrace a gay identity. The YMCA provided a perfect cover for men who denied their homosexuality; however, it also provided those who embraced their gay identity with the opportunity to become part of a gay subculture.

As these essays illustrate, the YMCA and the YWCA were much more than institutional and physical structures in the cities' landscape. Both associations furnished America's urban population with a spectrum of social services that no religious organization, civic group, or municipal agency was prepared to provide. In the process, the YMCA and YWCA not only helped ease the transition of the newly urbanized population but also created spaces which allowed men and women from all walks of life to explore their identities in a safe and supportive environment. Moreover, the associations brought together a heterogeneous group of city dwellers who otherwise would have had few opportunities to socialize. The interaction between the associations' middle-class volunteers and professional staffs and their urban constituents generated a dialogue about class, ethnic, racial, gender, and sexual relations that altered the attitudes of those involved in the discourse and helped to change the associations' structures, policies, and programs.

The Protestant middle-class reformers who established the associations in an attempt to control and discipline the behavior and attitudes of the urban masses encountered working-class members who brought their own ideals, values, and aspirations to the YMCA and YWCA. In response, association leaders gradually retreated from their strict definitions of proper middle-class conduct and demeanor and, in some cases, went so far as to support workers' efforts at labor reform. Similarly, the associations' work with immigrants and African Americans compelled YMCA and YWCA leaders to reexamine their ethnic and racial prejudices, and many started to support policies that challenged discrimination and segregation. The YWCA provided women with a place where they could develop leadership skills, set a reform agenda, and satisfy a desire to initiate social change outside the confines of a male-directed organization. For men, the YMCA has functioned as a venue for the exploration of issues surrounding the evolving definition of masculinity.

While the essays in this volume explore important aspects of the rich history of the YMCA and the YWCA in the urban setting, both associations remain fertile fields for scholarly inquiry. For a better understanding of the historical significance of these organizations, scholars will have to study the associations' missionary efforts abroad; their programs for students on college campuses; their services for boys and girls; their involvement in the civil rights movement; their attempts to desegregate local branches; and their services for Native Americans and Asian Americans, soldiers, sailors, defense workers, displaced persons, and prisoners of war. Both associations have also had a significant impact on some of the major public policy issues of this century. They have pioneered new methods of social work, as well as entered into the public debate on such topics as urban housing and planning, the homeless, and domestic violence. Scholars will have to address these and other questions to gain an understanding of the YMCA's and YWCA's place in American society.[10] A useful starting point for interested researchers is Nancy Robertson's and Elizabeth Norris' essay, the final one in this volume, on accessing archival collections and other information about the YWCA.

A cursory glance into the voluminous historical records of these organizations reveals the broad array of religious, social, educational, recreational, and vocational services that the YMCA and YWCA provided for generations of rural migrants, working men and women, immigrants, African Americans, families, Protestants, Catholics, Jews, and gay men who made the associations their home away from home. Today's YWCAs and YMCAs may be far removed from their original purpose of moral uplift and character building, but they still occupy a prominent place in the cities' social, cultural, and physical landscape.

NOTES

1. The YMCA and YWCA have published numerous studies of their work; however, few scholarly monographs trace the history of either association. Though commissioned by the YMCA, C. Howard Hopkins' *History of the YMCA in North America* (New York: Association Press, 1951) and Richard C. Lancaster's *Serving the U.S. Armed Forces, 1861–1986: The Story of the YMCA's Ministry to Military Personnel for 125 Years* (Schaumburg, Ill.: Armed Services YMCA of the U.S.A., 1987) are particularly useful for historians. Similarly, the YWCA has failed to attract the attention of a scholar willing to write a comprehensive history. Two books by Mary S. Sims, a long-time YWCA staff member, *The Natural History of a Social Institution—the Young Women's Christian Association* (New York: The Woman's Press, 1936) and *The YWCA—An Unfolding Purpose* (New York: The Woman's Press, 1950) and Anna V. Rice's *A History of the World's Young Women's Christian Association* (New York: The Woman's Press, 1947) provide helpful material on the structure and chronology of the organization.

2. Hopkins, *History of the YMCA in North America*, 117.

3. Sims, *The YWCA—An Unfolding Purpose*, 1–3; Anne Firor Scott, *Natural Allies: Women's Associations in American History* (Urbana: University of Illinois Press, 1991), 84.

4. Sims, *Natural History of a Social Institution*, 5–7; Elizabeth Wilson, *Fifty Years of Association Work Among Young Women* (New York: The Woman's Press, 1916), 53.

5. Sims, *Natural History of a Social Institution*, 46–49.

6. Mary Sims included a helpful timeline of YWCA history in *The YWCA—An Unfolding Purpose*, 141–152.

7. For a brief history of the Industrial Department of the National YWCA, see Mary Frederickson, "Citizens for Democracy: The Industrial Programs of the YWCA," in *Sisterhood and Solidarity: Workers' Education for Women, 1914–1984*, eds. Joyce L. Kornbluh and Mary Frederickson (Philadelphia: Temple University Press, 1984): 76–106; Margaret Spratt, "The Pittsburgh YWCA and Industrial Democracy in the 1920s," *Pennsylvania History* 59, 1 (January 1992): 5–14; Ken Fones-Wolf in *Trade Union Gospel: Christianity and Labor in Industrial Philadelphia, 1865–1915* (Philadelphia: Temple University Press, 1989) describes the complexities of the labor issue among the constituencies of that city's YMCA and YWCA.

8. Dorothy Height, *Interracial Policies of the Young Women's Christian Associations* (New York: The Woman's Press, 1948), 11–16.

9. Susan Lynn, *Progressive Women in Conservative Times: Racial Justice, Peace, and Feminism, 1945–1960* (New Brunswick, N.J.: Rutgers University Press, 1992), chap. 1.

10. In addition to the sources mentioned in the above notes, a number of books and essays highlight various historical aspects of the associations. Nina

Mjagkij's *Light in the Darkness: African Americans and the YMCA, 1852–1946* (Lexington: The University Press of Kentucky, 1994) is the only scholarly monograph tracing the history of the YMCA's work with African Americans. David I. Macleod's *Building Character in the American Boy: The Boy Scouts, YMCA, and Their Forerunners, 1870–1920* (Madison: University of Wisconsin Press, 1986) and Nancy K. Bristow's recent study, *Making Men Moral: Social Engineering during the Great War* (New York: New York University Press, 1996), are of particular interest to social and gender historians. Nancy Boyd's *Emissaries: The Overseas Work of the American YWCA* (New York: The Woman's Press, 1986) is dedicated to one aspect of the women's organization, and Carole Seymour-Jones examines the World YWCA in *Journey of Faith: The History of the World YWCA, 1945–1994* (London: Allison and Busby, 1994). Elizabeth Lasch-Quinn's *Black Neighbors: Race and the Limits of Reform in the American Settlement House Movement, 1890–1945* (Chapel Hill: University of North Carolina Press, 1993) includes chapters on YWCA history. Several recent journal articles and essays examine specific aspects of both organizations, including Stanley Warren, "The Monster Meetings at the Negro YMCA in Indianapolis," *Indiana Magazine of History* 91 (March 1995): 57–80; Jon Thares Davidann, "The American YMCA in Meiji Japan: God's Work Gone Awry," *Journal of World History* 6 (Spring 1995): 175–208; Clifford Putney, "Character Building in the YMCA, 1880–1930," *Mid-America* 73, 1 (1991): 49–70; Lillian S. Williams, "To Elevate the Race: The Michigan Avenue YMCA and the Advancement of Blacks in Buffalo, New York, 1922–1940," in Vincent P. Franklin and James D. Anderson, eds., *New Perspectives on Black Educational History* (Boston: G. K. Hall, 1978): 129–148 and "Black Communities and Adult Education: YMCA, YWCA, and Fraternal Organizations," in Harvey G. Neufeldt and Leo McGee (eds.), *Education of the African American Adult: A Historical Overview* (New York: Greenwood, 1990): 135–162; Jodi Vandenberg-Daves, "The Manly Pursuit of a Partnership between the Sexes: The Debate over YMCA Programs for Women and Girls, 1914–1933," *Journal of American History* 78, 4 (March 1992): 1324–1346; Sharlene Voogd Cochrane, "'Compelled to Speak': Women Confronting Institutional Racism, 1910–1950," *New England Journal of Public Policy* 7, 2 (Fall/Winter 1991): 47–59 and "'And the Pressure Never Let Up': Black Women, White Women, and the Boston YWCA, 1918–1948," in Vicki L. Crawford et al., eds., *Women in the Civil Rights Movement: Trailblazers and Torchbearers, 1941–1965* (Bloomington: Indiana University Press, 1993); M. Christine Anderson, "Home and Community for a Generation of Women: A Case Study of the Cincinnati Y.W.C.A. Residence, 1920–1940," *Queen City Heritage* 43, 4 (Winter 1985): 34–41; Marian J. Morton, "Seduced and Abandoned in an American City: Cleveland and Its Fallen Women, 1869–1936," *Journal of Urban History* 11, 4 (August 1985): 443–469; Richard Byrd, "Interracial Cooperation in a Decade of Conflict: The Denton (Texas) Christian Women's Inter-racial Fellowship," *Oral History Review* 19, 1–2 (Spring/Fall 1991): 31–53; Margaret

Ripley Wolfe, "Eleanor Copenhaver Anderson of the National Board of the YWCA: Appalachian Feminist and Author's Wife," *The Winesburg Eagle: The Official Publication of the Sherwood Anderson Society* 18 (Summer 1993): 2–9; Hilda Romer Christensen, "Among Flappers and Respectable Girls: Gender and Culture in the Danish YWCA, 1880–1940," *Nora* 1 (1994): 51–61; Judith Weisenfeld, "The Harlem YWCA and the Secular City, 1904–1945," *Journal of Women's History* 6, 3 (Fall 1994): 62–78; and Doug Rossinow, "'The Breakthrough to New Life': Christianity and the Emergence of the New Left in Austin, Texas, 1956–1964," *American Quarterly* 46, 3 (September 1994): 309–340.

Chapter One

"An Aggressive Christian Enterprise"

The Baltimore YMCA's Journey to Institutional Credibility and Religious Legitimacy, 1852–1882

Jessica Elfenbein

In 1851 Reverend John W. M. Williams became the pastor of the First Baptist Church of Baltimore, a church whose membership consisted of 36 men and 160 women. The dearth of men at First Baptist was so serious that observers suggested that its name be changed to the "First FEMALE Baptist Church of Baltimore" because, as Williams later remembered, the church was "without a deacon or a Sunday school superintendent, or a single male teacher, or a man who could lead in public prayer." Williams served the congregation for thirty-three years. He worked closely with the female majority, describing them as "wise, prudent, sensible, working women, who cheered the heart of their young pastor, and helped him in his work. Such women as Paul refers to who labor with us in the gospel.'" While Williams had faith in the women of his congregation, he was also concerned about the fate of young men in the city. This concern led Williams to attend the organizational meeting of the YMCA of Baltimore on November 18, 1852.[1]

While the 80 percent female membership at Baltimore's First Baptist Church represented an extreme gender imbalance, women had comprised the majority of church members in American Protestant congregations for a long time. Scholars have attributed the rise of women in reform and voluntary associations, and the emergence of women in the public sphere, to this "feminization" of American Protestantism.[2] This essay examines the effect of the feminized or emasculated church on the creation and growth of the Baltimore YMCA and the association's rise to institutional credibility and religious legitimacy from the time of its founding in 1852 until the arrival of William H. Morriss, its first General Secretary, in 1882.[3]

Baltimore has historical importance to many Christians. In addition to being the ecclesiastical center and earliest diocese of the Roman Catholic Church in America, Baltimore was the see city of the second diocese of the Protestant Episcopal Church and the birthplace of Methodism. Moreover, the city had long been a center of Presbyterian activity and an early stronghold of Quakers and Baptists. In 1859 there were 158 different church congregations in Baltimore, representing more than two dozen religious denominations. By the beginning of the twentieth century, Baltimore boasted nearly 600 church buildings.[4]

Despite the large number of congregations, some lay and clerical leaders were concerned about the paucity of male church members. In November 1852, a committee of five men of the Maryland Baptist Union appealed to the clergy of the city's white evangelical churches. Under the leadership of Franklin Wilson, a thirty-year-old Baptist minister, whose chronic respiratory problems precluded his employment as a congregational pastor, the committee urged the clergy to announce the formation of the YMCA from their pulpits and to ask young male congregants to attend a preliminary meeting. The committee members knew that men like themselves had already created YMCAs in Boston, New York, Philadelphia, and Washington, D.C., in an effort "to combine the young men of *all the Evangelical Churches* for the moral, mental, and religious improvement of themselves, and of all whom they can influence." To satisfy those goals, the YMCAs established libraries and reading rooms and charged members with welcoming newly arrived young men to the city by directing them to reputable boarding houses, churches, and the association itself. The YMCA hoped to welcome the newcomer and to "throw around him good influences, so that he may feel he is not a stranger, but that noble and Christian spirits care for his soul."[5]

News of the association's success elsewhere spurred the effort in Baltimore. In November 1852, more than 100 young laymen, representing nearly all of the city's white evangelical churches, attended the organizational meeting of the YMCA at the First Presbyterian Church.[6] Those who joined the enterprise recognized the critical need for a counteroffensive to the myriad sinful temptations that urban areas like Baltimore offered in the 1850s. The YMCA's organizers feared that neither the church nor the state was equipped to cope with the increase in population in urban areas and the challenges that the moral protection of so many newly arrived young males posed. The YMCA's early leaders quickly articulated the very real community needs of these young men and, under the auspices of the fledgling association, mobilized to provide for them.

YMCA members focused on ensuring the moral safety of young men adrift in the city, many of whom were naive farm boys. They urged the migrants to avoid temptations like the theater, the saloon, the ballroom, the gaming table, and prostitutes, whose "feet go down to death, and whose steps take hold on hell." The YMCA's organizers cautioned that these temptations paraded "their daily and nightly allurements in our midst, to drag into temporal and eternal ruin hundreds of young men." To attack "this deadly work," the self-proclaimed "lovers of God" who led the YMCA advocated using the "companionship and sympathy of the virtuous" as their ammunition.[7]

With an eye toward welcoming all those with even a modicum of interest in religious affairs, the Baltimore YMCA took into membership any moral young white Christian man. This policy was in vivid contrast to that of some of the European YMCAs, which required prospective members to answer a series of questions to prove not only their standing as church members but also their piety. Membership in the Baltimore YMCA grew quickly, and by 1853 the association reported having more than 500 members.[8]

Although the YMCA's leaders saw weaknesses in the churches' attraction to young men, they hoped that organizing through the city's congregations would give the nascent YMCA an air of respectability and an important network of contacts with socially responsible men. The YMCA sought formal links to all evangelical churches as both an affirmation of its commitment to "nondenominational Christianity" and a recruiting tool.[9] In 1852 the YMCA first organized Standing Committees to act as liaisons between individual church congregations and the association. YMCA leaders soon realized that, despite their faith in the redemptive qualities of nondenominationalism, it was impossible to attract representatives from each congregation of every denomination. YMCA Standing Committees were organized in only one-third of the city's eligible congregations. Advocates of YMCA work feared that this lack of church cooperation combined with the competition of other voluntary organizations favored by young men, such as the Mercantile Library, the Mechanics Institute, and the Odd Fellows, would slow the YMCA's growth.[10]

Initially, the YMCA's leaders thought that the most effective way for them to accomplish their goals was to avoid encroachment on what they broadly called "the proper work of the church."[11] At the beginning, this was not difficult because the YMCA's mission was to help young men adapt to the rapidly industrializing city, a job that appeared to be largely separate and distinct from church work. The goal of association members was to seek out newly arrived men and provide them with proper moral and religious influences by aiding them in finding suitable boarding places and employment and introducing them to the YMCA. Leading young men to "some place of worship on the Sabbath" and using "every means in their power" to surround the newcomer with "Christian associates" was part of the plan.[12]

This heavy suffusion of the YMCA's programs by Christianity quickly muddied the distinction between the association's mission and church work. Moreover, the YMCA's nondenominationalism had the largely unintended and unanticipated effect of supplanting the appeal traditional Protestant churches had for some young men. Thus, the YMCA's more masculine and nondenominational religiosity quickly upset the religious and social hegemony of the urban churches and their clergy.[13] In 1858, for example, J. Dean Smith, then the YMCA president, declared, "I speak from the depth of my inmost soul, when I say, that I owe to this means [the YMCA], under God, my happiest and most profitable religious hours, and my dearest Christian friends."[14]

The YMCA welcomed men with church affiliations, as well as those who were entirely unchurched. Going beyond the bounds of denominationalism was intended to help both young native Baltimoreans and those who were "constantly coming hither from surround and distant parts," men who the YMCA's leadership feared would "without right associations and influences . . . make shipwrecks of themselves forever." To provide the young men adrift in Baltimore with proper guidance and companionship, the YMCA's leaders repeatedly asked the city's ministers for their cooperation.[15]

Despite these appeals, ministerial involvement was limited. With the notable exceptions of Williams, Wilson, and a handful of other clerics, the vast majority of the association's early leaders and members were laymen. In 1854 Baltimore's YMCA reported only nine clergymen among its 512 members. While three of the ministers were YMCA officers that year, all of them had severed their ties with the association by 1858.[16] Perhaps the YMCA failed to attract larger numbers of ministers because its leaders sought to use the association to compensate for what they saw as the churches' shortcomings. Indeed, the organization of the YMCA itself represented an indictment of the churches' inability to reach young men. The relative absence of the city's clergy among the ranks of Baltimore's YMCA leadership is therefore not surprising.

Although association leaders remained apprehensive about alienating the churches, the association became gradually more aggressive in its religious work. After early attempts at public prayer meetings drew few takers, association leaders became savvier in their efforts to attract their targeted audience. In 1856, for example, the YMCA began to conduct religious services in the halls of the city's fire companies. The decision to customize prayer meetings for a particular audience was a harbinger of the YMCA's pragmatic practice of bringing programs to the people rather than waiting passively to be discovered by an appreciative public.[17]

In 1857 YMCA leaders eagerly pursued another avenue in attempting to reach young men adrift when Baltimore, like many other American cities, experienced an economic panic. The depression was serious, causing many of the nation's stock markets and banks to fail and leading to the collapse of a number of railroads. As prices plummeted and businesses and factories closed, thousands of workers were left unemployed. Nationwide, a total of 6,000 firms went under; however, the northeastern states were most seriously affected by the economic crisis.[18] The YMCA, seeing an opportunity for expansion, quickly mobilized to attract new members while also staving off labor unrest. In response to the panic, the YMCA started to increase its emphasis on religious programming and launched a series of noontime prayer meetings in November 1857.

In addition to the all-male prayer meetings in the YMCA's room on Fayette Street in downtown Baltimore, the association held as many as four public meetings each day in various churches and dance halls. In West Baltimore's China Hall, which had been "so often the scene of the gay revel," the YMCA conducted daily worship services. Association leaders proudly proclaimed that under their guidance China Hall, "which once echoed the sensual music, the obscene jester, the excited political harangue," was transformed into a site of moral activity. The most popular YMCA prayer meetings, however, were those held at the Maryland Institute, attracting between 2,000 and 4,000 people each day.[19] The YMCA's prayer meetings did not permanently transform the city's dance halls into moral and spiritual havens, but, the association's efforts excited religious fervor in the larger community and captured some of the time and attention of restless Baltimoreans. Perhaps the YMCA did help stave off labor unrest, an outcome surely attractive to the association's solidly middle-class leadership.[20]

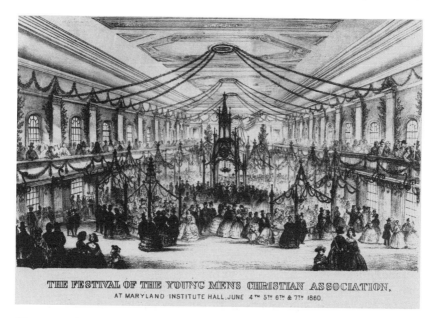

THE FESTIVAL OF THE YOUNG MENS CHRISTIAN ASSOCIATION.
AT MARYLAND INSTITUTE HALL, JUNE 4TH 5TH 6TH & 7TH 1860

Figure 1. The Union Festival, held by the Baltimore YMCA in 1859 and 1860, was very popular but failed to raise enough money for the construction of a new YMCA building. Use of print courtesy of The University of Baltimore Educational Foundation.

Part of the YMCA's success in organizing prayer meetings resulted from a deliberate avoidance of conflict with church services. YMCA prayer meetings, for example, were never scheduled for Sunday mornings. While the leaders of the Baltimore YMCA promoted nondenominationalism, they did not expressly seek to undercut the role of denominations in the Christian community. Many YMCA members were largely unconcerned about denominational differences, believing instead in the primacy of a true living church, which focused on satisfying a commitment to God through service to young men. Baltimore YMCA president J. Dean Smith, for example, denounced denominations and sects as "temporary and carnal," insisting that "the unity of the church is spiritual and eternal." Smith concluded that nondenominational unity was "the great foundation principle, upon which our associations stand; it is our creed, and the exemplification of, and the teaching, the power, and beauty, of this Christian oneness, is the great mission of these associations."[21]

While the association struggled to establish institutional legitimacy, it also sought a permanent place in the urban landscape. Since its inception, the Baltimore YMCA had occupied rented quarters in a variety of buildings in the downtown business district. In 1859, however, with the expe-rience of the prayer meetings of 1857 still fresh, YMCA leaders organized a "Union Festival" to raise money for the construction of a YMCA hall. The YMCA's Ladies' Auxiliary, with the support of women from various churches and denominations, made and sold a variety of goods to help raise funds for a building. The festival netted $6,500 in four days, which, though substantial, was not adequate for the acquisi-tion of land and the construction of a YMCA building.[22]

Lack of funds was not the only obstacle to YMCA work in the 1850s. Increasing sectional tensions also affected the association's success, as the debate over slavery divided not only Maryland's population but also the membership of Baltimore's YMCA. The sectional crisis threatened the very viability of the association as membership dropped precipitously. Since its inception, the YMCA had tried to remain neutral and banned any political discussions in its rooms, yet, the debate over slavery fre-quently affected association membership. When the Civil War started, many YMCA members left both the association and the city of Baltimore. Although the YMCA did not peter out entirely, it was mori-bund during the war years.[23]

It is likely that during the Civil War the membership of the Baltimore YMCA followed the model of associations in Washington, D.C., New York, and other cities and materially assisted the work of the United States Christian Commission. The Christian Commission, with its lead-ership drawn from YMCAs throughout the country, was a voluntary organization which acted as a clearing house for religious work in the armed forces of the North and South. Local associations raised funds, and the government provided suitable accommodations. Although some prosperous city associations were able to maintain services for their urban constituents while supporting the Christian Commission, many smaller associations merged into local branches of the Christian Commission. The Baltimore YMCA, like the associations in Chicago, New York, St. Paul, St. Louis, and Buffalo, served as a regional clearing house for the multitude of activities channeled through the Christian Commission. During the war, the Christian Commission recruited 5,000 men and women who went to the front to minister to the soldiers' reli-gious needs. In addition to providing one-on-one battlefield assistance, the volunteers of the Christian Commission distributed thousands of reli-gious tracts and Bibles. The Christian Commission's spiritual assistance to the soldiers of the Union and the Confederacy garnered much support for the YMCA in the postwar years.[24]

Once the Civil War ended, the Baltimore YMCA's work with the Christian Commission provided the association with the strength and respectability to overcome quickly much of the loss of membership it had suffered during the hostilities. In 1866 Baltimore's YMCA was reconstituted and in the following year the association admitted 347 new members, pushing membership to over 700. Those who joined the association, as well as those who assumed leadership roles in the YMCA following the war, were largely men who had not been involved in association work during the 1850s. By 1868, only a handful of the more than two dozen association officers and committee members had been affiliated with the YMCA prior to the war.[25]

Invigorated by new members and leaders and strengthened by its wartime service, the work of the YMCA shifted dramatically in the aftermath of the Civil War. By then the YMCA had become a religious association that no longer needed to operate within the confines of church-set agendas, but came to minister largely outside of the churches' domain.

In the postwar years the Baltimore YMCA began to employ innovative and proto-Progressive approaches to urban problems, bringing to the city the beginnings of scientific philanthropy, sophisticated workplace training, and a social service agenda, all of which were religiously infused. In 1866, for example, the YMCA founded as an experiment the News Boys' Home to help orphan boys locate gainful employment while "slowly but surely" developing "the foundations of character" so that they would grow up to be "honest and upright members of society."[26] The YMCA further extended its work with children in 1867. That year city authorities granted the association the free use of the Broadway Market Hall on Sundays to establish a large mission school. The YMCA also started to operate another mission school and conducted prayer meetings at a building it owned on East Baltimore's Abbott Street. Through these schools, YMCA leaders hoped to reach "many neglected children" who were not otherwise receiving religious training. To attract the young scholars, the YMCA distributed religious tracts and other ephemera. Many children who attended the mission schools were Sunday School scholars elsewhere who were attracted by the giveaways. In 1869 the YMCA reported that "quite a number of children after attending their own schools, would leave early in order to attend ours."[27]

In addition to new programs focusing on vulnerable children, Baltimore's YMCA established a Committee on Employment and Boarding. The Committee tried to help find "employment for the unfortunate" and maintained a list of "good eligible boarding houses . . . whose charges were moderate, and where Christian companionship would most likely be fostered." Perhaps as a gesture to unity in the postwar years, the leadership of the YMCA also helped scores of young southern men "without money or acquaintances in the city" obtain employment.[28] Moreover, the YMCA established a shelter for the city's homeless men when the number of unemployed rose in the aftermath of the panic of 1873. Starting in 1877 the Friendly Inn offered homeless patrons, many of whom "once lived in wealth and comfort and occupied high positions," food and shelter and assisted them in obtaining employment. The YMCA committee that operated the Friendly Inn proclaimed that there was "no better channel" for "Christian and other people who wish to practice charity in aiding needy and deserving men." To do so, association members sold meal and lodging tickets to concerned citizens for distribution to homeless men, who redeemed them at the Friendly Inn.[29]

As the YMCA expanded its services during the postwar years, association leaders tried to maintain a cooperative relationship with the city's clergy. Despite drawing many men to the association, the YMCA's literature and leadership continued to proclaim that a member's most important religious obligation was loyalty to a denominational church, with association activities filling only the leisure time that remained after professional, personal, and religious commitments were satisfied.[30]

Although the YMCA cultivated "handmaiden" rhetoric that promoted the image of the association and its work as "needed auxiliaries of the Church," participation in the association's religious programs did not always enhance membership in mainstream churches. For some association leaders and members the YMCA started to supersede the church's importance in their religious lives, and sometimes young men chose the association as their sole spiritual home. Baltimore's YMCA leaders, despite their public affirmation of the churches' religious authority, acknowledged the association's growing prominence as a spiritual institution. The YMCA, because of its nondenominational nature, they proclaimed, represented the "truest Christianity . . . that which best demonstrates the mission and sacrifices of Jesus Christ in the daily behavior of his disciples."[31]

In 1867 Baltimore's YMCA leaders tried to ameliorate the impact of the association's expanded religious appeal on relations with the city's clergy. They offered Baltimore's evangelical ministers a weekly meeting place in an attempt to gain "their affections which will the more readily secure us their personal sympathy and support." The ministers, however, did not flock to the YMCA, perhaps because they felt alienated from the association or perhaps because they simply preferred another venue. By 1868, association leaders regretfully reported "that there are but few of the ministers of our city who seem to take an interest in our operations, or who visit our rooms." Despite the clergy's apathy, YMCA leaders continued to invite the city's ministers to support the association's work, claiming that "their presence and encouragement would help us very much, and give tone and character to the enterprise in which we are engaged."[32]

The YMCA's growing religious appeal irked some clergy who apparently desired exclusive access to the spiritual lives of young men. Although ministers cloaked their criticism of the YMCA's encroachment on what they considered to be their turf, tensions between the clergy and the association's leadership surfaced during the postwar years.[33] At one point the YMCA's International Committee, the policymaking body of the North American association, had to intervene when some YMCA secretaries interpreted their jobs as formal ministry and started to wear ministerial collars. The International Committee instructed those secretaries to "avoid anything that smacks of the cloth," explaining that they had not been ordained as spiritual leaders and as YMCA secretaries were therefore not entitled to the "distinctive garb of the clergy."[34]

More important, the clergy's misgivings about the YMCA's work was caused by the expansion of the association's activities after the Civil War. In addition to serving young men adrift, Baltimore's YMCA launched new programs such as children's meetings, sick and poor visitations, mission schools, street preaching, and open-air gatherings. These new YMCA enterprises may have caused some concern among ministers who feared that the association's outreach to children, women, and destitute men would threaten the loyalty of the churches' traditional stalwarts.[35]

The YMCA's open-air meetings began in the summer of 1869. More than 150 speakers participated in twenty different weekly forums, each attracting between 100 and 1,000 people. Held near East Baltimore's Causeway on Eastern Avenue, a locality similar to New York City's Five Points neighborhood, these meetings aimed at combating the evil influences of "low groggeries [and] dance houses." The YMCA's open-air gatherings became more popular each year, perhaps because they provided free entertainment and a positive alternative to the neighborhood's more tawdry pastimes. Some Protestant ministers supported the open-air meetings because sermons were limited to topics on which evangelical Christians agreed, and the policy was neither to commend nor condemn any creed.[36]

Although some ministers, like those who participated in the open-air meetings, worked cooperatively with the YMCA, relations between the majority of clergy and the association remained distant. Association supporters repeatedly tried to reassure the clergy that the YMCA's work was not intended to replace their own. The church, YMCA leaders proclaimed, was eminently qualified for all religious work, and therefore it would be "simply absurd to suppose that the Association can be more effective." YMCA leaders assured the clergy that "we do not interfere in any way with the legitimate work of the church, or attempt to take out of her hands that which is peculiarly her own." To substantiate that claim, the YMCA reported that it tried only to reach the unchurched, its lay leaders taking the "simple truth" and bringing it to "those who avoid the sanctuary."[37]

No one ministered better to the unchurched than Dwight Lyman Moody, who held a series of revivals under the YMCA's auspices during the winter and spring of 1878 and 1879. In anticipation of Moody's visit, the Baltimore YMCA hastened the completion of its Central Building. Baltimore's association leaders had invited Moody not only to experience his evangelical ministry but also to garner his lobbying and fundraising assistance in support of the local YMCA. While in Baltimore, for example, Moody convinced John Work Garrett, president of the B&O Railroad, to support the establishment of a railroad YMCA in the city.[38]

Moody himself was part of the migration from farm to city. Born in rural Massachusetts in 1837, he arrived in Boston in 1854 and joined the local YMCA soon afterward. Moody, a "nominal Unitarian" before his conversion to Congregationalism, joined the association for social rather than religious reasons. In 1856 Moody moved to Chicago, where he joined the city's YMCA and soon became involved in its administration. After volunteering for the Christian Commission, Moody served as president of the Chicago YMCA and earned a national reputation for both his association work and his involvement in the Sunday School movement. By 1870 Moody had become not only a very successful merchant but also a committed Christian. He gave up his business enterprise, severed his official ties with the YMCA, and left Chicago to become a full-time evangelist.[39]

Moody's visit to Baltimore stirred up religious zeal and strengthened the association's role as a serious and legitimate participant in the city's religious life. At Moody's request and in the hope of winning some clerical support, the YMCA hosted a plenary meeting with representatives from ten Protestant denominations at the commencement of his stay. Moody's visit also coincided with the Annual Convention of the North American YMCA in Baltimore, where, against his will, he was elected national president of the YMCA.[40]

In June 1879 Moody completed his stay in Baltimore and returned to his home in Northfield, Massachusetts. Hoping to continue Moody's revival activities and his goal of extending the work of the "Church in Baltimore," YMCA leaders hired the evangelist E. W. Bliss to succeed Moody. In a letter sent to ministers throughout the city, YMCA leaders asserted that they expected Bliss to work without ministerial support, hoping that "this great Christian enterprise may be carried on without interfering with the regular work of the Ministry in your own congregation."[41]

Although the YMCA remained committed to basic courtesy in its interaction with the city's clergy, by 1880 the association had proven itself a viable and independent force within the city's religious life. While ministerial approval was desirable, it was no longer necessary to legitimize the YMCA's religious programming. Moody's visit proved to be the culmination of the association's postwar march toward religious independence and institutional legitimacy. There was now no question about the YMCA's ability to stand unsupported by the ministerial community.

In 1881, despite an accumulation of rhetoric to the contrary, the Baltimore YMCA publicly recognized that it had long been considered "an organization directly antagonistic to the church; working for its own ends, and laboring in a field properly coming under church government."[42] But that would all change, the YMCA promised, as the association refocused its attention to ministering exclusively to the needs of young men. In 1882 the YMCA hired as its General Secretary William Morriss, who spearheaded the association's return to its original institutional commitment to bringing young men to Jesus. Under Morriss' leadership, the YMCA excluded women and children, and boys and men regained the association's exclusive attention. Moreover, the YMCA sought to reach a more diverse group of young men, including railroad workers, college students, German immigrants, and African American migrants. Morris, a Quaker and proselytizing evangelist, saw the YMCA's fluctuating membership as a boon to his ministry. Early in his forty-one-year tenure with the Baltimore YMCA, Morriss realized that it was rare for the YMCA's religious work alone to reach young men. Thus he advocated the use of athletic, educational, and social programs, as well as housing facilities, to attract young men to the association. This he believed would increase the possibility of exposing them to the YMCA's religious mission and ultimately lead them to Jesus. "That this is not done effectively or completely does not lessen the fact that it is our recognized aim," he concluded.[43]

In the thirty years following the founding of the Baltimore YMCA in 1852, its leaders and members affirmed their need for a religion that was masculine, accessible, and nondenominational. At its inception, the Baltimore YMCA had a tightly focused mission of reaching the flood of young men who entered the city and whom the established churches were largely failing to attract. Some leading members of the city's Protestant clergy supported the formation of the YMCA, concerned that "the lovers of sin," with their array of "daily and nightly allurements," were winning the battle for the souls of young men. In turn, the YMCA in its first years sought legitimization from the churches. The Standing Committees, in particular, were means not only of attracting new YMCA members but of attempting to work *with* and *through* the churches. The YMCA's mission and its companion efforts to promote nondenominationalism bred a comforting, reassuring rhetoric that cast the association as an auxiliary of the churches.

By the end of its first decade, however, the YMCA's rhetoric had already begun to clash with the realities of its programmatic efforts. The YMCA responded to the panic of 1857 and the resulting economic dislocations by taking the lead in organizing religious programming for an audience far broader than just young men. If it was using techniques which the established churches had not employed, the YMCA was now reaching not only the unchurched, but also women and children whom the churches had often successfully cultivated.

While the coming of the Civil War led to a contraction in the YMCA's activities, after the war the YMCA emerged as an extremely confident organization embarking on a wide-ranging effort to provide services not only to men but also to children and women. The rhetoric of the YMCA during this period, however, remained committed to the notion of a limited mission, devoted to serving the needs of young men, and to the very politic, deferential language of serving as the churches' auxiliary. Although early association rhetoric described the YMCA's goal as supplementing the work of the church, for some men the association quickly replaced or superseded the role of Protestant churches. By 1882, when William Morriss filled the position of General Secretary, the Baltimore YMCA had emerged as an independent and legitimate institutional presence within the city's religious infrastructure.

Finding an appropriate niche on the religious landscape was a central goal of the YMCA throughout the United States. Thus, it is likely that the issues and challenges faced by the Baltimore YMCA in establishing institutional credibility and religious legitimacy were also encountered by associations in other American cities, as they, too, promoted a kind of applied Christianity that took its ministry well beyond the framework of the mainstream Protestant churches.

NOTES

1. J. W. M. Williams, *Reminiscences of a Pastorate of Thirty-Three Years in the First Baptist Church of Baltimore, Maryland* (Baltimore: J. F. Weishampel, 1884), 6; and Baltimore YMCA, 1854, *Annual Report*, 17.

2. Nancy Cott argues that as early as the mid-seventeenth century, women outnumbered men in the New England churches. It was, however, not until the nineteenth century that the feminization of Protestantism became conspicuous. See Nancy F. Cott, *The Bonds of Womanhood: Women's Sphere in New England, 1780–1835* (New Haven: Yale University Press, 1977), 126–132. Barbara Welter coined the term "feminization of religion" in "The Feminization of Religion in Nineteenth-Century America" in Mary Hartman and Lois Banner, eds., *Clio's Consciousness Raised* (New York: Harper Torchbooks, 1973), 305–332. For other examples of scholars concerned with the feminization of Protestantism, see also Carroll Smith-Rosenberg, "The Cross and the Pedestal," in Carroll Smith-Rosenberg, *Disorderly Conduct: Visions of Gender in Victorian America* (New York: Oxford University Press, 1985), 129–164; Mary P. Ryan, *Cradle of the Middle Class: The Family in Oneida County, New York, 1790–1865* (Cambridge: Cambridge University Press, 1981), 60–144; and Gail Bederman, "'The Women Have Had Charge of the Church Work Long Enough': The Men and Religion Forward Movement of 1911–1912 and the Masculinization of Middle-Class Protestantism," *American Quarterly* 41 (September 1989): 432–465.

3. Morriss served as the General Secretary of the Baltimore YMCA for more than forty years. Under his leadership the YMCA pioneered in making the change from traditional almsgiving to an allegedly scientific philanthropy. The association, for example, encouraged the growth of a meritocracy by establishing a web of schools. Moreover, it served *in loco parentis* to nurture and house young men and boys in locations throughout the city, reached out to workers in a variety of industrial settings, and began formal service to ethnic and racial minorities. For a more detailed discussion, see Jessica Elfenbein, "Urban Offering: The Baltimore YMCA and Metropolitan Change" (Ph.D. diss., University of Delaware, 1996).

4. *Baltimore American*, October 21, 1859; and Lawrence W. Wroth, "Churches and Religious Organizations in Baltimore," in *Baltimore: Its History and Its People* (New York: Lewis Historical Publishing Co., 1912), 678.

5. Franklin Wilson, *The Life Story of Franklin Wilson as Told by Himself in His Journals* (Baltimore: Wharton & Barron, 1897); Baltimore YMCA, 1854, *Annual Report*, 4–5; and original notice for the formation of the YMCA of Baltimore, November 12, 1852 (emphasis in the original) in Franklin Wilson Papers, MS 833, Box 3, Maryland Historical Society, Baltimore, Maryland (hereinafter cited as MHS).

6. Only eight clergymen attended the meeting. In addition to Williams, John Chester Backus of First Presbyterian, Joseph T. Smith, D.D., of Second

Presbyterian, John Henry Van Dyke of Christ Church, and the ministers from the Westminster Presbyterian, First German Reformed, and Methodist Episcopal churches were present. Baltimore YMCA, 1854, *Annual Report*, 16 and 17. In its early years, the YMCA distinguished between members of evangelical and nonevangelical churches, allowing only the former to be *active* members, while the latter were *associate* members. By 1869, reflecting the YMCA's increased emphasis on nondenominationalism, the association removed this disparity in membership status, reasoning that if any young man was "willing to work with us in saving young men, and persuading them to give up their evil habits and associations, why not let them do so without stopping to inquire what their particular views are in regard to abstruse questions of theology or what theological teachings they believe in. " Baltimore YMCA, 1869, *Annual Report*, 6.

7. Original notice for the formation of the YMCA of Baltimore, 12 November 1852, Franklin Wilson Papers, MHS, MS 833, Box 3. See also Karen Haltunnen, *Confidence Men and Painted Women: A Study of Middle-Class Culture in America, 1830–1870* (New Haven: Yale University Press, 1982), especially chapter 1.

8. Baltimore YMCA, 1854, *Annual Report*, 19, 20.

9. Baltimore YMCA, 1921, *Annual Report*, 1–2.

10. Baltimore YMCA, 1854, *Annual Report*, 8, 19, 20.

11. Ibid., 3.

12. Excerpt from the 1858 Constitution, Baltimore YMCA, 1858, *Annual Report*, 14.

13. Paul Boyer and Allan Stanley Horlick, in their works on young men in the cities, have largely accepted the YMCA's rhetoric identifying the association as an auxiliary to the churches. Both argue that the YMCA represented a nostalgic form of middle-class social control born of status anxiety and xenophobia. Yet, the YMCA was also a harbinger of American modernity that challenged the monopolistic role of the churches in the shaping of urban religiosity. See Paul Boyer, *Urban Masses and Moral Order in America, 1820–1920* (Cambridge: Harvard University Press, 1978), 108–120; and Allan Stanley Horlick, *Country Boys and Merchant Princes: The Social Control of Young Men in New York* (Lewisburg, PA: Bucknell University Press, 1975), 226–243.

14. Baltimore YMCA, 1858, *Annual Report*, 6.

15. Earlier attempts at interdenominational work in Baltimore were shortlived. Baltimore YMCA, 1857, *Annual Report*, 3, and 1854, *Annual Report*, 3; and Bernard C. Steiner, "Maryland's Religious History," *Maryland Historical Magazine*, XXI (March 1926): 12–13.

16. In 1854 the Reverends William I. Hoge, J. W. M. Williams, and Franklin Wilson served on the YMCA's board, the last as its Recording Secretary. In addition, Hoge served on the YMCA's Committee on Publication, and Williams and Wilson were members of the Committee on Lectures. Baltimore YMCA, 1854, *Annual Report*, 4–5, 17; and 1858, *Annual Report*, 18–19.

17. Baltimore YMCA, 1857, *Annual Report*, 4.

18. Marion Bell, *Crusade in the City: Revivalism in Nineteenth Century Philadelphia* (Lewisburg, PA: Bucknell University Press, 1977), 176.

19. Baltimore YMCA, 1858, *Annual Report*, 8–9. Several historians have argued that YMCAs were "the chief motivating force and promotional agency of the nation-wide revivals" that followed the panic of 1857. See, for example, Hopkins, *History of the Y. M. C. A.*, 45; Robert H. Bremner, *The Public Good: The Impact of the Civil War* (New York: Alfred A. Knopf, 1980), 11; and Bell, *Crusade in the City*, 182–183.

20. Baltimore YMCA, "Mirror of the Festival," May 24, 1859, Baltimore YMCA, Box 74, Folder 5, University of Baltimore Archives, Baltimore, Maryland (hereinafter cited as UBA).

21. Baltimore YMCA, 1858, *Annual Report*, 3–4.

22. Baltimore YMCA, Notice, April 19, 1859, UBA, Box 7, File 1; "Mirror of the Festival," May 24, 1859, UBA, Box 74, Folder 5; and Open Letter from J. Dean Smith, July 1, 1859, UBA, Box 7, File 1.

23. The leadership of the YMCA resolved "to take no part in any political question," Baltimore YMCA, Minutes of Board of Managers, October 19, 1854, UBA, Box 7, File 1. Unlike the neutral stance of the YMCA, many of Baltimore's churches supported either the Union or the Confederacy. For more information on sectional church ties, see Steiner, "Maryland's Religious History," 8, 18–19. For the period between May 1860 and 1866, no records for the Baltimore YMCA have survived.

24. M. Hamlin Cannon, "The United States Christian Commission," *Mississippi Valley Historical Review*, 38 (1951–1952): 61–80; Hopkins, *History of the Y.M.C.A.*, 89–92; and Richard C. Lancaster, *The Story of the YMCA's Ministry to Military Personnel for 125 Years* (Schaumburg, IL: Armed Services YMCA of the USA, 1987), 1–19.

25. Baltimore YMCA, 1859, *Annual Report*, 14; and 1868, *Annual Report*, 3, 5, 22–23.

26. By 1869, the News Boys' Home was incorporated as a separate organization, Baltimore YMCA, 1869, *Annual Report*, 26–27.

27. Baltimore YMCA, 1868, *Annual Report*, 6; 1869, *Annual Report*, 23; and 1871, *Annual Report*, 7.

28. Baltimore YMCA, 1868, *Annual Report*, 5, 16; and *Proceedings of the Meeting in Aid of the Young Men's Christian Association of Baltimore, December 22, 1870*, 25, UBA.

29. In 1877 the Friendly Inn furnished 14,015 meals and assisted 291 men in obtaining employment. During that year the Friendly Inn absorbed nearly 50 percent of the total YMCA expenditures of $7,820. By 1879 the Inn either subsidized or provided free of charge more than 50,000 meals and reported nearly 19,000 overnight stays of destitute men. The Friendly Inn, like the News Boys' Home, was short-lived, perhaps because of the YMCA's high financial commitment. Baltimore YMCA, 1883, *Annual Report*, 15–17; and Minutes, Executive Committee, January 12, 1880; *Weekly Bulletin*, 1, #2 (November 11, 1877); and *Weekly Bulletin*, 1, #8 (December 23, 1877), UBA, Box 70.

30. In 1877 the YMCA declared that "Our organization is one composed of Christian Workers, from the various denominations, banded together to work for 'The Master.' We hold to our respective churches, and consider our first duty belongs there, but in the many intermediate hours of leisure, we can find plenty of time to engage in YMCA work. " Baltimore YMCA, *Weekly Bulletin*, 1, #4 (November 25, 1877), UBA, Box 70.

31. Baltimore YMCA, "Mirror of the Festival," May 24, 1859, UBA, Box 74, Folder 5.

32. Baltimore YMCA, 1868, *Annual Report*, 4, 10.

33. The hostility between some rabbis and Baltimore's Young Men's Hebrew Association (YMHA) was more overt than the tensions between the YMCA and the city's Protestant clergy. The Baltimore YMHA, established in 1854, was the first association of its kind in the United States. It is likely that the founders of the YMHA were inspired by the successful model of the Baltimore YMCA. Unlike its Protestant counterpart, the YMHA engendered strong opposition from some rabbis who feared competition for the loyalty and membership of young men. Letters of David Philipson, January 24, 1870; and Letter from Rosenau to William Levy, January 15, 1917, cited in Isaac M. Fein, *The Making of an American Jewish Community: The History of Baltimore Jewry from 1773 to 1920* (Baltimore: Jewish Historical Society of Maryland, 1971), 132, 219.

34. John F. Moore, *The Story of the Railroad "Y"* (New York: Association Press, 1930), 68–69, 137.

35. In 1868 members of the YMCA also became involved in "Street and Park Preaching," Baltimore YMCA, Executive Committee Reports, September 15, 1868, UBA, Box 11, Folder 3; and 1869, *Annual Report*.

36. In 1874, the YMCA's secretary commented that the open-air meetings would remain a program of the association because both laymen and clergy saw them as being "of immediate importance" and something from which neither group could be absolved. Solving the problems endemic to this neighborhood apparently required the cooperation of all concerned citizens. Baltimore YMCA, 1874, *Annual Report*, 7, 17; and *Weekly Bulletin*, 1, #5 (December 2, 1877), UBA, Box 70.

37. Baltimore YMCA, 1869, *Annual Report*, 10; and 1871, *Annual Report*, 17.

38. During his Baltimore revival, Moody attended many YMCA meetings and delivered some 270 sermons at the city's churches, attracting an average attendance of 1,500 to 1,800 men. Thomas M. Beadenkopf and W. Raymond Stricklen, *Moody in Baltimore* (Baltimore: A. S. Abell & Co., 1879), 6; James F. Findlay, Jr., *Dwight L. Moody, American Evangelist, 1837–1899* (Chicago: University of Chicago Press, 1969), 344; Baltimore YMCA, "Address by John W. Garrett, Delivered on the 30th of January, 1883, before the YMCA of Baltimore on the Occasion of their Thirtieth Anniversary" (Baltimore, 1883); and Hopkins, *History of the Y.M.C.A.*, 344.

39. Findlay, *Dwight L. Moody*, 46–47, 63, 92–118.

40. Baltimore YMCA, *Weekly Bulletin*, 1, #5 (December 2, 1877), 6–8, UBA, Box 70; Beadenkopf and Stricklen, *Moody in Baltimore*, 27; and Hopkins, *History of the Y.M.C.A.*, 188.

41. James Carey Thomas, Chairman, YMCA Committee, to Baltimore's Ministers, June 27, 1879, UBA, Box 7, File 1.

42. Baltimore YMCA, *Weekly Bulletin*, 3, #6 (June 18, 1881), UBA, Box 70.

43. Baltimore YMCA, 1921, *Annual Report*, 5–6.

Chapter Two

Manhood Factories

Architecture, Business, and the Evolving Urban Role of the YMCA, 1865–1925

Paula Lupkin

On December 2, 1869, members of the New York YMCA gathered to dedicate their new headquarters located on the corner of Fourth Avenue and 23rd Street in lower Manhattan. At a cost of nearly half a million dollars, this five-story Second Empire structure was a prominent addition to the fashionable Victorian shopping and entertainment district known as the "Ladies Mile." Hundreds of New Yorkers attended the opening ceremony, and prominent religious, business, and political leaders addressed the crowd, including Schuyler Colfax, Vice-President of the United States, and John T. Hoffman, Governor of New York. The spectators had gathered to witness the unveiling of a new kind of religious building that was designed to impart Protestant values through mental, physical, and spiritual means.[1]

The New York YMCA was not the first building constructed specifically for association use. In 1859 the Baltimore YMCA had erected a small structure, and the associations in San Francisco, Chicago, and Washington, D.C., had dedicated buildings in the years following the Civil War. The New York building, however, was the first modern YMCA. Unlike earlier association structures, which resembled churches and functioned primarily as revival halls, New York's YMCA was a secular-religious hybrid. It housed under one roof a revival hall, gymnasium, library, employment office, social parlor, and classrooms. Designed to compete with the city's commercial amusements, the New York YMCA came to serve as the model for other associations that erected buildings during the late nineteenth century. More important, it helped to trans-

THE STRANGER.

Y.M.C.A.

RAILWAY STATION

ROOMS TO RENT

POOL ROOM WELCOME SALOON WELCOME

Y.M.C.A.
GYMNASIUM
BATHS
SWIMMING TANK
READING ROOMS
BILLIARDS AND POOL
DAY AND NIGHT SCHOOL
RESTAURANT
LECTURES
SOCIAL ENTERTAINMENTS
GOOD BOARDING PLACES REC-
OMMENDED.
EMPLOYMENT BUREAU
EMPLOYE S CHECKS CASHED.
FROM $5<u>00</u> TO $25<u>00</u> PER YEAR.

Figure 2. This 1908 front page cartoon in the *Chicago Tribune* illustrates the centrality of architecture in the YMCA's institutional identity. Warm and welcoming facilities were an essential tool in the struggle to compete with the city's commercial amusements. Copyrighted *Chicago Tribune* Company. All rights reserved. Used with permission.

form the YMCA from a fledgling evangelical group into a national network of efficient manhood factories designed to socialize young men adrift in the cities.[2]

The New York YMCA building was a visionary response of the city's business community to the problems precipitated by the influx of large numbers of young men from the countryside. Starting in the first half of the nineteenth century, ambitious young men left their rural homes and families in increasing numbers and flocked to the cities in search of financial and personal freedom. Members of New York's mercantile elite, who employed the rural migrants, were concerned about the moral welfare of the young men, as well as their potentially disruptive impact on urban society. The migrants, they feared, were adrift in a vacuum of moral authority, lacking proper guidance from the traditional sources of Christian socialization such as the church and the home. The city's mercantile elite tried to supplement the waning influence of churches and families by providing an institution of socialization that promoted Protestant virtues useful in business life such as thrift, honesty, temperance, industriousness, and benevolence.[3]

The 1869 dedication of New York's YMCA building, conceived and financed by prominent laymen from the business community, represented a pivotal development in the history of the American YMCA. Prior to the Civil War, the YMCA had provided services similar to those of hundreds of voluntary men's societies and mercantile libraries. Competing with these associations, the YMCA had offered inspirational lectures, Bible study classes, and wholesome recreation in an attempt to promote religious and moral values among young urban businessmen. Yet these programs had limited appeal and the YMCA remained financially unstable, relying on a volunteer workforce and operating in rented and often inadequate rooms.[4] Although some ambitious association leaders made several attempts to construct buildings prior to the Civil War, there was insufficient financial support for what most Protestants perceived as a radical venture.[5]

Following the Civil War, the tide began to turn when prominent members of the cities' commercial and financial elite assumed leadership roles in the YMCA. These businessmen brought not only their managerial skills but also their considerable financial fortunes with them.[6] Their sudden interest in the YMCA was sparked by a concern about proper business conduct that accompanied the emerging incorporation of America. Prior to the Civil War, the apprenticeship system had helped to maintain the good name of the business community by providing men with vocational training as well as moral supervision. Young migrants arriving in the cities often worked closely with their employers, and some even boarded with them. A clerkship in a shop not only taught the young man necessary skills and proper values such as thrift, duty, philanthropy, and sobriety, but also shaped his future commercial transactions and helped regulate the business practices of the mercantile community.[7]

After the Civil War, however, the apprenticeship system disintegrated when the onset of massive industrialization created the complex and often impersonal structure of the modern corporation. The introduction of machines into the manufacturing process altered traditional patterns of work and slowly replaced the craftsman with the wage laborer and the merchant with the corporate magnate. The explosion of economic and industrial activities also contributed to the physical growth of cities. This spatial expansion, accompanied by innovations in transportation, resulted in the fragmentation of the urban landscape according to function and class, dividing the rich from the poor and separating the residential neighborhoods from the shopping districts.[8]

As cities and companies grew in size, the relationship between employers and employees became increasingly impersonal. Clerks ceased to live above the shop and sought affordable rooms in boardinghouses or cheap hotels, which often catered to a transient and disreputable crowd.[9] Moreover, many boardinghouses were located at a distance from the homes of the affluent employers and often in close proximity to entertainment districts filled with saloons and other disreputable establishments. While the young men's physical distance from their employers increased their autonomy, it also exposed them to the dangers of city life. Typically raised in a slow-moving, close-knit agrarian society, rural migrants, some no older than fifteen, were forced to adjust quickly to this aggressive, impersonal urban culture. Without the close supervision of parents, ministers, and employers, they took to the streets in search of brightly lit, warm social spaces, companionship, and cheap meals.[10]

There were few respectable, attractive, and affordable leisure-time alternatives for the young men. Neither the city's philanthropic institutions, which were mostly dedicated to the causes of poverty and disease, nor the churches adapted themselves to the specific needs of the migrants. Most Protestant denominations viewed leisure and sport as the devil's tools and made little provision for them within the religious sphere of life. Nonsectarian institutions like Sunday Schools, voluntary associations, and mercantile libraries stepped into the gap, but these groups were ill equipped to compete for the attention of young men in the emerging marketplace of commercial leisure.[11]

Unlike the cities' religious groups and voluntary societies, commercial entrepreneurs adapted quickly to the social changes sparked by migration and industrialization. Saloons, cheap theaters, and dance halls offered young men attractive and nonrestrictive spaces to spend their leisure hours. The saloon keepers were particularly enterprising, offering free lunches, warm and inviting social rooms, the services of a savings bank, an employment bureau, and, occasionally, a cheap hotel. Not surprisingly, saloons often became the unofficial social centers for many young men adrift in the cities.[12]

The older generation of urban merchants, successful at fording the rapids of modern city life, feared that young men in the clutches of saloons would be exposed to greed and self-indulgence but to none of the values they held dear. Businessmen concerned about ensuring the survival of their values and ethics in this new corporate age took a growing interest in the work of the YMCA. The association seemed an appropriate vehicle for the businessmen's agenda, but the YMCA's limited facilities were inadequate to cater to the ever-growing number of young men who migrated to the cities in the second half of the nineteenth century.[13]

The moment had arrived for the YMCA's transformation, and the New York association took the lead. In 1865 the city's YMCA members elected a new Board of Directors, bringing a group of prominent business leaders, including James Stokes, William E. Dodge, and J. P. Morgan, to the helm of the association. These men set out to make the YMCA a more viable force able to compete with the city's commercial leisure facilities. A building specifically designed for YMCA use, the Board believed, would attract the growing number of young single men. The building they envisioned would combine the functions of a library, school, revival hall, and social club. It would house lecture, reading, and conversation rooms, circulating and reference libraries, and a gymnasium, as well as suitable accommodations for religious, literary, recreational, and social activities. The building did not contain dormitories but offered a boardinghouse register with a list of approved establishments.[14] YMCA leaders were hesitant to place young men in a single-sex living environment. By limiting themselves to recreational and educational facilities, they did not challenge the sanctity of the home, even a substitute home in a boardinghouse.[15]

In addition to providing young men with a morally sound urban refuge, YMCA leaders hoped that a building would give the association a physical and thus a more permanent place in society, lending it stability and status and elevating it from a fledgling voluntary organization to an institution of note.[16] Without a building, they argued, it would be difficult to be taken seriously by the public, the press, or the young men the association purported to serve. Moreover, a building dedicated to God's work in the commercial heart of the city was good publicity because it served as a monument to the civic-mindedness of the business community. Thus, the YMCA had to combine in a single structure a building that was welcoming to young men, impressive to the public, efficient in the production of proper values, and financially self-supporting.[17]

The YMCA's architectural design was the product of collaboration between William E. Dodge, chair of the association's building committee, YMCA Secretary Robert McBurney, and the architect, James Renwick, Jr.[18] Like other contemporaries, these men were influenced by the nineteenth-century debate about the effects of the physical and social environments on the individual's moral and religious development. These concerns first shaped American architecture during the Jacksonian period, when penitentiaries, hospitals, and asylums were designed to remove patients or criminals from a negative environment and place them in positive surroundings where they could be cured of vice or illness.[19]

Nineteenth-century concerns about the impact of the physical and social environments also affected religious architecture. Sunday School officials, for example, believed that the proper physical arrangement of classrooms played a crucial role in instilling in their students religious values and respect for authority. In 1839 the American Sunday School Union advocated a floor plan that placed several classes of different age groups in a single room. Each class was seated on a semicircular bench, hierarchically positioned to focus the attention of the students on the teacher and the superintendent, the latter sitting on a raised platform at the front of the room. The arrangement of the room "gave visual notice that this was to be an orderly social environment in which every individual had a clearly defined place." Like an engine that transformed raw material into a finished product, the Sunday School floor plan was designed to transmit the Protestant work ethic in the most efficient manner and mold children into productive, contented workers.[20]

In 1867 this social machinery was improved by Lewis Miller, inventor of the buckeye mower and reaper and superintendent of a Sunday School in Akron, Ohio. Miller devised a new floor plan based on the panopticon, a prison and factory design popularized by Jeremy Bentham in the late eighteenth century.[21] Instead of arranging semicircular benches within a square or rectangular room, Miller advocated that the room itself be semicircular, divided like a pie, with partitions forming classrooms for different age groups. The superintendent, seated on a platform at the center of the semicircle, was able to monitor efficiently the conduct of all students. The semipanoptic Akron plan was published widely in the religious press, copied by Sunday Schools throughout the country, and adopted by New York's YMCA leaders.[22]

The New York association building, similar to contemporary Sunday Schools, was designed to serve as an efficient socialization mechanism.[23] On the outside, the five-story building looked like a combination of an office building and the new department stores that had recently been constructed by YMCA contributors like A. T. Stewart, the Lord brothers, and John Wanamaker. Stores on the ground level and studios on the fifth floor were rented to businessmen and artists to generate funds for the association's operating expenses. The interior design of the building was plain but dignified. The rooms were furnished to promote a homelike atmosphere, and edifying paintings such as Thomas Cole's "The Cross and the World" lined the walls, contrasting sharply with the gaudy decor of many saloons. The physical arrangement of the association's rooms represented an adaptation of the Sunday School's panoptic floor plan. The entrances, exits, stairways, parlor, reading rooms, and classrooms were organized in a semicircle around a central reception area, staffed by a desk clerk who was able to monitor all activities from a single vantage point. This modified use of the panoptic plan was intended to reduce the number of paid staff while allowing for proper supervision of the men who visited the association.[24]

After the inauguration of the New York building, the city's YMCA leaders launched a campaign to convince other American associations of the "Advantages of a Permanent Home."[25] For this purpose, New York's association leaders operated through the Central Committee, the policy-making body of the North American YMCA. The Central Committee, renamed the International Committee in 1879, was not only dominated by New Yorkers but also occupied an office in the city's newly constructed association building. Throughout the 1870s and 1880s, the Committee moved to replicate the New York model in communities across the country.[26]

The YMCA's "Building Movement" was modeled on the corporations that the Committee members owned or dominated. Headquartered in New York, it was composed of a central office, a board of management, and traveling salesmen equipped with promotional tools. The Committee published thousands of pamphlets to popularize its new permanent home and hired association secretaries who rode the rail lines promoting the construction of YMCA buildings. These traveling salesmen distributed pamphlets and fundraising information and presented illustrated lectures in cities across the nation, seeding the continent with hundreds of associa-tion buildings. Appealing to civic pride and moral duty, traveling YMCA secretaries maintained that the size and appearance of an association building served as material evidence of the community's character. By 1890 even small towns were convinced that a YMCA building was essen-tial, not only to combat urban malaise but also to boost civic pride.[27]

Once a local group had decided to construct a YMCA the International Committee provided props, tools, and manuals to help launch a fundraising campaign.[28] Occasionally the Committee sent a YMCA secretary from New York to assist a local association in the orga-nization of a building campaign. In many cases, however, the Committee dispensed fundraising and architectural advice through its journals *Association Monthly* and *The Watchman*. The launching of these YMCA publications coincided with the advent of the Building Movement, and each issue featured on the front page a drawing and detailed description of a recently erected association building.[29] These reports provided important data for local architects and builders, who often worked under severe budgetary constraints and lacked the experience to implement the New York building on a smaller scale. Especially difficult was the trans-lation of the YMCA's novel conception of a public, dignified, and imposing yet homelike, attractive, and welcoming space that provided for ease of supervision.[30]

Although the New York building was the primary architectural model for American YMCAs, local associations often included different facili-ties tailored to their sites, budgets, needs, and tastes. The buildings, designed in Richardsonian Romanesque, neoclassical, Italianate, Second Empire, and Victorian Gothic styles, reflected the eclecticism that charac-terized architectural design in the late nineteenth century. Some associations had meeting halls and classrooms; others emphasized the parlor or included a gymnasium in their buildings. Despite these varia-tions, local association buildings continued to reproduce the panoptic floor plan first used in New York. The buildings' exteriors resembled that of New York's association, with ground-level stores and at least three additional stories for YMCA programs.[31]

By the 1890s, however, the New York YMCA had started to lose its status as the model for new associations. Libraries had become part of the urban infrastructure and were no longer an essential aspect of the association. The fussy parlor, a vestige of Victoriana, was replaced by a flexible series of social rooms that could be used for different purposes. The revival hall, an important element of the New York building, dimin-

The first home of the Dayton Association, in 1870, was in the old Journal Building—

In 1908 was removed into this large building, but the work continued to expand until another move was mandatory. In the fall of this year the Association will move again into the modern home shown below.

Then, upon reorganization in 1874, it occupied this building, which it outgrew—

and in 1886, built this home which became too small for the rapidly growing work, which—

Figure 3. This montage traces the history of the Dayton, Ohio, YMCA through the successive acquisition and construction of five buildings in only fifty-eight years. The constant replacement of facilities was necessary as membership grew and the association's building changed to meet new programmatic and technological requirements. Reprinted from Association Men (January 1929), with permission from YMCA of the USA Archives, University of Minnesota Archives.

ished in size or was eliminated altogether when the YMCA recognized exercise as a worthy character-building activity. As recreational and athletic programs started to overshadow religious activities, gymnasiums, locker rooms, and swimming pools became standard features of the YMCA, creating complex technological demands. Always eager to employ the latest and most efficient machinery for its manhood factories, the YMCA adopted the steel frame, as well as elaborate heating, lighting, and ventilation systems.[32]

The YMCA's venture into athletics also changed the exterior form of the association building. Reluctant to relinquish valuable space to storekeepers, associations started to experiment with alternative ways of generating their operating funds. In 1887 the associations in Harrisburg, Milwaukee, and Dayton introduced dormitories as a new source of income. The removal of ground-level stores and the addition of bedrooms transformed the appearance of the YMCA from that of an urban commercial structure to a clubhouse or modest hotel.[33]

Another factor that influenced the form of the modern YMCA building was the introduction of boys' work at the turn of the century. Most of the associations that offered programs for boys carved out a space for their adolescent members within the main building, yet removed from the adult facilities. However, concerns that the noise and juvenile behavior of rowdy boys would repel adults convinced some associations to purchase separate buildings, while others adopted a "twin building" design that linked side-by-side structures.[34]

In addition to providing special buildings for boys, many associations started to erect branches in residential neighborhoods. The new discipline of urban sociology and the passion for city planning, set off by the World's Columbian Exposition in 1893, focused public attention on the need for neighborhood-based recreation centers. This inspired YMCA leaders to expand the scope of their activities from a single building to a network of social centers under the supervision of a centralized metropolitan management. By 1901 ten cities had adopted the "metropolitan" system, setting off a wave of YMCA building construction.[35]

The increased construction activity strained the informal system of building advice developed by the International Committee in the 1870s and 1880s.[36] In response, in the early 1880s the International Committee appointed Erskine Uhl, one of its secretaries, to assist local associations as part of his duties. Supplementing the work of the traveling secretaries and the existing advice literature and displays, Uhl systematically gathered information about the cost, dimensions, and facilities of local association

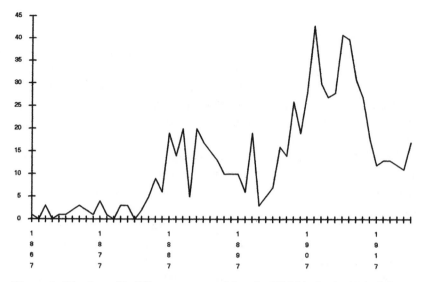

Figure 4. Number of buildings constructed for city YMCAs in the United States and Canada, 1867–1922. Data from *Yearbook of the Young Men's Christian Associations of America, 1898* (New York: International Committee, YMCA, 1898), 54–63, and "Table Showing Investments in City YMCA Buildings in U.S. and Canada, 1900–1925," Historical Records, Buildings and Furnishings Service, YMCA of the USA, Chicago.

buildings. Drawing on the data collected, Uhl advised local associations in the process of erecting buildings. Under his leadership, the International Committee published model floor plans and compiled architectural data in handbooks such as *The Book of Young Men's Christian Association Buildings* and *A Handbook of the History, Organization and Methods of Work of the Young Men's Christian Associations*.[37]

Despite these efforts, the International Committee continued to be overwhelmed by the growing demand for building assistance. At the turn of the century, answering local calls for guidance and support, the Committee assigned a field secretary, Charles S. Ward, to assist associations with their building projects. Ward, who had served as association secretary in several cities before accepting the field secretary position, was instrumental in shaping the YMCA's fundraising campaigns. He introduced standard fundraising procedures, most notably the "short-term building campaign," and promoted the patronage of a small group of architects specializing in constructing functional, low-cost buildings.[38] A handful of men, including Louis E. Jallade and John F. Jackson in New York and the Chicago firm of Shattuck & Hussey, and later Shattuck & Layer, were responsible for the majority of the nearly 200 YMCA buildings constructed between the turn of the century and the First World War. These architects gained familiarity with and expertise in the special requirements of YMCAs and served as the main sources of information about association building design.[39]

As a result of the employment of a small number of architects, YMCA buildings started to display uniformity in style and floor plan. The typical YMCA building designed by these architects was a simple rectangular Georgian or Renaissance Revival clubhouse of brick or stone with classical detail ornamenting the fenestration, cornice, and entrance. The consistent use of universal classical formulas replaced regional stylistic traditions like Romanesque Revival in the Northeast and Spanish Colonial Revival in the Southwest. Similarly, the interior design of YMCA buildings reflected a uniform style adhering to one key principle: a panoptic plan allowing for efficient and economic administration. This floor plan, placing the staff offices in the center of the social rooms, with direct sight lines to all entrances, exits, and staircases, was honed down to a formula and adapted to fit every possible site.[40]

Despite the sponsorship of Charles Ward, however, the specialist architects enjoyed only a brief period of popularity with YMCA building committees. By 1910 their buildings came under attack. Some association leaders were critical because the responsibility for designing YMCA buildings was placed in the hands of individuals whose goals were profit and self-promotion rather than the socialization of young men. Other association officials were apparently concerned about the business practices of Shattuck & Hussey, who were not well regarded in the architectural community. The American Institute of Architects received a half dozen strongly worded letters suggesting that Shattuck & Hussey were retained as YMCA specialists, not because of their skill but because Hussey was Ward's brother-in-law. Hussey's critics alleged that he had used this connection to secure YMCA commissions.[41]

Criticism of the architects and the buildings they designed was particularly strong at the local level. Hired to implement the YMCAs' practical priorities, the architects seemed content to replicate a functional and cheap plan, without regard to local needs or demands. Furthermore, many local associations complained about the architects' use of substandard materials and the poor quality of construction, which necessitated frequent repairs.[42] This rendered the buildings a hindrance rather than a help, as secretaries had to devote an increasing amount of time to fundraising campaigns in an effort to supplement maintenance and repair costs. One YMCA official compared the hap-

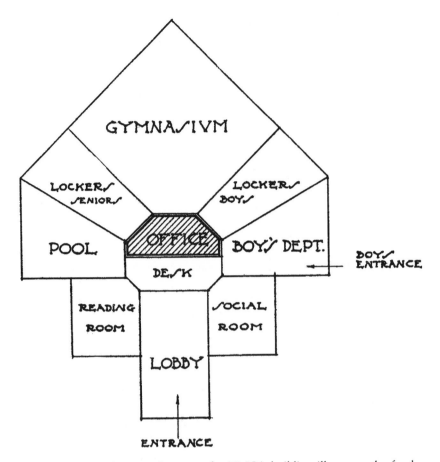

Figure 5. This schematic diagram of a YMCA building illustrates the fundamental principle of YMCA architecture: economy of administration. Association buildings were organized around a central observation post to offer the greatest degree of supervision with the least possible amount of manpower. From *The Association Building: Supervision and Circulation*, Part 1 (1913), YMCA of the USA Archives. Reprinted with permission from YMCA of the USA Archives, University of Minnesota Archives.

hazard building procedures of the time to a modern tower of Babel in danger of toppling.[43] A 1911 editorial in *Association Men* admitted that the incompetence and inefficiency of the building system "have cost not only thousands of dollars to repair, but have wasted thousands each year in [the] cost of extra supervision."[44]

By 1912 frustrated local YMCA secretaries started to petition the International Committee, urging it to provide sufficient supervision for the construction of association buildings.[45] Even the YWCA and the British YMCA, which built only a fraction of the number of buildings erected by the North American YMCA, had already addressed this problem and hired building experts.[46] While the American YMCA had devised highly efficient and systematic plans for fundraising campaigns, it had done little to secure proper spending of those funds. As an editorial in *Association Men* pointed out:

> The organized effort which secures millions each year for new buildings is conceded to be the best in the world. Now that we have gained the confidence of the people sufficiently to have them entrust their money to us, ought we not make adequate provision to ensure its wise expenditure?[47]

For a bureaucratic organization acknowledged by architectural critics as a leader in institutional design, this lack of a systematic approach to design was glaring.[48]

Responding to requests from its constituency, the International Committee began considering the creation of a special department in early 1912 and officially sanctioned its formation at the annual YMCA convention in 1913.[49] Initially the department made little progress, largely because the International Committee failed to delineate clearly its responsibilities and duties. However, this situation changed in 1915 when the International Committee hired Neil McMillan, who had not only an architectural degree but also association experience. The Committee placed McMillan in charge of a new planning division known as the Building Bureau, while Ward continued to supervise the fundraising campaigns.[50]

McMillan's first job was to determine the specific function of the Building Bureau. In the past, local associations had used either general-practice architects or the specialists endorsed by Ward; both groups had produced unsatisfactory results. The general-practice architects appeared to be more concerned with the artistic quality of their buildings than with their ability to function effectively; the opposite was true of the specialist architects. McMillan devised a system that aimed to combine both groups by placing the YMCA's own efficient building experts in charge of supervising talented general-practice architects. In the months prior to America's entry into World War I, he sketched the shape of a new planning service but was unable to implement it under wartime building restrictions. During the war McMillan toured YMCAs across the country, collecting and analyzing building data. He compiled records of different types of construction materials and maintenance procedures, studied the use of facilities at different hours of the day and night, and drafted plans for the standardization of buildings.[51]

Following World War I the Building Bureau, augmented by additional architects, engineers, and experts in building management, was ready for peacetime construction. The Bureau, stopping short of offering complete architectural services to local YMCAs, provided advisory design services, as well as assistance with a furnishings plan.[52] When a building committee hired the Building Bureau, its specialists helped them select a site and an architect, and developed plans for the financing and supervision of the construction. This service cost 2 percent of the building's projected budget. For this fee, the Bureau provided preliminary drawings of special details like swimming pool drainage and standard specifications to the architect, and reviewed his plans and contract. The architect, however, maintained control over the final drawings, artistic touches like the façade, and the construction of the building. For an additional 1.5 percent of the building's cost, the Furnishings Service of the Bureau took care of decorating decisions, transforming the YMCA's image from spare simplicity to comfortable, attractive masculinity. The Furnishings Service not only provided artistic services, but also used its buying power to obtain bulk discounts and even commission furniture specifically designed for YMCA buildings.[53]

With the introduction of the Furnishings Service, the YMCA acknowledged the distinction between the artistic and financial aspects of constructing an association building. The YMCA was no longer just a social machine; it was also a work of art. To differentiate the aesthetic from the utilitarian, the YMCA established a separate Financial Service Bureau to supervise fundraising campaigns and renamed the Building Bureau the Architectural Bureau.[54]

The services of the YMCA Building Bureau were very popular and widely used during the building boom of the postwar years. By 1920, forty-two American associations had contracted with the Bureau in the construction of fifty-three buildings. Within five years, nearly 90 percent of the association's new buildings were using the Bureau's services. The Building Bureau was so successful that the YMCA opened a branch office in Chicago.[55]

By the 1920s the association building had become a central part of the YMCA's identity. Yet, the YMCA's decision to rely heavily on buildings to achieve its goals was also a liability.[56] The public often failed to distinguish between the YMCA's physical structure and its programs. Association officials constantly refuted the idea that the YMCA was a building, insisting that it was just a "tool, to be used widely in producing our objectives."[57] Moreover, many YMCAs in smaller towns were ruined by the debt incurred through overly ambitious building programs. Cumbersome and expensive, the YMCA building was in many ways a burden. The process of erecting a building was by necessity a long one, often taking several years from fundraising to furnishing. By the time a building was finished, it was often considered outdated according to the standards of the International Committee. Change came slowly and expensively because the buildings' existing facilities and arrangement of rooms often hampered flexible programming. The YMCA, which had once tested the boundaries of acceptable Protestantism, became a conservative institution locked into the role of maintaining aging buildings.[58]

But this fact does not compromise the importance of buildings in the history of the YMCA. In the 1870s, when the YMCA started its building program, the association's business leaders turned to architecture as a means of efficiently dispensing moral values. As the YMCA continued to invest heavily in buildings, the moral component was overshadowed by recreational programs as the association strove to retain its membership while competing with commercial leisure institutions. The YMCA building, by providing a space in which leisure time could be interpreted in Protestant moral terms, helped ease the transition between a theocracy and a secularized American commercial culture.

NOTES

1. M. Christine Boyer, *Manhattan Manners: Architecture and Style 1850–1900* (New York: Rizzoli, 1985), 84; Jay E. Cantor, "The Public Architecture of James Renwick, Jr.: An Investigation of the Concept of an American National Style of Architecture During the Nineteenth Century" (M.A. thesis, Winterthur, 1967), 154–158; Rosalie Thorne McKenna, "James Renwick, Jr. and the Second Empire Style in the United States," *The Magazine of Art* 44 (March 1951): 97–101; "Dedication of the New Building of the Young Men's Christian Association of the City of New York," 1869, published by the Association, 23rd Street Branch Materials, Archives of the YMCA of Greater New York, New York City; hereinafter cited as NY Archives; Joseph P. Thompson, "The Association in Architecture," *Association Monthly* 1 (January 1870): 3–4; and "The Young Men's Christian Association," *Harper's New Monthly Magazine* 41 (October 1870): 644.

2. For a detailed discussion of YMCA architecture see Paula Lupkin, "YMCA Architecture: Evangelical Equipment for the American City, 1867–1920" (Ph.D. diss., University of Pennsylvania, 1996). See also Christine

Bogrette, "The Abington YMCA: A Case Study of an American Institutional Building Type" (M.A. thesis, University of Pennsylvania, 1993); and Paula Lupkin "A Temple of Practical Christianity," *Chicago History* 24 (Fall 1995): 22–41. Studies of related religious and secular social reform buildings include Deborah E. B. Weiner, *Architecture and Social Reform in Late-Victorian London* (Manchester: Manchester University Press, 1994); Ellen Weiss, *City in the Woods: The Life and Design of an American Camp Meeting on Martha's Vineyard* (New York: Oxford University Press, 1987); Guy Szuberla, "Three Chicago Settlements: Their Architectural Form and Social Meaning," *Journal of the Illinois State Historical Society* 70 (May 1977): 114–129; Ellen Christensen, "A Vision of Urban Social Reform," *Chicago History* 22 (March 1993): 50–61; Helen Lefkowitz Horowitz, "Hull House as Women's Space," *Chicago History* 12 (Winter 1983–1984): 40–55; David Glassberg, "The Design of Reform: The Public Bath Movement in America," *Journal of American Studies* 20 (2) (Fall 1979): 5–21; and Abigail Van Slyck, *Free to All: Carnegie Libraries and American Culture* (Chicago: University of Chicago Press, 1995).

3. The literature on this subject is voluminous. See Colleen McDannell, *The Christian Home in Victorian America, 1840–1900* (Bloomington: Indiana University Press, 1986), 1–52; Stuart Blumin, *The Emergence of the Middle Class: Social Experience in the American City, 1760–1900* (Cambridge: Cambridge University Press, 1989), 179–191; Ann Douglas, *The Feminization of American Culture* (New York: Knopf, 1977); Nancy Cott, *The Bonds of Womanhood: "Woman's Sphere" in New England, 1780–1835* (New Haven: Yale University Press, 1977); Mary Ryan, *Cradle of the Middle Class: The Family in Oneida County, New York 1790–1865* (Cambridge: Harvard University Press, 1981); Karen Halttunen, *Confidence Men and Painted Women: A Study of Middle-Class Culture in America, 1830–1870* (New Haven: Yale University Press, 1982); Michael W. Hughey, *Civil Religion and Moral Order: Theoretical and Historical Dimensions* (Westport, CT: Greenwood Press, 1983), 87–89; and Martin E. Marty, *Righteous Empire: The Protestant Experience in America* (New York: Dial Press, 1970), 107–109. Recent scholarship questions the concept of a distinct female domestic sphere and the prominence of mothers as role models for children. See, for example, Margaret Marsh, "Suburban Men and Masculine Domesticity, 1870–1915," in Mark C. Carnes and Clyde Griffen, eds., *Meanings for Manhood: Reconstructions of Masculinity in Victorian America* (Chicago: University of Chicago Press, 1990).

4. C. Howard Hopkins, *History of the Y.M.C.A. in North America* (New York: Association Press, 1951), 57. For the literature on urban voluntary associations see Paul Boyer, *Urban Masses and Moral Order in America, 1820–1930* (Cambridge: Harvard University Press, 1978), 14–21, 22–53; Blumin, *Emergence of the Middle Class*, 192–230; and Ryan, *Cradle of the Middle Class*, 127–136. For information on young men's societies in Britain and the United States see John Campbell, *Memoirs of David Nasmith: His Labours and Travels in Great Britain, France, the United States and Canada* (London: J. Snow, 1844);

John C. Symons, *The History and Advantages of Young Men's Associations* (Melbourne: George Nicholls, 1856); Clyde Binfield, *George Williams and the Y.M.C.A.: A Study in Victorian Social Attitudes* (London: Heinemann, 1973), 134–149; Richard D. Altick, *The English Common Reader: A Social History of the Mass Reading Public, 1800–1900* (Chicago: University of Chicago Press, 1957), 188–212; and Allan Stanley Horlick, *Country Boys and Merchant Princes: The Social Control of Young Men in New York* (London: Associated University Presses, 1975), 252–266.

5. In 1852, the New York YMCA appealed to the city's business community to help erect a building, and in 1857 the Brooklyn association made plans to construct a building housing a gymnasium, bowling alleys, classrooms, and reading rooms, as well as a library. *First Annual Report of the New York YMCA, 1852*, NY Archives, 7; and *Proceedings of the Fourth Annual Convention of the Young Men's Christian Associations of the United States and British Provinces*, Richmond, Virginia, May 21–23, 1857, 14; YMCA of the USA Archives, University of Minnesota Libraries, St. Paul, Minnesota, hereinafter cited as *Proceedings*.

6. Hopkins, *History of the Y.M.C.A.*, 102, 117. For a discussion of the involvement of businessmen in the YMCA and other evangelical philanthropic organizations see Aaron Abell, *The Urban Impact on American Protestantism, 1865–1900* (Hamden, CT: Archon, 1962), 3–18; Robert H. Bremner, *The Public Good: Philanthropy and Welfare in the Civil War Era* (New York: Knopf, 1984), 181–185, 208–211; and Alan Trachtenberg, *The Incorporation of America: Culture and Society in the Gilded Age* (New York: Hill and Wang, 1982).

7. For a discussion of the effect of industrialization on business practices see Blumin, *Emergence of the Middle Class*, 68–107; Glenn Porter, *The Rise of Big Business, 1860–1910* (Arlington Heights, IL: H. Davidson, 1973); and Alfred D. Chandler, Jr., *The Visible Hand: The Managerial Revolution in American Business* (Cambridge: Harvard University Press, 1977). Robert McBurney's entry into New York's business world is illustrative of the apprenticeship system of the early nineteenth century. See L. L. Doggett, *Life of Robert R. McBurney* (Cleveland: F. M. Barton, 1902), 17–19. See also Horlick, *Country Boys and Merchant Princes*, 11–15, 73–74; and Ryan, *Cradle of the Middle Class*, 128–129.

8. Charles N. Glaab and A. Theodore Brown, *A History of Urban America* (New York: Macmillan, 1967), 107–132, 139–140, 147–152; and Blumin, *Emergence of the Middle Class*, 163–179.

9. Ryan, *Cradle of the Middle Class*, 129, 255; and *A Memorandum Respecting New-York as a Field for Moral and Christian Effort Among Young Men* (New York: Young Men's Christian Association, 1866), 3, New York Public Library, hereinafter cited as NYPL. For a humorous description of the difficulties of boardinghouse life in New York in the 1850s see Thomas Butler Gunn, *The Physiology of New York Boarding-Houses* (New York: Mason Brothers, 1857).

10. Contemporary concern for these young men resulted in the creation of a genre of literature devoted to the plight of young men in the city. Advice books, novels, and lurid city guidebooks like Edward Winslow Martin's *The Secrets of the Great City* chronicled the sad end of many gullible young farm boys who sought companionship in the city's saloons. Some men were killed, stripped of their valuables, and dumped in the river. More common was the fate of the young men who were brought up in the bosom of home and church and then led into lives of debauchery and drunkenness. See the frontispiece of Edward Winslow Martin, *The Secrets of the Great City* (Philadelphia: Jones Brothers, 1868); Junius Henri Browne, *The Great Metropolis: A Mirror of New York* (Hartford, CT: America Pub. Co., 1869; reprint ed., New York: Arno Press, 1975); and James D. McCabe, Jr., *Lights and Shadows of New York Life; or the Sights and Sensations of The Great City* (Philadelphia: National Publishing Company, 1872).

11. Abell, *Urban Impact*, 6–7; and R. Laurence Moore, *Selling God: American Religion in the Marketplace of Culture* (New York: Oxford University Press, 1994), 4–6, and 91–95.

12. Perry R. Duis, *The Saloon: Public Drinking in Chicago and Boston: 1880–1920* (Urbana: University of Illinois Press, 1983), 184–197; and Jon M. Kingsdale, "The Poor Man's Club: Social Functions of the Urban Working Class Saloon," *American Quarterly* 25 (October 1973): 472–489.

13. Verranus Morse's speech, "Improvement of the Social Condition of Young Men," articulates these concerns; in *Proceedings*, Albany, New York, June 1866, 53.

14. "Historical Sketch of the Building of the Association," *Seventeenth Annual Report of the New York Young Men's Christian Association*, 1870, 54, NY Archives; *A Memorandum*, 4–10; *Proceedings*, Montreal, June 1867, 51; Rev. William Adams, *The Duty of Christian People to Those in their Employ* (New York: Robert Carter and Brothers, 1866); Verranus Morse, *Amusements: An Essay Read before the Young Men's Christian Association of New York City, November 7, 1867* (New York: James L. Hastie, 1868), both in the NY Archives.

15. This decision was questioned as early as 1872, when the boarding-house committee petitioned William Dodge, Jr., to consider the construction of YMCA hotels to serve the needs of young men. W. W. Hoppin to William Dodge, "Boarding Houses," January 1872, Branch Materials, 23rd Street Box, NY Archives.

16. The businessmen who launched the YMCA's building campaign had looked to architecture as a means of giving identity to their own enterprises. They had been the patrons of the first skyscrapers and were conscious of the symbolic value of buildings. See Winston Weissman, "New York and the Problem of the First Skyscraper," *Journal of the Society of Architectural Historians* 12 (March 1953): 13–21; and Kenneth Turney Gibbs, *Business Architectural Imagery in America, 1870–1930* (Ann Arbor: UMI Research Press, 1984), 15–17, 20–40.

17. See Robert A. Orr, "The First Year's Experience in a New Association Building," 1885, 4; E. S. Turner, "What Advantages have Accrued to Work for Young Men as a Result of Securing Association Buildings?" 1885, 4; and Leland Hume, "Successful and Safe Methods for Securing Money for Current Expenses or Buildings," 1888, 2, Buildings and Furnishings Records, box 1, YMCA of the USA Archives, University of Minnesota Libraries, St. Paul, Minnesota; hereinafter cited as YMCA Archives.

18. Doggett, *Life of McBurney*, 74; and Hopkins, *History of the Y.M.C.A.*, 151. Renwick had gained experience designing diverse types of buildings, including educational institutions such as the Smithsonian and Vassar College, as well as fashionable New York churches, hospitals, and theaters. See Cantor, "The Public Architecture of James Renwick."

19. The effects of environment were articulated and popularized by John Ruskin, *The Seven Lamps of Architecture* (New York: John Wiley, 1849); Andrew Jackson Downing, *The Architecture of Country Houses* (New York: Appleton & Co., 1850); Charles Darwin, *On the Origin of the Species; and, the Descent of Man* (New York: Modern Library, 1992); and Horace Bushnell, *Views of Christian Nurture, and of Subjects Adjacent Thereto* (Delmar, NY: Scholars' Facsimiles & Reprints, 1975). For a discussion of the impact of Bushnell's religious thinking on environmentalism, see Clifford E. Clark, Jr., "Domestic Architecture as an Index to Social History: The Romantic Revival and the Cult of Domesticity in America, 1840–1870," in *Material Life in America, 1600–1800*, ed. Robert Blair St. George (Boston: Northeastern University Press, 1988), 539–540. See also David J. Rothman, *The Discovery of the Asylum: Social Order and Disorder in the New Republic* (Boston: Little, Brown, 1971), 82; and Stanley Schultz, *Constructing Urban Culture: American Cities and City Planning* (Philadelphia: Temple University Press, 1989), 114.

20. General Assembly of the Presbyterian Church of the United States of America, *Minutes*, Philadelphia, 1844, 373; 1866, 6; 1867, 4, Presbyterian Historical Society, Philadelphia, Pennsylvania; and Boyer, *Urban Masses and Moral Order*, 46; see also the diagram in the group of illustrations between pages 36 and 37.

21. Marion Lawrance, *Housing the Sunday School* (Philadelphia: Westminster Press, 1921), 83–92; and Herbert Francis Evans, *The Sunday-School Building and its Equipment* (Chicago: University of Chicago Press, 1914), 5–13.

22. Michel Foucault, *Discipline and Punish: The Birth of the Prison* (New York: Vintage Books, 1979), 195–228; Robin Evans, *The Fabrication of Virtue: English Prison Architecture, 1750–1840* (Cambridge: Cambridge University Press, 1982), 195–235; Rothman, *The Discovery of the Asylum*, 83–88; Anne M. Boylan, *The Sunday School: The Formation of an American Institution, 1790–1880* (New Haven: Yale University Press, 1988), 101–114; and L. L. Doggett, *Life of McBurney*, 20.

23. YMCA literature often used machine metaphors when discussing association buildings. See Nelson F. Evans, "The Work of the Young Men's Christian

Association," *Proceedings*, San Francisco, May 11–18, 1887, 90; and E. S. Turner, "What Advantages?" 1885, 1, Buildings and Furnishings Records, box 1, YMCA of the USA.

24. "Young Men's Christian Association of the City of New York, Building Committee Report," March 21, 1871, 4–8, Branch Materials, 23rd Street Box, NY Archives; Winston Weissman, "Commercial Palaces of New York: 1845–1875," *Art Bulletin* 36 (December 1954): 285–302; Christine I. Oaklander, "Studios at the YMCA, 1869–1903," *Archives of American Art Journal* 32, 3 (1992): 14–22; "The Cross and the World," published by the Association, n.d., Branch Materials, 23rd Street Box, NY Archives; and "Conversational Intelligence," *Association Notes* 4 (February 1889): 6, NY Archives.

25. Rev. T. G. Darling, *Advantages of a Permanent Home for a Young Men's Christian Association* (New York: George F. Nesbitt & Co., 1881), Buildings and Furnishings Records, box 1, YMCA of the USA.

26. Paul Boyer chronicles the proliferation of public buildings constructed to effect social reform in the late nineteenth century: *Urban Masses and Moral Order*, 233–251.

27. Hopkins, *History of the Y.M.C.A.*, 117; and Darling, *Advantages of a Permanent Home* and *Why Should we have a Young Men's Christian Association in our Town?* (New York: International Committee, 1888), 12–14, 26, 33, Buildings and Furnishings Records, box 1, YMCA of the USA.

28. *Ten Reasons Why it Paid*, n.d., n.p., marked no. 86; *Plan of a Canvass for a Young Men's Christian Association Building*, n.d., n.p., marked no. 202; Richard C. Morse, *The Young Men of Our Cities* (privately printed, 1885); and Darling, *Why Should we have a Young Men's Christian Association in our Town?*.

29. The YMCA began publication of *Association Monthly* in 1870 and of *The Watchman* in 1874. William E. Dodge, Jr., "How to Secure a Building," *The Watchman* 5 (May 1, 1879): 99; W. H. Morriss, "The Association Building, or Headquarters: Number, Arrangement, and Care of Rooms," *The Watchman* 8 (April 15, 1882): 116; "Why Should We Have a New Association Building?" *The Watchman* 8 (June 15, 1882): 181; "Where Should the Gymnasium be Located?" *The Watchman* 14 (June, 15, 1888): 181; and H. B. Gordon, "Association Architecture: External Appearance and Interior Arrangements," *Young Men's Era* 16 (April 17, 1890): 241 and *Young Men's Era* 16 (April 24, 1890): 257.

30. Andrew Saint, *The Image of the Architect* (New Haven: Yale University Press, 1983), 82.

31. Richard Longstreth, *The Buildings of Main Street: A Guide to American Commercial Architecture* (Washington, DC: Preservation Press, 1987), 24–51, 76–99.

32. "Passing Things in Association Architecture," *Association Men* 30 (May 1905): 378; "Association Reconstruction—An Example," *Association Men* 38 (March 1913): 28–29; Robert B. Reeves, "Changes at the Twenty-Third Street Branch," *Men of New York* 40 (January 1925): 16; "The New and Vast

Reception Room, West Side New York," *Association Men* 38 (February 1913):
229; *Hints about the Construction of Association Buildings* (New York:
Association Press, 1909), 30. On the introduction of athletics see Clifford
Putney, "Character Building in the YMCA, 1880–1930," *Mid-America* 73
(January 1991): 60–64; Harvey I. Allen, "Artificial Light for Gymnasiums,"
Physical Training 7 (May 1911): 20–23; M. I. Foss, "Equipment and
Construction of the Physical Department," *Physical Training* 7 (May,
September–October 1910): 3–7, 19–24, 18–21; and "Heating of Young Men's
Christian Association Buildings," *Radiation* 2 (May 1913): 10–14.

    33. Dormitories and cafeterias were controversial additions to the YMCA.
Many association leaders were concerned about the difficulty of managing them,
and they did not become a standard feature of YMCA buildings until after the
turn of the century. In 1901, YMCA construction guides began to include eating
facilities as necessary elements of association buildings. Dormitories, however,
were not considered essential until 1910. The Chicago (1913) and Buffalo
(1910) associations also erected separate YMCA hotels to serve their patrons,
but most associations incorporated living space into their buildings. Chester D.
Barr, "Y.M.C.A. Dormitories: Theory and Practice" (M.A. thesis, Ohio State
University, 1927), 6–7, Residences/Dormitories, box VI, 725, YMCA of the
USA; "What Part of the Building Should be Used by the Association?" *The
Watchman* 14 (July 1, 1888): 202–203; "The Report of an Informal Conference
on Young Men's Christian Association Buildings," Buffalo, 1901, 15, Buildings
and Furnishings Records, box 1, YMCA of the USA; *Hints about the
Construction of Association Buildings* (New York: Association Press, 1909), 3,
Buildings and Furnishings Records, box 1, YMCA of the USA; A. G. Studer,
"Large Modern Buildings," *Proceedings*, Toronto, October 28–31, 1910, 79;
and *How to Establish a City Young Men's Christian Association with Modern
Building and Equipment* (New York: Association Press, 1916), 17.

    34. The YMCA had offered some programs for boys starting in the 1860s;
however, there was no systematic approach until the International Committee
established the Boys Work Department in 1900. Hopkins, *History of the
Y.M.C.A.*, 200–207; and David Macleod, *Building Character in the American
Boy: The Boy Scouts, YMCA, and Their Forerunners, 1870–1920* (Madison:
University of Wisconsin Press, 1983), 74–78; H. S. Ninde, J. T. Bowne, and
Erskine Uhl, eds., *A Handbook of the History, Organization, and Methods of
Work of Young Men's Christian Associations* (New York: International
Committee of the Young Men's Christian Associations, 1892), 166, YMCA of
the USA; and Edgar M. Robinson, "Provision for Boys' Work in Association
Buildings," *American Youth* (August 1914): 195–257.

    35. Hopkins, *History of the Y.M.C.A.*, 419–420. On the influence of the
Columbian Exposition see M. Christine Boyer, *Dreaming the Rational City: The
Myth of American City Planning* (Cambridge: MIT Press, 1983), 46–56.

    36. *Yearbook of the Young Men's Christian Association of North America*,
1883, 3, YMCA of the USA Archives.

37. "Typical Building Plans," *Association Notes* 21 (December 1, 1906): 2–4; Ninde, Bowne, and Uhl, eds., *A Handbook*; I.E. Brown, *Book of Young Men's Christian Association Buildings* (Chicago: Young Men's Era, 1895); *Hints About the Construction*; Walter Wood, *Association Buildings* (New York: International Committee of the Young Men's Christian Associations, n.d.); and *The Report of the Buffalo Building Conference* (n.p., 1901); all in Buildings and Furnishings Records, box 1, YMCA of the USA.

38. Scott M. Cutlip, *Fund Raising in the United States: Its Role in American Philanthropy* (New Brunswick: Rutgers University Press, 1965), 41; and Hopkins, *History of the Y.M.C.A.*, 599. The "short-term building campaign" replaced the inefficient and labor-intensive process of soliciting individual wealthy donors with a communitywide event. Prepared by advance publicity in local newspapers, competing teams of young men armed with a list of prospects, a special system of donation slips, and recordkeeping equipment canvassed the city systematically to raise funds within a given amount of time, usually a month. This freed YMCA staff from the constant and overwhelming need to raise funds.

39. These architects did not automatically receive all YMCA commissions. Some associations, especially those in large cities, held competitions to select an architect. Frank E. Sickels, *Fifty Years of the Young Men's Christian Association in Buffalo: A History* (Buffalo: published by the Association, 1904), 79; Philadelphia YMCA, Building Committee Minutes, February 1, 1906, Philadelphia YMCA Collection, Acc 151 and 173, box 7, Temple University, Urban Archives, Philadelphia, Pennsylvania; Louis Allen Abramson, "The Planning of a Young Men's Christian Association, I, II, III," *The Brickbuilder* 22 (March–May 1913): 49–54, 77–80, 127–131. Abramson was the partner of Louis Jallade and the architect of the Young Women's Hebrew Association building on Central Park North in New York City. Louis E. Jallade, "Suggestions for Furnishings," *Association Men* 36 (October 1911): 11; and John F. Jackson, "Constructive Criticism on Association Building," *Association Men* 36 (March–April, June–July 1911): 263, 303, 401–405.

40. Louis E. Jallade, *The Association Building, 1. Supervision and Circulation*, with an introduction by Thornton B. Penfield (New York: Association Press, 1913).

41. Report of the Special Committee Appointed to Review General Policies and Budget Problems of the Architectural Bureau, 1928, Buildings and Furnishings Records, box 1, YMCA of the USA Archives; and Walter F. Shattuck, Biographical Files, American Institute of Architects Archives, Washington, DC.

42. Charles C. May, "A Post-War Construction Program: The Building Bureau of the International Committee of the YMCA," *Architectural Record* 42 (March 1919): 217. The poor quality of construction materials and craftsmanship may have been due in part to extremely tight budgets. See "Statement for Consideration of the Special Committee on the Architectural Bureau's Policy

and Charges," Meeting at the Yale Club, New York City, September 10, 1928; YMCA of the USA Buildings and Furnishings Service, Historical Collection, YMCA of the USA corporate headquarters, Chicago; hereinafter cited as BFS.

43. Sherman Dean, "Putting Character into Buildings," *Association Men* 43 (January 1928): 215.

44. "A National Building Expert Needed," *Association Men* 36 (June 1911): 376.

45. "The Builders' Bureau," *Cleveland's Young Men*, May 2, 1912, Buildings and Furnishings Records, box 1, YMCA of the USA.

46. "A National Building Expert Needed," *Association Men* 36 (June 1911): 376; and "Report of the National Council," *Yearbook of the Young Men's Christian Association of Great Britain and Ireland, 1902–3*, 21, English Materials, box E2, YMCA of the USA.

47. L. H. Martin, "A Building Expert Needed," *Association Men* 36 (December 1911), 123.

48. Fiske Kimball, "The Social Center," *Architectural Record* 45 (May 1919): 433.

49. Executive Committee of the International Committee of the YMCA, Minutes, "Report of the Commission Appointed at the Atlantic City Conference to Further Consider and Propose Desirable Re-adjustments in the Work of the International Committee," December 12, 1912, 50, Administrative Records, YMCA of the USA.

50. *Proceedings*, Cleveland, 1916, 69.

51. International Committee of the Young Men's Christian Association, Minutes, September 12, 1918, 331, Administrative Records, YMCA of the USA; and *Proceedings*, Cleveland, 1916, 69.

52. The architectural community, represented by the American Institute of Architects, was not pleased with the Building Bureau's policies. See Board of Directors of the American Institute of Architects, *Minutes*, December 9–10, 1928, 21, and April 27, 1929, 21, Archives of the American Institute of Architects, Washington, DC.

53. "Statement for the Consideration of the Special Committee on the Architectural Bureau's Policy and Charges," Meeting at the Yale Club, New York, September 10, 1928, BFS. This fee structure was borrowed from the American Institute of Architects, which had just recently established its standard fee at 6 percent. Saint, *Image of the Architect*, 94; Neil McMillan, "Building Bureau Service," in *The Building Enterprise of a City Young Men's Christian Association*, n.p., 1919, 11–13, and *Report of the International Committee of the Young Men's Christian Association to the National Council*, 1924, 94, Buildings and Furnishings Records, box 1, YMCA of the USA Archives; and Obsolete Furniture Designs, Furnishings Service, Building Bureau, Buildings and Furnishings Records, box 6, YMCA of the USA.

54. Dean, "Putting Character into Buildings," 216.

55. In 1923 the Bureau had contracts with associations for sixty-four buildings, the total cost of which exceeded $15 million. In 1924 the Bureau was

retained on seventy-five building projects worth $22 million. "Report of the Architectural Bureau To The National Council of YMCA's for the period from December 1, 1924 to October 5, 1925," 4, Building and Furnishing Records, box 1, YMCA of the USA Archives.

56. For an extended discussion of some of the negative effects of the YMCA building program see Owen Pence, *The Y.M.C.A. and Social Need: A Study of Institutional Adaptation* (New York: Association Press, 1939), 254.

57. O. M. Brunson, "Function of the Y.M.C.A. Building in the Association's Program," n.d., Buildings and Furnishings Records, box 1, YMCA of the USA Archives.

58. In the early twentieth century the YMCA experimented with nonbuilding programs, called "Community" or "Nonequipment" work. Responding to the proliferation of recreational facilities, settlement houses, and parks, the YMCA attempted to provide its character-building services without the assistance of a specially designed physical environment. Nonequipment programs utilized existing neighborhood facilities such as churches, empty store fronts, and schools. Although this type of work was particularly useful during the Depression, when the construction of new buildings was severely limited, those who participated usually campaigned for a building. See Hopkins, *History of the Y.M.C.A.*, 483–485.

Chapter Three

Contested Spaces
The YMCA and Workingmen on
the Railroads, 1877–1917

Thomas Winter

In late-nineteenth-century America, urbanization generated a proliferation of new public spaces such as libraries, playgrounds, parks, and settlement houses, as well as YWCAs and YMCAs. Many urban elites, including middle-class reformers and philanthropy-minded entrepreneurs, helped create these spaces, hoping to regulate the attitudes and behavior of the cities' masses.[1] The spaces reflected the sense of mission of this self-conscious urban elite and were designed to promote the values reformers and philanthropists held dear: self-restraint, civic duty, a reverence for genteel cultural ideals, and, above all, Christian morality.[2]

Concerns about the proper demeanor and conduct of the city's working classes also permeated the leadership ranks of the YMCA, which were dominated by members of the urban elite. The YMCA began to experiment with ways to carry the association's message of Christian manhood to the working classes in 1877. That year the YMCA created a Railroad Department to reach out to transient railroad workers. Under the auspices of this Department, the YMCA offered railroad employees Bible classes and entertainments, and opened its reading rooms and exercise facilities to them.[3] Association officials hoped that workers would shed their propensity for political radicalism and industrial unrest once they adopted the YMCA's higher ideals of manhood, rooted in Christian values such as brotherhood,

Figure 6. Many railroad workers embraced the YMCA's ideal of Christian manhood, but they also challenged the association's control over the buildings
designed to turn them into reliable workers. Reprinted from *Railroad
Association Men* 5, 22 (May 1916), with permission from YMCA of the USA
Archives, University of Minnesota Libraries.

service, cleanliness, and temperance. Thus, YMCA programs aimed at
defusing the workers' potential for industrial unrest by involving them
in a web of uplifting activities, all of which were designed to make them
better men and more loyal employees.[4] Many railroad managers shared
the YMCA's concern with proper standards of manliness, and railroad
companies, troubled by the mounting discontent of their workers,
often supported the YMCA in an effort to ensure allegiance among
their workforce.[5]

Despite the conservative intentions of the YMCA's Railroad
Department, large numbers of workers joined the associations. In 1886,
when the YMCA's *Yearbook* first recorded railroad association statistics,
fifty-eight branches reported 9,506 members. By 1917, the number had
increased to 225 associations with a membership of 107,870.[6] While railroad YMCAs were at least in part designed to mold workers into morally
reformed individuals, better men, and more dedicated employees, the
associations did not necessarily reinforce the cultural hegemony of the
urban elite. Although many railroad workers shared the YMCA's ideals
of manhood, they also contested the control over the spaces designed to
shape their behavior off and on the job.[7]

The working-class members of railroad YMCAs were particularly successful in shaping the programs of local associations due to the YMCA's administrative structure. The International Committee, the main governing body of the North American YMCA, had largely an advisory function, which limited its power to influence local association management. The International Committee, for example, could advise local branches and recommend candidates for employment as professional YMCA secretaries. Moreover, the Committee set policies regulating the participation of YMCA members in national association governance. Members who wished to vote or hold office in the association had to sign the Evangelical Test, a compilation of New Testament phrases that the International Committee considered to be central tenets of orthodox Protestant doctrine. Yet, the YMCA of North America was essentially a confederation of autonomous local associations, each maintaining control over its own governance and budget. The administrative and fiscal autonomy of local branches opened avenues for power struggles between YMCA officials, company sponsors, and working-class patrons.[8]

Railroad YMCAs were usually established in response to demands initiated by the YMCA, the workers, or company management. In many cases, a YMCA official, either a member of the International Committee or the secretary of an already existing city association, established contacts with the management of a railroad company to launch the founding of an association. Occasionally, however, railroad workers took the initiative and instigated the creation of a YMCA branch without initial aid from the International Committee. YMCA officials or workers interested in establishing an association then presented their case to the railroad company's management to obtain a pledge of funding and permission to drum up support among its employees. Railroad companies, which represented the largest source of income of the YMCA's Railroad Department, usually provided buildings and partial funding of the secretary's salary, as well as the association's running expenses. Yet, company support often depended on sufficient interest in the YMCA among employees, and company managers frequently required the association to raise matching funds through membership fees. Once a railroad branch was established, the workers appointed from their ranks a Committee of Management, which hired a full-time professional YMCA secretary. The workers' involvement in the establishment, funding, and governance of local associations provided them potentially with a considerable voice in the affairs of railroad branches.[9]

Railroad YMCAs drew the majority of their members from the ranks of the "running services," composed of highly skilled railroad engineers and conductors as well as semiskilled brakemen and firemen. In 1908, for example, a Chicago trainman obtained the signatures of 360 railroad employees petitioning the city's YMCA to organize a Railroad Department on the South Side. The workers who signed the petition represented more than thirty skilled and semiskilled occupations; however, only two of the signers identified themselves as laborers. Membership figures of the New York railroad YMCA also indicate that skilled and semiskilled workers displayed the strongest interest in association work. Employees in the running services were often eager to join the association because their jobs forced them to travel frequently and the YMCA proved convenient while on the road.[10]

Skilled railroad workers not only welcomed the YMCA for pragmatic reasons but also embraced the association's ideals of manhood. Engineers and conductors, among the highest-paid railroad employees, regarded the YMCA as a means of initiating their fellow workers into their male craft culture. As skilled workers, they believed that a man established self-esteem and earned the respect of his fellow workers, superiors, and the community through industry, sobriety, duty, civility, and responsibility.[11] Skilled railroad workers not only hoped to perpetuate their craft culture but also felt the need to guard their reputations, afraid that they would be judged by the behavior of their less reputable fellow workers.[12] The governance of railroad YMCAs was largely in the hands of these aristocrats of labor, who considered the association's notion of manliness central to the individual's social, moral, and economic uplift.[13]

Semiskilled workers of the running services often joined the YMCA not only because they shared the manhood ideals of the aristocracy of labor but also in the hope of bolstering their careers. Firemen and brakemen, recruited from among the unskilled workers, viewed their positions as stepping stones to professional and economic advancement. Firemen aspired to become engineers, and brakemen hoped to become conductors. A brakeman, who may have hoped to advance one day to the position of conductor, praised the YMCA for promoting manliness among railroad workers: "I have often wanted to tell you that the `Y' has made me a better man. . . . You should be proud you are in the Business of Bettering Men." By joining the YMCA, workers signaled their superiors that they subscribed to the values which both company management and the skilled aristocracy of the railroad workforce embraced.[14]

Some labor unions, such as the Brotherhood of Locomotive Engineers and the Order of Railroad Conductors, also praised the YMCA's efforts to promote Christian manhood among the workingmen. Peter M.

Arthur, Grand Chief Engineer of the Brotherhood of Locomotive Engineers, for example, associated manliness with rugged individualism, achievement, and self-improvement, claiming that "a person endowed with a true manly spirit finds little fault with the conditions of his life." A true man, Arthur asserted, will strive for individual accomplishment and take pride in his work, and he concluded that the YMCA's programs greatly benefited the railroad workers because they helped them to become not only better workers but also "better men." Crediting the YMCA for its efforts to ameliorate industrial conflict through moral reform, Arthur asserted that "there is a better feeling between the men and those over them, a better understanding of the fact that all men can meet on the common plane of religion and Bible study as well as manliness and honesty."[15] Warren S. Stone, Arthur's successor, concurred and insisted that an important goal of any union should be the advancement of manhood among its members. "[T]he labor union which looks after the wage scale of its members and does not strive to uplift the man to a higher standard of citizenship and manliness," Stone proclaimed, "falls short of its mission."[16]

Railroad managers often promoted ideals of manhood among their employees that were virtually identical to those of the Railroad Brotherhoods and the YMCA. Theodore Vorhees, for example, Vice-President of the Philadelphia & Reading Railroad and former Superintendent of the New York Central & Hudson River Railroad, declared "that it is very much the business of the company to make sober, moral men of their employees, and that any money successfully expended for that end is well invested." Not surprisingly, many railroad officials, concerned about maintaining a disciplined and loyal workforce, believed that support of the YMCA was in the best interest of their companies.[17]

While some labor unions shared the conservative goals of the YMCA and the railroad companies' management, others believed that association buildings and their genteel surroundings might very well serve the interests of organized labor and stir the workers into action. The *Union Pacific Employee Magazine*, a Knights of Labor publication, pointed to the possible multiple uses of a YMCA building. The paper acknowledged that YMCAs were designed to prevent workers from organizing but also insisted that the amenities of association buildings could serve purposes other than those of its corporate sponsors. Association buildings, the paper pointed out, could "be made the most effective ally in the work of labor advancement." Exposed to the genteel environment of the YMCA parlor, the paper predicted, workers would develop "the desire to have them all the times [sic]." They would gain a sense "of very unjust and unnecessary conditions" and search for remedies. Therefore, the paper concluded, "labor organizations everywhere should encourage the growth of the demand of such places and see that they are patronized. . . . If possible make the lecture rooms their assembly rooms." The *Union Pacific Employee Magazine* encouraged its readers to explore ways in which workers could infuse YMCA facilities with meanings of their own.[18]

In some cases, the working-class patrons' determination to exercise more control over railroad associations resulted in the complete separation of railroad branches from the YMCA. By 1879, only two years after the inauguration of the YMCA's Railroad Department, five of the existing thirty-two railroad associations decided to separate from YMCA governance. The separation of the railroad associations of Cleveland; Indianapolis; Elmira, New York; Meadsville, Illinois; and Altoona, Pennsylvania, from their respective city branches challenged the very integrity of the fledgling Railroad Department.[19]

The reasons for these separations are difficult to assess, but strictures of YMCA governance and a feeling that affiliation with the city branches would stifle the expansion of the railroad association movement played key roles. Some of the separatists apparently feared that the rapidly growing railroad work might be bogged down by the city branches, which set association policy on the local level and controlled the purse strings of the railroad branches.[20] Henry Stager, President of the Railroad Men's Christian Association of Cleveland, explained that prior to separation, railroad workers had to join the city association, which then transferred funds to the railroad branch. Cleveland's separatists were convinced that their affiliation with the city branch—which, like most city associations, was controlled by the urban business leaders—hampered their ability to attract railroad workers. By severing its ties with the city association, Cleveland's railroad YMCA tried to gain control over its own membership's contributions. This, Stager claimed, would place "the association in full control of those directly interested" and likely attract more workers.[21]

Other railroad branches separated from the YMCA because of its forbidding attitude toward games, which apparently limited the association's appeal to workers. George Cobb, secretary of the separatist Indianapolis railroad association, claimed that the lack of games alienated workers and drove them into saloons. Cobb urged the introduction of "innocent" games such as checkers and parlor croquet as a strategy to keep the workers out of disreputable places. Moreover, Cobb cautioned other YMCA secretaries "not to plaster the walls of our rooms with 'don't do this' and 'don't do that,' for as a result the boys don't come in." Cobb warned that these restrictive policies prevented many workers, who were apparently "a little suspicious" of the YMCA's objectives, from entering association buildings. Only after the Indianapolis railroad association separated from the city YMCA was Cobb able to remove these suspicions. Scolding his fellow railroad secretaries, Cobb added that "there have been mistakes made by the Y.M.C.A. We might as well confess that."[22]

Even though only a few branches sought independence from YMCA governance, separatist sentiments among railroad associations challenged the leverage of the YMCA in negotiations with railroad companies for further funding. Influential railroad officials such as Cornelius Vanderbilt urged autonomous associations, which depended on railroad contributions and used railroad property, to reunite with the YMCA. Association representatives and railroad officials also assured the workers that they would continue to have a voice in the management of railroad YMCAs. By 1883 the issue was settled in favor of the YMCA, and it appears that all separatist branches renewed their affiliation with their respective city associations.[23]

Yet, the lesson that the YMCA had to do more to attract workers was not lost on YMCA Railroad Department officials. In the aftermath of the separatist movement, the Railroad Department made efforts to become more attractive to the workers, but it did not abandon its primary goal of morally uplifting the railroad men. Indeed, YMCA officials believed that games could be incorporated into the association's grand strategy of improving men by means of moral reform. Edwin D. Ingersoll, the International Committee's General Secretary for Railroad Work, recognized that many workers might not be interested in prayer meetings and Bible classes. But Ingersoll hoped to use games to attract workers to YMCA buildings, and he predicted that those men would soon become interested in other "social and musical entertainments, or in illustrated newspapers and magazines."[24]

Ingersoll considered more uplifting forms of entertainment only a first step in the process of morally regenerating the workers. As railroad workers took part in genteel leisure activities, he predicted, amusements would become less crucial in attracting the worker once he "has learned to want and use something better. Thought is stimulated. His social instincts are satisfied with healthful associations." Ingersoll believed that once the association's working-class members experienced good literature, enlightened debates, and classical music, their entertainment preferences would be transformed. As men were led to desire more genteel ways to use their leisure, he speculated that "beer gardens and billiard rooms" would become "less attractive than our rooms."[25] Indeed, he concluded that the "social, literary and musical attractions . . . cheerful rooms and good influences" of the YMCA left "no excuse . . . to any employee to use stimulants or seek harmful surroundings for society, refuge and rest in leisure hours."[26] Once exposed to the inspiring environment of a YMCA building, Ingersoll surmised, workingmen would turn their back on traditional forms of working-class culture. This change, Ingersoll believed, would also affect the worker's behavior on the job, as he "becomes a better man, a better citizen, [and] a more intelligent and loyal servant of the corporation."[27]

Even when the YMCA broadened its program to include games, association officials continued to insist on instilling in workers a sense of gentility in the hope of turning them into more faithful employees. Nonetheless, games remained a controversial subject. The YMCA had begun to accept chess and checkers, but games such as billiards were identified with gambling and drinking and therefore detrimental to the association's goal of building Christian manhood. Yet, by the early twentieth century, workers had forced the YMCA to make concessions and to accept billiards, smoking rooms, and bowling alleys.[28]

Railroad workers challenged YMCA regulations and introduced billiards despite the association's ban of the game in its rooms. In 1899, for example, rank-and-file workers of the railroad association in Hoboken, New Jersey, inaugurated billiards. Most likely aware of the controversial nature of the subject and in lieu of the appropriate equipment, the workers introduced billiards in a piecemeal process. For a while, the YMCA parlor must have been an amusing sight as the workers started playing pool on a croquet table "using cues instead of mallets; then a few adventurous [ones] undertook to play a kind of mongrel game of billiards on the croquet table, in spite of the disadvantages of the wickets." Eventually, "the wickets were taken out, a new cloth provided for the table, and billiards were played on a house-made table." Finally, the Superintendent of Construction of a local railroad assembled "a billiard table, which seemed to answer the purpose very well."[29]

The workers' introduction of billiards put the secretary of Hoboken's railroad branch in an awkward position. While local donations and membership dues provided for the secretary's salary, he was also a representative of the International YMCA and as such was required to uphold association policy, including the ban on billiards. The general secretary of

Figure 7. Initially, YMCA officials resented billiards as a danger to Christian manhood. Despite YMCA opposition to the game, railroad workers successfully established billiards in railroad associations by the early twentieth century. Reprinted from *Railroad Men* 27, 12 (September 1914), with permission from YMCA of the USA Archives, University of Minnesota Libraries.

the Hoboken railroad YMCA, therefore, had to absolve himself of any responsibility for the situation. The introduction of billiards, he claimed, was "the natural result of a chain of circumstances beyond the control of the leaders in the Christian work of the Association, who were opposed to the movement." However, the secretary tried to assure his fellow YMCA officials that "he did all in his power to promote the best interests of the scheme, immediately taking precautions to surround the playing of billiards in the Association with proper safeguards." YMCA officials particularly feared that games such as billiards would encourage gambling and urged secretaries to be wary of "unwholesome competition." Although the secretary did not elaborate on the precautions he took, close supervision of the workers' activities surrounding the table was certainly among them.[30]

Despite the secretary's opposition, the Committee of Management of Hoboken's railroad YMCA welcomed the introduction of billiards. The engineers and conductors who dominated the Committee claimed that billiards could very well aid in weaning less reputable workers away from saloons. Thus, they launched a fundraising campaign among the patrons for the acquisition of a billiard table. By embracing billiards, skilled railroad workers espoused a rather pragmatic vision of the YMCA's mission. A conductor argued: "I consider billiards a good thing for the Association, as it keeps men in the building, and away from objectionable places." This conductor certainly did not think that billiards would hamper the YMCA's effort to promote higher ideals of manhood among the workers. Another railroad worker expressed similar sentiments, insisting that "if you are going to rob the saloon of its patronage, you must rob it of its games, when they are not necessarily wrong." In particular, the members of the Committee of Management, who represented the aristocracy of railroad labor, expressed the hope that billiards would aid in drawing the men away from saloons and other places of ill repute and bring them under proper guidance within the YMCA.[31]

Given the interest of the workers and the support of the Committee of Management, billiards became a permanent feature of the Hoboken association despite the YMCA's and the secretary's opposition to the game. A month after first reporting that workers had introduced billiards, the Hoboken secretary wrote: "we are still studying the billiard table problem." The secretary's reservations about the game, however, were already obsolete, as he admitted: "there is no doubt that with us the game has come to stay."[32]

While the secretary at Hoboken had lost control over the leisure activities of the association's members, elsewhere workers were not as successful in undermining the YMCA's policy. The members of the railroad YMCA of Mechanicville, New York, for example, tried to introduce billiards without success. When Lucien C. Warner, chairman of the YMCA's New York State Committee, heard about the incident, he immediately dispatched the committee's railroad secretary, John Ferguson Moore, to investigate the matter. Within a day Moore had "the offending table taken apart and stored securely behind the locked door of a closet."[33] Whether billiards made it into the rooms of a local YMCA apparently depended to a large degree on the ability of the local Committee of Management to resist interference from state and national authorities.

Only after the turn of the century did YMCA railroad officials embrace billiards. George A. Warburton, general secretary of the New York City railroad branch and the influential editor of *New York Railroad Men*, acknowledged that "the games and the smoking rooms have been a large factor in helping the Association to compete with the saloons for the patronage of railroad men." Games, Warburton claimed, were "a distinct help, each appealing to men with different social and intellectual tastes."[34] Warburton recognized that although games were not directly linked to the promotion of moral uplift, they could nonetheless fulfill a useful role within the YMCA's strategy of moral reform. In the end, the YMCA accepted billiards and other previously undesirable activities, but association officials remained convinced that they could use games and smoking rooms as part of a larger strategy designed to create morally reformed men.

Whatever the motives, billiards and other games drew far more workers into YMCAs than the quest for religious salvation. Between January and July 1913, the Grand Trunk Railroad YMCA conducted thirty-five religious interviews with workers, but not a single men joined the church. Yet, during the same period more than 3,000 men requested games, such as chess and checkers, and more than 4,000 men played billiards.[35] The general secretary of the Chicago & Eastern Illinois branch reported similar figures. Between February and September 1913, ninety-one patrons requested a religious interview. While no men converted or joined the church as a result of these interviews, more than 1,600 men played pool during the same time period.[36] At other locations, however, religious programs were apparently more popular. During March 1899, for example, 547 railroad workers with the Chesapeake & Ohio Railroad attended religious meetings at eight railroad associations located throughout Kentucky and Virginia, whereas only 165 workers participated in YMCA entertainment programs.[37] By and large, however, workers clearly did not go to the YMCA to satisfy spiritual needs.

Apathy and resentment best describe most workers' reactions to the religious programs of the railroad YMCA. In East St. Louis, for example, lack of interest led to the discontinuation of religious work in 1899. Due to space constraints, the branch's secretary had conducted gospel meetings in the association's reading room, which "resulted in driving out a number of men who were not interested" and instead "made an adjacent saloon their place of resort until the meetings were over."[38] A brakeman with the Pennsylvania Railroad expressed what many workers must have felt about the YMCA's attempts to minister to them. Complaining to the YMCA secretary, he charged: "I have been bothered with Bible-study lessons lately; I believe they came through you . . . I wish you'd have them discontinued."[39] The workers' objection to the YMCA's religious programs also affected the association's ability to attract new members. The general secretary at Dearborn Station in Chicago noted that whenever he asked workers to take out memberships in the YMCA, they responded by complaining about "dull times."[40] Few of the railroad workers who joined the association considered membership in the YMCA as a long-term commitment, and membership turnover was generally high among them. Some of the fluctuation was due to workforce turnover, but many workers simply stopped paying dues.[41]

Substantial numbers of railroad workers used the YMCA's facilities and services without joining the association. The secretary at Dearborn Station, for example, noted that some men who "made a convenience of the rooms in disagreeable winter weather, absent themselves as the weather is more pleasant outdoors."[42] Railroad workers who patronized the association without taking out memberships often felt that the services they rendered to the company entitled them to the free use of the YMCA. Thus, many railroad workers not only failed to pay dues but also refused to settle their bills at the YMCA. Along the Pennsylvania Railroad, the problem apparently became so prevalent that the Chicago YMCA requested that the company introduce a system of payroll deductions. However, company managers rejected the request, arguing that it exceeded their responsibility.[43]

While some workers declined to pay for association privileges, others used the facilities without showing much respect for what YMCA officials considered to be proper conduct and behavior. Ward Adair, YMCA secretary in Scranton, Pennsylvania, for example, criticized workers whose "idea is that the place was built for the use and abuse of railroad men irrespective of membership." Adair particularly disapproved of the general lack of respect for etiquette among some of the workers. The "mossback," Adair complained, "spits on the new floor as he did on the old [and] his used up quids are thrown in the general direction of the cu[s]pidor, but he cares little where they land." Adair alerted his fellow secretaries that when such a worker "patronizes the washroom, it will be well to search his side-pockets for soap before he leaves the place." Adair griped, "should he be so reckless as to take a bath, look in his calaboose for your missing bath towel."[44] While Adair's grousing sounds amusingly petty, it also illustrates that workers had little respect for YMCA officials' concerns about standards of respectable behavior. The workers' violation of etiquette, however, turned out to be a minor concern compared to the problems that an association had to face during a strike.

Strikes represented the most severe challenge to the relationship between YMCA secretaries and railroad workers. During industrial conflicts the YMCA tried to maintain a neutral position in an attempt to appease both employers and employees. Preserving the association's neutrality, however, was a difficult task. While companies generally insisted that their financial contributions entitled them to put up strikebreakers at the YMCA, the dues-paying working-class members also demanded loyalty from the association for their cause.[45] If a secretary rejected the demands of the employer to accommodate strikebreakers, the railroad company usually cut its financial support of the association. In 1911, for example, when the secretary of the Waterloo, Illinois, YMCA refused to put up strikebreakers, the Illinois Central Railroad Company responded by stalling plans to expand association work along its lines.[46]

Yet, those secretaries who resisted the attempts of employers to intervene in the management of associations earned the workers' respect. In July 1910, for example, during a strike along the Grand Trunk Railroad, the company's superintendent at Niagara Falls, New York, tried to order the secretary's assistant to evict two of the strikers and refund their money. The assistant not only "refused point blank to do so" but also prevented the railroad superintendent from entering the building to remove the offending workers himself. The YMCA secretary reported that "this episode was heralded all along the line and did not a little toward softening the feeling of the strikers toward the Association."[47] The secretary's defiance of the railroad company and his support of the striking workers was apparently not an isolated incident. In 1908, during a strike in Van Buren, Mississippi, one of the strikebreakers went to the YMCA's lunch counter but an association employee sympathetic to the strikers refused to serve him.[48]

Workers not only demanded that the YMCA refuse to support railroad companies during strikes, but on several occasions they took matters into their own hands to prevent strikebreakers from entering association buildings. In 1902, for example, a fight broke out at the Cleburne Railroad YMCA between striking workers and railroad company guards when the latter tried to carry an injured strikebreaker into the YMCA building.[49] In another incident a YMCA secretary employed as a porter a man who had lost his job during a previous strike. When one of the former strikebreakers visited the association, a group of men led by the porter attacked him outside the building. The YMCA secretary, who witnessed the ensuing fistfight from a window, tolerated the porter's actions and neither fired nor reported him to the YMCA's Board of Directors.[50]

Workers along the railroads both embraced and contested the YMCA's provision of leisure-time activities in an exclusively male environment.

Despite amicable relations between YMCA secretaries and railroad workers and their unions, only a few men took the association's offering lock,
stock, and barrel. Workers remade railroad YMCA branches to reflect
their leisure-time preferences, often in defiance of association standards of
etiquette and propriety. The contest over the use of YMCA facilities particularly escalated during strikes. Situated at a critical junction of
industrial relations, railroad YMCAs could not escape the conflicts
between workers and management. On such occasions, railroad workers
made it clear that they expected the YMCA to serve their purposes and
interests. By defying the YMCA's expectations about appropriate behavior inside the association buildings and by challenging company control
over railroad branches during strikes, workers contested the YMCA's
intentions to produce more loyal servants of the corporation.

NOTES

1. For a discussion of the relationship between bourgeois culture, public
spaces, and voluntary associations, see Jürgen Habermas, *The Structural
Transformation of the Public Sphere: An Inquiry into a Category of Bourgeois
Society* (Cambridge, Mass.: MIT Press, 1989); Geoff Eley, "Nations, Publics,
and Political Cultures: Placing Habermas in the Nineteenth Century," in:
Culture/Power/History: A Reader in Contemporary Social Theory, ed. by
Nicholas B. Dirks, Geoff Eley, and Sherry B. Ortner (Princeton: Princeton
University Press, 1993), 297–335; Kathryn J. Oberdeck, "Religion, Culture, and
the Politics of Class: Alexander Irvine's Mission to Turn-of-the-Century New
Haven," *American Quarterly* 47 (June 1995): 236–79; Michael Schudson, "Was
There Ever a Public Sphere? If So, When? Reflections on the American Case,"
in: *Habermas and the Public Sphere*, ed. by Craig Calhoun (Cambridge, Mass.:
MIT Press, 1992), 143–163; and David Scobey, "Anatomy of the Promenade:
The Politics of Bourgeois Sociability in Nineteenth-Century New York," *Social
History* 17 (May 1992): 203–27.

2. For a more detailed discussion of the expansion of cities and the response
of urban reformers, see Samuel P. Hays, *The Response to Industrialism,
1885–1914* (Chicago: University of Chicago Press, 1957), 94–115; Robert
Wiebe, *The Search for Order, 1877–1920* (New York: Hill and Wang, 1967),
44–75, 111–32; Alan Trachtenberg, *The Incorporation of America: Culture and
Society in the Gilded Age* (New York: Hill and Wang, 1982), 101–39; Stuart M.
Blumin, *The Emergence of the Middle Class: Social Experience in the American
City, 1760–1900* (Cambridge: Cambridge University Press, 1989), 192–229;
Raymond A. Mohl, *The New City: Urban America in the Industrial Age,
1860–1920* (Arlington Heights, Ill.: Harlan Davidson, 1985), 165; Paul Boyer,
Urban Masses and Moral Order, 1820–1920 (Cambridge: Harvard University

Press, 1978); Allan Stanley Horlick, *Country Boys and Merchant Princes: The Social Control of Young Men in New York* (Lewisburg: Bucknell University Press, 1975); Henry F. May, *Protestant Churches and Industrial America* (New York: Harper & Row, 1949); Jean Quandt, *From the Small Town to the Great Community: The Social Thought of Progressive Individuals* (New Brunswick: Rutgers University Press, 1970); Paul A. Carter, *The Spiritual Crisis of the Gilded Age* (DeKalb: Northern Illinois University Press, 1971); Donald K. Gorrell, *The Age of Responsibility: The Social Gospel in the Progressive Era, 1900–1920* (Macon: Mercer University Press, 1988); Robert M. Crunden, *Ministers of Reform: The Progressives' Achievement in American Civilization, 1889–1920* (New York: Basic Books, 1982); and Susan Curtis, *A Consuming Faith: The Social Gospel and Modern American Culture* (Baltimore: Johns Hopkins University Press, 1991).

3. For a discussion of the YMCA's railroad work, see John F. Moore, *The Story of the Railroad "Y"* (New York: Association Press, 1930); Richard C. Morse, *My Life With Young Men: Fifty Years in the Young Men's Christian Association* (New York: Association Press, 1918), 391–95; Morse, *History of the North American Young Men's Christian Associations* (New York: Association Press, 1919), 207–16; C. Howard Hopkins, *History of the Y.M.C.A. in North America* (New York: Association Press, 1951), 227–36, 390–91, 475–79; and Clarence J. Hicks, *My Life in Industrial Relations: Fifty Years in the Growth of a Profession* (New York: Harper & Brothers, 1941), 18–40. Gilded Age religious reformers noted with great concern that the workers increasingly refrained from attending church. See Carter, *The Spiritual Crisis of the Gilded Age*, 135–50; and Herbert George Gutman, "Protestantism and the American Labor Movement: The Christian Spirit in the Gilded Age," *American Historical Review* 72 (October 1966): 74–101. On conflicts between workers and reformers over the relation between Christianity and labor issues, see Kenneth Fones-Wolf, *Trade-Union Gospel: Christianity and Labor in Industrial Philadelphia, 1865–1915* (Philadelphia: Temple University Press, 1989).

4. For a discussion of middle-class ideals of manhood, see E. Anthony Rotundo, "Body and Soul: Changing Ideals of American Middle-Class Manhood, 1770–1920," *Journal of Social History* 16 (Summer 1985): 23–35; Rotundo, *American Manhood: Transformations in Masculinity from the Revolution to the Modern Era* (New York: Basic Books, 1993); Clyde Griffen, "Reconstructing Masculinity from the Evangelical Revival to the Waning of Progressivism: A Speculative Synthesis," in: *Meanings for Manhood: Constructions of Masculinity in Victorian America*, Mark C. Carnes and Clyde Griffen, eds. (Chicago: University of Chicago Press, 1990), 183–204; Ted Ownby, *Subduing Satan: Religion, Recreation, and Manhood in the Rural South, 1865–1920* (Chapel Hill: University of North Carolina Press, 1990); Mark C. Carnes, *Secret Ritual and Manhood in Victorian America* (New Haven: Yale University Press, 1989); Mary Ann Clawson, *Constructing Brotherhood: Class, Gender, and Fraternalism* (Princeton: Princeton University Press, 1989); Judy

Arlene Hilkey, *"The Way to Win: A Search for Success in the New Industrial Order, 1870–1910"* (Ph.D. diss., Rutgers, The State University of New Jersey, 1980), 146–68; and Gerald Franklin Roberts, "The Strenuous Life: The Cult of Manliness in the Era of Theodore Roosevelt" (Ph.D. diss., Michigan State University, 1970).

5. B. D. Caldwell, "The Railroad Employee as a Man," *New York Railroad Men* 14 (November 1900): 58–62. See also Olivier Zunz, *Making America Corporate, 1880–1920* (Chicago: University of Chicago Press, 1990), 125–48; Robert Ozanne, *A Century of Labor-Management Relations at McCormick and International Harvester* (Madison: University of Wisconsin Press, 1967); Bruno Ramirez, *When Workers Fight: The Politics of Industrial Relations in the Progressive Era, 1898–1916* (Westport: Greenwood Press, 1978); Stephen J. Scheinberg, *Employees and Reformers: The Development of Corporation Labor Policy, 1900–1940* (New York: Garland, 1986); Oscar Nestor, *A History of Personnel Administration, 1890–1910* (New York: Garland, 1986); Stuart D. Brandes, *American Welfare Capitalism, 1880–1940* (Chicago: University of Chicago Press, 1976); Gerald Zahavi, *Workers, Managers, and Welfare Capitalism: The Shoeworkers and Tanners of Endicott Johnson, 1890–1950* (Urbana: University of Illinois Press, 1987); Howard Gitelman, "Welfare Capitalism Reconsidered," *Labor History* 33 (Winter 1992): 5–31; David Montgomery, *The Fall of the House of Labor: The Workplace, the State, and American Labor Activism, 1865–1925* (Cambridge: Cambridge University Press, 1987); Shelton Stromquist, *A Generation Of Boomers: The Pattern of Railroad Labor Conflict in Nineteenth-Century America* (Urbana: University of Illinois Press, 1987); and Paul K. Edwards, *Strikes in the United States, 1881–1974* (New York: St. Martin's Press, 1981).

6. *Year Book of the Young Men's Christian Associations of the United States and the Dominion of Canada, For the Year 1886* (New York: International Committee, 1917), 156, hereinafter cited as *Yearbook*; and *Year Book, 1917* (New York: Association Press, 1917), 54. The Railroad Department mostly served white workers and operated only one facility for African Americans at Bluefield, West Virginia. See *Railroad Association Magazine*, 3 (November 1914): 34; Jesse E. Moorland, "The Colored Railroad Man," *Railroad Association Magazine*, 4 (January 1915): 4–6. On the YMCA's work with African Americans in cities, see Nina Mjagkij, *Light in the Darkness: African Americans and the YMCA, 1852–1946* (Lexington: The University Press of Kentucky, 1994).

7. For the ways in which hegemony and domination can also open possibilities for counterhegemonic contest, see Richard Hoggart, *Uses of Literacy* (Harmondsworth: Penguin, 1990); James C. Scott, *Domination and the Art of Resistance: Hidden Transcripts* (New Haven: Yale University Press, 1991); and Stuart Hall, "Notes on Deconstructing `the Popular'," in *People's History and Socialist Theory*, ed. by Raphael Samuel (London: Routledge & Kegan Paul, 1981), 227–40. For studies exploring how reformers attempted to use public

spaces to transmit their values, see Dominick Cavallo, *Muscles and Morals: Organized Playgrounds and Urban Reform, 1880–1920* (Philadelphia: University of Pennsylvania Press, 1981); and George Cotkin, *Reluctant Modernism: American Thought and Culture, 1880–1900* (New York: Twayne, 1992), 101–9, 116–19. On contests between workers and reformers over proper use of leisure time, see Roy Rosenzweig, *Eight Hours for What We Will: Workers and Leisure in an Industrial City, 1870–1920* (Cambridge: Cambridge University Press, 1983).

8. The Evangelical Test was adopted at the 1869 convention in Portland, Maine, and remained in force until 1931. See *Young Men's Christian Association Handbook* (New York: n.p., 1892), 66–130; Hopkins, *History*, 18–19, 48, 62, 65, 115–16, 362–69; and S. Wirt Wiley, *History of Y.M.C.A.-Church Relations in the United States* (New York: Association Press, 1944), 2–3, 17–18.

9. See David L. Lightner, *Labor on the Illinois Central Railroad, 1852–1900: The Evolution of an Industrial Environment* (New York: Arno Press, 1977), 275–78; Hicks, *My Life in Industrial Relations*, 18–28; Moore, *Story*, 16–20; Pierce Williams and Frederick E. Croxton, *Corporation Contributions to Organized Community Welfare Service* (New York: National Bureau of Economic Research, 1930), 13, 228–29; F. Emerson Andrews, *Corporation Giving* (New York: Russell Sage Foundation, 1952), 25–26, 28; and *Proceedings of the Second International Conference of the Railroad Young Men's Christian Associations of the United States and British Provinces, held at Altoona, Pennsylvania, September 18–21, 1879* (New York: Executive Committee of Young Men's Christian Associations of the United States and British Provinces, 1879), 32, box 5, Railroad Convention Proceedings, YMCA Railroad Department Records, 1877–1987, YMCA of the USA Archives, University of Minnesota, St. Paul, Minnesota, hereinafter cited as YMCA Railroad Records.

10. See Biebesheimer Petition, 1908, South Chicago Railroad Department, Petitions, box 17, folders 16–18, Series II, Board of Trustees, 1861–1975, Subseries 3, Vault Materials, 1861–1966, YMCA of Metropolitan Chicago Papers, Chicago Historical Society, Chicago, Illinois, hereinafter cited as YMCA of Chicago; "Classification of Membership," *New York Railroad Men* 4 (February 1891): 94–95; "Classification of Membership," *New York Railroad Men* 10 (October 1896): 170; "Classification of Membership," *Railroad Men* 11 (February 1898): 153; "Classification of Membership," *Railroad Men* 12 (February 1899): 194; "Classification of Membership," *Railroad Men* 13 (February 1900): 200; "Classification of Membership," *Railroad Men* 14 (February 1901): 220; "Classification of Membership," *Railroad Men* 15 (February 1902): 202; "Classification of Membership," *Railroad Men* 18 (February 1905): 188.

11. Nick Salvatore, *Eugene V. Debs: Citizen and Socialist* (Urbana: University of Illinois Press, 1982), 22–30; David Montgomery, "Workers' Control of Machine Production in the Nineteenth Century," *Labor History* 17 (Fall 1976): 491; David Bensman, *The Practice of Solidarity: American Hat*

Finishers in the Nineteenth Century (Urbana: University of Illinois Press, 1985), 68–88; Patricia A. Cooper, *Once a Cigar Maker: Men, Women, and Work Culture in American Cigar Factories, 1900–1919* (Urbana: University of Illinois Press, 1987), 75–89, 123–52, 322–23; Ava Baron, "Questions of Gender: Deskilling and Demasculinization in the U.S. Printing Industry, 1830–1915," *Gender & History* 1 (Summer 1989): 178–99; Baron, "An 'Other' Side of Gender Antagonism at Work: Men, Boys, and the Remasculinization of Printers' Work, 1830–1920," in *Work Engendered: Toward a New History of American Labor,* ed. by Ava Baron (Ithaca: Cornell University Press, 1991), 47–69.

12. E. C. Dixon, "How Can Christian Railroad Men Furnish to Their Comrades the Antidote and the Substitute for the Tippling," in *Proceedings of the First International Conference of the Railroad Young Men's Christian Associations of the United States and British Provinces, held at Cleveland, Ohio, October 25–28, 1877* (New York: Executive Committee of Young Men's Christian Associations of the United States and British Provinces, 1877), 27, box 5, Railroad Convention Proceedings, 1877–1894, YMCA Railroad Records. See also A. M. Watt, "The Relation of the Railroad Department to the Spiritual Life of Railroad Men," *Proceedings of the Ninth International Conference of the Railroad Department of Young Men's Christian Associations of North America, held at Fort Wayne, Indiana, October 20–23, 1898* (New York: International Committee of Young Men's Christian Associations, 1898), 32, box 6, Railroad Convention Proceedings, 1895–1905, YMCA Railroad Records.

13. Lists of delegates available for several YMCA railroad conferences support this point. Among the 308 delegates present at the seventh YMCA railroad conference in New York City in 1894, shopmen ranked first, with 38 delegates, and engineers second, with 35. Firemen and brakemen ranked sixth and seventh, with nine and eight delegates, respectively. The following year, at the eighth YMCA railroad conference at Clifton Forge, Virginia, 469 delegates were present. Among them, engineers ranked first, with sixty-six delegates, followed by sixty clerks, fifty-two shopmen, thirty-one conductors, twenty-five firemen, and twenty brakemen. This pattern was replicated at the ninth YMCA railroad conference at Fort Wayne, Indiana, in 1898: among the 643 delegates, engineers were in the lead, with 84 delegates, followed by 81 shopmen, 51 clerks, 48 conductors, 43 brakemen, and 28 firemen. Overall, engineers continued to send the largest numbers of delegates to YMCA railroad conferences. See *Proceedings of the Seventh International Conference of the Railroad Department of Young Men's Christian Associations of North America, held in New York City, March 29 to April 1, 1894* (New York: International Committee of Young Men's Christian Associations, n.d.), 14, box 5, Railroad Convention Proceedings, 1877–1894, YMCA Railroad Records; *Proceedings of the Eighth International Conference of the Railroad Department of Young Men's Christian Associations of North America, held in Clifton Forge, Virginia, September 13–15, 1895* (New York: International Committee of Young Men's Christian Associations, n.d.), 16, box 6, Railroad Convention Proceedings, 1895–1905, ibid.; and

Proceedings of the Ninth International Conference of the Railroad Department of Young Men's Christian Associations of North America, held in Fort Wayne, Indiana, October 20–23, 1898 (New York: International Committee of Young Men's Christian Associations, n.d.), 20, ibid. For further examples, see the following: *Proceedings of the Tenth International Conference of the Railroad Department of Young Men's Christian Associations of North America held in Philadelphia, Pa., October 11 to 14, 1900* (New York: International Committee of Young Men's Christian Associations, n.d.), 30, ibid.; *Proceedings of the Eleventh International Conference of the Railroad Department of Young Men's Christian Associations of North America, held at Topeka, Kansas, April 30–May 3, 1903* (New York: International Committee of Young Men's Christian Associations, n.d.), 35–36, ibid.; and *Proceedings of the Twelfth International Conference of the Railroad Department of Young Men's Christian Associations of North America, held at Detroit, Michigan, September 28–October 1, 1905* (New York: International Committee of Young Men's Christian Associations, n.d.), 31–32, ibid.

14. "The Railroad Men of a Continent," *Association Men* 36 (March 1911): 271; "Why I Joined," *Railroad Association Magazine* 5 (November 1916): 8; and "As They See It," *Railroad Association Magazine* 4 (November 1915): 13.

15. Peter M. Arthur, "A Labor Leader's Views of the Christian Association, delivered at the dedication of the John M. Toucey Memorial Building, Mott Haven Department, New York, January 19, 1902," *Railroad Association Magazine* 15 (February 1902): 172–74.

16. Quoted in "Christian Brotherliness, The Great Conference Theme of Railroad Men of All Ranks at St. Louis," *Association Men* 34 (July 1909): 453.

17. "The Railroad Department of the Young Men's Christian Associations," undated brochure, Promotional Materials, 1880–1899, box 1, YMCA Railroad Records, YMCA Archives; *Proceedings of the Twenty-Fifth International Convention of Young Men's Christian Associations, Held at Milwaukee, Wis., May 16–20, 1883* (New York: International Committee of Young Men's Christian Associations, 1883), 59–60; Stromquist, *A Generation Of Boomers*, 106–7; and Walter Licht, *Working for the Railroad: The Organization of Work in the Nineteenth Century* (Princeton: Princeton University Press, 1983), 79–124.

18. "Railroad Branches Y.M.C.A.," *Union Pacific Employee Magazine* 5 (August 1890): 196–98.

19. *Altoona Proceedings, 1879*, 12, box 5, YMCA Railroad Records; Moore, *Story*, 47–48, 51–63; and Hopkins, *History*, 230–31.

20. Moore, *Story*, 58.

21. "First Annual Report of the Railroad Men's Christian Association Cleveland, Ohio, 1878-9" (Cleveland: J. S. Savage, 1879), 3, box 38, folder 1, Collinwood Branch, Annual & Monthly Reports, 1872–1886, YMCA of Cleveland, Western Reserve Historical Society, Cleveland, Ohio, hereinafter cited as YMCA of Cleveland; "Railway Branch Young Men's Christian Association,

Monthly Report for May, 1878," box 38, folder 1, Collinwood Branch, Annual & Monthly Reports, 1872–1886, YMCA of Cleveland; and Owen Pence, *The Y.M.C.A. and Social Need: A Study of Institutional Adaptation* (New York: Association Press, 1939), 246–47.

22. George W. Cobb, "Conversation and Amusement Rooms," *Altoona Proceedings, 1879*, 44, box 5, Railroad Convention Proceedings, 1877–1894, YMCA Railroad Records.

23. Moore, *Story*, 47–48, 51–63.; Hopkins, *History*, 230–31; and "Work of Edwin D. Ingersoll," *Yearbook, 1882–83*, 25–26; Cornelius C. Vanderbilt to Cephas Brainerd, September 15, 1879, box 1, Correspondence, 1879–91, YMCA Railroad Records. See also *Altoona Proceedings, 1879*, 29–30, box 5, Railroad Convention Proceedings, 1877–1894; and Herbert E. Brown, "The History of the Railroad Young Men's Christian Association." graduation thesis, Institute and Training School of Young Men's Christian Associations, Chicago, May 25, 1905, 35.

24. "Work of Edwin D. Ingersoll," *Yearbook, 1882–83*, 26.

25. Ibid.

26. "Report of Edwin D. Ingersoll," *Yearbook, 1884–85*, 75.

27. "Work of Edwin D. Ingersoll," *Yearbook, 1882–83*, 26.

28. For a discussion of the controversial ban of billiards in the YMCA, see Hopkins, *History*, 381–82; Charles T. Rea, "History of the Railroad Young Men's Christian Associations," thesis, Springfield Training School, 1904, 66–67, 78.

29. "Billiards Pro and Con," *Railroad Association Magazine* 12 (May 1899): 343.

30. Ibid., 343–44; and *Among Industrial Workers (Ways and Means): A Handbook for Associations in Industrial Fields* (New York: Industrial Department, International Committee of Young Men's Christian Associations, 1916), 38.

31. "Billiards Pro and Con," 344–45.

32. "Hoboken, NJ," *Railroad Association Magazine* 12 (June 1899): 384.

33. Quoted in Moore, *Story*, 161.

34. George A. Warburton, "A Study of the Success of the Railroad Work of the Young Men's Christian Association from the Standpoint of the Men," *New York Railroad Men* 18 (March 1904): 226.

35. Grand Trunk, 1913, box 9, folder 6, Series I, Historical Records, 1853–1973, Subseries I, Indexed Records, 1853–1962, YMCA of Chicago.

36. Monthly Reports, February to September 1913, box 9 folder 5, Chicago & Eastern Illinois, 1913, Series I, Subseries I, YMCA of Chicago.

37. "Comparative Statement of the Chesapeake & Ohio R.R. Departments, Y.M.C.A. For the Month Ending March 31st, 1899," *New York Railroad Men*, 12 (May 1899): 307.

38. "18th Annual Report of the Railroad Branch, Young Men's Christian Association, East St. Louis , Ill," enclosure G. Parker to Hamilton Fish, February 24, 1899, Hamilton Fish, In-letters, vol. 243, Illinois Central, Series 1, Subseries

F 2.2, Illinois Central Papers, Newberry Library, Chicago. For a similar illustration of the problem, see also Minutes of the Committee of Management, November 11, 1895, box 35, vol. 2, Collinwood Branch, Board of Managers, Minutes, 1887–1894, YMCA of Cleveland.

39. "A Pennsylvania Railroad Combine," *Association Men* 31 (October 1906): 20.

40. Monthly Report, February 1889, box 9, folder 8, Dearborn Station, 1889–90, 1917, Series I, Subseries I, YMCA of Chicago.

41. In 1899, for example, 590 new members joined the New York railroad association and 473 discontinued their membership. Of those workers who canceled their memberships, 238 had left the company, 94 did not state a reason for their decision, and the remainder failed to pay dues. See "The Result for 1897 in Figures," *Railroad Men* 11 (February 1899): 152; "The Result for 1898 in Figures," *Railroad Men* 12 (February 1899): 193; "The Result for 1899 in Figures," *Railroad Men* 13 (February 1900): 199; "The Result for 1900 in Figures," *Railroad Men* 14 (February 1901): 219; "The Result for 1901 in Figures," *Railroad Men* 15 (February 1902): 201; and "Partial Report of the Railroad Branch of the Young Men's Christian Association of New York City for 1904," *Railroad Men* 18 (February 1905): 187.

42. Monthly Report, March 1889, box 9, folder 8, Dearborn Station, 1889–90, 1917, Series I, Subseries I, YMCA of Chicago.

43. Holcomb to James McCrea, May 25, 1900, Pennsylvania Lines, 1897–1900, box 9, folder 4, Series I, Subseries I, YMCA of Chicago.

44. Ward W. Adair, "About Railroaders," *Association Men* 29 (March 1904): 275.

45. Hopkins, *History*, 478; and Moore, *Story*, 164–73.

46. Report of A. G. Knebel, October 1911, box 4, Reports Railroad Secretaries International Committee Railroad Department, 1908–12, YMCA Railroad Records.

47. Report of J. M. Dudley, July 1910, box 4, Reports Railroad Secretaries International Committee Railroad Department, 1908–1912, YMCA Railroad Records.

48. Report of Edwin L. Hamilton, July 1908, box 4, Reports Railroad Secretaries International Committee Railroad Department, 1908–12, YMCA Railroad Records.

49. Monthly Report of George D. McDill, September 1902, box 4, Reports Railroad Secretaries International Committee Railroad Department, 1901–7, YMCA Railroad Records.

50. "An Unusual Incident," *Railroad Association Magazine* 1 (May 1912): 6. For a similar occurrence, see Report of Arthur G. Knebel, April 1912, box 4, Reports Railroad Secretaries International Committee Railroad Department, 1908–12, YMCA Railroad Records.

Chapter Four

Negotiating White Womanhood
The Cincinnati YWCA and White Wage-Earning Women, 1918–1929

Sarah Heath

In the early decades of the twentieth century, white working-class women in American cities found themselves in an unenviable situation. Typically relegated to unskilled and low-paying jobs, white independent wage-earning women (those who lived and worked apart from their families) often led a hand-to-mouth existence. Nonetheless, these young women flocked to the cities in search of employment and to seek lives away from their families. Rapid industrialization had given rise to a new demand for women workers, especially in factories and service industries. Young white women were also attracted to urban centers because of the new amusements they could find there. Moving pictures, restaurants, dancing, and drives in automobiles were just some of the activities available to an urban consumer culture, and young white working-class women were among their most avid participants.

The attractions of city life, though, were offset by the realities of economic hardship that often characterized working women's lives. By the end of 1920, all workers nationwide earned an average weekly wage of $28.71, but women workers earned an average of just $17.09 per week.[1] Because of their low wages, working women struggled to provide for their own needs when they lived alone in industrializing cities. The costs of food, clothing, entertainment, and especially housing challenged women's ability to live independently in cities. Nor did the high cost of rooms necessarily guarantee a safe or respectable environment for working women.[2] Thus, reformers of that time worried that women workers would be drawn into a situation of decreasing finances and declining morality. Specifically, a common fear was that women who lacked money might turn to a life of prostitution to avoid starvation.

The YWCA was one of several organizations which emerged to address the perceived plight of young working women. By the end of the nineteenth century, middle-class reformers had established local branches of the YWCA in most American cities, and their activism focused predominantly on the uplift of working women. The YWCA provided the Rooms Registry service, which evaluated and recommended available rooms for women who traveled alone or who were new to cities and were looking for work. Local associations also provided job training and referral for young women. By the turn of the twentieth century, the YWCA in many cities had turned its attention to the question of women in industry. Local associations of the YWCA engaged in studies of women's workplaces and encouraged employers to assist in the moral and physical protection of female employees. Thus, although the stated philosophy of the YWCA was to encourage the spiritual development of young women, the actual programs of many local branches were devoted to the social and economic conditions confronting young wage-earning women.[3]

Using this approach, middle-class women of the YWCA attempted to prescribe and protect an ideal of womanhood in the working-class women who came to the association. Indeed, in the early decades of the twentieth century, new notions of acceptable behavior for women and men meant that traditional ideals of gendered behavior were being confronted by new social norms and practices. Women reformers in the YWCA held values that were more commonly associated with nineteenth-century Victorian values. They encouraged young women to meet prospective mates in a chaperoned setting and hoped that when women were married, they would be able to leave the workforce to bear and raise children.

But by the 1910s and 1920s, white wage-earning women began to adopt the image of the "new woman," who was much more resilient, self-sufficient, and assertive than many middle-class reformers liked their protégées to be. New women, more often than those of previous generations, were willing to smoke, to drink alcohol, to dance, and to experiment with their sexuality. As Kathy Peiss has argued in *Cheap Amusements*, the ideal of the new woman encouraged "a new sense of female self, a woman who was independent, athletic, sexual, and modern."[4] Thus reformers in the YWCA were confronted with different concepts of womanhood that conflicted with their preferred notions of behavior, sexuality, and moral upbringing.[5]

Recent historical literature on female reformers and working-class women emphasizes the ability of the charges to reshape the middle-class ideals of the reformers.[6] This essay will illustrate that women did in many instances reconstruct the prescribed notions of womanhood that the YWCA hoped to encourage. It will demonstrate that the programs offered by the YWCA gave young white working women a structured but supportive community that fostered the development of a new role for themselves. The YWCA was just one organization which touched the lives of thousands of working women. The accounts of the YWCA are thus an important touchstone for understanding the lives of working women in industrial cities of the post–World War I era and their relationships with one group of female reformers at that time.

The conflict over definitions of womanhood was especially apparent in the Cincinnati YWCA from 1919 to 1929. From the founding of the association in 1869, its middle-class members believed that the problem of working women's low wages presented the threat of disastrous social consequences. In the 1920s, 29 percent of a sample group of such women earned a median wage of just $13 a week, and they generally expected to pay about $12 a week for room and board.[7] Thus, the association felt that it could provide a buffer against these social evils if it developed an organized program of reform on behalf of young working women.

With this concern in mind, the Cincinnati YWCA first embarked on a campaign in the late nineteenth century to assist working women. It directed its efforts toward working women in order to "bring them under moral and religious influences by aiding them in the selection of suitable boarding places and employment."[8] This concern was well founded in Cincinnati, where women constituted a relatively high percentage of all wage earners. In 1920, for example, Cincinnati's 50,344 working women comprised 31.8 percent of the workforce. Of that number, 41,941 women were single, representing 26.5 percent of all laborers that year.[9]

The YWCA tried to impose its traditional middle-class values on the working women with whom it came into contact. By the early twentieth century, the Cincinnati YWCA offered cheaper housing that provided a more protective environment than residences elsewhere in the city. Following the guidance of the YWCA's National Board, the Cincinnati YWCA arranged inspections of rooms and houses in the city to meet standards high enough to be placed on the Rooms Registry.[10] It held evening classes for women workers to provide both personal enrichment and vocational training. The association also provided noontime classes and lectures at various factories in Cincinnati and urged the passage of protective legislation, such as the eight-hour day and the reduction of night work for women.

Indeed, the close ties that some young women developed through the YWCA programs allowed them to survive their experience as independent wage earners. Working-class women conflicted with the YWCA on appropriate notions of womanhood precisely because the YWCA offered them a sense of community and security in which they could create new norms of behavior and conduct. But white working women used the stability gained by the YWCA programs and residences to strike out in directions hardly intended by the association. Cincinnati's working women pursued options which enabled them to find stability in a homosocial network, gave them an increased sense of self-worth, and helped them to shape their own lives. The issues of power, reform, culture, and values that were played out in Cincinnati's YWCA were thus simply one part of the transition characterizing the whole country in the 1910s and 1920s.

The white working women who came in contact with the Cincinnati YWCA had many common characteristics. They were young, ranging in age from eighteen to thirty-five, but almost always in their twenties. Many did not live with family members on whom they could depend for food or money. They often held low-skilled, poorly paying jobs, sometimes in factories where the risk of injury was prevalent. Work also tended to be sporadic, so periodic unemployment was common for these women. Similarities such as these helped the women to identify common interests and, to some extent, lay behind their behavior and their responses to YWCA programs.

The women who lived at the YWCA and participated in its programs were decidedly working class. In 1919, the association offered a brief report on the earnings of its ninety-two residents:

Weekly Earnings	Percent of Residents
$5–7	14%
$7–9	30%
$9–12	20%
$12–14	20%
$14+	16%

The YWCA found it a "distressing fact" that 44 percent of the young women were earning less than $9 each week; this sum was insufficient to support a single independent wage earner. Further, although it may appear that women at the top of this wage scale could have lived quite comfortably, even outside the YWCA residence, these figures are deceptive. The YWCA established a $15 weekly wage limit to qualify a young woman for residence in the YWCA building. Any woman earning more than that had to prove that she supported dependents. Thus, the women who lived at the YWCA building truly strained to meet the demands of living alone in the Queen City.[11]

The experiences of white wage-earning women in Cincinnati had antecedents in the nineteenth century. The Cincinnati YWCA was founded in 1869 as the Woman's Christian Association and clearly defined its objective as aiding "the temporal, moral and religious welfare of women, especially young women, who are dependent on their own exertions for support."[12] In the beginning, the YWCA focused on two projects to assist working women. First, it established a residence which charged rent in proportion to income. Thus, no matter how low a woman's wages were, she could still afford to live in the YWCA's protective and hospitable environment. The YWCA also established a system whereby young women new to the city and in need of work could be referred to places of employment that were hiring. By screening potential employers who wanted to advertise for workers with the YWCA, the association hoped that it could protect women employees from overwork, unsafe factory conditions, and possible sexual advances by unscrupulous employers.

By the 1920s, the YWCA, like other reform groups, supported the passage of legislation to remedy the working conditions of wage-earning women. The association supported such demands as "an eight hour day, no night work for women, one day [of] rest in seven, a living wage, equal pay for equal work, collective bargaining, [and] the abolition of child labor."[13] In addition to legislative approaches, the YWCA led a campaign to visit groups of women workers at their places of employment. Most often factory visits involved hanging posters which advertised night programs at the YWCA building. Also, the association organized lunchtime classes and discussion groups designed to spark the interest of the young women and usually to offer some sort of educational improvement, with topics ranging from English language or literature to Bible study.[14]

The reformers of the Cincinnati YWCA tried to respond to innumerable requests from women workers and were often impressed with the young laborers' initiative: "In a clothing factory your secretary asked the girls *why* they had asked for a noon day talk. This was the reply: 'Because we want to get some education somehow.'"[15] While continuing the practice of referring women to job openings, the YWCA felt that factory visits were in many ways more important. Through visits and poster campaigns, the YWCA reached women who otherwise would not have approached the association. Moreover, by visiting job sites in person, women reformers probably assured themselves that female laborers were working in an acceptable environment. The YWCA visited a number of stores and factories throughout the 1910s and 1920s.[16] Typically, the association first approached factory owners in person or in writing and received permission to enter the factory. The YWCA directed its efforts to companies that were receptive to their advances. For example, reform women frequently visited the Crown Overall factory. Its owner, Oscar Berman, was well known for his receptivity to progressivism in industry. An entire floor of his factory was devoted to physical recreation, offering a gymnasium, roomy locker facilities, and showers. His factory was also known for its quality working conditions. Berman himself received the endorsement of the United Garment Workers Local 99 when he ran for the Cincinnati City Council in 1937.[17]

In other factories, however, the YWCA was not welcome; the specter of social and industrial reform apparently preceded the Y women. Many companies "politely refused" admission to the YWCA; others avoided the reform women by not responding to requests at all.[18] Although the association endorsed legislative remedies to industrial ills, generally it was not willing to adopt an aggressive posture in its direct dealings with businesses. Instead, the Cincinnati association preferred to do work where it was already welcome. Indeed, the YWCA was busy enough working in the companies that accepted the reform women. In 1929, the YWCA estimated that it had contacted about 4,500 working women through factory visits.[19]

In addition to daytime work in factories, the YWCA offered a program of night classes to provide opportunities to "girls who have never had a chance to better themselves or their position."[20] Night classes met once a week at the YWCA building; they were free for YWCA members and available at a nominal fee for nonmembers. Staff members designed classes to attract large numbers of women and to appeal to a wide range of interests. In 1920, for example, women chose from gym, dramatics, beadwork, ukelele classes, dressmaking, chorus, millinery, "star talks," current events, basketry, English literature, and embroidery.[21] The YWCA also worked closely with the YMCA and sent women to the YMCA Commercial School for bookkeeping, accounting, and salesmanship courses.[22]

For middle-class reformers in the YWCA, one advantage of the night classes was that they fostered a positive social atmosphere in which working women could enjoy diversions otherwise not available to them. Beyond that, however, the association had more serious goals. The classes drew women to the YWCA in large numbers, and the association intended to instill in these women certain attitudes about the benefits of a Christian moral upbringing: "Because we believe that if a right viewpoint controls individuals, it will through them control society. Because today's world insists on an intelligent right-visioned, righteously-acting prepared womanhood."[23]

The message of social control presented by the Cincinnati YWCA represented a serious effort to instill in working-class women an ideal to which they could aspire and one that would reinforce traditional values of the middle-class reformers.[24] The YWCA recognized the fact that young women were joining the workforce in increasing numbers and that many of these women depended on their own labor for subsistence. The association's training of young white women for professional occupations, primarily in clerical work, was one way that they could help wage earners provide for themselves. Nonetheless, the reformers of the association believed that independent women should be only a temporary part of the workforce.

The Cincinnati YWCA presented a clear message to working-class women that reinforced what the association believed to be its proper role: as soon as a young woman married, she would leave the labor force in order to fulfill her role as a domestic caretaker. Thus, while some of the evening classes that the YWCA offered seemed to encourage public and professional occupations for women, the association maintained that "Encouragement is given to courses which contribute to homemaking, including the care of children, so that young women may go to their homes knowing right care and management, and may raise their community standards through enacting principles for right living that are ethically and scientifically sound."[25] In this way, the Cincinnati YWCA reformers subtly suggested to wage-earning women what their proper role was to be in the future.

Besides providing vocational training, factory visits, and support of protective legislation, the YWCA deepened its commitment to the provision of safe and affordable housing for working women. By the late 1910s and into the 1920s, the YWCA residence in Cincinnati accommodated between 90 and 100 permanent residents and some 20 to 30 transient guests nightly.[26] Although the YWCA occasionally housed young married couples who needed reasonably priced lodging, most transient guests were women traveling alone who needed an affordable room. However, some women came to the YWCA claiming that they were abandoned by husbands, fiancés, or boyfriends. Others said that they had lost their purse or that they had nowhere else to go.

Middle-class members of the association believed that one of their most important assignments was to safeguard the physical and sexual well-being of young women in the city. They feared that any lone female who was denied access to the safety of the YWCA residence could easily fall prey to the dangerous and crime-ridden streets of Cincinnati. One report illustrated the particular care with which YWCA reformers tried to preserve young women's virginity: "We are thankful too, for the sheltering arms of our association that encircled a little runaway girl of twelve years, who came in at eleven o'clock at night. At two o'clock we were able to return her to her almost crazed parents. Yes, we were more than thankful, knowing what awful thing might have befallen her."[27] In this case, the YWCA extended its efforts to someone who was clearly not yet old enough to be independent of her family or to be employed fulltime. Regardless of her age, the YWCA women apparently felt that the child's personal safety was at risk and that the association was a source of protection for her.

The YWCA extended its facilities to any woman that it perceived as needing the protection of its "sheltering arms." Above all, however, the YWCA felt that its residence provided the best help to independent women. Women from the National Board of the YWCA commended local association members for the "attractive home touches" of Cincinnati's residence for working women.[28] Primarily, the home offered a surrogate family for women alone in Cincinnati. More important, reformers used every opportunity to inculcate in young residents a specific model of behavior and decorum. Residents were required to obey a nightly curfew. Male guests were allowed only in visitors' parlors at designated hours. The residence secretary or the house matron oversaw coeducational activities. Women who left the residence for short periods of time were asked to sign a register informing the staff of their whereabouts.[29] Residents were discharged for such transgressions as smoking, having been married previously, drug use, insubordination, and general undesirability of character. While most of these standards reflect the YWCA's desire to maintain a specific code of behavioral conduct, the rule regarding women's previous marriage may also reflect the association's particular concern with protecting the young women's innocence.[30]

Beyond promoting a code of conduct, the YWCA encouraged young women to adopt other practices which upheld the mores of white middle-class Christian reform women. Charm classes addressed standards of dress, speech, posture, and conduct. The association sent the names of residents to local churches to encourage attendance at services by facilitating contact between young women and local ministers. After 1920, the YWCA helped eligible residents register to vote. Staff members at the house used "motherly council" and "heart to heart talks" with the occupants, feeling that "these little family circles are doing much to broaden the vision of our girls and to bring into their life the right ideals."[31] The YWCA installed baths in the residence in 1920, creating a momentous change for some young working women: "One girl rises 45 minutes earlier than need be every morning for fear she will lose her chance at the shower. If cleanliness comes next to Godliness, we are progressing."[32]

Apparently, some young women were unaccustomed to the standards of cleanliness and decorum that the YWCA established. Nonetheless, they flocked to the residence in search of affordable and respectable housing. While the Consumers' League of Cincinnati claimed that workers should expect to pay about $12 per week for room and board, the YWCA offered rooms for as little as $7 per month. With board costs added to this rate, women still paid just over $7 per week, substantially less than the $12 weekly average.[33] Working women also found that living at the YWCA residence increased their chances of procuring employment: "It is *said by many* of our girls that it is easier to secure a good position when the employer knows they live at the YWCA. In a girl's words, 'You don't know how much it helps.'"[34]

Additionally, the house offered services that were probably not available in residences elsewhere in the city. Doctors attended to young women who fell ill at the residence. In serious cases, the association arranged a woman's transport to the hospital. Extreme cases of poverty, unemployment, or abandonment resulted frequently in a free night's lodging, meals, or a ride home. Living at the YWCA house also gave women a valuable social network of peers who shared their backgrounds and experiences.

Yet, for all the benefits that the YWCA residence offered, many working women found that there were some sources of conflict as well. The YWCA's traditional values confronted the continually developing model of the new woman in the YWCA residence.[35] Indeed, the YWCA noted in 1925 that "girls of today are fearless questioners; unbound by traditions and mentally alert to the facts of everyday life and work."[36] In the face of these changing norms of heterosocial contact and sexual behavior, the YWCA attempted to provide women with strict rules and models of behavior that the association believed would help to preserve women's decency.

The Cincinnati YWCA envisioned itself as a surrogate family whose key responsibility was to safeguard the health, safety, and morals of its young flock. Of these ideals, the goal of protecting young women's sexual reputations was paramount. One way that the YWCA tried to regulate women's social contact with men was by enforcing a homosocial atmosphere at the residence. But in a society that encouraged marriage, the association also had to arrange for carefully supervised contact between young women and men in order to prepare their charges for their eventual roles as wives and mothers.

In the residence, the association observed strict rules of contact between women and men. Men could enter the building but had to register with the house matron and were allowed only in visitors' lounges. The residence staff was extremely vigilant during men's visits. Even so, evenings at the residence were sometimes punctuated by the discovery of unexpected and unwelcome visitors: "One girl was awakened at 6 o'clock and found a colored man at her bedside, holding her hand. Some of the other girls saw a negro bare headed going down the fire escape."[37] The issue of race, as well as the threat of male sexual aggression against residents in their own rooms, shocked the YWCA. Association members feared that their young charges were threatened sexually and physically. More often than not, however, the YWCA maintained and controlled a single-sex atmosphere at the residence. Frequently the association prided itself on the "jolly time" that young workers had together at women-only functions. The YWCA sponsored evening sporting events in which teams of women competed with one another. Afternoon teas held at the YWCA reinforced women's proper social roles. Often groups of women hosted parties for their female friends. In 1928, for example, a group of Hughes High School girls hosted a Valentine party; their guests were other female students from Withrow High School.[38]

The YWCA also held two to three dances each month as important social functions. Often dances were for women only. This, however, did not stop the YWCA from reinforcing its images of proper heterosocial and heterosexual contact. One party attracted eighty-five young women: "On the first of December a Christmas party was given for the Industrial and business girls. The party took the form of a 'boy and girl party', some of the girls disguising as boys and escorting the girls."[39] This type of gathering was a common social event at the YWCA and reflects the traditional values of the YWCA women. For many of them, large gatherings of women as well as intense female friendships simply indicated that women were fulfilling appropriate and meaningful social roles in the absence of male friends.[40] The fact that women also dressed as boys in this party perhaps indicates that the YWCA was trying to illustrate in practical terms the roles which young women would eventually be playing, that is, as wives who depended on the emotional and financial support of men.

Men were invited to attend dances only on the last Friday of the month. Not surprisingly, these tended to be the most popular of all the gatherings at the YWCA.[41] Frequently, the association invited men from the YMCA for these parties in an effort to control the character of the men who attended YWCA functions. Even if they did trust YMCA men, women of the YWCA made a firm resolution to protect the morals of the young women at these dances. The YWCA leadership adopted strict rules enforcing acceptable behavior, including restrictions on body contact, "exaggerated positions," and the type of dance music to be used: no "syncopated music from which most of the objectionable forms of dancing arise."[42] The YWCA thus strictly regulated the type and the time of contact between single women and men. At the same time, however, the association reflected the desire to see their young women married. Many of the activities appeared to try to pair off eligible young women and men for eventual betrothal. For example, the YWCA noted with delight that young men from Trinity Methodist Episcopal Church held functions to which young women were invited. Apparently, some young couples were formed as a result: "Trinity slogan is 'Come to Trinity twice and get a boy friend.' One of our girls already engaged to a Trinity boy, other prospects later."[43]

Moreover, the association expressed approval at the return of former residents who were married. Sometimes former residents maintained contact with the association women. The YWCA frequently took note of and appreciated that correspondence. For example, one recently married woman wrote "from Findlay, their new home, [and said,] 'It sounds wonderful to be a Mrs.'"[44] Sometimes, married women returned to the association building to allow "the inspection of new babies brought in by two of our former residence girls. The Residence Grandmother heartily approving."[45]

But as much as some young women appeared to adopt some of the traditional values of womanhood that the YWCA espoused, others also embraced a new self-image that sharply contrasted with the roles the YWCA urged. Whether at the workplace, at YWCA functions, or in the residence, working women both actively and unconsciously challenged some of the behavioral norms that the YWCA tried to promote. Further, although the association women looked askance at the way their residents behaved, they were also forced to accept certain aspects of working women's new model of womanhood. The behavior and attitudes of the young women thus shaped gradual and perceptible changes in YWCA policies.

For example, the Cincinnati YWCA adopted an ambivalent stance toward working women on the issue of unionism. The association clearly believed that women suffered under conditions of low pay and hazardous environments. Yet reform women disapproved of radical unionism. Rather, they worked to help "promote a right understanding of the means of cooperation between employer and employees." In doing so, the association not only sought to "improve the conditions affecting young women in industry," primarily through the passage of protective legislation, but also strove "to increase the efficiency of the young women in industry."[46] However, the YWCA did permit some expression of pro-union sentiment. At one point, YWCA secretaries in Cincinnati vowed to "ask some of the members to tell us about their respective unions some club night, and what they consider to be the benefits of trade unionism."[47] Thus, the YWCA apparently felt that the workplace could be an arena for peaceful negotiation between employers and laborers and that such negotiation would resolve the industrial ills from which working women suffered.

The limited attention to some labor issues in the YWCA residence was mirrored by the National Board's commitment to the protection of women workers. In fact, both the Cincinnati branch of the YWCA and its National Board engaged in numerous forms of activism that they believed would promote a better understanding of the conditions facing working women. To this end, the National Board of the YWCA sponsored national industrial conferences in which they focused on particular issues, such as the improvement of working conditions or working women's wages.[48] More important, members of the YWCA on the local and national levels believed that they could present a unified demand for solutions to the worst problems affecting America's working women. For instance, the Cincinnati YWCA reported in 1921 that it endorsed the passage of a minimum wage bill being considered in the Ohio State legislature. A month later, the association was especially proud that a young resident at the YWCA, Maude Baker, testified before the legislature in support of this bill.[49]

The General Secretary of the Cincinnati YWCA claimed that the organization was "closely linked up to the National YWCA" and that it
"derived much of its program and thinking from National sources." The
local association also welcomed the visit of National Industrial Secretary
Lucy Carner to Cincinnati in 1927 and believed that such contacts were
helping to streamline their program of industrial action. The Cincinnati
association closely followed directions from the National Board in planning their next course of action in industrial work. In 1925, on the
recommendation of the National Board, the Cincinnati YWCA engaged
in a campaign to "secure the signatures of employers who endorsed the
Child Labor Amendment."[50] While efforts to pass protective legislation
did not necessarily make the YWCA pro-union, the association's concern
about working women's problems helped to lay the groundwork which
allowed working-class women to bring about a slow change in the extent
of association women's activism.

Many of the women workers became labor activists and over time
convinced the YWCA to take up their causes. The association noted that
several young women who lived at the residence were active union
members. In 1922, for instance, a survey of employed women in the
YWCA residence found that women participated in the United Garment
Workers of America, the Boot and Shoe Workers Local 364, and the
Amalgamated Clothing Workers of America.[51]

Association leaders, fond of recording the popularity of evening
classes and social events at the Cincinnati building, blamed union activity for the declining attendance at these functions. They warned that
"everyone has an idea that all is well and that there are no problems. . . .
Some of our most loyal Y.W.C.A. girls are most actively concerned in the
strike of garment workers and cap makers. More than once they have
excused themselves to attend their union meetings."[52] Working women
pushed the YWCA to reevaluate its own standards of conduct appropriate to women. Indeed, the YWCA concluded its pessimistic report by
acknowledging that "we owe them [working women] an intelligent study
of the situation."

Although it balked at some of the changes that young women instituted at the association, the Cincinnati YWCA eventually supported
some campaigns that working women undertook. The association was
founded on the premise that working women's precarious economic
status threatened their morals. Thus, the YWCA was willing to adopt an
antagonistic stance toward employers if it felt that working women were
being treated unfairly. When a group of young women instituted a boy-

Figure 8. Gym class at the Cincinnati YWCA. Photo courtesy of the Cincinnati Historical Society.

cott of Allen-A Hosiery in 1929 and "decided to investigate the brands of hose that were sold at the stores where they usually buy, in order to be sure to buy hose that were manufactured by concerns that were fair to labor," the YWCA willingly complied with the boycott.[53] In this case, under the initiative of the working women, the YWCA assumed an unusually public and aggressive role on behalf of its constituents.

Young working women also expanded the range of opportunities that the YWCA offered them, particularly in the evening functions at the YWCA building. The change was evident in the evening athletic classes. As part of its progressive approach to working women, the YWCA offered gym classes in order to foster wellness in the working population. The association believed that athletics provided several benefits for working women: increased stamina, improved posture, self-confidence, and an appreciation for teamwork.[54] Yet the YWCA never acknowledged that women enjoyed athletics for its simple entertainment value, nor did it encourage the competitiveness that grew between teams.

The YWCA originally offered athletic contests outside the association (such as with high schools in the area) as well as interclass games (played among different teams, all of which were affiliated with the YWCA, as opposed to high school or industrial teams). Later, however, the YWCA changed its tack, deciding that "the stress will be put on intergroup ath-

letics rather than competitive games with groups outside the association." Thereafter, the association emphasized enjoyment of games in a
"spirit of friendly rivalry" and especially praised good sportsmanship.[55]
For the YWCA, then, the importance of athletics was simply the value of
group interaction and team spirit, not necessarily the development of
skills for the sake of competition.

The YWCA offered evening classes and tournaments in volleyball,
baseball, basketball, and later swimming. While in 1919 the YWCA
offered just three evening gymnasium classes, by the end of 1920 the
number of classes had increased to seven.[56] The YWCA had a difficult
time meeting the demands of the working women in the gym building. So
many young women attended that the YWCA gymnasium was seldom
empty, and the association struggled to offer all the activities promised:
"Interclass games in basket ball have taken place this month but difficulty is experienced in finding time for such, as the gymnasium is in
constant use in the evening."[57]

The general policy of trying to meet the demands of the women with
whom it worked became especially problematic to reformers in the
YWCA. Some of the reformers (the Industrial Committee in particular)
felt that their best work was done by attracting large numbers of women
to the association building. Their approach decidedly emphasized the
social over the religious for early contact with working women; the
intent was to attract them to "more serious" programs later. They thus
scrambled to meet the innumerable requests by women workers for night
athletic events: "It is a source of regret that the accommodations are so
limited, especially in the gym work. . . . There is no doubt but that we
could fill larger quarters, and that we could offer more serious courses
and reach a greater number of girls."[58] Yet not all of the association
women approved of this method. Some women felt that the program of
evening recreation "was successful from the point of view of numbers,
but whether it did more than this can't be said. It is a big job to try to
inculcate the ideal standards, but we are trying to do it." Some association reformers adopted an even more hostile stance toward the sudden
increase in the number of athletic programs: "the physical department
has a waiting list of ninety girls to say nothing of groups of girls anxious
to come but who know it is useless. Two more classes are being formed
making seven gym classes in all. *Because of this something else will suffer
and it should not.*"[59] In the end, however, the YWCA continued to devote
funds to athletic events and facilities. Responding to working women's
requests, the YWCA eventually diversified its program to include base-

ball, volleyball, and tennis, and in 1929 finally offered the use of a swimming pool.[60] Thus, in this instance, working women exerted a definite influence on YWCA policies and eventually made their outreach programs decidedly more social and secular in character, deviating from the earlier philosophy of Christian outreach.

All women, not just YWCA building residents, could attend evening athletic events. The desire of the association to attract large numbers of women may imply that it adopted a more flexible approach only when it was in contact with women who were not under the direct guidance of the reformers. However, even the women who lived at the YWCA building influenced certain changes in association policies. The YWCA started with a strict set of regulations for its young residents. In fact, association women once complained that the young women "rearrange our correctly placed furniture once in a while."[61] Gradually, however, as a result of working women's requests and their own model of appropriate behavior, the YWCA women altered their standards of acceptable conduct in the residence.

For one thing, young women apparently frustrated direct efforts by the YWCA to Christianize its residents. As early as 1920, YWCA women noted that they had "tried earnestly to raise the standard of Sunday observance among our girls, but small progress can be reported." Although the association women were disappointed, they should have expected some failures. First, the diverse religious practices of YWCA residents made it difficult to oversee each young woman's attendance at a service. Second, some women apparently preferred to investigate many other sources of amusement that Cincinnati had to offer. In a recreational survey conducted in 1919, the YWCA found that Cincinnati offered a wide range of diversions: "theatres, moving pictures, dance halls, skating rinks, playgrounds, parks, and recreation centres."[62] The YWCA explained its failures accordingly: "We are set in the midst of so many temptations here in the heart of the city, and we have so many beliefs in our family."[63] Thus, the YWCA could not convince women workers to uphold the behavior that the association had long regarded as being at the core of true womanhood.

In some cases, the association acknowledged that the best influences on the behavior of young women were often those of other young women in the building, not necessarily association women. The YWCA gave particular praise to young women who served as role models to several (often younger) women. One such woman, named Beth in a YWCA report, apparently served as a "big sister" to six or eight younger colleagues and inspired the reformers to note that "We hope to multiply the Beths who will hold in check the reckless little sister who thoughtlessly goes away for the night, leaving no word of her whereabouts."[64] Thus, it appeared that, although the standards of YWCA reformers and young women sometimes differed, some "Beths" proved to be as capable as the association women of promoting a sense of order within the confines of the residence.

Young women not only managed to make some changes in YWCA expectations about their behavior, they also worked directly to relax specific house rules. For example, while women could be expelled from the residence for smoking in 1921, by 1929 the rule had changed significantly. In May of that year, forty-three residents held a meeting to discuss the issue of smoking. The YWCA noted approvingly that "Thirty-two [out] of forty-three girls agreed not to encourage it in the residence, [believing] a higher standard should prevail in a Y.W.C.A."[65] However, while smoking was not entirely accepted at the YWCA, it was obvious that the association women did not penalize it as strictly as they once had.

Working women also approached the association directly on the issue of entertainment in the building. Early in 1928, residents asked the YWCA leaders for permission to play card games in the building. The YWCA expressed consternation; card playing was still not acceptable for women and carried with it the stigma of gambling. Still, because these were "older girls" who did not "dance or have other pleasures," the YWCA cautiously approved of "a little social game without the prize, not on Sunday and under the supervision of Mrs. Lester [the house matron] or the secretary in charge." Only a few months later, regular reports reflected with delight that working women often entertained "their young men" at social games of cards, and that these games were "thoroughly enjoyed" and always "perfectly proper."[66] Thus, what seemed to the YWCA to be a serious test of the proper role for women was offset by the positive influence of entertaining men in a carefully supervised social setting.

Nowhere was the transformation in YWCA outlook toward working women more apparent than in its approach to women's sexuality. Early in the 1920s, the YWCA exercised firm and maternal control over women's relationships with men. Clearly, the early association policy of a woman seeing men at the residence only when chaperoned reflected the suspicion that young men might be able to seduce innocent and unwitting women. For instance, in 1920, one young woman was abandoned at the YWCA building by a man who had reportedly promised to marry her. Although there was no mention of sexual indiscretion on the woman's part, the YWCA concluded: "The remarkable thing was that though the girl seemed intelligent and made an excellent appearance, she seemed to have no sense whatever of the damage to character and the insult the man had offered her. She only thought that she had lost the man she loved!"[67]

However, by the end of the decade, the YWCA acknowledged that many women were sexually involved, and it attempted to address that issue in an open forum with residents. A report of the meeting indicated that "Many girls were interested in the [charm] school and are especially interested in the talks on Marriage and Petting." Discussions following these talks might have included: "Is a kiss or petting [permissible] before engagement? How to encourage the boys without permitting it? The effect of petting upon both parties?"[68] Instead of viewing working-class women as hopelessly naive and potential victims of malicious and lustful men, the YWCA began to acknowledge that women's new public role and the pressures that accompanied it needed different types of responses. Thus, the YWCA program changed in several ways as a result of women's evolving roles and their own notions of acceptable conduct.

Indeed, the 1920s was a significant period of transformation in the YWCA on several issues, with 1929 as a benchmark year. The YWCA finally acquired a new building as a result of an aggressive fundraising campaign.[69] The onset of the Great Depression also meant that the YWCA adopted a different outlook about women working and about the association's function as a service organization. Even more than that, however, the changing social norms that had at first scandalized middle-class members of the YWCA became socially acceptable, legitimized through film, radio, and advertising. Thus, by the end of the 1920s, the YWCA in Cincinnati was transformed. What had been a strongly Christian organization with a social program in the late 1910s became a more social organization informed by a Christian philosophy by the 1920s.

Clearly, the YWCA had an agenda set on inculcating in women workers middle-class traditional moral values. The association tried to offer women all the benefits of a comfortable lifestyle supported by their own hard work. Women benefited from the YWCA programs in several ways. They had access to a comfortable, protective, and homelike setting in which they formed lasting friendships. The YWCA offered them access to entertainment that they otherwise could not have enjoyed, such as dances, parties, and athletics. YWCA classes also offered women important social and vocational skills that they valued. Finally, for many young women who found themselves alone in Cincinnati for the first time, the YWCA provided the "sheltering arms" that offered them the comfort and protection they sought.

Yet the values of many young women clashed with the traditional ideals of the YWCA reformers. These were women who exerted pressure for change on the YWCA, either by refusing to adopt the association's ideals or, more frequently, by reaching for a middle ground. The women who lived at the YWCA did not necessarily offer a radical reappraisal of women's roles; rather, they slowly but perceptibly enacted change in the YWCA's programs. In the final analysis, the 1920s were years of transformation for the YWCA and for working-class women. The multifaceted approach of YWCA reforms and the variable responses of the women with whom it came in contact provide a rich tapestry of social change that took place in the early decades of the twentieth century.

NOTES

I would like to thank Thomas Winter, Joanne Meyerowitz, Bruce Levine, and Margaret Spratt for their helpful suggestions on earlier drafts of this essay.

1. National Industrial Conference Board, Inc., *Wages in the United States, 1914–1930* (New York: National Industrial Conference Board, 1931): 52, 59.

2. For some accounts of working women and the challenges they faced in American cities, see Joanne Meyerowitz, *Women Adrift: Independent Wage Earners in Chicago, 1880–1920* (Chicago: University of Chicago Press, 1988); Carol Groneman and Mary Beth Norton, eds., *"To Toil the Livelong Day": America's Women at Work* (Ithaca, NY: Cornell University Press, 1987); Kathy Peiss, *Cheap Amusements: Working Women and Leisure in Turn-of-the-Century New York* (Philadelphia: Temple University Press, 1986); Leslie Woodcock Tentler, *Wage-earning Women: Industrial Work and Family Life in the United States, 1900–1930* (New York: Oxford University Press, 1979); and Stephen H. Norwood, *Labor's Flaming Youth: Telephone Operators and Worker Militancy, 1878–1923* (Urbana: University of Illinois Press, 1990).

3. Several scholars have focused on the character of the YWCA as a social agency. See, for instance, Marion W. Roydhouse, "Bridging Chasms: Community and the Southern YWCA" in Nancy Hewitt and Suzanne Lebsock, eds., *Visible Women: New Essays on American Activism* (Urbana: University of Illinois Press, 1993): 270–295; Diana Pederson, "'Building Today for the Womanhood of Tomorrow': Businessmen, Boosters, and the YWCA, 1890–1930," *Urban History Review* 15 (Autumn 1987): 225–242; Dawn Sebire, "'To Shield from Temptation': The Business Girl and the City," *Urban*

History Review 17 (Autumn 1989): 203–208; and Margaret A. Spratt, "The Pittsburgh YWCA and Industrial Democracy in the 1920s," *Pennsylvania History* 59 (January 1992): 5–20.

4. Peiss, *Cheap Amusements*, 7.

5. Definitions of the "new woman" have changed considerably over time. For various discussions of the new woman, see Nat Arling, "What Is the Role of the 'New Woman'?" *Westminster Review* 150 (November 1898): 576–587; Florence Hayllar, "Woman's Ideal of Womanhood," *Westminster Review* 171 (March 1909): 309–313; Meyerowitz, *Women Adrift*, esp. 116, 126, 132; Peiss, *Cheap Amusements*, esp. 7; Carroll Smith-Rosenberg, "The New Woman as Androgyne," in *Disorderly Conduct: Visions of Gender in Victorian America* (New York: Oxford University Press, 1985); Margaret Spratt, *"Women Adrift" and "Urban Pioneers": Self-Supporting Working Women in America, 1880–1930* (Ann Arbor, MI: University Microfilms International, 1988).

6. See, for instance, Richard Hoggart, *The Uses of Literacy: Aspects of Working-Class Life, with Special References to Publications and Entertainments* (London: Chatto and Windus, 1967); Lawrence W. Levine, *Highbrow/Lowbrow: The Emergence of Cultural Hierarchy in America* (Cambridge, MA: Harvard University Press, 1988); Meyerowitz, *Women Adrift*; Peiss, *Cheap Amusements*; M. Christine Anderson, "Home and Community for a Generation of Women: A Case Study of the Cincinnati Y.W.C.A. Residence, 1920–1940," *Queen City Heritage* 43, 4 (Winter 1985): 34–41; Meyerowitz, *Women Adrift*, 118–20, 123–26; Peggy Pascoe, *Relations of Rescue: The Search for Female Moral Authority in the American West, 1874–1939* (New York: Oxford University Press, 1990); Peiss, *Cheap Amusements*, 163–84; Jodi Vandenberg-Daves, "The Manly Pursuit of a Partnership between the Sexes: The Debate Over YMCA Programs for Women and Girls, 1914–1933," *Journal of American History*, 78, 4 (March 1992): 1324–46; Roydhouse, "Bridging Chasms," 270–95; and James C. Scott, *Domination and the Arts of Resistance* (New Haven, CT: Yale University Press, 1990).

7. Frances R. Whitney, *What Girls Live On—and How: A Study of the Expenditures of a Sample Group Employed in Cincinnati in 1929* (Cincinnati: Consumers' League of Cincinnati, 1930): 9; National Industrial Conference Board, *The Cost of Living Among Wage Earners, Cincinnati, Ohio, May, 1920*, Special Report Number 13 (New York: National Industrial Conference Board, 1929): 13; and Edith M. Hadley, "The Housing Problem as It Affects Girls," *The Survey* 30 (April 14, 1913): 92–94. See also the Report of the Residence Committee, October 1, 1919, Cincinnati YWCA Manuscripts Collection, housed at the Cincinnati Historical Society (hereafter cited as YWCA), box 8, folder 28, 4, in which the YWCA secretary claimed: "Young women earning less than $15 weekly can find almost nothing respectable within their ability to pay, and often too the girl earning more can find nothing under $12."

8. First Annual Report of the Cincinnati Women's Christian Association (Cincinnati, 1869), YWCA, box 1, folder 1, 8; see also Carol J. Blum, "The

Cincinnati Women's Christian Association: A Study of Improvisation and Change, 1868–1880," *Queen City Heritage* 41 (Winter 1983): 56–64.

9. Department of Commerce, Bureau of the Census, *Fourteenth Census of the United States Taken in the Year 1920. Occupations* (Washington, DC: Government Printing Office, 1923): 817. For all cities with a population of over 100,000, an average of 32.5 percent of women over the age of sixteen were considered "gainfully occupied." Department of Commerce, Bureau of the Census, *Women in Gainful Occupations 1870–1920* (Washington, DC: Government Printing Office, 1929): 11, 31. For discussions about working women in Cincinnati, see Anderson, "Home and Community," 34–41; Blum, "The Cincinnati Women's Christian Association"; and Andrea Tuttle Kornbluh, *Lighting the Way: The Woman's City Club of Cincinnati, 1915–1965* (Cincinnati: Young and Klein, Inc., 1986).

10. *Fiftieth Annual Report*, 1919, YWCA, 6. In 1919, Miss Martha Chase of the National Board visited the local buildings and "put her stamp of approval on houses for girls and women" recommended by the local YWCA. See also YWCA, box 7, folder 3, Reports of the Cincinnati YWCA to the National Board for 1922, in which the secretary submitting the report reinforced the desire of her local branch to follow closely the policies of the National YWCA.

11. Report of the Residence Committee, October 1, 1919; YWCA, box 8, folder 28, 1, 3. For another detailed report of resident women's wages and occupations, see the Report of the Residence Department, December 1929, YWCA, box 9, folder 5, 1.

12. *First Annual Report of the Woman's Christian Association of Cincinnati, Ohio*, 1869, YWCA, box 1, folder 1, 6.

13. Industrial Committee Report, June 1919, YWCA, box 8, folder 22, 2.

14. For some examples of the YWCA's numerous visitation programs, see *YWCA Forty-Eighth Annual Report 1917*, YWCA, box 1, volume 3, 8; Report of the Industrial Committee, March 5, 1919, YWCA, box 8, folder 22, 5; Report of the Immigration Committee, March 15, 1919, YWCA, box 8, folder 21, 1–2; Report of the Industrial Department, November 1919, YWCA, box 8, folder 22, 13; and Report of the Industrial Department, February 27, 1920, YWCA, box 8, folder 37, 1–2.

15. For some examples of the YWCA's numerous visitation programs, see *YWCA Forty-Eighth Annual Report 1917*, YWCA, box 1, volume 3, 8; Report of the Industrial Committee, March 5, 1919, YWCA, box 8, folder 22, 5; Report of the Immigration Committee, March 15, 1919, YWCA, box 8, folder 21, 1–2; Report of the Industrial Department, November 1919, YWCA, box 8, folder 22, 13; Report of the Industrial Department, February 27, 1920, YWCA, box 8, folder 37, 1–2.

16. For example, in 1929 the YWCA visited the following establishments: five clothing or garment factories, five laundry or linen establishments, six tailoring companies, one chocolate factory, one biscuit factory, two shoe factories, two radio companies, six stores, one art establishment, one printing company,

one tea and spice company, and four other companies. See the Report of the Industrial Committee, February 1929, YWCA, box 11, folder 29, 1. Refer also to the *YWCA Forty-Eighth Annual Report 1917*, YWCA, box 1, volume 3, 8, for another extensive list of factory visits.

17. Cincinnati *Enquirer*, November 29, 1916, 16; Cincinnati *Enquirer*, November 1, 1917, 5; Cincinnati *Enquirer*, May 4, 1919, 14; Nellie Berrard to United Garment Workers Local 99, October 1937. Part of the Crown and Headlight Collection housed at the Cincinnati Historical Society. Berrard was then president of the union local.

18. Report of the Industrial Department, March 29, 1920, YWCA, box 8, folder 37, 1.

19. Report of the Industrial Committee, February 1929, YWCA, box 11, folder 29, 1.

20. *Young Women's Christian Association Fifty-Third Annual Report 1922*, YWCA, box 1, volume 3, 7.

21. Report of the Industrial Department, July 6, 1920, YWCA, box 8, folder 37, 1.

22. *YWCA Fifty-Third Annual Report 1922*, YWCA, box 1, volume 3, 7.

23. *YWCA Fifty-Fifth Year Book 1924*, YWCA, box 1, volume 3, 2.

24. For more analysis of social control in reform movements, see Lois W. Banner, "Religious Benevolence as Social Control: A Critique of an Interpretation," *Journal of American History* 60, 1 (June 1973): 23–41; Don S. Kirschner, "The Ambiguous Legacy: Social Justice and Social Control in the Progressive Era," *Reflexions Historiques* 2 (Summer 1975): 69–88; and Kenneth L. Kusmer, "The Functions of Organized Charity in the Progressive Era: Chicago as a Case Study," *Journal of American History* 60, 3 (December 1973): 657–78.

25. *YWCA Fifty-Third Annual Report 1922*, YWCA, box 1, volume 3, 7.

26. See, for example, the Annual Report of the House Committee, 1920, YWCA, box 8, folder 26, 1. A transient guest was one who needed only temporary lodging (one or two nights).

27. *The Young Women's Christian Association of Cincinnati, Ohio: Year Book, 1916*, YWCA, box 1, volume 3, 17.

28. Report of the Residence Department, November 1922, YWCA, box 9, folder 26, 2.

29. Report of the General Secretary, March 1927, YWCA, box 10, folder 45, 2–3.

30. See, for example, Joanne Meyerowitz, *Women Adrift*, in which she argues that the women of the Chicago YWCA were similarly concerned about the virginity of their young charges.

31. Report of the Colored Branch, May 28, 1920, YWCA, box 8, folder 30, 3–4.

32. Report of the Residence Secretary, July 1920, YWCA, box 8, folder 44, 1.

33. Report of the Residence Department, February 1922, YWCA, box 9, folder 26, 2–3. These figures are based on a small survey of residents with varying incomes. Women averaged $24.90 per month in food expenditures.

Assuming that a woman lived in a $7.00 per month room, she could average as little as $7.36 each week for room and board.

34. Annual Report of the Residence Department, 1925, YWCA, box 10, folder 33, 1; emphasis in the original.

35. Refer to note 5 for some discussion of the new woman.

36. *Young Women's Christian Association Year Book 1925*, YWCA, box 1, volume 3, 10.

37. Report of the Residence Department, December 1925, YWCA, box 10, folder 33, 1. According to this report, no one was able to see the perpetrator clearly except to identify his race and sex. The YWCA assumed that any man who had so easily gained access to the building must have had keys to the residence (e.g., employed there). On the advice of a security company (Cal Crim), the YWCA decided to dismiss a black male employee. See also a brief account of a similar incident in the Report of the Residence Secretary, April 1920, YWCA, box 8, folder 43, 1.

38. Report of the Girl Reserve Committee, January 1928, YWCA, box 11, folder 11, 3.

39. Report of the Industrial Department, December 1923, YWCA, box 10, folder 4, 1.

40. See, for example, "The Female World of Love and Ritual," in Carroll Smith-Rosenberg, *Disorderly Conduct* (New York: Alfred A. Knopf, 1985): 53–76.

41. See, for example, Report of the Residence Committee, January 1919, YWCA, box 8, folder 26, 1; Annual Report of the Residence Department, 1922, YWCA, box 9, folder 26, 2; and Report of the General Secretary, March 1925, YWCA, box 10, folder 25, 2.

42. Report of the Health Committee, December 1920, YWCA, box 8, folder 34, 1.

43. Report of the Residence Committee, March 1928, YWCA, box 11, folder 17, 1.

44. Report of the Residence Committee, May 1928, YWCA, box 11, folder 17, 1.

45. Report of the Residence Committee, August 1928, YWCA, box 11, folder 17, 1.

46. Report of the Industrial Department, 1922, YWCA, box 9, folder 23, 1.

47. *Federation News* (mimeo newsletter), 1, 1, September 22, 1921, YWCA, box 9, folder 4, 6.

48. Industrial Committee Report, November 1919, YWCA, box 8, folder 22, 1–2; Year Book 1923, YWCA, box 1, folder 3, 5.

49. Industrial Committee Report, February 28, 1921, 2; March 1921, 1–2. Both from YWCA, box 9, folder 9.

50. Annual Report of the General Secretary, 1922, YWCA, box 9, folder 19, 7; Report of the General Secretary, November 1927, YWCA, box 10, folder 45, 2; Report of the Industrial and Mercantile Department, December 1927, YWCA, box 10, folder 47, 1; Minutes of the Industrial Committee, May 1925, YWCA, box 10, folder 28, 1.

51. *Federation News* (mimeo packet printed by YWCA residence women), 1, 1 (September 1922), YWCA, box 9, folder 4, 6; Industrial Department Report, February 1922, YWCA, box 9, folder 23, 1–2; Industrial Committee Report, June 1929, YWCA, box 11, folder 29, 2.

52. Report of the Industrial Department, April 1919, YWCA, box 8, folder 22, 1. For other accounts of declining attendance at YWCA functions and labor unrest in Cincinnati, see the Report of the General Secretary, March 1921, YWCA, box 9, folder 4, 1–2; and Report of the Industrial Department, January 31, 1921, YWCA, box 9, folder 9, 2.

53. Report of the Industrial Committee, March 1929, YWCA, box 11, folder 29, 2.

54. See, for example, William Leach, *True Love and Perfect Union: The Feminist Reform of Sex and Society* (Middletown, CT: Wesleyan University Press, 1980): 64–69; and Roy Rosenzweig, *Eight Hours for What We Will: Workers and Leisure in an Industrial City, 1870–1920* (New York: Cambridge University Press, 1983): 128–52.

55. Report of the General Secretary, January 1925, YWCA, box 10, folder 25, 2; Report of the General Secretary, November 1925, YWCA, box 10, folder 25, 1; Report of the Industrial Department, February 1925, YWCA, box 10, folder 28, 2; Report of the General Secretary, November 1927, YWCA, box 10, folder 45, 5.

56. Girls' Work Committee Report, January 8, 1919, YWCA, box 8, folder 19, 1; and Physical Education Committee Report, November 1920, YWCA, box 8, folder 40, 1.

57. General Secretary's Report, February 1925, YWCA, box 10, folder 25, 2.

58. Report of the Industrial Department, October 2, 1920, YWCA, box 8, folder 37, 2.

59. Report of the Physical Education Department, November 1920, 2, October 1920, 1, YWCA, box 8, folder 40; emphasis added.

60. Annual Report of the General Secretary for the Year 1929, January 1930, YWCA, box 11, folder 25, 4.

61. Report of the Industrial Department, June 1919, YWCA, box 8, folder 22, 1.

62. Report of the Girls' Work Committee, March 5, 1919, YWCA, box 8, folder 19, 1.

63. Annual Report of the Residence Secretary, 1920, YWCA, box 8, folder 44, 2. Kathy Peiss has argued that newly available entertainment options in New York may have increased a secular element among working women related to the change from Victorian values to the role of the new woman. See Peiss, *Cheap Amusements*.

64. Report of the General Secretary, March 1921, YWCA, box 9, folder 4, 2–3.

65. Residence Committee Report, May 1929, YWCA, box 11, folder 33, 1.

66. Minutes of the Residence Committee, January 1928, 1; Report of the Residence Committee, February 1928, 1; Minutes of the Residence Committee,

May 24, 1928, 1; Report of the Residence Committee, May 1928, 1; all from YWCA, box 11, folder 17.

67. Report of the Residence Secretary, September 1920, YWCA, box 8, folder 44, 1.

68. Report of the Residence Committee, January 1929, YWCA, box 11, folder 33, 1.

69. Cincinnati *Enquirer,* November 12, 1926, 24; November 13, 1926, 20. The initial campaign set a goal of $700,000 for the erection of the building now located at Ninth and Walnut Streets; eventually it raised $772,000 from 13,000 donations.

Chapter Five

Cultural Pluralism in Immigrant Education
The YWCA's International Institutes,
1910–1940

Raymond A. Mohl

Recent work in the history of American education has reflected a new awareness and appreciation of the diversity of educational agencies and institutions in the United States. Traditional work emphasized the role of the public school, often ignoring the full range of educational processes at work in American communities, especially in urban areas. The heavy focus on public education tended to suggest that education was something that went on only in public schools, a process that occurred only within the formal structure of the classroom. New research has demonstrated the importance of other institutions and agencies involved in the educational and socialization process—family, church, parochial school, settlement houses, social groups, community organizations, the workplace, newspapers and other mass media, and others. The formal and informal education sponsored by such institutions often rivaled that of the public schools in importance. Some of this alternative education supplemented and reinforced public schooling, but this was not always the case. This case study of several immigrant social service agencies sponsored by the YWCA and known as International Institutes demonstrates how such alternative educational institutions functioned to promote cultural pluralism and ethnic adjustment in American cities.[1]

Between 1820 and 1930, approximately 35 million immigrants came to the United States from Europe, Asia, and Western Hemisphere nations such as Canada and Mexico. The arrival of such massive numbers of new-comers, especially in the last decades of the nineteenth century and in the early years of the twentieth, posed a special challenge for American edu-cators. The new immigrants, according to educational historian Raymond E. Callahan, "constituted an educational problem unparalleled in human history." Ethnic and racial minorities came to the United States with dif-ferent languages, cultures, traditions, and values. Fearful of the social consequences of mass immigration and insensitive to ethnic cultural dif-ferences, most native-born Americans placed a special importance on the public school as an Americanizing agency. American society expected the public schools to assimilate immigrant children and adults, to teach them the English language, to prepare them for citizenship, and to incorporate them into the structure of American society as rapidly as possible.[2]

As a homogenizing agent, as an institution designed to secure confor-mity to the American way, the public school thus took on the task of breaking down and destroying ethnic and racial cultures. In cities throughout the nation, the public schools became melting pots in which immigrants were melted down into Americans. Ellwood P. Cubberley, one of the nation's leading educators, articulated the goals of the Americanizers in 1909: "Our task is to break up these groups or settle-ments, to assimilate and amalgamate these people as a part of our American race, and to implant in their children, so far as can be done, the Anglo-Saxon conception of righteousness, law and order, and popular government, and to awaken in them a reverence for our democratic insti-tutions and for those things in our national life which we as a people hold to be of abiding worth." The public schools became, as Boston Superintendent of Schools Frank V. Thompson wrote in 1920, "the chief instrument of Americanization."[3]

The public schools were Americanizers, but immigrant and ethnic groups built networks of indigenous institutions, many of which sought to maintain old country culture and traditions. The Irish, Germans, Poles, Lithuanians, and other Catholic immigrant groups supported extensive parochial school systems that fostered ethnic religions, lan-guages, and cultures; in some cities, parochial schools enrolled upward of 20 or 30 percent of the total school-age population. Some immigrant groups, especially Jews, Chinese, and the various Eastern Orthodox denominations, organized ethnic "folk" schools that children attended daily after public school classes had ended. Immigrants found in the ethnic folk school a means of maintaining their language and passing the old culture and heritage on to their children. Other ethnic institutions such as churches and Sunday schools, fraternal and social groups, music and dramatic organizations, and the immigrant press served educational functions and often encouraged pluralism and culture maintenance. They muted the harsh impact of Americanizing agencies and eased the adjustment process for the immigrants.[4]

The International Institutes were among the agencies that engaged in immigrant education, encouraged cultural pluralism, and aided ethnic adjustment in urban America. Immigrant social service agencies with unique purposes and programs, International Institutes were established in most of the heavily ethnic cities. The first Institute was organized in New York City in 1910 under the sponsorship of the Young Women's Christian Association. The moving force behind the new YWCA experiment was Edith Terry Bremer, a young social welfare and settlement worker. Hired by the National Board of the YWCA in 1909 to direct the agency's work with immigrant women and girls, Bremer pushed for the establishment of an educational and social service center in Greenwich Village, one of New York City's heavily populated immigrant districts. As Bremer conceived of the new center, its purpose was to serve newcomers by providing English classes, recreational and club activities, and aid in dealing with housing, employment, naturalization, and other problems. Not yet a cultural pluralist, Bremer envisioned the New York International Institute as a service and adjustment agency much like the social settlements. Promoted aggressively by Bremer, the Institute idea of work with immigrant women spread to other cities. By the mid-1920s, some fifty-five International Institutes had been organized by local YWCAs in such cities as Boston, Providence, Baltimore, Buffalo, Detroit, Pittsburgh, Cleveland, Philadelphia, Brooklyn, St. Louis, Milwaukee, San Antonio, Los Angeles, San Francisco, and a host of others.[5] The YWCA is usually noted for its religious and missionary orientation. It is clear, however, that by the early twentieth century the agency had awakened to the emerging women's movement and had moved beyond pure moral uplift to such social issues as public health, labor reform, temperance, political reform, women's suffrage, the peace movement, and other issues affecting women. Religious proselytizing became less important than protection and social service as women's historical agency began to reshape YWCA programs. The development of the International Institute movement was a reflection of the YWCA's new concern for women as women rather than as potential evangelical converts. For several decades the Institutes remained tied to the YWCAs, but in the 1930s most of them severed this connection and merged to create a new national organization—the National Institute of Immigrant Welfare. In 1943 the agency changed its name to the American Federation of International Institutes (AFII). Another merger took place in 1959, when the AFII joined with the Common Council for American Unity to create the American Council for Nationalities Service, which still exists.[6]

Edith Bremer was the moving and guiding force behind the International Institute movement. A dynamic and creative woman, Bremer headed the Institutes during the YWCA period and as independent agencies until her retirement in 1954, thus providing a long period of centralized direction and leadership. Bremer graduated from the University of Chicago in 1907. For three years prior to beginning YWCA work, she served as a researcher for the Chicago Women's Trade Union League, a field investigator for the Chicago Juvenile Court, a resident in Chicago and New York settlement houses, and a special agent for the United States Immigration Commission. Thus, she came to YWCA immigration work with a relatively brief but diverse background in social service experience.[7]

Bremer had studied and worked with the Chicago network of social workers and university scholars interested in immigration and social problems. The members of this group—Jane Addams, Julia Lathrop, Graham Taylor, Mary E. McDowell, Margaret Robins, Edith and Grace Abbott, and University of Chicago sociologist William I. Thomas, among others—were essentially "liberal assimilationists" on the immigration issue. They were sympathetic to the human and social plight of the immigrants in the new land and sensitive to the importance of their historical and cultural traditions, and they rejected harsh demands for immediate Americanization. However, they believed that the social forces of modern American life—the mass media, the public school, the city, the factory, the consumer society—would eventually undermine ethnic cultures and communities, leading to immigrant assimilation in the long run.[8] To serve and protect new immigrants during the adjustment process, the Chicago social work network, especially those like Bremer involved in the Women's Trade Union League, established the Immigrants' Protective League of Chicago in 1908.[9] Bremer shared the views of the liberal assimilationists and was thoroughly familiar with the philosophy and goals of the Immigrants' Protective League.

Edith Bremer brought these views and experiences to her YWCA work, and they had a shaping influence on the development of the International Institute movement. She conceived of the International Institutes as service-oriented agencies designed to protect immigrant women, address their problems, and facilitate their adjustment to life in the United States. As early as 1911, she rejected the "prevailing notion that work for immigrants must be either shaking hands on Ellis Island or making them learn English." A much broader and more coherent program of education, recreation, and case work was required. As the various International Institutes implemented such programs during the teens, Bremer gradually moved toward a cultural pluralist position. She was especially disturbed by the nativist and anti-immigrant tenor of the Americanization campaign of the World War I years and the postwar red scare. Bremer was alarmed at the fear, hate, ignorance, and blind patriotism which the new nativism encouraged. She fought against the "arrogant assumption that everything American was intrinsically superior to anything foreign." Americanization, she argued, represented "a nationalistic and political effort" to make conformity and assimilation compulsory for the immigrants. By the 1920s, Bremer led the Institutes to a new emphasis on the importance of ethnic cultures and traditions in easing the adjustment process. In an important statement of purpose in 1923, Bremer wrote that "there is no richer material for cultural growth than that that can be saved for the foreigner out of his own inheritance." These ideas not only helped facilitate immigrants' adjustment to life in the United States but also shaped institute programs that sought to preserve the immigrant heritage, transmit the old culture to the second generation in America, and generally promote cultural pluralism.[10]

Bremer's shift to a pluralist position stemmed partially from her experience in immigrant work and her hostility to the wartime Americanization campaign. Her views were also given form by the writings of such pluralist advocates as Horace M. Kallen, Isaac B. Berkson, and Julius Drachsler. Bremer knew of the work of Kallen, who first enunciated the ideology of cultural pluralism in a series of articles in *The Nation* in 1915. Interestingly, in January 1916 Bremer and Kallen both published articles in the first issue of *Immigrants in America Review*, a short-lived publication of the Committee of Immigrants in America. Kallen's brand of cultural pluralism called for a permanent "federation of nationalities," each nourished by ethnic languages, religions, and cultures.[11] Kallen was never very specific as to how these ethnic federations would operate in actual practice, and his vague prescription for a pluralist society never won support.[12]

However, Bremer and other Institute people were influenced by the work of Berkson, a Jewish educator in New York City, whose 1920 book *Theories of Americanization* advocated a "community theory" of immigrant adjustment. Berkson rejected Americanization or assimilation through the melting pot, insisting rather on the value of the ethnic group "as a permanent asset in American life." As one scholar has noted, Berkson's theory of adjustment posited that "each ethnic group which desires to do so should be permitted to create its own communal life, preserving and developing its cultural heritage while at the same time participating effectively in the broader life of the nation as a whole." Ethnic communities and cultures would coexist alongside American culture, but they would share in the common economic and political life. Assimilation might take place over time, but this was acceptable as long as no compulsion was involved.[13] Julius Drachsler proposed a similar sort of "cultural democracy" in his book *Democracy and Assimilation*, also published in 1920.[14] The programs of the International Institutes in the 1920s and early 1930s closely matched the immigrant adjustment theories of Berkson and Drachsler.

In the 1930s, the pluralist vision was elaborated anew. The leading advocate of cultural pluralism during the depression decade and the World War II years was Louis Adamic, a Slovenian immigrant who became a successful journalist and writer in the United States. In a series of articles and books, Adamic established himself as an articulate and sensitive pluralist. He was especially concerned about the so-called second-generation problem—the conflict between ethnic newcomers and their American-born children. He sought to overcome the sense of inferiority that prevailed among ethnic minorities in the United States through a sort of ethnic renewal that would build pride in ethnic origins and culture. As Rudolph J. Vecoli has suggested, "the ideological thrust of Adamic's argument was that a new conception of America was necessary, one which recognized that America was no longer an Anglo-Saxon country and that the children of immigrants should not be expected to become Anglo-Saxons." Adamic sought the eventual integration of ethnic and racial groups into a new "universal" American ideal, and this made him a "short-term pluralist." However, Adamic opposed assimilation that would destroy the cultural qualities of any individual ethnic groups. The United States, Adamic contended, was "a nation of nations," and only a new vision of America could accommodate cultural diversity. As Vecoli has noted, "Adamic strove tirelessly to move America toward a new definition of itself—one in which Ellis Island would be regarded as historically important as Plymouth Rock."[15]

Just as the work of Berkson and Drachsler influenced the direction of the International Institutes in the 1920s, Adamic's writings helped

International Institute leaders focus and elaborate their thinking during the decades of depression and world war. Recently described as a "symbolic personification of ethnic America" during these years, Adamic spoke to large and admiring audiences at many Institutes, obviously articulating unspoken but deeply felt attitudes and feelings of the newcomers. The Institutes also drew on the ideals of the intercultural education movement—an organized effort during the 1930s to enhance the status of racial and ethnic minority groups in the United States and to use the public schools to eliminate prejudice and intolerance.[16] Thus, over a period of three decades after the founding of the first International Institute in 1910, Bremer and her Institute colleagues gradually moved from the liberal assimilationist position to the cultural pluralism or cultural democracy of Berkson and Drachsler and then to the more refined pluralist-integrationist position of Louis Adamic. By the 1930s, paradoxically, the Institutes were both promoting cultural and ethnic pluralism and seeking better integration of immigrants and their children into American society. Like Adamic, International Institute people conceived of the goals of pluralism and integration as complementary rather than contradictory. Bremer and her colleagues in the 1920s and 1930s did not think of integration of the immigrant as a preliminary stage leading to total assimilation. According to William S. Bernard, who succeeded Bremer as head of the Institute movement in the 1950s, the Institutes thought of integration "as meaning the acceptance of immigrants by the American public, and their full participation in American life while they were still ethnically different and part of a culturally pluralistic society and not assimilated." In other words, Bernard has written, "cultural identity and integration could go hand in hand and assimilation was at the other end of the scale entirely. The Institutes thought cultural pluralism was good for the immigrants and also good for America." Read Lewis, who worked closely with Bremer and the International Institutes as director of the Foreign Language Information Service, described Institute goals in a similar way. According to Lewis, there was no inconsistency between "integrating immigrants and their children fully into the mainstream of American life," on the one hand, and encouraging them and their descendants "to maintain and enjoy their ancestral languages, religions, customs and cultures," on the other hand.[17] Reflecting the influence of Adamic and the intercultural educators, this dual emphasis on pluralism and integration came to shape the International Institute movement during the depression years.

The work of the individual International Institutes generally conformed to the ideals and purposes articulated by Bremer, thus giving the

Figure 9. Children representing nationality groups attending the International Institute in Gary, Indiana, 1922. Photo courtesy of the Calumet Regional Archives, Indiana University, Northwest.

whole movement a unified direction over many decades. Although beginning as YWCA agencies designed to aid immigrant women, the Institutes moved quickly to family case work, since women and their individual problems could not be treated separately from the immigrant households and ethnic communities in which they lived and worked. Thus, each Institute engaged in traditional social service work in the immigrant neighborhoods. Institute workers divided their time between individual and family case work and group and community work. Much of the case work consisted of handling the often complicated naturalization and citizenship problems of the immigrants. Institute people became experts on immigration law and its application—an area of social service generally neglected by the settlement houses and other agencies. Moreover, Institute case workers mediated between the newcomers and various government agencies, translated letters and documents, helped immigrants find jobs and housing, and directed those with special problems to the appropriate office, bureau, or agency. Typical family case work problems involved conflicts between husband and wife, and between immigrant parents and second-generation children. The group and community social work of the International Institutes was considered a natural corollary to case work. By bringing newcomers together in organized groups for education, recreation, or special projects, Institute workers hoped to overcome the immigrants' sense of powerlessness and give them a shared feeling of participating and belonging. For the Institutes, group and community work was "an integral part of a therapeutic case work plan."[18]

What made the International Institutes unique was the utilization of foreign-born and second-generation women as case workers. Called "nationality workers," these women were usually college educated, with additional professional social work training. They knew the languages of the newcomers, and they understood the various ethnic backgrounds and cultures. As one observer noted in 1920, the Institute nationality workers could "get inside the immigrant groups." The settlement houses and other charitable agencies, by contrast, were generally staffed by middle-class American women, who were often ignored or looked upon suspiciously in the immigrant communities. The nationality workers were not nativists or Americanizers, but instead saw the value and importance of ethnic culture. Thus, they not only helped to give the immigrants the skills and knowledge they needed to adjust to life in urban America, but they also sought to build consciousness and pride in the immigrant heritage. They urged the newcomers to retain their languages, traditions, and folkways. At the same time, through various programs, they encouraged Americans to understand immigrant customs and recognize ethnic contributions to American life.[19] During the nativist and intolerant years from World War I through the Great Depression, few other agencies promoted the immigrant cause as persistently and effectively as the International Institutes.

The YWCA's International Institutes recognized the importance of educational programs in carrying out their multifaceted social service tasks. Thus, each Institute sponsored a variety of educational activities ranging from formal classroom instruction to informal cultural programs. The Institutes generally offered classes in English, citizenship instruction in American history and government, and courses in such practical subjects as nursing, child care, first aid, homemaking, sewing, cooking, and vocational guidance. Much of this instruction took the form of explaining American customs, institutions, and laws to the immigrants. At the center of each Institute's educational effort, however, were classes and clubs studying old country languages, music, art, literature, history, and culture. Similarly, the Institutes sponsored, organized, or helped immigrant groups put on ethnic folk festivals, pageants, plays, concerts, and handicraft exhibits. These events had broad, if somewhat informal, educational functions in the immigrant communities, especially among the American-born children of the immigrants.

The educational programs of the International Institutes in San Francisco, Philadelphia, and Boston typified the work of the movement as a whole. Local YWCA leaders founded the San Francisco Institute in 1918 to conduct service-type work with immigrant women. Nationality workers were engaged to work in the city's Greek, Italian, Russian, Slavic, Scandinavian, and Spanish-speaking communities. By 1920, the Institute had absorbed the functions of the Chinese and Japanese YWCAs, both begun in earlier years, and nationality workers were added for these two groups of Asian immigrants. In 1934 the San Francisco Institute separated from the YWCA and joined with other Institutes in the National Institute of Immigrant Welfare.[20] The Philadelphia International Institute was established in 1921, and it too became independent in 1934 and joined the new national agency headed by Edith Bremer. By the end of the 1920s, the Philadelphia Institute had nationality workers for the city's Russian, Ukrainian, Czech, Hungarian, Polish, German, Italian, and Armenian communities.[21] Founded in 1924 as a YWCA agency, the Boston International Institute had become independent by 1935. Following the Institute pattern of using multilingual case workers, the Boston agency began with Armenian, Greek, Syrian, Russian, Polish, and Italian nationality secretaries. A Chinese worker was added in the early 1940s.[22] As in the other Institutes, these nationality workers came from the immigrant communities and were at the center of the various Institute programs.

These three International Institutes were typical of the wider movement in that each pursued both cultural pluralism and social integration of newcomers in American society. Emphasizing this pluralist-integrationist stance, the San Francisco Institute described itself in its 1936 annual report as "an agency whose purpose in every activity [is] to promote the interests and understanding of the nationality communities of San Francisco, to work for the conservation of the aesthetic values in their culture, to cooperate with them in their efforts to become a part of American life." Similarly, the 1935 constitution of the Boston Institute suggests the motives of service, pluralism, and adjustment:

> The purpose of this organization shall be to provide a centre for information, service, education, and assembly for the use of people of all nationalities; to develop international fellowship and understanding; to consider and promote the welfare of our foreign population as a whole and

as a matter of social concern; to specialize in problems of the foreign born; to maintain contact with the social forces within nationality communities; to cooperate with other social agencies primarily interested in cultural, civic and economic welfare; to preserve and stimulate an interest in racial cultural values; to assist the older and newer citizenry in their orientation.

In pursuing such varied goals, the International Institutes placed special importance on educational programs and events. Institute leaders conceived of immigrant education as necessary both to help newcomers adjust to the new land and to maintain their old cultures, traditions, and languages.[23]

Education for immigrant adjustment and to aid ethnic integration into American society took several forms in the various Institutes. In providing English language instruction, for instance, the International Institutes served real needs in the immigrant communities. Institute workers rejected Americanization and the assimilationist position, but they envisioned only advantages in teaching immigrants helpful language skills. They focused at first on immigrant women who often were confined to home and neighborhood, while immigrant men and children generally picked up English in the workplace and the public schools. Thus, both in Boston and Philadelphia, the International Institutes first organized small and informal English classes for foreign-born women in immigrant homes or in neighborhood nationality halls. Usually organized on a nationality basis, these informal meetings had social and recreational purposes as well. Moreover, they satisfied the reluctance or fear of immigrant women to leave the neighborhood for formal classes, as well as the opposition of immigrant husbands, who did not want their wives venturing far from the household.[24]

During the 1920s, English language instruction gradually became more formal, with regular classes held at Institutes. In Philadelphia, for example, sixteen separate English classes with a total enrollment of 252 met regularly at the International Institute during 1928.[25] Similar instructional programs for foreign-born women were conducted at the Boston Institute, where Armenians, Greeks, Syrians, Poles, Russians, and others attended regular English-language classes taught by nationality workers and multi-lingual volunteers.[26] In San Francisco, a slightly different pattern prevailed. The Institute there considered English-language classes for immigrant women and girls a central part of the program, and a "director of English teaching" was hired in addition to several nationality workers. English classes were held at Institute centers in the Chinese, Japanese, Russian, Italian, and Greek districts of the city. By 1921, attendance at these classes totaled almost 7,000. By the mid-twenties, however, in order to devote more time to case work, the San Francisco Institute convinced the city's board of education to assume responsibility for these classes. This pattern continued into the next decade, as the Institute people, through their case work contacts, enrolled foreign-born women in special public school English classes.[27]

In the 1930s, while the San Francisco Institute phased out its own English-language classes, the Boston and Philadelphia agencies began sponsoring English classes for foreign-born males. With thousands of immigrants out of work during the depression, and with a sustained federal campaign against aliens, Institutes in the two eastern cities expanded their programs of language instruction. The foreign-born sought such instruction in large numbers, for the loss of jobs or the threat of deportation gave immigrants a real reason for learning the language, taking out citizenship papers, and becoming naturalized. In both cities, these expanded language programs received government support in the form of WPA-paid teachers. In Philadelphia, the Institute's executive director, Evelyn Hersey, conducted a special training seminar on immigrant backgrounds necessary for successful teaching of foreign-born adults. In the late 1930s, when the number of refugees from war-torn Europe increased substantially, the Boston Institute initiated special WPA English classes for European refugees.[28] The increased case work loads of the Institute nationality workers during the depression years meant that they had less time for teaching, so the New Deal teaching programs were especially welcomed. In all of this language instruction, the Institute sought only to serve and protect the foreign-born. Institute workers did not think of English teaching as preparation for Americanization. Rather, the learning of English was simply a skill that immigrants needed to survive and adjust to life in the American industrial city. At the same time, most Institutes periodically organized classes in American history and government for those newcomers who sought citizenship. In Boston and Philadelphia, these activities were most pronounced during the 1930s, when the currents of nativist bigotry and intolerance ran strong. Noncitizens were discriminated against in employment and denied public relief, the government required aliens to register, and federal officials pursued an active deportation policy. Immigrants who had resided in the United States for many years now recognized the urgency of naturalization. "Too much cannot be said these days regarding the advisability of acquiring citizenship," Boston Institute director Marion Blackwell noted in 1938. "More and more, discrimination is being made against the noncitizen."[29] For the immigrants, the practical aspect of citizenship was that it was a means of avoiding deportation, securing or maintaining a job, getting on the welfare or work relief rolls, and generally protecting one's investment in America.

Thus, the International Institutes became clearing houses for information on naturalization, deportation, repatriation, immigration law, and citizenship procedures. In addition, the case work of the nationality workers in the thirties was heavily weighted toward technical immigration and naturalization problems. Naturally, therefore, most Institutes moved to provide the formal instruction required for foreign-born clients seeking citizenship. In San Francisco, however, there were few such classes at the Institute. The city's role as an immigrant-receiving center (San Francisco's Angel Island was second only to New York's Ellis Island as an immigrant reception station) created an extra heavy case work load, leaving nationality workers little time for teaching. The city's public schools seem to have absorbed the burden of such citizenship instruction. Like the English-language instruction, Institute citizenship education was informational rather than propagandistic.[30]

In addition to English language and citizenship classes, each International Institute sponsored formal and informal instruction in a wide variety of practical subjects. Typically, at different times, the Philadelphia Institute offered classes in Red Cross training, public speaking, typing, bookkeeping, and similar subjects. Similarly, throughout the twenties and into the thirties, the San Francisco Institute provided classes in piano, violin, cooking, sewing, knitting, millinery, dress making, child care, and social hygiene, as well as lectures on immigration law, naturalization procedures, international relations, and world affairs.[31]

The immigrant communities themselves often initiated the demand for this sort of practical and general education. Indeed, much of it was provided through the nationality clubs and ethnic organizations sponsored by the Institutes. For instance, the South Boston Armenian Women's Club, organized at the Boston Institute in 1927, sponsored a class in the Armenian language with lectures on cooking, child care, home health and hygiene, current events, and American and Armenian history. In 1932 the Institute's Syrian Mothers' Club organized classes in nursing and cooking.[32] In Philadelphia, Armenian, Russian, and Italian clubs at the International Institute sponsored foreign-language lecture programs on child care, mental hygiene, home economics, world affairs, and other practical subjects.[33] In San Francisco, the Institute's Russian-American Club formed a study group in 1925 to study "the principles of American business" and attended lectures by American businessmen twice a month. A Mexican women's club went on educational trips through the city, visiting banks, government offices, and other agencies. A Chinese women's group organized a library of 300 Chinese books for their community, a Japanese girls' club studied business, Japanese women studied literature and politics, and a Mexican mothers' group learned methods of home hygiene and health care.[34] Nationality workers in the Institutes, then, taught and helped organize a variety of classes on subjects of practical utility and general interest among immigrants and their children.

In their efforts to bring knowledge and information to the immigrant communities, most International Institutes used media such as foreign-language programs and the foreign-language press. During the 1930s, the Philadelphia Institute sponsored radio programs in English, Russian, Italian, German, and other languages.[35] A series of radio programs put on by the Boston Institute in 1931 and the San Francisco Institute in 1935 discussed American laws, especially naturalization and deportation procedures, and publicized the educational, recreational, and social service work of the International Institutes.[36] The immigrant press had an important influence in the ethnic communities, and the Institutes also used this medium to publicize their activities and promote their educational goals, often working closely with the Foreign-Language Information Service, another offshoot of YWCA immigration work.[37] Generally, this sort of informal education sought to explain American institutions and laws to the newcomers and dealt with such subjects as naturalization, deportation, the legal rights of aliens, housing, employment, relief, and other things about the United States that immigrants needed to know and about which there was a great deal of misinformation. Reaching out to the foreign-born through their own media and in their own language, Institute people believed, would have a positive educational impact. As a Philadelphia Institute committee noted in 1934, "American customs introduced to them in their own language by a person of their own nationality can be better understood . . . less terrifying and much more likely to be tolerated."[38] In addition, both the Boston and Philadelphia Institutes had their own monthly newsletters by the end of the thirties—the *International Beacon* in Boston and *Internationality News* in Philadelphia. The San Francisco Institute did not begin publishing its *News Bulletin* until 1944, but as early as 1927 the Institute's Japanese center published its own bulletin, with columns both in English and Japanese.[39] In all of these media efforts, the Institutes sought to educate and inform the newcomers and to facilitate their adjustment to the new land.

The foregoing activities supplied an essential part of each International Institute's program. However, the Institutes had an equally important task—the preservation of immigrant languages and cultures and the building of respect for ethnic heritages among the American-born children of the immigrants. Edith Bremer believed that the immigrant cultural inheritance "should be kept an active force among the children and young people growing up in America." She was especially concerned about language maintenance, and in a 1930 address, Bremer urged every Institute to provide "mother tongue classes" for the immigrant children. Such classes, she suggested, would not only encourage pride and respect in the old country background, but address the "second-generation problem" and help "to bridge the generations."[40]

Over the years, the various Institutes adhered closely to the goals laid down by Bremer. In Boston, for instance, Institute director Marion Blackwell fully agreed with Bremer's thinking on maintaining ethnic pluralism. In a 1938 letter to the Armenian newspaper *Hairenik*, Blackwell wrote: "I believe it is disastrous to sever old-country traditions and ties, and I do not believe in the melting pot idea which would make all people in America one kind." Thus, one of the important functions of the Boston Institute was to instill second-generation children "with the respect which their parents' culture and tradition truly deserve." Similarly, Annie Clo Watson, director of the San Francisco Institute from 1932 until the 1950s, asserted that "we do not want the people who come from older countries to become Americanized"; rather, Watson contended, "our purpose is . . . to help them feel at home in the American community while keeping their own customs."[41] Consequently, through group and community education work, Institute nationality workers sought to preserve and pass on the old country traditions and tongues, thus fostering ethnic pluralism and cultural diversity.

The educational and group work of the Boston International Institute reveals the variety of the pluralist program. The South Boston Armenian Women's Club, for example, had classes not only in American history but also Armenian history. The club also sponsored classes in the Armenian language for the American-born children of Armenian immigrants. Similarly, an Italian girls' club met weekly at the Institute to study Italian history, language, and literature. These activities, according to the Italian nationality workers, would "give the girls a feeling of pride in acknowledging the greatness of their ancestry." The Institute's Greek nationality worker helped organize an Orthodox Young People's Christian Association, which studied Greek language and history and put on plays and concerts. The South End Greek Mothers' Club met at the Institute to study Arabic, and a Syrian Mothers' Club met for lectures in Arabic and to sing Arabic songs. Ukrainians, Russians, Germans, and Swedes gathered at the Institute for folk dancing and folk singing, Finns for Finnish musical activities, Russians for Russian language classes, and Poles for the study of Polish history and culture. Russian and Czech groups sponsored lectures on the history of their respective homelands. And in the mid-thirties, the Boston Institute conducted a series of weekly radio broadcasts celebrating the musical accomplishments of Poles, Swedes, Finns, Russians, Greeks, Chinese, and other ethnic groups.[42] In all of these ways, the Boston International Institute encouraged and supported education for cultural pluralism. At the same time, these activities countered the often harsh Americanizing influences of the public schools and other agencies working with immigrants and their children.

In Philadelphia, the International Institute was engaged in a similar kind of pluralist education designed, as the agency's 1940 annual report noted, "to encourage the preservation and sharing of cultural heritages." Retention of old country languages was an essential first step. Thus, throughout the 1930s the Institute sponsored formal language classes in French, German, Russian, Italian, Spanish, Swedish, Greek, and other languages. The Institute's monthly bulletin, *Internationality News*, urged second-generation young people to "learn the language of your forefathers." As in Boston, most of the Institute's cultural programs were carried out through group work with numerous affiliated clubs. A Polish Students' Club, for instance, had classes in the Polish language and put on Polish plays in the community. An Armenian Girls' Club, organized to study Armenian literature, made it a point "to carry on all their meetings in Armenian so that they may have practice in the language of their parents." The Young German Circle was interested in "rescuing old traditions" and in the revival of old German folk songs, folk dances, folk costumes, and art. Another German club of high school students published a monthly paper in German, while a third German society pursued "German gymnastics." Several Italian clubs studied Italian art, music, and literature. A Russian Young Peoples' Club studied Russian language, literature, and history, while a second group, the Russian Singers, learned "to sing Russian folk and classical pieces in Russian." Other Institute-affiliated groups included a German Glee Club and Finnish, Swedish, and Ukrainian folk dance clubs. Some forty-three language and culture groups met regularly at the Philadelphia International Institute during 1933—a typical year—and total attendance surpassed eighteen thousand.[43]

A similar pattern prevailed in the San Francisco International Institute, although a heavy emphasis on social service and case work often cut into group and cultural work in the 1930s. Nevertheless, the west coast Institute sponsored a variety of language classes and such diverse groups as Armenian, Polish, German, Mexican, and Swedish folk dance clubs, an Italian Choral Club, a Russian Literary Society, a Mexican singing society, Russian, Greek, and Danish orchestras, a Japanese Girls' Club that studied Japanese literature, a Filipino Mothers' Club that put on plays in the Filipino community, and in 1933 fourteen separate Chinese cultural groups and classes.[44] Unique to the San Francisco Institute was the agency's "Studio" department—"a place where the foreign people who are interested in the arts, may come to meet each other, to practice, to have a sort of genial art home."[45]

In all of these group activities and programs promoting immigrant language and culture maintenance, the International Institutes emphasized strongly old country musical, dramatic, artistic, dancing, and handicraft traditions. Clubs and groups involved in these activities met regularly at the Institutes for rehearsals and performances. The Institutes were also used for the celebration of immigrant festival days, holidays, and saints' days—occasions when cultural and religious traditions were emphasized. Most of the Institutes had special "nights" highlighting the culture of separate nationality groups. In Philadelphia, for example, the International Institute held such "nationality nights" monthly, each focusing on "the artistic worth of each nationality." The ethnic communities themselves organized the programs, which typically included folk dancing, folk singing, handicraft and folk art exhibits, old country food specialties, perhaps a film, even lectures and discussions by community leaders or invited speakers.[46]

Such efforts at intercultural education were common at the Boston and San Francisco Institutes as well. According to Annie Clo Watson, the San Francisco Institute director, "the most important purpose of 'nationality nights' is to foster the spirit of tolerance by joining native and foreign-born citizens in events which proclaim the contributions to our national culture which have come to us thru our immigrant citizens from across seas and boundaries."[47] By demonstrating the colorful and rich cultures of the old countries, these "nationality nights" fostered cooperation and understanding among different ethnic groups and between newcomers and native-born Americans.

Similarly highlighting immigrant cultures were the big folk festivals sponsored by most International Institutes throughout the 1920s and

1930s. The folk festivals brought people from the ethnic communities together for work on a common project, they stimulated pride in the homeland and its traditions, and they made native-born Americans more appreciative of immigrant cultures.[48] Most Institutes also put on a variety of international banquets, handicraft exhibits, harvest balls, Christmas festivals, and similar events that built a spirit of pluralism, cooperation, and community among the newcomers. Programs of this kind at the Philadelphia Institute, for instance, included "folk story nights" at which Institute clubs used music, dramatics, and puppetry to illustrate nationality legends and folk tales; "internationality dinners" featuring immigrant songs and dances as well as foods; and Christmas parties and festivals portraying Christmas customs in many lands.[49] Suggesting the cultural variety of such events, the program of an international Christmas party at the San Francisco Institute in 1930 consisted of "Russian kindergarten children, Chinese girls singing Christmas carols, Russian soloists, Greek group dancing, Swedish Christmas songs and dances, English carolers and finally the singing in unison of "Holy Night" by the various nationalities, each in his own native tongue."[50]

All of these events had broad, if somewhat informal, educative results in the immigrant communities. They built bridges of understanding between the old and the new, between children and parents, and between newcomers and old-stock Americans. They contributed to ethnic cultural and language maintenance. Immigrants gained a measure of pride in their heritage. The second generation came to appreciate and respect the native customs and traditions of their parents. The essential message of the International Institutes was that diversity rather than conformity, that cooperation rather than conflict, was the essence of American democracy. Clearly, these Institute cultural activities were extraordinary efforts at community education.

Throughout the 1920s and 1930s, the YWCA's International Institutes pursued the dual objectives outlined by Edith Bremer. They sought a better adjustment and integration of the immigrants in American society. Simultaneously, through their group and community activities, they encouraged the newcomers to retain their languages and cultures and to take pride in their old-country heritages. The Institutes fought for the immigrant cause and defended ethnic communities and their traditions. As Bremer noted in a 1934 talk in Boston, the International Institutes were "about the only organization that has stood up and said that the foreign-born are not dangerous."[51] The task was far from easy during the decades of nativism, intolerance, and depression.

Indeed the Great Depression had an important impact on the Institute movement as a whole. The downturn in the American economy cut into American philanthropy, eventually causing severe budget problems for the individual Institutes. With less operating capital, most Institutes reduced their staffs, put remaining nationality workers on part-time, closed for summer months, and took other austerity measures. By the mid-thirties, these measures began to cut rather deeply into cultural and educational programs. Nationality workers still on the job spent an increasing amount of their time on naturalization and immigration case work problems. This pattern intensified by 1940, when Congress passed the Alien Registration Act—a measure which further increased naturalization work at the International Institutes. During World War II the Institutes emphasized consensus and patriotic war work in the immigrant communities, thus hastening the demise of cultural pluralist programs. In the immediate postwar years, most Institutes devoted attention to the resettlement of European refugees in the United States. In San Francisco, the Institute launched a major effort to aid in the resettlement of the Japanese Americans who had been incarcerated during the war. Since the 1950s, while many Institutes still sponsor an occasional folk festival, International Institute work has been devoted almost solely to technical immigration and naturalization case work.

Irrespective of their limited role after 1940, the International Institutes served important functions during the twenties and thirties. Institute cultural programs and educational activities during those years both aided in the adjustment of new immigrants and promoted the ideals of diversity and pluralism. Following the lead of founder Edith Bremer, the International Institutes rejected demands for Americanization and immediate assimilation, working instead for a gradual integration of the newcomers into the American mainstream. Institute workers conceived of pluralist educational programs as essential ingredients in immigrant adjustment. Through their group and community cultural and language programs, the International Institutes were providing the immigrants and their children with a very different sort of education from that encountered in the public schools and in official adult education and Americanization classes. Much like the ethnic folk schools, the immigrant churches, the foreign-language press, and other immigrant organizations, the International Institutes served as alternative educational agencies, muting the impact of public schools and countering pervasive nativist demands for conformity.

Study of the International Institutes adds important perspectives on twentieth-century American immigration and ethnic history. The educational activities of the various Institutes suggest the range and diversity of educational experiences among immigrants and their children. The technical and immigration case work of Institute nationality workers illustrates a neglected dimension of American social welfare history, and especially of the history of the YWCA. Education and social service were two significant dimensions of Institute work, and the pluralist framework from which the Institutes functioned made these programs distinctive. Most studies of cultural pluralism in America deal only with the ideas of intellectuals and writers; they discuss the place of cultural pluralism in American social thought. The great advantage of studying the International Institutes is the ability to examine the practice as well as the ideology of pluralism. Case study of the Institutes provides an opportunity to see how the ideology of cultural pluralism worked at the level where it affected people, to examine how it was applied to human problems in actual situations. There is still much to learn about the Institute movement, about the Institutes as an early expression of feminist agency, about the diverse ways in which Institutes empowered immigrant women and ethnic communities, about the special role of the nationality workers, about Institute political agendas, and the like. Despite what remains to be learned, however, it should be clear that the International Institutes of Boston, Philadelphia, and San Francisco differed in significant ways from most other agencies working with immigrants and ethnic communities. They gave the newcomers a different perception of themselves and of their place in the new land. That they did so under the organizational umbrella of the YWCA provides further evidence of the diversity and ubiquity of the parent agency and its wide-ranging influence in the modern American city.

NOTES

The author acknowledges the support of the Florida Atlantic University Division of Sponsored Research, the Immigration History Research Center at the University of Minnesota, and the American Council of Learned Societies.

1. The reinterpretation of American educational history began with Bernard Bailyn's *Education in the Forming of American Society* (Chapel Hill: University of North Carolina Press, 1960). Later studies that pursued Bailyn's approach include Lawrence A. Cremin, *American Education: The Metropolitan*

Experience, 1876–1980 (New York: Harper and Row, 1988); Vincent P. Franklin, *The Education of Black Philadelphia: The Social and Educational History of a Minority Community, 1900–1950* (Philadelphia: University of Pennsylvania Press, 1979); William J. Reese, *Power and the Promise of School Reform: Grassroots Movements during the Progressive Era* (Boston: Routledge and Kegan Paul, 1986); Ronald D. Cohen, *Children of the Mill: Schooling and Society in Gary, Indiana, 1906–1960* (Bloomington: Indiana University Press, 1990).

2. Raymond E. Callahan, *Education and the Cult of Efficiency: A Study of the Social Forces That Have Shaped the Administration of the Public Schools* (Chicago: University of Chicago Press, 1962), 15. The most comprehensive studies of immigration history are John Bodnar, *The Transplanted: A History of Immigrants in Urban America* (Bloomington: Indiana University Press, 1985); Thomas J. Archdeacon, *Becoming American: An Ethnic History* (New York: Free Press, 1983); and Roger Daniels, *Coming to America: A History of Immigration and Ethnicity in American Life* (New York: HarperCollins, 1990).

3. Ellwood P. Cubberley, *Changing Conceptions of Education* (Boston: Houghton Mifflin, 1909), 15–16; Frank V. Thompson, *Schooling of the Immigrant* (New York: Harper, 1920), 1.

4. On parochial schools, see James W. Sanders, *The Education of an Urban Minority: Catholics in Chicago, 1833–1965* (New York: Oxford University Press, 1977). On ethnic folk schools, see Joshua A. Fishman, *Language Loyalty in the United States* (The Hague: Mouton, 1966), 92–126. For an analysis of immigrants and education in a single city, taking into account multiple educational institutions, see Ronald D. Cohen and Raymond A. Mohl, *The Paradox of Progressive Education: The Gary Plan and Urban Schooling* (Port Washington, N.Y.: Kennikat Press, 1979), 84–109.

5. For initial YWCA interest in the immigration problem, see YWCA, *Some Urgent Phases of Immigrant Life* (New York: National Board of the YWCA, 1910); for Bremer's early reports on International Institute work, see YWCA, Department of Immigration and Foreign Communities, Reports, 1910–1921, Archives of the National Board of the YWCA, New York City (hereafter cited as YWCA Archives). See also "The International Institute for Young Women in New York," *Women's International Quarterly*, 1 (October 1912): 56–57; "Educational Work of the Young Women's Christian Association," United States Bureau of Education, *Bulletin*, no. 26 (Washington, D.C., 1923), 13–16; Mary S. Sims, *The First Twenty-Five Years: Being a Summary of the Work of the Young Women's Christian Association of the United States of America, 1906–1931* (New York: Womans Press, 1932), 17, 33; Julia Talbot Bird, "The International Institutes of the Young Women's Christian Association and Immigrant Women" (M.A. thesis, Yale University, 1932), 35–60.

6. Grace H. Wilson, *The Religious and Educational Philosophy of the Young Women's Christian Association* (New York: Teachers College, Columbia University, 1933), 15–46; Sheila M. Rothman, *Woman's Proper Place: A History of Changing Ideals and Practices, 1870 to the Present* (New York: Basic Books,

1978), 74–76; Mary S. Sims, *The Natural History of a Social Institution—The Young Women's Christian Association* (New York: Womans Press, 1936), 92; Raymond A. Mohl, "American Federation of International Institutes," in *Greenwood Encyclopedia of American Institutions: Social Service Organizations,* ed. Peter Romanofsky, 2 vols. (Westport, Conn.: Greenwood Press, 1978), 1: 59–63. For recent discussion of "women's historical agency," see Linda K. Kerber et al., *U.S. History as Women's History: New Feminist Essays* (Chapel Hill: University of North Carolina Press, 1995).

    7. "Information Regarding Edith Terry Bremer," November 1939, in American Council for Nationalities Service Papers, Shipment 8, Box 20, Immigration History Research Center, University of Minnesota (hereafter cited as ACNS Papers); Raymond A. Mohl, "Edith Terry Bremer," in *Notable American Women: The Modern Period,* eds. Barbara Siccherman and Carol Hurd Green (Cambridge, Mass.: Harvard University Press, 1980), 105–107.

    8. R. Fred Wacker, "Assimilation and Cultural Pluralism in American Social Thought," *Phylon,* 40 (December 1979): 325–327. See also Robert E. L. Faris, *Chicago Sociology, 1930–1932* (San Francisco: Chandler, 1970), 3–36; William I. Thomas, *Old World Traits Transplanted* (1921; reprint ed. Montclair, N.J.: Patterson Smith, 1971), vii–xv; Stephen J. Diner, *A City and Its Universities: Public Policy in Chicago, 1892–1919* (Chapel Hill: University of North Carolina Press, 1980); Mary Jo Deegan, *Jane Addams and the Men of the Chicago School, 1892–1918* (New Brunswick, N.J.: Transaction Books, 1988). For surveys of the settlement house movement, see Allen F. Davis, *Spearheads for Reform: The Social Settlements and the Progressive Movement, 1890–1914* (New York: Oxford University Press, 1967); Judith Ann Trolander, *Professionalism and Social Change: From the Settlement House Movement to Neighborhood Centers, 1886 to the Present* (New York: Columbia University Press, 1987); Mina Carson, *Settlement Folk: Social Thought and the American Settlement Movement, 1885–1930* (Chicago: University of Chicago Press, 1990).

    9. Robert Buroker, "From Voluntary Association to Welfare State: The Illinois Immigrants' Protective League, 1908–1926," *Journal of American History,* 57 (December 1971): 643–660; Henry B. Leonard, "The Immigrants' Protective League of Chicago, 1908–1921," *Illinois State Historical Society Journal,* 66 (Autumn 1973): 271–284.

    10. Edith B. Terry, "A Report on the Immigration Work of the National Board," 24 March 1911, YWCA Archives; Edith Terry Bremer, "Report of Department on Work for Foreign Born Women," 2 October 1919, ibid.; Edith Terry Bremer, "Immigrants and Foreign Communities," *Social Work Yearbook,* 1929 (New York: Russell Sage Foundation, 1930), 215; Edith Terry Bremer, *The International Institutes in Foreign Community Work: Their Program and Philosophy* (New York: Womans Press, 1923), 10.

    11. Horace M. Kallen, "Democracy Versus the Melting Pot," *The Nation,* 100 (February 18 and 25, 1915): 190–194, 217–220, reprinted in Horace M. Kallen, *Culture and Democracy in the United States: Studies in the Group*

Psychology of the American Peoples (New York: Boni and Liveright, 1924), 67–125. See also Horace M. Kallen, "Nationality and the Hyphenated America," *Menorah Journal,* 1 (1915): 79–86; Horace M. Kallen, "The Meaning of Americanism," *Immigrants in America Review,* 1 (January 1916): 12–19; Edith Terry Bremer, "Foreign Community and Immigration Work of the National Young Women's Christian Association," ibid., 73–82.

12. For an analysis of Kallen's pluralism, see Milton M. Gordon, *Assimilation in American Life: The Role of Race, Religion, and National Origins* (New York: Oxford University Press, 1964), 141–149; John Higham, *Send These to Me: Jews and Other Immigrants in Urban America* (New York: Atheneum, 1975), 196–230; Arthur Mann, *The One and the Many: Reflections on the American Identity* (Chicago: University of Chicago Press, 1979), 136–148; F. H. Matthews, "The Revolt Against Americanism: Cultural Pluralism and Cultural Relativism as an Ideology of Liberation," *Canadian Review of American Studies,* 1 (Spring 1970): 4–31; James Henry Powell, "The Concept of Cultural Pluralism in American Social Thought, 1915–1965" (Ph.D. dissertation, University of Notre Dame, 1971), 1–36.

13. Isaac B. Berkson, *Theories of Americanization: A Critical Study* (New York: Teachers College, Columbia University, 1920), 98; Gordon, *Assimilation in American Life,* 154.

14. Julius Drachsler, *Democracy and Assimilation: The Blending of Immigrant Heritages in America* (New York: Macmillan, 1920), 214–216.

15. Rudolph J. Vecoli, "Louis Adamic and the Contemporary Search for Roots," *Ethnic Studies,* 2 (1978): 32; Louis Adamic, *Two-Way Passage* (New York: Harper, 1941), 11–14. See also Carey McWilliams, *Louis Adamic and Shadow-America* (Los Angeles: Arthur Whipple, 1935), and Adamic's important writings, including *The Native's Return* (New York: Harper, 1934); *My America* (New York: Harper, 1938); *From Many Lands* (New York: Harper, 1940); *What's Your Name?* (New York: Harper, 1942); and *A Nation of Nations* (New York: Harper, 1945).

16. Richard Weiss, "Ethnicity and Reform: Minorities and the Ambience of the Depression Years," *Journal of American History,* 66 (December 1979): 569; Ronald K. Goodenow, "The Progressive Educator, Race and Ethnicity in the Depression Years: An Overview," *History of Education Quarterly,* 15 (Winter 1975): 365–394; Stewart G. Cole, "Intercultural Education," in *One America,* eds. Francis J. Brown and Joseph S. Roucek (rev. ed.; New York: Prentice-Hall, 1945), 561–571; Nicholas V. Montalto, *A History of the Intercultural Education Movement, 1924–1941* (New York: Garland Publishing, 1982). For an example of International Institute discussion of these issues, see San Francisco International Institute, "Conference on Intercultural Relations," 6 December 1936, mimeo transcript, San Francisco International Institute Papers, located in the offices of the San Francisco International Institute (hereafter cited as SFII Papers).

17. William S. Bernard to author, 10 September 1978; Read Lewis to author,

14 August 1978. See also William S. Bernard, *American Immigration Policy: A Reappraisal* (New York: Harper, 1950), 109–111.

18. Philadelphia YWCA, Consulting Committee, "Study of the International Institute," 1934, typescript, Philadelphia YWCA Papers, Box 13, folder URB/I/163, Urban Archives Center, Temple University (hereafter cited as TUUA). For an example of the range of activities in a typical Institute, see Raymond A. Mohl and Neil Betten, "Ethnic Adjustment in the Industrial City: The International Institute of Gary, 1919–1940," *International Migration Review*, 6 (Winter 1972): 361–376.

19. John Daniels, *America via the Neighborhood* (New York: Harper, 1920), 301. See also Edith Terry Bremer, *The Field of the International Institute and Its Place in Social Work* (reprint of a paper given at the Seventh Annual Conference of International Institutes, 1925; New York: Womans Press, 1926); Edith Terry Bremer, "The Foreign Language Worker in the Fusion Process: An Indispensable Asset to Social Work in America," National Conference on Social Work, *Proceedings* (1919), 740–746; Marian Lantz, "The Place of the Nationality Secretary in an International Institute," n.d. (c. 1940), mimeo, Philadelphia Nationalities Service Center Papers, Series 1, Box 14, TUUA (hereafter cited as PNSC Papers). In 1963 the Philadelphia International Institute changed its name to Philadelphia Nationalities Service Center. For a study critical of the assimilating tendencies of the settlements, see Rivka Shpak Lissak, *Hull House and the New Immigrants, 1890–1919* (Chicago: University of Chicago Press, 1989).

20. On the origins of the San Francisco Institute, see "History of the San Francisco International Institute," 1930, typescript, SFII Papers. For the Institute's separation from the YWCA, see Annual Report, 1934, typescript, SFII Papers.

21. For the early history of the Philadelphia Institute, see "Forty-five Years of Service of the Nationalities Service Center of Philadelphia," 1966, typescript, PNSC Papers, Acc. 368, Box 34, TUUA.

22. On the beginnings of the Boston Institute, see "Confidential Report on the International Institute of Boston," 1935, typescript, Boston International Institute Papers (hereafter cited as BII Papers). Since my examination of materials and records at the offices of the Boston International Institute, these papers have been deposited at the Immigration History Research Center, University of Minnesota.

23. San Francisco International Institute, Annual Report, Papers; Boston International Institute, Constitution, 7 May 1935, typescript, BII Papers.

24. Edith Terry Bremer, "Education for 'Immigrant Women': What Is It?" *Educational Foundations*, 27 (1916): 289–297; Bird, "The International Institutes," 108–109.

25. For English-language instruction in Philadelphia, see Committee of Management, Minutes, 27 December 1927, 14 March, 3 April 1928, PNSC Papers, Series 1, Box 1, folder 1, TUUA; *Fifty-Eighth Annual Report of the Philadelphia Young Women's Christian Association* (Philadelphia: Philadelphia YWCA, 1929), 54, ibid., Box 25.

26. See Monthly Reports of Nationality Workers, 1930s, BII Papers.

27. "History of the San Francisco International Institute," SFII Papers; Annual Reports, 1922–1930, SFII Papers.

28. On WPA teachers in Institutes programs, see "WPA Workers in Literacy and Americanization," 1936, transcripts of class meetings, PNSC Papers, Series 1, Box 10, folder III, TUUA; "Report of Work with Refugees," 12 March 1940, typescript, BII Papers.

29. (Boston) *International Beacon*, 5 (15 June 1938); Edith Terry Bremer, "A Forward Look for International Institutes," 1930, mimeo, in SFII Papers. See also Edith Terry Bremer, "How Is It With the Non-Citizens?" *The Womans Press*, 24 (December 1930): 847–848, 856; Edith Terry Bremer, "The Jobless `Alien'—A Challenge to Social Workers," *The Survey*, 65 (15 December 1930): 316–317. For typical examples of anti-immigrant hostility in the 1930s, see Isaac F. Marcosson, "The Alien in America," *The Saturday Evening Post*, 207 (6 April 1935): 22–23, 110, 112–113; Raymond G. Carroll, "The Alien on Relief," ibid., 208 (25 January 1936): 23, 82, 84–86, 89; Louis Adamic, "Aliens and Alien-Baiters," *Harpers Magazine*, 173 (November 1936): 561–574. For Institute activities in one city opposing nativism in the 1930s, see Neil Betten and Raymond A. Mohl, "From Discrimination to Repatriation: Mexican Life in Gary, Indiana, During the Great Depression," *Pacific Historical Review*, 42 (August 1973): 380–385.

30. On International Institute work at the Angel Island immigration station, see Sarah Ellis, "At the Golden Gateway: Something of the Port Work of the Y.W.C.A. at Angel Island," *The Womans Press*, 21 (November 1927): 768–769, 816.

31. (Philadelphia) *Internationality News*, 15 November 1939; San Francisco International Institute, Annual Reports, 1922–1934, SFII Papers.

32. Bird, "The International Institutes," pp. 108–109; (Boston) *International Beacon*, January 1933; Monthly Reports, January–March 1932, BII Papers.

33. Philadelphia YWCA, Consulting Committee, "Study of the International Institute," 1934, typescript, PNSC Papers, Series 1, Box 21, TUUA.

34. San Francisco International Institute, Annual Reports, 1925, 1926, 1928, 1930, 1932, SFII Papers.

35. Philadelphia YWCA, "Supporting 1934 Budget, International Institute," 1934, typescript, Philadelphia YWCA Papers, Box 13, URB/I/165, TUUA.

36. Radio Script, 7 May 1931, BII Papers; San Francisco International Institute, Annual Report, 1935, SFII Papers.

37. Edith Terry Bremer, *American Foreign Language Service Bureaus* (New York: National Board of the YWCA, 1917); Annual Report of the Work of the Department for Foreign Born Women, 1920–1921, YWCA Archives. On the work of the Foreign Language Information Service, see Lynn Ann Schweitzer, "Foreign Language Information Service," in *Greenwood Encyclopedia of American Institutions: Social Service Organizations*, ed. Romanofsky, 1:311–315; Daniel E. Weinberg, "The Ethnic Technician and the Foreign-Born:

Another Look at Americanization Ideology and Goals," *Societas—A Review of Social History,* 7 (Summer 1977): 209–227.

38. Philadelphia YWCA, Consulting Committee, "Study of the International Institute," 1934, typescript, Philadelphia YWCA Papers, Box 13, folder URB/I/163, YUUA.

39. San Francisco International Institute, Annual Report, 1927, SFII Papers.

40. Edith Terry Bremer, "The International Institute: A Re-Analysis of Our Foundations," Confidential Proceedings of the Conference on International Institute Work, 1923, mimeo, 22, in YWCA; Edith Terry Bremer, "A Forward Look for International Institutes" 1930, mimeo, SFII Papers.

41. (Boston) *Hairenik,* 15 July 1938, clipping, BII Papers; WPA, Federal Writers Project, "Statement on the International Institute of Boston," April 1939, BII Papers; (Tokyo) *Nippon Times,* undated clipping, Annie Clo Watson Papers, Immigration History Research Center, University of Minnesota.

42. (Boston) *International Beacon,* January 1933, 14 November 1934, 15 September 1935; Monthly Reports, March 1931, December 1931, December 1932, September 1935, December 1935, January 1936, November 1937, BII Papers; Boston International Institute, Annual Reports, 1937, 1940, 1941, ibid.; Minutes, International Institute Board of Directors, 5 June, 26 June, 12 November 1935, ibid.

43. Philadelphia International Institute, Annual Report, 1940, PNSC Papers, Series 1, Box 1, folder 16, TUUA; (Philadelphia) *Internationality News,* 21 October, 15 November 1939; Minutes, International Institute Committee of Management (renamed Board of Directors in 1934), 14 March, 3 April 1928, 24 October 1935, 13 January 1941, PNSC Papers, Series 1, Box 1 TUUA; "Field Work of the International Institute of the Philadelphia YWCA," 1932, typescript, ibid., Box 1, folder 14; (Philadelphia) *YWCA News,* 9 (February 1933), ibid., Box 1, folder 9; Catherine Shimkus, "Report of the Russian Worker in the International Institute," n.d. (c. early 1930s), typescript, ibid., Box 4, folder 117; Philadelphia International Institute, "For a United America," unpaginated pamphlet, ibid., Box 1, folder 10.

44. San Francisco International Institute, Annual Reports, 1928–1934, SFII Papers.

45. San Francisco International Institute, Annual Report, 1927, SFII Papers.

46. Philadelphia International Institute, Minutes, Board of Directors, 16 January 1935, PNSC Papers, Series 1, Box 1, folder 9; Invitations to Open House Nights, Scrapbook, 1940–1942, ibid., Box 11.

47. San Francisco International Institute, Annual Report, 1933, SFII Papers.

48. For typical material on Institute folk festivals, see Dorothy G. Spicer, *Folk Festivals and the Foreign Community* (New York: Womans Press, 1923); Dorothy G. Spicer, "The Folk Festival and the Community," *Foreign-Born: A Bulletin of International Service,* 3 (August–September 1922): 208; Alice L. Sickels, *Around the World in St. Paul* (Minneapolis: University of Minnesota Press, 1945); Allen H. Eaton, *Immigrant Gifts to American Life* (New York:

Russell Sage Foundation, 1932), 92–94; Louis Adamic, "The St. Paul Festival of Nations," *Common Ground* (Summer 1941): 103–110.

49. Philadelphia International Institute, *News Notes,* 25 February 1940, PNSC Papers, Box 11, TUUA; Invitations, 1940, Scrapbooks, 1940–1942, ibid.

50. San Francisco International Institute, Annual Report, 1930, SFII Papers.

51. "Notes from Mrs. Bremer's Talk," 13 March 1934, BII Papers.

Chapter Six

True Manhood
The YMCA and Racial Advancement, 1890–1930

Nina Mjagkij

In recent years, many historians have discovered gender as a useful tool for historical analysis; however, much of the scholarship has been limited to the study of women. As E. Anthony Rotundo has pointed out: "Nearly everything we know about human behaviour in the past concerns men and yet it is equally—and ironically—true that we know far more about womanhood and the female role than we know about masculinity or the man's role."[1] The lack of scholarly studies examining manhood prompted Michael S. Kimmel, author of *Manhood in America*, to pose the question: "How is it that men have no history?" Books about men, Kimmel claimed "are not about men as men . . . American men have no history as gendered selves."[2] This is particularly true of African American men. Scholars of the black experience have produced a considerable body of literature examining African American women, yet they have paid little attention to the gender roles and identities of African American men.[3] Similarly, the increasing number of publications exploring American manhood center almost exclusively on white middle-class men and neglect the gendered experiences of black men.[4]

Historical studies of African Americans have largely sought to explain the black experience in the context of race and class. As a result, scholars have examined African American men either as members of a racial group or as representatives of an economic class, but they have failed to study black men as men. Undoubtedly, race and class analyses are critical

Good Citizens!

Its tried and tested programs—developed out of many years' experience—appeal to boys of every type, under many conditions. Boys like it—enter into it—and grow into sturdy manhood through it.

This program is comparatively inexpensive. Our public schools average over $65 per pupil per year. The Young Men's Christian Association program the country over costs about $12 per boy per year — and the boys put in part of this.

CRIME waves are with us. Our papers are full of murder and gunmen. And who are they? Largely young fellows!

There is much talk about causes and remedies but fundamentally it's lack of character, due to wrong environment, little home training, and scant appreciation of right or wrong.

Start boys right, give them the proper perspective of life, show them their responsibility to society and give them an outlet for excess steam and you stop criminal tendencies at the source.

The Young Men's Christian Association is making heroic efforts to reach many more boys.

Because many boys or their parents are needy—and can not afford to pay all costs—the work requires funds.

Such work needs your support, both moral and financial. It requires men as well as money. It is much less expensive than courts or reformatories.

May we count on you to help to just as great an extent as possible?

With *your* support, we can take our boys off the front page of yellow journals and put them in the blue book of good citizens.

YMCA

Figure 10. African American YMCA leaders hoped to achieve racial advancement through the display of good citizenship, sound character, and true manhood. They accepted segregated YMCAs to provide African American men and boys with the opportunity to build their manhood while shielding them from racial humiliation. Reprinted with permission from the Moorland-Spingarn Research Center, Howard University.

for an understanding of the African American experience, yet for many black men their manhood was equally important in defining their identity. In particular, African American men who led the movement to establish separate black YMCAs at the turn of the century attributed great importance to their masculine identity. For them the attainment and display of proper manhood was more than a search for individual identity or personal fulfillment, it was also a crucial element in their struggle for racial advancement.

Founded in 1852, the American YMCA initially did not even consider association work for African Americans. After all, the YMCA was dedicated to building Christian character in men, and most African Americans were slaves and thus legally property. Only after the Civil War did the YMCA start to encourage freedmen to establish their own associations and to join the Christian brotherhood on separate-but-equal terms. During Reconstruction, African American men established numerous associations. However, limited by lack of financial resources as well as administrative support from the national YMCA, most of these associations had only a brief existence.[5]

It was not until the late nineteenth century that African American association work began to thrive when the national YMCA hired two black men to supervise the creation of separate black branches. In 1891 Canadian-born William A. Hunton joined the YMCA's International Committee and became the highest-ranking black association official in the United States. During the 1890s Hunton organized numerous associations on black college campuses and promoted YMCA work in the black urban communities. Hunton's efforts generated a growing African American interest in association work, and in response the International Committee hired an additional black YMCA secretary. In 1898 Jesse E. Moorland, a black minister from Ohio, joined Hunton and assumed responsibility for the supervision of black association work in cities. Moorland was particularly successful in mobilizing the support of a growing number of African American urban professional and business men who embraced the YMCA's mission to develop "the whole man—body, mind, and spirit."[6]

Members of the black urban middle class and elite welcomed the YMCA as a means to affirm and assert their masculinity, particularly at a time when white society refused to recognize black men fully as men. Although African Americans had gained their freedom, black men continued to face social, political, economic, legal, and physical emasculation in the years following Reconstruction. African Americans were deprived of the ballot, Jim Crow laws established the legal segregation of nearly all aspects of life, sharecropping created a system of economic bondage, and lynchings reached "staggering proportions."[7]

White Southerners further challenged African American masculinity in their public interaction with black men. Drawing on a body of customs that governed relations between the races, white Southerners used the rules of etiquette in an attempt to restore the social order and racial hierarchy of the Old South. White men refused to bestow on black men the public attribute of masculinity and refrained from addressing them as "Mister." Instead they called African American men by their first names or referred to them as either "boy" or "uncle."[8]

Trapped in a system of economic dependency that provided little, if any, legal protection, many African Americans responded to their racial subordination without openly challenging Jim Crowism. Rather than promoting protest and confrontation, they advocated racial solidarity and self-help in an effort to achieve equality. Through self-reliance and cooperation, they hoped to acquire wealth and social status, expecting to gain "the respect of white men and thus be accorded the rights as citizens."[9]

African American men who led the YMCA movement in the cities pursued a similar strategy. Adopting an accommodationist and gradualist approach, they decided not to challenge the YMCA's Jim Crow policy. It was better, they argued, to serve African Americans in separate associations and "hope for a final adjustment . . . that would be fair and Christian than to withhold services from the disadvantaged group until the millennium could come."[10] Although black YMCA leaders embraced the doctrines of self-help and racial solidarity, they questioned economic prosperity as a means of achieving equality. African American men, they insisted, could not earn the respect and esteem of whites through the acquisition of wealth but rather through the manifestation of their manhood. Unlike Booker T. Washington, who advocated economic advancement through industrial education, and W. E. B. Du Bois, who stressed the leadership role of the "talented tenth" as a means of racial uplift, black YMCA leaders insisted that "true manhood" was the key to racial equality. A black YMCA pamphlet confidently proclaimed: "The test of a race's greatness is the kind of men it brings forth."[11]

The kind of men black YMCA leaders tried to marshall under the association banner were those who embraced an ideal of manhood that combined the virtues of traditional Victorian gentility with the manly display of muscular prowess: men who were industrious, thrifty, self-reliant, honest, pious, and culturally refined Christian gentlemen, as well as physically fit and healthy individuals ready to face the demands of a rapidly industrializing society. Placing their faith in a concept of manhood that was universal rather than race specific, black YMCA advocates believed that gentlemen of all races shared a set of values and observed a code of conduct that transcended racial lines. Like other members of the educated and professional black elite, they assumed that African Americans "would be accepted or assimilated into American society on a purely individual basis as each demonstrated merit and worthiness."[12] Racism, discrimination, and segregation, while regrettable, were not overwhelming obstacles to success, they insisted, but merely challenges African American men had to face like real men. Once black men displayed all the characteristics of true manhood, YMCA leaders reasoned, they could command the respect of any man and no white gentleman would withhold justice from them.

In their quest for true manhood and equality, black urban professional and business men launched a nationwide movement to establish YMCAs. Separate associations, they believed, would provide African American men with the opportunity to develop their manhood, which would disprove white claims of black inferiority and earn black men the respect and esteem of whites. By 1930 African American men had created a network of sixty black-controlled YMCAs in cities across the nation, boasting a membership of nearly 34,000 men and boys.[13]

The tremendous growth of black YMCA work at the turn of the century was largely the product of the increasing migration of African Americans from the countryside to the cities. A growing number of African Americans left the plantations and moved to the cities of the North and the South, searching for employment and educational opportunities as well as a less racially oppressive environment. Largely due to this population shift, the percentage of African Americans living in cities rose from 13 percent in 1870 to nearly 44 percent in 1930.[14]

In the urban communities, rural black migrants encountered the members of a fledgling group of African Americans who "were better fed and housed, had more money, entertained themselves differently, and belonged to different organizations and churches."[15] Many African Americans who considered themselves to be part of this upwardly mobile, cultured, and educated urban elite were alarmed by the influx of large numbers of rural blacks into their communities. They perceived the lower-class migrants as a destabilizing force contributing to the physical decay of black neighborhoods and exacerbating crime rates. Newcomers to the cities, they predicted, would be forced to "live like animals huddled together, without any regard for decency, morality, or health."[16] Overcrowding and lack of recreational facilities and economic opportunities, as well as the migrants' "lax moral habits," Du Bois observed in *The Philadelphia Negro*, created "a pressing series of social problems" destined to "rear young criminals for our jails."[17]

The "better class" of African Americans were also troubled by what they considered to be the disreputable public behavior and the "careless appearance" of many migrants. The display of improper manners by any member of the race, many black elites feared, would not only result in the decline of their own social standing but was also "responsible for much of the legal and extralegal discrimination against the whole race."[18] As Du Bois noted: "the great number of raw recruits who have from time to time precipitated themselves upon the Negroes of the city . . . have made reputations which, whether good or bad, all their race must share."[19] Afraid that white society would make "little allowance for their culture or means," black elites tried to avoid affiliation with the "lower masses of their people" in an attempt to preserve their own social status.[20] Aspiring to achieve respectability, the better class of African Americans stressed the importance of "proper conduct and refined behavior in public." Etiquette books circulating among African Americans, such as *On Habits and Manners* and *The Negro in Etiquette*, defined correct deportment and propagated "genteel performance" as a means of overcoming racism.[21]

Members of the African American elite, however, not only distanced themselves from the black urban masses but also tried to discipline and regulate their behavior. African American professional and business men who spearheaded the YMCA movement were particularly concerned about the plight of single young men who migrated to the cities. These "unknown *strangers, poor,* and *green*," they claimed, were at risk of being destroyed by the temptations of the "wicked city." Impressionable young men were "an easy prey to the vicious and deadly influences" surrounding them: "the gambling den—that false promiser of an easy road to wealth—the saloon, the house of vice, and a thousand less flagrant evils." These "death traps," they warned, lured "young men into the way that leads to certain moral and spiritual ruin."[22]

The young men's descent into the "wilderness of sin and shame," black YMCA advocates feared, was inevitable because most schools, homes, and churches failed to provide proper guidance and support. The schools, they lamented, "stop at a point with most of our youth where the danger is greatest," and the majority of black homes were unable to provide a stimulating environment. "What ought to be homes among us," one black YMCA leader complained, "are largely only places in which to eat and sleep. . . . Many of our so-called homes positively drive the boys out and send them a-drifting."[23] Du Bois, in his study of the black communities in Philadelphia and New York, expressed similar concerns. The low wages of African American men, he found, forced many black women to seek employment outside the homes, leaving "children without guidance or restraint for the better part of the day," while high rents compelled many black families to take in lodgers, destroying "the privacy and intimacy of home life."[24]

The churches, African American YMCA supporters bemoaned, also failed to address the needs of most young black men in the cities. Many black ministers responded to the influx of migrants into their communities by constructing larger churches; however, few established any social services for the newcomers.[25] The ministers' failure to provide adequate and attractive social programs for the migrants, black YMCA advocates insisted, alienated many young men and drove them out of the churches. A 1905 YMCA study of Chicago's African American population claimed that only 26 percent of the city's black men regularly attended church, and of those, only 13 percent were church members. The author of the study concluded that this was largely due to the churches' inability to "compete in attractiveness with the dance halls, [and] wine and gambling resorts of the city."[26] Jesse E. Moorland, a black YMCA official and former minister, agreed, admitting that the churches "are regarded by the young as a dreary place."[27] While some black migrants may have found more appealing places to socialize, others made a conscious decision to take "advantage of the move to the city to break free of confining church traditions in rural areas."[28] These single young black men without church or family ties, many members of the black urban elite feared, would succumb to the sinful temptations of the cities, bringing shame to their families as well as to their race.[29]

In an effort to protect the rural migrants from moral turpitude and to thwart the disruptive impact of their influx on the urban communities, African American men established an ever-growing number of YMCAs. Through the associations they hoped to supply the newcomers with a homelike environment, proper companionship, and role models, as well as moral guidance, in order to draw them away from the unwholesome attractions of the cities. More important, though, they insisted that the YMCA's programs could provide the young men with the means for per-sonal and racial advancement by allowing them to build true manhood.[30]

Although black YMCA advocates claimed to work on behalf of the rural migrants, they made no special efforts to recruit them. Instead of going to the taverns, pool halls, and gambling dens, where they suspected the newcomers gathered, they waited for men who took the initiative and sought out the YMCA's services. The absence of membership drives specifically designed to attract the migrants suggests that black YMCA supporters were less interested in building manhood among the lower classes than they were in preserving the manhood of members of their own rank. Existing records do not indicate the socioeconomic back-ground of black YMCA members; however, membership requirements illustrate that the association was not concerned about rescuing those who had already fallen from grace. Only men who were active members of a Protestant church, subscribed to the ideals promulgated by the YMCA, and were able to pay a small membership fee were eligible to join. Despite their rhetoric, champions of black YMCA work largely tried "to save and keep saved the flower of the race," and associations

A CALL TO MEN OF BROOKLYN
AT THE
Carlton Ave. Branch Y. M. C. A.
405 Carlton Avenue   Brooklyn, N. Y.

Sunday afternoon, February 18, 1923
AT 4 O'CLOCK SHARP

A Men's Meeting you cannot afford to miss; address: "A Call to Men of Brooklyn" by Dr. J. E. MOORLAND, Senior Secretary, International Committee Y. M. C. A. Good fellowship. Bring another man.   Be on time.   We begin on the dot. All men welcome.

DR. J. E. MOORLAND

SPECIAL:- MR. CHARLES WATERS, TENOR, WILL SING

Figure 11. Black YMCAs tried to appeal to all African American men, regardless of social or economic status. The YMCA's leadership, however, was recruited exclusively from the ranks of the college-educated black elite. Reprinted with permission from the Moorland-Spingarn Research Center, Howard University.

tended to serve predominantly middle-class and elite men, who tried to safeguard their manhood against the encroachment of what Du Bois called the "dangerous class" of "criminals, gamblers, and loafers."[31] For those African American men who were struggling to build or preserve their manhood, the YMCA provided a fourfold program that catered to their physical, educational, spiritual, and social needs.

Physical exercise programs became a standard feature of association work in the 1890s when the YMCA officially recognized fitness as a crucial factor in the development of manhood.[32] The YMCA's endorsement of athletics was in part a response to a contemporary debate about the virtues of exercise, which was sparked by the discovery of a new disease. Neurasthenia, or nervous exhaustion, some members of the medical profession claimed, afflicted mostly middle-class men who engaged in sedentary occupations. Too much "brain work" and too little exercise, they reasoned, was bound to lead to the mental and physical breakdown of white-collar workers.[33] While some physicians prescribed relaxation therapy to restore their patients' emotional stability and physical strength, others tried to revitalize masculine prowess and prevent its further erosion through vigorous exercise.

The YMCA became one of the leading champions of Muscular Christianity, a religiously inspired exercise philosophy that maintained that the body represented "a fundamental and intrinsic part in the salvation of man."[34] Muscular Christianity, however, was not only the product of concerns over nervous exhaustion or religious salvation; it was also fueled by nativist fears and infused with the rhetoric of Social Darwinism. As a growing number of immigrants from southern and eastern Europe flocked to the United States in the late nineteenth century, members of the white Protestant middle class "foresaw a debilitated, native-born workforce yielding to muscular immigrant 'hordes'."[35] Similar to many whites in the YMCA who embraced athletics as an antidote to race suicide, black association leaders advocated exercise as a means to prevent the decline of physical male prowess in the members of their own race. Living and working conditions in the expanding cities, they claimed, deprived men of the benefits of vigorous outdoor labor. Black men, they predicted, were in danger of losing their physical power because city life denied them the opportunity of "homely exercise" such as "sawing wood, tilling the small garden to the rear of the house and other out-door work."[36]

Yet, black association leaders launched athletics not only to strengthen the male physique but also to instruct African American men in the ethics of proper manhood. The associations' physical exercise programs were broadly designed to provide men with strong, healthy bodies, as well as the moral and spiritual fortitude to resist unsavory habits, carnal desires, and urban temptations. Basketball games instilled team spirit and cooperation and fostered a sense of racial solidarity, while drill exercises stressed the importance of proper masculine deportment and trained men "to stand erect and to look a man in the eye when they are addressed." Moreover, physical exercise programs were often accompanied by personal hygiene and health lectures that emphasized bodily cleanliness as an essential component of masculine fitness, vigor, and virility. Maintaining a clean, healthy body, YMCA leaders proclaimed, was the mark of a true Christian gentleman who valued his body because it was "the temple of the Holy Ghost." To keep "His temple . . . clean and blemishless" required not only soap and water but moral integrity and a wholesome lifestyle. Through lectures and pamphlets, black association leaders advocated sexual purity for single men and in "heart to heart talks" urged those who were married to remain monogamous. By shunning promiscuous behavior and assuming their responsibilities as husbands and fathers, African American men would not only gain the respect of their wives, children, and the black community but also forestall white claims of black men's insatiable sex drive, which frequently served as a rationale for lynchings.[37]

In addition to a muscular masculine appearance, proper public

Figure 12. This 1920 gathering of the Atlanta Business Men's Club at the city's Butler Street YMCA provided not only an opportunity for physical exercise but also an occasion for male bonding and professional networking. Reprinted with permission from the Moorland-Spingarn Research Center, Howard University.

deportment, and an exemplary lifestyle, black association leaders emphasized education as a crucial factor in the making of true manhood. Education, they argued, not only fostered self-respect and thus liberated African American men from the shackles of mental slavery but also helped them cope with racism.[38] As Jesse E. Moorland pointed out: "No man is a slave whose brain is free. You may be inconvenienced by this or that, but if you have a trained brain, you simply build a bridge with your thoughts over the difficulties and go on the other side."[39] Thus, YMCAs launched a variety of educational ventures, including reading rooms, lecture series, debating clubs, and literary societies, to provide black men with intellectual stimulation.[40]

Most of the educational programs of African American YMCAs, however, were more pragmatic, and aimed at enhancing black men's vocational and professional training in order to increase their "commercial value." For this purpose, associations established night schools that offered a variety of classes, including English, typewriting, architectural and mechanical drawing, stenography, barbering, accounting, painting, printing, auto mechanics, and driving lessons, as well as study courses for college entrance and civil service exams. Black association leaders acknowledged that necessity often forced African American men "to remain in poorly paid employment because they have no means for training and education." But they insisted that these obstacles could be overcome through personal initiative. Embracing the doctrine of rugged individualism, they encouraged men to use their spare time to pursue the American Dream and improve themselves, assuring them that "There is room on top. Developed minds and skilled hands are constantly in demand."[41]

Although the YMCA's educational programs were primarily designed to cultivate marketable skills and increase black men's chances of employment as well as their earning power, they also served as a tool in the struggle for racial advancement. Better-paying jobs, association leaders argued, would enable black men "to become more self-sustaining" and "to care for those who depend upon them," allowing their wives to remain at home and raise the children without having to contend with the disruptive influence of boarders. Striving for the middle-class ideal of the single-income household, black YMCA advocates hoped to enhance black men's marital and parental authority, ensure family stability, and disprove white stereotypes that cast African American men as lazy, shiftless, indolent, and irresponsible.[42]

In addition to providing physical and educational programs, black YMCA leaders stressed the importance of social environment, proper male companionship, and role models in the development of manhood. "The social element is one of the potent factors in destroying men," Moorland warned, because a "man becomes like his companions and his state falls to the level of his surroundings." With the creation of YMCA lounges, reading rooms, and dormitories, association men hoped to provide physical spaces allowing for appropriate social interaction, male bonding, and professional networking.[43]

Although the YMCA primarily served men in their struggle to attain true manhood, the association also tried to reach black boys. Many YMCAs, for example, hosted father-son banquets to provide boys with proper role models and to foster "close companionship between fathers and boys, better environments in the home, higher education and a Christian life." Concerned parents could rest assured that a son who spent his afternoon or evening at the YMCA was using his leisure time constructively. As one mother, expressing her gratitude to the YMCA in Washington, D.C., noted: "Before this building was opened I did not know where my boy was. Now I rest content, knowing that his leisure is being properly directed."[44]

Creating a positive social environment, building strong bodies, and developing sound minds were important aspects of black YMCA leaders' efforts to foster true manhood, yet the "capstone to all" was Christian character. Only a man whose life was inspired by Christian principles, black YMCA advocates believed, was truly a gentleman, a man who implicitly knew right from wrong and whose decisions were guided not by personal gains but by service to his family, community, and race. In its attempt to build Christian character the YMCA promoted a nondenominational Christianity, hoping to attract as many men as possible without alienating the Protestant clergy. Hence, black association leaders assured African American ministers that they did not compete with the work of the churches but complemented it. The YMCA, they proclaimed, was the "Right Arm of the Christian Church," and they promised that the association's religious programs would neither coincide with those provided by local churches nor discuss denominational differences. Instead the YMCA's gospel meetings and Bible study classes tried to instill a sense of civic stewardship, and the Christianity black association leaders envisioned was "a form of social consciousness" rather than endorsement of a particular church.[45]

The strategy for racial advancement that African American YMCA leaders advocated was unique. Instead of promoting industrial training or academic education, YMCA leaders insisted that the key to racial advancement was the physical, moral, religious, and intellectual strength of the race's manhood. African American men, they hoped, would become prime examples of the type of men whites aspired to be and thus prove to white men that indeed they were gentlemen who deserved to be treated as such. While the YMCA's call for true manhood represented an alternative to the racial advancement strategies advocated by Booker T. Washington and W. E. B. Du Bois, it also combined elements of both. Not surprisingly, Washington and Du Bois praised those aspects of YMCA work that best reflected their own doctrine of racial progress.

Washington shared with black YMCA leaders an abiding faith in rugged individualism. Advocating personal initiative and hard work as essential tools for racial advancement, he applauded the "strong, constructive and stimulating influences" of the association on those men who "are leaving the simple and comparatively healthy life of the plantation and are joining the already overcrowded throngs in the cities."[46] Washington also praised the YMCA's work because the accommodationist and gradualist approach of black association leaders resembled his own strategy. Both he and the black YMCA leaders placed the burden of racial progress on the shoulders of African Americans—they had to improve in order to advance. Washington urged African Americans to acquire the necessary skills and trades to become successful businessmen and property owners, insisting that "No one will very long object to a man's voting who owns the largest business establishment and is the largest tax-payer in his community."[47] Association leaders likewise believed in the power of individual achievement. Working within the confines of Jim Crowism, they tried to provide black men with the opportunity to improve body, mind, and spirit and thus demonstrate their manhood to whites.[48]

Although Washington praised the YMCA for preserving "the young manhoood of my race," he insisted that industrial training was, at least for the time being, more important for the advancement of African Americans than the association's programs.[49] "A race," Washington argued "improves in its morals and Christian education, as a rule, after it gets an industrial foundation. It is a hard thing to make a good Christian of a man who is hungry and lives in a rented one-room cabin."[50] Washington's reservations about the value of YMCA work reflected his concern for the plight of the masses of black sharecroppers in the South rather than criticism of the association.

Du Bois also paid tribute to the YMCA, recalling his involvement as a boy in a New England association as "a source of pleasure—an inspiration." Du Bois, who linked the advancement of the race to the ability of a leadership group, particularly praised the association's efforts to build black manhood among the urban elite. The "Negro race, like all other races, is going to be saved by its exceptional men," Du Bois predicted, and he demanded that schools also "make manhood the object" of their work.[51]

Although Du Bois conceded that the YMCA provided black urban youths with the opportunity to build their manhood, he remained critical of the association's Jim Crow policy. Addressing a group of white YMCA members in New York City, Du Bois professed a "distinct feeling of distaste and antagonism" and attacked his audience, charging that the existence of segregated YMCAs "*is neither an exhibition of manhood nor in accordance with the right ideals of youth nor in accordance with the ethics of Jesus Christ.*" Despite his condemnation of the YMCA's Jim Crow policy, however, Du Bois did not assail black association leaders. Perhaps Du Bois realized that while he merely called on the talented tenth to lead the masses in the struggle for equality, YMCA leaders labored to provide black men with the opportunity to test, exercise, and improve their leadership skills.[52]

When members of the black urban professional and business elite created a network of YMCAs in cities across the nation, they also created safe havens for large numbers of African American men and boys. Black-controlled YMCAs shielded African American men and boys from racial humiliations and allowed them to build true manhood without losing their dignity and self-esteem. Indeed, associations served as sanctuaries which preserved African American masculinity and prepared men and boys for their leadership in the struggle for equality that lay ahead.[53] At a time when black men faced emasculation through lynchings, race riots, disfranchisement, and Jim Crow laws, YMCAs provided them with a place where African American men could be men and African American boys could become men. Aside from churches, YMCAs were frequently the only places where large numbers of African Americans could gather comfortably and without white interference. Businessmen's clubs, merchant associations, ministers, choirs, mutual aid societies, and professional, fraternal, and civic groups, as well as NAACP and Urban League chapters, often convened for their weekly meetings at the YMCAs. In 1915, for example, when Carter G. Woodson organized the Association for the Study of Negro Life and History, he assembled the charter group at the Wabash Avenue YMCA in Chicago.[54]

Black association men, like their white urban middle-class counterparts, embraced a conservative model of manhood that was grounded in the promise of the American Dream. African American YMCA members were convinced that professional success, financial prosperity, and personal recognition could be achieved through the attainment and display of true manhood. In the past, they believed, black men had failed to internalize and exhibit the traits of proper manliness, not due to inability but because they had lacked the opportunity to develop their manhood. However, this situation changed when YMCAs started to cater to black men, providing them with programs and spaces designed to cultivate and nurture their masculine identity. Henceforth, black association leaders argued, African American men had an obligation to attain true manhood not only in the interest of personal advancement but, more important, to serve their race. True manhood, they believed, was rooted in middle-class values but cut across color lines. It provided a crucial bond between black and white men that would prove to be stronger than racism. Through the display of their manhood, black YMCA leaders claimed, African American men could earn the esteem and respect of whites and ultimately secure civil rights and racial equality.

While black association leaders advocated racial advancement, they did not challenge traditional Victorian gender ideals. Instead YMCA programs were designed to strengthen the role of the husband and father by promoting single-income households that preserved a patriarchal family structure and maintained separate gender spheres. A woman's place was in the home, where she could best assist her husband and son by providing a caring and supportive domestic environment conducive to the development of manhood.

The manhood ideal black YMCA members aspired to did not differ from that of white association men. Yet, African Americans pursued this ideal for entirely different reasons than their white counterparts. For turn-of-the-century white middle-class men, industrialization, immigration, urbanization, and "the expanding demands of women created a confusing 'crisis of masculinity.'"[55] Afraid of losing their status in society, white middle-class men responded to their anxieties by celebrating their manhood. To reassure themselves of their virility and manliness, they invented the cult of masculinity.

Black middle-class men did not share the insecurities of white men, who were clinging to the past in an effort to maintain their masculinity. For black men the pursuit of true manhood did not represent a reaction to the forces of modernization but a rehearsal for the future. While white men sought comfort in traditional gender roles in the hope of resisting change, African Americans were determined to use them to propel change in the interest of racial progress. By demonstrating their manhood, black association men hoped to dispel stereotypical white images of African American men and shame whites into ending Jim Crowism.

Although black YMCA leaders pursued an accommodationist and gradualist approach, relying on persuasion rather than protest, their strategy enjoyed some success. Working within a Jim Crow institution that was based on Christian brotherhood, African Americans did arouse the conscience of some white association leaders. After World War I, whites in the YMCA responded to the discrepancy between what the association was preaching and how it was acting. During the 1920s white association leaders launched the interracial movement, which, while not devoted to ending segregation, was at least interested in improving segregation. Subsequent years of interracial dialogue paved the way for the YMCA's decision to adopt a desegregation policy in 1946, two years before the United States Army initiated desegregation and eight years before the *Brown* decision reversed the separate-but-equal ruling.

NOTES

1. E. Anthony Rotundo, "Learning about Manhood: Gender Ideals and the Middle-Class Family in Nineteenth-Century America," in J. A. Mangan and James Walvin (eds.), *Manliness and Morality: Middle-Class Masculinity in Britain and America, 1800–1940* (New York: St. Martin's Press, 1987), 35.

2. Michael S. Kimmel, "How Is It That Men Have No History?" *The Chronicle of Higher Education* (December 8, 1993), B5, and *Manhood in America: A Cultural History* (New York: Free Press, 1996).

3. Notable exceptions are Eugene D. Genovese, "Husbands and Fathers," in Elizabeth and Joseph Pleck (eds.), *The American Man* (Englewood Cliffs, NJ: Spectrum Books, 1980), 173–183; Gwendolyn Captain, "Enter Ladies and Gentlemen of Color: Gender, Sport, and the Ideal of African American Manhood and Womanhood During the Late 19th and Early 20th Centuries," *Journal of Sport History* 18, 1 (Spring 1991): 81–102; Jim Cullen, "'I's a Man Now': Gender and African American Men," in Catherine Clinton and Nina Silber (eds.), *Divided Houses: Gender and the Civil War* (New York: Oxford University Press, 1992), 76–91; Wilson J. Moses, "Where Honor Is Due: Frederick Douglass as Representative Black Man," *Prospects* 17 (1992): 177–189; James Oliver Horton and Lois E. Horton, "Violence, Protest, and Identity: Black Manhood in Antebellum America," in James Oliver Horton (ed.), *Free People of Color: Inside the African American Community* (Washington, DC: Smithsonian Institution Press, 1993), 80–96; and Martha Hodes, "The Sexualization of Reconstruction Politics: White Women and Black Men in the South after the Civil War," in John C. Fout and Maura Shaw Tantillo (eds.), *American Sexual Politics: Sex, Gender, and Race since the Civil War* (Chicago: University of Chicago Press 1993): 59–74. For a discussion of the historical literature on African American women see Darlene Clark Hine, "Lifting the Veil, Shattering the Silence: Black Women's History in Slavery and Freedom," in Darlene Clark Hine (ed.), *The State of Afro-American History: Past, Present, and Future* (Baton Rouge: Louisiana State University Press, 1986), 223–249; John H. Bracey, Jr., "Afro-American Women: A Guide to Writings from Historical and Feminist Perspectives," *Contributions in Black Studies* 8 (1986–1987): 106–110; and Elizabeth Higginbotham and Sarah Watts, "The New Scholarship on Afro-American Women," *Women's Studies Quarterly* 1 and 2 (1988): 12–21. See also the special edition of *The Journal of Men's Studies* 1, 3 (February 1993).

4. Recent studies reflecting the growing interest in the history of masculinity include Kimmel, *Manhood in America*; Gail Bederman, *Manliness and Civilization: A Cultural History of Gender and Race in the United States, 1880–1917* (Chicago: University of Chicago Press, 1995); George Chauncey, *Gay New York: Gender, Urban Culture, and the Making of the Gay Male World, 1890–1940* (New York: Basic Books, 1994); E. Anthony Rotundo, *American Manhood: Transformations in Masculinity from the Revolution to the Modern Era* (New York: Basic Books, 1993); Kevin White, *The First Sexual Revolution:*

The Emergence of Male Heterosexuality in Modern America (New York: New York University Press, 1993); Robert L. Griswold, *Fatherhood in America: A History* (New York: Basic Books, 1993); Peter Stearns, *Be a Man!: Males in Modern Society,* 2nd ed. (New York: Holmes & Meier, 1990); David D. Gilmore, *Manhood in the Making: Cultural Concepts of Masculinity* (New Haven, CT: Yale University Press, 1990); Mark C. Carnes and Clyde Griffen (eds.), *Meanings for Manhood: Constructions of Masculinity in Victorian America* (Chicago: University of Chicago Press, 1990); Ted Ownby, *Subduing Satan: Religion, Recreation, and Manhood in the Rural South, 1865–1920* (Chapel Hill: University of North Carolina Press, 1990); Mark C. Carnes, *Secret Ritual and Manhood in Victorian America* (New Haven, CT: Yale University Press, 1989); Mary Ann Clawson, *Constructing Brotherhood: Class, Gender, Fraternalism* (Princeton, NJ: Princeton University Press, 1989); Harry Brod (ed.), *The Making of Masculinities: The New Men's Studies* (Boston: Allen & Unwin, 1987); Michael S. Kimmel (ed.), *Changing Men: New Directions in Research on Men and Masculinity* (Newbury Park, CA: Sage Publications 1987); Peter G. Filene, *Him/Her/Self: Sex Roles in Modern America* (Baltimore: Johns Hopkins University Press, 1986); Norman Vance, *The Sinews of the Spirit: The Ideal of Christian Manliness in Victorian Culture and Religious Thought* (Cambridge, MA: Cambridge University Press, 1985); Barbara Ehrenreich, *The Hearts of Men: American Dreams and the Flight from Commitment* (New York: Anchor Press/Doubleday, 1983); David G. Pugh, *Sons of Liberty: The Masculine Mind in Nineteenth-Century America* (Westport, CT: Greenwood Press, 1983); Elizabeth H. Pleck and Joseph H. Pleck (eds.), *The American Man* (Englewood Cliffs, NJ: Prentice-Hall, 1980); and Joe L. Dubbert, *A Man's Place: Masculinity in Transition* (Englewood Cliffs, NJ: Prentice-Hall, 1979).

5. For histories of the YMCA see C. Howard Hopkins, *History of the YMCA in North America* (New York: Association Press, 1951), and Nina Mjagkij, *Light in the Darkness: African Americans and the YMCA, 1852–1946* (Lexington: The University Press of Kentucky, 1994).

6. Mjagkij, *Light in the Darkness,* 35–52.

7. C. Vann Woodward, *The Strange Career of Jim Crow* (Oxford: Oxford University Press, 1955), 43. For detailed discussions of race relations in the late nineteenth century see also Rayford W. Logan, *The Negro in American Life and Thought: The Nadir, 1877–1901* (New York: Dial Press, 1954); C. Vann Woodward, *Origins of the New South, 1877–1913* (Baton Rouge: Louisiana State University Press, 1951); Thomas F. Gossett, *Race: The History of an Idea in America* (New York: Schocken Books, 1965); and Joel Williamson, *The Crucible of Race: Black-White Relations in the American South Since Emancipation* (Oxford: Oxford University Press, 1984).

8. See Horton, "Violence, Protest, and Identity"; William J. Harris, "Etiquette, Lynching, and Racial Boundaries in Southern History: A Mississippi Example," *American Historical Review* 100, 2 (April 1995): 387–410; Bertram W. Doyle, *The Etiquette of Race Relations in the South: A Study in Social*

Control (Port Washington, NY: Kennikat Press, 1937), 142–143; and Bertram Wyatt-Brown, *Southern Honor: Ethics and Behavior in the Old South* (New York: Oxford University Press, 1982).

9. August Meier, *Negro Thought in America, 1880–1915: Racial Ideologies in the Age of Booker T. Washington* (Ann Arbor: University of Michigan Press, 1963), 42.

10. Jesse E. Moorland, "The YMCA: A Potent Agency in the Salvation of Young Men," ca. 1902, 2, Jesse E. Moorland Papers, Moorland-Spingarn Research Center, Howard University, Washington, DC, box 126-27, folder 563, hereinafter cited as JEM Papers; Channing H. Tobias to Carl Murphy, April 23, 1936, Records Relating to YMCA Work With Blacks, 1891–1979, YMCA of the USA Archives, St. Paul, Minnesota, box 6, folder Colored Work Department— Local, State and Area Associations—L-R, 1916–42, hereinafter cited as Black YMCA Records; and Channing H. Tobias, "Visits in the Central, Western and Southern Region," October 17, 1930, JEM Papers, box 126-67, folder 1294.

11. "Conference of Christian Workers," Asheville, North Carolina, July 14–18, 1898, 13–14, JEM Papers, box 126-38, folder 802; YMCA, International Committee, *The Colored Men's Department of the YMCA* (New York, 1894), Black YMCA Records, box 3, folder Colored Work Department— Pamphlets—1894–1904; and Druid Hill Avenue YMCA, "Fundraising Program," ca. 1918, JEM Papers, box 126-23, folder 349.

12. Willard B. Gatewood, *Aristocrats of Color: The Black Elite, 1880–1920* (Bloomington, IN: Indiana University Press, 1990), 209.

13. Mjagkij, *Light in the Darkness*, 134, 138.

14. Daniel O. Price, *Changing Characteristics of the Negro Population* (Washington, DC: Government Printing Office, 1960), 11. Recent studies that examine the causes, processes, and impacts of the black urban migration include Alferdteen Harrison (ed.), *Black Exodus: The Great Migration from the American South* (Jackson: University Press of Mississippi, 1991); Joe William Trotter, Jr. (ed.), *The Great Migration in Historical Perspective: New Dimensions of Race, Class, and Gender* (Bloomington: Indiana University Press, 1991); Nicholas Lemann, *The Promised Land: The Great Black Migration and How It Changed America* (New York: Alfred A. Knopf, 1991); Earl Lewis, *In Their Own Interest: Race, Class, and Power in Twentieth Century Norfolk* (Berkeley: University of California Press, 1991); James R. Grossman, *Land of Hope: Chicago, Black Southerners, and the Great Migration* (Chicago: University of Chicago Press, 1989); Carole Marks, *Farewell—We're Good and Gone: The Great Black Migration* (Bloomington: Indiana University Press, 1989); and Peter Gottlieb, *Making Their Own Way: Southern Blacks' Migration to Pittsburgh, 1916–30* (Urbana: University of Illinois Press, 1987).

15. Howard N. Rabinowitz, *Race Relations in the Urban South, 1865–1890* (Urbana: University of Illinois Press, 1980), 238.

16. "Conference of Christian Workers," Asheville, North Carolina, July 14–18, 1898, 7–8, JEM Papers, box 126-38, folder 802.

17. W. E. B. Du Bois, *The Philadelphia Negro: A Social Study* (1899; reprint, New York: Benjamin Blom, 1967), 67, 80–82.

18. W. E. B. Du Bois, *The Black North in 1901: A Social Study* (New York: Arno Press, 1969), 26; Du Bois, *Philadelphia*, 81; and Gatewood, *Aristocrats of Color*, 208.

19. Du Bois, *Philadelphia*, 283.

20. Du Bois, *Black North*, 29.

21. Mary Frances Armstrong, *On Habits and Manners* (Hampton, VA: Normal School Press, 1888); Elias McSails Woods, *The Negro in Etiquette: A Novelty* (Saint Louis: Buxton and Skinner, 1899); Edward S. Green, *National Capital Code of Etiquette* (Washington, DC: Austin Jenkins Co., 1920); Gatewood, *Aristocrats of Color*, 187; and John F. Kasson, *Rudeness and Civility: Manners in Nineteenth-Century Urban America* (New York: Hill and Wang, 1990), 54. See also W. E. B. Du Bois, *Morals and Manners among Negro Americans* (Atlanta: Atlanta University Press, 1914); and Guy Szuberla, "Ladies, Gentlemen, Flirts, Mashers, Snoozers, and the Breaking of Etiquette's Code," *Prospects* 15 (1990): 169–196.

22. Carole Marks, in her study of the Great Migration, claims that the typical migrant was "a black male between the ages of twenty-five and thirty-four," Marks, *Farewell*, 35; Jesse E. Moorland, untitled speech, ca. 1893, 2, JEM Papers, box 126-27, folder 569; William A. Hunton, "Colored Men's Department of the YMCA," *Voice of the Negro* 2, 6 (June 1905): 390; and YMCA, International Committee, *The Colored Men's Department of the YMCA* (New York: YMCA, International Committee, 1894), Black YMCA Records, box 3, folder Colored Work Department—Pamphlets—1894–1904.

23. S. G. Atkins, "The Mental Improvement of Colored Men," *Men* (December 18, 1897), 253; and Jesse E. Moorland, "The Work of the Young Men's Christian Association Among Colored Young Men," ca. 1901, 5, JEM Papers, box 126-27, folder 554.

24. Du Bois, *Black North*, 12, and *Philadelphia*, 194.

25. C. Eric Lincoln and Lawrence H. Mamiya, *The Black Church in the African American Experience* (Durham, NC: Duke University Press, 1990), 119–121; and Gunnar Myrdal, *An American Dilemma: The Negro Problem and Modern Democracy* (New York: Harper and Brothers, 1944), 862–863.

26. B. Emanuel Johnson, "The Colored Men of Chicago," graduation thesis, The Institute and Training School of YMCA, May 25, 1905, 7, 11, JEM Papers, box 126-28, folder 593.

27. Moorland, untitled speech, ca. 1893.

28. Lincoln and Mamiya, *The Black Church*, 120.

29. Jesse E. Moorland, "The Association Today," n.d., JEM Papers, box, 126-23, folder 334.

30. Moorland, untitled speech, ca. 1893, 8; Moorland, "The Association Today"; Moorland, "Y.M.C.A. Work Among Colored Young Men," *Home Mission Monthly* 16 (April 1902): 131; Sumner A. Furniss to Moorland, July

10, 1902, JEM Papers, box 126-18, folder 229; Moorland, "The Association's Part in the Making of a Race," n.d., JEM Papers, box 126-23, folder 335; and YMCA International Committee, "Helping to Supply the Nation's Need," ca. 1910, Black YMCA Records, box 1, folder Fundraising Pamphlets, 1920s.

31. Jesse E. Moorland, "The YMCA: A Potent Agency in the Salvation of Young Men," n.d., JEM Papers, box 126-27, folder 563; and Du Bois, *Black North*, 28.

32. For a discussion of the role of physical exercise in the YMCA see Clifford Putney, "Character Building in the YMCA, 1880–1930," *Mid-America* 73, 1 (January 1991): 49–70; and William J. Baker, "To Pray or to Play? The YMCA Question in the United Kingdom and the United States, 1850–1900," *The International Journal of the History of Sport* 11, 1 (April 1994): 42–62.

33. See Bederman, *Manliness and Civilization*, 14.

34. Quoted in Putney, "Character Building," 54; see also his forthcoming *Muscular Christianity: A Protestant Celebration of American Manhood, 1880–1920* (Chicago: University of Chicago Press, 1998).

35. Putney, "Character Building," 55.

36. A. G. Clyde Randall, "Settled Principles of Association Work," Louisville Colored Conference 1909, 9, JEM Papers, box 126-47, folder 950; YMCA International Committee, "Helping to Supply the Nation's Need"; and Hunton, "Colored Men's Department," 388.

37. Moorland, "Practical Plans for Physical Department," ca. 1898, JEM Papers, box 126-25, folder 472; John Glover to Moorland, April 5, 1899, JEM Papers, box 126-18, folder 232; and Moorland, "The YMCA: A Potent Agency in the Salvation of Young Men." See also Gail Bederman, "'Civilization,' the Decline of Middle-Class Manliness, and Ida B. Wells' Antilynching Campaign (1892–94)," *Radical History Review* 52 (Winter 1992): 5–30.

38. Atkins, "Mental Improvement," 252; and Jesse E. Moorland, untitled speech, n.d., JEM Papers, box 126-27, folder 561.

39. Jesse E. Moorland, "End of Education," April 2–6, 1908, New Orleans, JEM Papers, box 126-24, folder 386; and Moorland, untitled speech, n.d., JEM Papers, box 126-27, folder 561.

40. YMCA, *The Colored Men's Department*, 23; Moorland, "The YMCA: A Potent Agency in the Salvation of Men," 3; and Mjagkij, *Light in the Darkness*, 154–201.

41. *A Great Opportunity* (New York: Carlton Avenue Branch YMCA, ca. 1923), JEM Papers, box 126-51, folder 1026; Moorland, untitled speech, n.d., JEM Papers, box 126-27, folder 561; Moorland, "The Opportunity and Responsibility of the International Secretaries in the Progress of the Department," January 1, 1913, JEM Papers, box 126-60, folder 1149; William A. Hunton, "Colored Men's Department," 389; YMCA International Committee, "Helping to Supply the Nation's Need"; "YMCA Broadside 1901," JEM Papers, box 126-38, folder 790; and Mjagkij, *Light in the Darkness*, 154–201.

42. Moorland, "The Opportunity and Responsibility of the International Secretary in the Progress of the Department," 9.

43. "Colored Men's Department," 1904, Black YMCA Records, box 3, folder Colored Work Department—Pamphlets—1894–1904; and Moorland, "The YMCA: A Potent Agency in the Salvation of Men," 3.

44. Dayton Forum, 2-18-1921, JEM Papers, box 126-7, folder 127; and "Washington's Modern Building for Colored Men," *Association Men* (January 1913): 203.

45. Moorland, "The YMCA: A Potent Agency in the Salvation of Men," 4, 6; John B. Watson, "Report of Service at Conference of Secretaries, Colored Men's Department," January 1, 1913, 2–3, Black YMCA Records, box 3, folder Colored Work Department—Secretaries Reports—1910–1924; Moorland, "Religion; the Hope of Human Unity," 11-23-24, JEM Papers, box 126-25, folder 485; Moorland "The Relation of the YMCA to the Church and the Relation of the Church to the YMCA," n.d., JEM Papers, box 126-25, folder 483; Hunton, "Colored Men's Department of the Young Men's Christian Association," 389; YMCA, *Colored Men's Department*, 15, 23; Randall, "Settled Principles of Association Work," JEM Papers, box 126-47, folder 950; "YMCA Work Among Colored Young Men," n.d., JEM Papers, box 126-27, folder 559; and Robert J. Macbeth to Moorland, September 17, 1902, JEM Papers, box 126-20, folder 264.

46. "Booker T. Washington on the Negro in the American City and his Needs," *Association Men* (January 1911): 149.

47. Ibid.

48. Jesse E. Moorland, "End of Education," April 2–6, 1908, JEM Papers, box 126-24, folder 386; and YMCA International Committee, "Leadership, Environment, Fellowship: For the Colored Men and Boys of North America," 3, Black YMCA Records, box 1, folder Fundraising Pamphlets, 1920s.

49. William A. Hunton, *Testimonies and Statistics, 1876–1901*, 12, Black YMCA Records, box 3, folder Colored Work Department—Pamphlets—1894–1904.

50. Booker T. Washington, "The Future of the Negro Race," *Men* (March 27, 1897), 1.

51. *The Horizon* 5 (March 1910): 3; and W. E. B. Du Bois, "The Talented Tenth," in Booker T. Washington et al., *The Negro Problem: A Series of Articles by Representative American Negroes of To-Day* (1913; reprint, Miami: Mnemosyne Publishing, 1969), 33.

52. *The Horizon* 5 (March 1910): 3.

53. Moorland, "The Association Today," n.d., JEM Papers, box 126-23, folder 334; and "The Work of the YMCA among Colored Young Men," ca. 1901, 5, JEM Papers, box 126-27, folder 554.

54. Minutes, Joint Meeting of the Colored Work Department Committee and Executive Committee of the Semi-Centennial Celebration," October 19, 1941, Biographical Records, YMCA of the USA Archives, University of

Minnesota, St. Paul, Minnesota, folder Tobias, Channing H.—Colored Work Department—Minutes, 1919–43, folder 10; Moorland, "The Association Today," n.d., JEM Papers, box 126-23, folder 334; and "The Work of the YMCA among Colored Young Men," ca. 1901, 5, JEM Papers, box 126-27, folder 554; Moorland, "Report on Colored YMCA Building," January 15, 1920, YMCA of Metropolitan Chicago Records, box 92, folder 8, Chicago Historical Society, Chicago, Illinois; and August Meier and Elliott Rudwick, *Black History and the Historical Profession, 1915–1980* (Urbana: University of Illinois Press, 1986), 13–16.

55. Clyde Griffen, "Reconstructing Masculinity from the Evangelical Revival to the Waning of Progressivism: A Speculative Synthesis," in Carnes and Griffen (eds.), *Meanings for Manhood*, 183.

Chapter Seven

Struggle among Saints
African American Women and the YWCA, 1870–1920

Adrienne Lash Jones

> I am not with these YWCA women. I am ashamed to say it
> but I have never been. . . . You would not expect anything
> different from a business man, a farmer, etc. but when the
> saints come along you expect them to be different.[1]

When Margaret Murray Washington wrote these words to her friend Lugenia Burns Hope in 1920, she was expressing the disappointment, frustration, and growing impatience of numerous African American club women. As the immediate past president of the umbrella organization for black women's clubs, the National Association of Colored Women, Washington had worked tirelessly in the forefront for social reform for nearly twenty-five years, along with an impressive number of black women leaders. While many so-called women's issues were the same for both black and white women, race and political agendas separated their efforts.

Washington's impatience with the Young Women's Christian Association was understandable. In spite of the association's enormous popularity among black college students and the unprecedented growth in the number of black members, through an aggressive war work campaign, the association's National Board remained ambivalent about and at times insensitive to the concerns of black women. Further, although by the end of World War I the organization could boast of having the largest multiracial membership of women in the nation, its local and national structures essentially protected prevailing segregationist practices. Separate branches served black women, and the National Board had no black representation.

Yet, the YWCA was unique among women's organizations. When the association consolidated all of the local women's associations which claimed its name and organized a National Board and staff in 1906, black student organizations and city associations were already in place. Thus the challenge to the new organization was to find a way to recognize and include these associations and their black members without offending the racial sensibilities of the majority white membership. At a time when southern states were rapidly passing laws to separate the races and the number of lynchings of blacks was reaching unprecedented numbers, the task of managing diversity within one organization was indeed daunting.

From the time the YWCA was first organized in the United States, black women as well as whites recognized the potential for resolving some of society's most pressing problems. The combination of "effective religious appeal with a humanitarian social-service emphasis upon a better environment for the tempted"[2] appealed to Christian club women. First, the interdenominational character of the association encouraged women to work together across religious lines. Second, the association provided a means to extend individual benevolence in more coherent, organized, and efficient ways to respond to the needs of increasingly large numbers of women workers. Third, and most important for black women, the YWCA provided the possibility of interracial cooperation among women. Particularly at a time when white women were expressing the virtues of social equality for themselves, black women felt that it was critical to gain their support to end racial inequality. Thus, the YWCA became a centerpiece of the struggle for Christian women as they sought to find common ground within one organization.

This essay will explore the actions and efforts of African American women within the YWCA movement between 1870 and 1920, with emphasis on the work of the National Board and policies determined by the organization at conventions and meetings. Records indicate that by 1870, the first YWCA for black women was already in existence. Fifty years later, a group of club women including Lugenia Burns Hope, Lucy Laney, and Mary McCrorey, claiming to represent the interests of some "300,000 Negro women of the South," went to the national convention to challenge the membership to confront what they called "the trouble existing in the work of the YWCA among colored women."[3] In this post–World War I era, not only was the association considered sufficiently important to the women and their communities to command their time and attention, but black women were convinced of their own importance to the organization. Thus the dramatic confrontation between black and white members in 1920 proved to be a watershed in the history of the association.

As young women migrated to cities to look for work in factories and personal service, black and white middle-class women were inspired to organize to minister to "the temporal, moral and religious welfare of young women who [were] dependent on their own exertions for support."[4] Older models of Christian benevolence, which mostly relied on individual acts of charity, could not respond sufficiently to the needs of the rapidly increasing number of women who made up the new urban working class. Thus, in the wake of shifting population demographics, and the accompanying changes in race and gender relationships which followed America's Civil War, the time was ripe for testing new ideas to achieve social uplift.

For the founding mothers of the Women's Christian Association, the YWCA's predecessor, the definition of membership and their sense of obligation to serve those of their own sex did not necessarily extend to black women. A few black domestic workers and factory workers were among the women who became members during the early years, but a lack of records makes it impossible to identify members by race. However, general race policies in the majority of urban cities toward the end of the nineteenth century suggest that the number of black women who had access to membership was very limited.[5]

African American women during this period were also expanding their community service efforts. The antebellum model of providing material aid to freedom-seeking slaves through denominational church organizations was dated. With increasing numbers of blacks migrating to cities, more complex problems and needs required new strategies to provide social services, especially for women. Therefore, it is not surprising that the earliest records of association work specifically for black women came from organizations of black women themselves. The model for interdenominational, evangelical social service, which was already underway for men through black branches of the YMCA, was undoubtedly one which seemed appropriate for black women as well.

The earliest record of organized association work among black women can be found in the minutes of the Philadelphia association in

1870, when a group of black women, representing a Colored Women's Christian Association, appealed to the local all-white Women's Christian Association for support.[6] A black domestic worker heard of the work of the Women's Christian Association while cleaning buildings in downtown Philadelphia. After several years of unsuccessful lobbying of black and white churches, she turned to the all-white women's group for help in establishing a black women's association.[7]

The Colored Women's Association of Philadelphia struggled until about 1900, with small residences in two locations. However, although it sent representatives to participate in the 1875 International Convention of the Women's Christian Association, the group was unable to gain support or recognition from the Philadelphia association. When a special National Board worker visited the city in 1908, she was unable to recommend the Colored Women's Association of Philadelphia as a charter member of the new national organization because it no longer represented work with or for young women. The residences closed because of a lack of sufficient operating funds, but the organization continued to work with children and older women.[8]

A group African American women in Dayton, Ohio, established the Women's Christian Association #2 in 1893. The women were members of a small sewing club sponsored by a local African Methodist Episcopal (AME) church. The group was never a part of the white Christian Women's Association but appears to have enjoyed good relations with the white women. Also, black women maintained a sense of belonging to a larger national movement of Colored Women's Associations through their correspondence and their relationship with the older Philadelphia organization. In 1900 the Dayton women purchased a building from funds raised in their own community and with the support of the white association. The association maintained its affiliation with the National Board until 1918, when it became an affiliated branch of the all-white Dayton association. This special cooperative relationship between the two groups gives Dayton the distinction of claiming the oldest continuously affiliated branch for black women in the United States. Similar independent associations were organized by black women in New York City, Baltimore, Brooklyn, and Washington, D.C., before 1906.

Without a doubt, it was the spread of the YWCA movement through black college campuses which had the most direct effect on the makeup of the earliest membership of the national movement. The missionary nature of the growing YWCA movement on college campuses was perfectly complementary to the spirit which characterized the founding of the majority of black colleges in the South. The mostly Protestant denominational financial support made learning and religion practically synonymous in the curricula of the colleges, with the specific resolve that graduates of the institutions should spread out and minister to the needs of the race. The Christian-based YWCAs and YMCAs, with their evangelistic emphasis, were heartily encouraged as wholesome and desirable activities for students by white faculty members and administrators.

The earliest black YWCA student association on record was organized at Baptist-sponsored Spelman College, where the predominantly white faculty labored to ensure fulfillment of the school's primary objective: to "develop Christian women." The Spelman YWCA was organized in 1884, with every student and teacher enrolled in the membership. According to Cynthia Neverdon-Morton, in her study of black women's activities in the South, three of the most active committees of the organization concentrated on missionary work, young converts, and temperance.[9] This mission was consistent with the early YWCA movement on white campuses, where women students joined, along with their YMCA counterparts, to concentrate their efforts in a Volunteer Movement for Foreign Missions. The Spelman YWCA not only carried on missionary work in the poor sections of Atlanta's black neighborhoods, but the school's most distinguished department was its Missionary Training Department, which encouraged missionary work in Africa.[10]

At Wilberforce University, an African Methodist Episcopal denomination-sponsored coeducational school, when the YWCA organized in 1895, the founders listed as their aims "To form a more perfect union, to promote general welfare and to aid in the preparation for the great responsibilities of life."[11] In addition to holding prayer services, YWCA women at Wilberforce furnished a "rest room" for women students, in keeping with the current emphasis of the national movement to secure comfortable gathering spaces for women. Members of the organization also helped purchase books and clothing for needy students.

These examples illustrate the major thrust of Christian missionary work in student YWCA organizations. In fact, by 1908, when Addie Waite Hunton was hired by the National Board to visit black colleges, she reported that seven of fourteen affiliated chapters were devoting themselves to "real association work," meaning that the students were actively involved in religious recruiting in their communities. She also reported that in her travels she had been "brought into contact with 2300 young black women" and was "awake to the possibility of a larger and fuller womanhood for them thro' the association movement, realizing in the Association the greatest possible factor in the work of uplifting her race."[12] By some accounts, student associations at black colleges in 1913 covered twenty-eight states, with eighty chapters claiming the name YWCA.[13] The student movement's membership rolls reportedly represented over half of the enrolled female population at black colleges.

After careful study, Hunton recommended only four colored city associations for National Board affiliation under the original charter. These were located in Washington, D.C., Baltimore, Brooklyn, and New York City. Hunton also recommended for charter membership three of the fourteen black student associations which had formerly been affiliated with the American Committee. They were found at Spelman College, Tuskeegee Institute, and Agricultural and Mechanical College at Normal, Alabama. Soon afterward, following visits to the south and midwest, Hunton expanded the list to include a number of other student associations, followed by a few independent black city associations.

From the beginning, the race question posed a delicate problem for the YWCA. In 1906, when the association set out to become the largest and most influential grass-roots women's social organization in the nation, legal segregation was determined to be the natural order in the south, and racial separation was accepted in the north and west. Thus, the YWCA faced a unique challenge. Its deep roots in the Christian faith, which served as a basis for all the policies of the organization, could be interpreted to mean that women of all races should be included in their services and membership. This interpretation was most profoundly expressed through the work of the World's YWCA, founded in 1894 by women in Europe. Before the turn of the century this group solicited the aid of American missionaries to organize association work in India, China, Japan, and South America. As a result, one of the first and strongest departments in the new national organization was its foreign division.

On the North American continent, the association had also reached out to diverse populations. Its work with Indian girls on reservations dated back to the 1890s, when Christian missionaries started organizations at the Indian schools. These missions were isolated, and for the most part the girls who left the reservations were few enough in number to be absorbed into the student movement or into various city associations in northern and western cities. Also, student associations in many colleges and universities included Asian and other non-European members. However, this model could not apply to black associations. For one thing, race laws and racial separation practices throughout the nation applied most stringently to black Americans in that era. Black women could not be absorbed into the majority organizations in the south, and in the northern and western states they were not welcome in most white central associations. Therefore, in most cases, the black city associations came into existence because white associations failed to include black women in their membership. Most were founded and supported by blacks themselves. Unlike the student organizations, the work was self-initiated, and there was little support or recognition from their white counterparts.

Perhaps even more important, however, was the issue of the mission of the association itself. White Christian women were faced with a major contradiction when they ignored the black women who upheld the same Christian faith and who were eager to join the whites in efforts to uplift women in their communities. At a time when black women were routinely excluded from most other white women's organizations, the challenge for the YWCA was to find a way to build a movement which, while fulfilling its mission, would not violate the sensibilities of the majority.

As one of her first actions as president of the new National Board, Grace Dodge called a conference to discuss the situation in the south and to recommend a race policy which would be satisfactory to already established associations. The conference was held in Asheville, North Carolina on June 7–17, 1907, with sixty white invited participants and no blacks, even though two black southern city associations in Baltimore and Washington, D.C., and student associations on southern black college campuses were charter members of the national organization. At that time, black association work was already underway in such cities as Norfolk, Charleston, and Columbia, South Carolina.[14] To make matters more complicated, several northern cities had separate black associations and association work in black communities.

The records of the Asheville meeting contain conflicting interpretations of the participants' recommendations. According to one account, the group agreed that "no work was to be undertaken by our Southern Advisory Committee . . . to promote association work in the cities in the south. It would be all right to affiliate student associations already organized and go on organizing, asking that that be done from headquarters."[15] Another participant reported that "after much discussion . . . these women stated that they were quite anxious and willing to help . . . but on account of the prejudice, they did not think it best to attempt it at that time."[16] Apparently, the white southerners were not inclined to cut off work that was already underway, but were unwilling to support any work to encourage the addition of more black associations. The group was concerned that white women could be faced with the inconceivable embarrassment of attending nationally sponsored conferences where black women from the same city might be in attendance. In her report to the National Board, a staff member observed that she "came away [from Asheville] with the feeling that we were under a certain amount of obligation not to make it too difficult for these [white] women who had conceded a great deal."[17]

Following the Asheville conference, in September 1907 Addie Waite Hunton, a former teacher, active club woman, and wife of the Administrative Secretary of the Colored Men's Department of the International YMCA, was hired by the National Board as a temporary consultant. Her original charge—to spend three months visiting and assessing the work in black associations—was extended very quickly when it became clear that this assignment was a much bigger task than originally anticipated by the Board. Between September and December, Hunton traveled to college campuses across the south and to cities where YWCA work was reportedly already underway. After her first round of visits, she recommended that the National Board hire a permanent staff member to work with local black staffs and their volunteers and another to work with student organizations. She also recommended affiliation for fifteen additional student organizations.[18]

In October 1908, Elizabeth Ross (Haynes) was hired as the first permanent "special worker for colored students," with the responsibility to continue to travel to black colleges where there were student associations or where organizations existed with the potential for affiliating as chapters of the association. She included visits to city organizations where black women were organized and interested in affiliating with the new national YWCA. However, Ross also found that there was too much work for one staff person, and it was impossible to devote time to both the city and student organizations. Consequently, Hunton was asked to remain as a consultant and to continue her work with local city associations. The two women traveled to campuses and cities throughout the south and east to survey organizations which called themselves Young Women's (or Colored) Christian Associations. After her first round of visits, Ross reported that black organizations raised many critical questions as to how the national organization planned to deal with the particular problems they faced in their segregated communities. Many of the independent black city associations were frustrated because they were struggling to survive and in some cases did not know the method of work espoused by the YWCA. Frequently, local leaders confronted Ross with questions as to "why the National Board ha[d] not shown more interest in city work for colored people and [has] refused to encourage one association which sought membership in the National movement."[19] These were questions for which the National Board had no easy answers.

Because there was no clear interpretation of the policy regarding black associations, the special workers undoubtedly devised their own working definition of how those organizations should be handled, and apparently Ross and Hunton responded to requests wherever they were located. Thus, as early as January 1909, Ross reported that there were interested groups working toward affiliation in fourteen cities, including several in the south.

Although she pressed the National Board to clarify its position on the matter of southern association work, Ross continued to work with the local members, most of whom were also active members of the National Association of Colored Women (NACW). In fact, leadership roles in the two organizations were often almost duplicate, and their goals were quite consistent. This large network of clubs provided black women with an incredibly effective system for communication and organization whereby they could address issues of racial and sexual oppression. The NACW was composed of various local clubs that were affiliated with city, state, and regional arms of the organization, with a national federated umbrella association. The organization was founded in 1896, in response to the exclusion of black women by majority national women's associations, and quickly developed the reputation of being the representative voice for black women. According to author Paula Giddings, "their job was to help—by word and by deed—to create opportunity and environment for all black women."[20] The middle-class leadership of the NACW saw the interracial YWCA as an organization where black women could form alliances with white women in the struggle against societal prejudice.

In spite of complaints from black women about the apparent ambivalence of the organization's leadership in regard to work in the south, where the majority of blacks lived, Ross and Hunton were convinced that in cases where there was consent and cooperation between the white associations and an active black constituency, the black associations could succeed, especially in the North and West. Both women, however, recognized that a separate strategy for working with southern women would be necessary because of the rigid segregation laws.

By 1910 the issue of a systematic policy toward black city association work could no longer be postponed. After the Asheville conference, although the National Board confined their "encouragement and help" to efforts of black women in city organizations in the northwest and east, they recognized that "there were many organizations calling themselves Colored YWCAs springing up through the south."[21] Without the support of trained YWCA staff, the organizations were not consistently performing association work. Some were working principally among the elderly and others with children, while the work with young women was hardly visible. Thus, there was the issue of standards and training requirements for paid and volunteer workers in the associations.

The all-white National Board was concerned that the growing swell of requests for association work in black communities could put them in the position of giving fiscal and/or social responsibility to reluctant white YWCAs. While keeping the national network of associations from becoming embroiled in a split over the race issue, the board was hard pressed to come up with a reasonable policy.

In response to these concerns, in 1910 the National Board passed a resolution stating, "In certain cities where there is no central association, or where the central association is weak or where the organization of a branch is not feasible, if the colored population is sufficiently large and able to support its own work, an association called the Colored Young Women's Christian Association shall be organized." The Board also outlined an administrative plan which placed all new black association work under the supervision of a national worker and mandated direct affiliation with the National Board. However, as soon as possible, these associations were to become branches of their local YWCAs.[22]

In response to requests for information about the YWCA's policy, Hunton organized two mass meetings in New York City. Her purpose was twofold. First, she wanted to recognize the work in the black community which was already underway. The work in New York City dated back to 1905, when a group of black women organized a Colored Women's Association and requested affiliation with the Central New York Association. Another association for black women in Brooklyn was also in operation when the National Board was organized. Hunton's second purpose for holding the mass meetings was to stimulate more national attention to the movement. Both meetings were successful, with large numbers in attendance, and gained national notice in black newspapers. This kind of attention was most helpful when the National Board hired a second special student worker for colored work to assist Ross, and Hunton was freed to work with city associations. In her new and more focused position, Hunton concentrated on building strong fiscal and community support in established associations and encouraging work in cities where association work was taking shape.

The new national staff assignments quickly brought results, with a black association opening in St. Louis and a revitalized "Colored Association" opening in Philadelphia. A year later, Hunton organized the first "Conference of Volunteer and Employed Workers in Colored YWCAs" in New York. The conference attracted twenty-five delegate presidents and workers from five states and the District of Columbia.

During the same period, Hunton initiated the first survey to investigate industrial conditions for black women in factories in Winston-Salem, Fayetteville, and Durham, North Carolina. In this report, she described working conditions for the women in the towns as "a story too dark, too depressing, too long to be unfolded." To remedy some of the problems, she encouraged black women in the towns to take the initiative to remedy some of the most unsavory living conditions and to organize for better working conditions. Hunton reported that the plan was "heartily welcomed by superintendents and owners who were glad to aid in any movement for the uplift of their workers." In response to her report, the National Board endorsed a plan to organize industrial work among the black women in the mills and to encourage black middle-class women in the towns to work toward "upliftment among colored mill workers."[23]

When Ross and Hunton announced their intent to leave their positions with the National Board, the Board finally assigned a permanent, full-time staff employee to work with black city associations. This decision took on more urgency when Addie Hunton reported on her work for the city committee at the national convention and moved the membership to pledge an "emphasis on colored work, where conditions [were] favorable for model associations." The convention's action specified that in order to join the national movement, interested groups should provide "permanent and adequate equipment, and there should be funds available to employ a competent secretary for at least a year." For their part, the national staff was asked to make provisions for training employed leadership.[24]

The need for more black national staff was also emphasized when two white workers who were assigned to help organize an association in Montclair, New Jersey, reported that their work among blacks in that city had to be postponed because they were unable to communicate with black women to determine if they had a real interest in starting a YWCA. In this unusual case, white women proposed to build an association to serve the large population of black women who had recently come into the city to work as domestics. According to the national guidelines, this proposal needed approval from the black women themselves before any further steps could be taken. Only after Addie Hunton's intervention were black women willing to commit to cooperating with whites, and the new association opened without problems. In that same year, 1913, Hunton proudly announced to the National Board that black women across the nation "had paid for [YWCA] homes with an aggregate value of $16,000 . . . and associations employing secretaries [had] usually raised their first year's expense budget before a Secretary was actually on staff."[25]

When the National Board failed to secure outside funding from philanthropist Julius Rosenwald, the position of Secretary for Colored Work was included as part of the headquarters' regular budget. Once again the Board made a brilliant appointment. Eva del Vakia Bowles, a former teacher, case worker, and, most recently, the Secretary of the Colored Branch of New York City, became the first full-time employee whose assignment was to work exclusively with the black city associations.

Soon after her appointment to the staff, Bowles assembled an interracial "Sub-Committee on Colored Work" to help plan appropriate policy and activities for the national organization. The committee included National Board members and selected black women who would help guide policies and programs to facilitate the work. At their first meeting, Bowles optimistically noted:

> Until recently the problem of the Negro girl has been approached with indifference . . . discussion has served often as an excuse for doing nothing. We believe that things may be actually done and handled effectively, if we are able to deal more intelligently with the problems through mutual understanding and sympathies.[26]

With the support of her committee, Bowles proceeded with deliberate speed to represent her special constituency at every level of association life. She regularly contributed to deliberations in the Department of Method (where her position was housed), wrote for national publications, and made numerous appearances at meetings of black club women. Most important, she worked with established associations and responded to interested groups in cities throughout the northeast and mid-west. From the beginning of her tenure on the national staff, Bowles was committed to integrating the work of black associations into the mainstream of the organization.[27]

Shortly after it was established, Bowles' special committee recommended that a more representative conference than the 1907 Asheville one should be convened to discuss the policy for work in southern cities.

The committee spent most of the first year planning the meeting, with the goal of finding some agreement between white and black southern women and recommending a more responsive policy for relationships between the black associations, their white counterparts, and the National Board. The committee felt that without the presence of black women to represent their own interests, no progress could be made. Besides, some of the mistrust and ill feelings between the groups needed to be mediated if the association was to continue to provide services for black women in the region.

The second Conference On Work With Southern Women was held in Louisville, Kentucky, on October 15–16, 1915, with twenty-eight persons in attendance. Invited participants included four white women and three white men who were considered to be representative leaders "in constructive work among colored people in the south," seven representatives of the YWCA's South Atlantic and South Central Field Committees, six black women who represented various movements in the south, and eight representatives from the National Board. The group reached a consensus on three important principles. First, an interracial committee would be appointed by the National Board, composed of black and white women either living in or originating from the south. Second, volunteer and staff leadership training were to be provided for colored associations in the south. Third, and perhaps most important, the group reportedly recognized that the "best method for cooperating in city associations [was] through branch relationship."[28]

Following the meeting, however, interpretations of the third point, the principle of having only one association in any community, once again proved to be problematic. For some struggling black associations with aspirations to become affiliated branches, this principle encouraged all-white central boards to support their efforts. However, other black associations complained that this arrangement was limiting and that this particular principle threatened to end their direct affiliation with the National Board, thus placing them at the mercy of prejudiced southern whites. Bowles agreed with the former position and regularly defended the notion that branch affiliation at the local level would ultimately prove to be beneficial for black members. Bowles supported a general pattern of organization whereby black associations would have direct affiliation as branches of local central associations. Black branches were to be managed by all-black committees of management. The branch committee and the local central board of directors would then appoint equal numbers of their members to serve on a joint "Committee on

Colored Work," with a white board member as the chair. The responsibility of this group was to serve as advisors and counselors to achieve racial understanding. Black branch secretaries (directors) and staff members were, by virtue of their positions, employees of the central associations, serving with the approval of the branch management committees.[29] Although variations of this arrangement persisted for nearly half a century, neither Bowles nor the national organization could anticipate the changes in race dynamics which profoundly altered the relationships within the association during and after World War I.

During the decade before World War I, one author described the YWCA as "inter-group" rather than interracial in its relations. Another noted that the emphasis was on "bi-racial" cooperation, with an uneven distribution of power between blacks and whites.[30] However, the national leadership preferred to describe a "cross-section" organization. For them, black women and girls were only one special constituency. Student work, the foreign department, industrial work, and work with young girls and adolescents were also designated as special interest work. Nevertheless, the issue of service to black women required special solutions. Therefore the Louisville Conference of 1915 provided a unique opportunity for black and white women to negotiate ways to cooperate as members of the same organization. Perhaps the recommendation "to establish interracial regional committees" provided the most critical opportunity for black and white women of similar education and interests to work together in the south. In other parts of the country the plan also provided a model for interracial cooperation, especially since the majority of associations in all regions were segregated. Without this agreement, there were few other opportunities for contact between the two groups, since black women were not represented on either the national or local central boards, except for the staff. The association considered the newly formed field (regional) committees to be a first step toward giving black volunteers an official voice in the association's policy making.

For the times, the opportunity for biracial cooperation was unique among women's organizations. Although the association carefully guarded the principle and practice of racial separation, both black and white women claimed to believe that a policy of working together would "furnish a working knowledge . . . [toward] interrelationship."[31] For the most part, even though most blacks despised segregation, they agreed that their communities were best served by black professionals. However, interpretation of roles within this dual system of service differed a great deal. Although conceding that segregated facilities might be most practical, black women were not willing to give in to the dictates of the all-white central boards. This determination to maintain control of the branches led to much dissension in the organization during the postwar period.

Although the majority of the black leaders who were active in the association were also members of organizations affiliated with the NACW, many of whom served as regional and national officers, the intergroup spirit of the YWCA was attractive. Because the organization extended across race and class lines, African American leaders believed that its Christian mission essentially mandated them to lead as a new phase of the women's movement was evolving. This spirit was articulated in a speech by Mabel Cratty, Executive Secretary of the National Board, to the National Convention in 1915, when she asked her audience, "What are some of the reasons which give us some right to expect that this particular woman's movement should or may shape the trend of the stream in this nation? First, it is the Church's stake in the whole woman movement. Second, it is a movement of all types of women, all communities are represented in it. Third, it is perfectly sure of its goal, and many of these streams are not. Fourth, being a Christian movement, it is to be expected that its vision should outrun that of any other."[32]

In this spirit, the National Board Council on Colored Work followed with an even stronger statement on the challenge of interracial cooperation in shaping the women's movement. At a meeting on race relations sponsored by the NACW, representatives of the new Council sent a resolution that stated: "Because the full strength of the womanhood of America is needed and must be conserved and utilized in this re-construction period, it is the duty of women of both races to accept the challenge and face squarely the opportunity and together work out, therefore, moral, economic and social destiny."[33]

In spite of this and other proclamations from the YWCA, however, the women of the NACW remained suspicious and failed to ratify the resolution. Undoubtedly, black women shared concern for the women's issues which were foremost on the agenda of the YWCA. Yet, they were concerned that while white women reformers like the leadership of the YWCA expressed some interest in interracial cooperation, the larger women's movement was becoming increasingly dependent on racist arguments to gain suffrage rights and political opportunity. Black women felt that for the most part, white women leaders preferred to ignore and indict blacks as responsible for their own low social and economic condition, without regard for the history of racism that held them hostage in this society. Relationships between the races, especially in local associations, were often strained at best. White central boards were not always sympathetic to the aspirations and needs of their black members, and too often used supervisory positions over the personnel and activities of the branches to impede the progress of the black branches. Black women could point to the fact that the leadership of the YWCA at the national and local levels failed to express or exhibit urgency in the work to relieve racial oppression. Rather, the association's reform agenda and the structural arrangements of the organization demonstrated more willingness to accommodate to the status quo than to challenge white racial hegemony.[34] For example, when black women requested the use of a YWCA pool in Lakewood, New Jersey, the Small Town and Country Committee, as well as the City Committee of the National Board, resolved that "Because of a necessary policy and an understanding entered into by the National Board with the Southern Associations, it would not seem wise to . . . advise this being done."[35]

In spite of these worries, black women employees of the association found that the opportunity for professional training in the YWCA overwhelmed many other concerns. At a time when few white-collar jobs were available to women, and especially black women, a position in the YWCA was not only prestigious but offered the additional attraction of allowing them to function as managers and program developers. Moreover, the association's reputation for hiring college graduates, and its many nationally sponsored conferences and conventions, provided access to a very supportive national network of women with similar education and interests.

From the time Addie Hunton made her first report to the National Board, she and her successors constantly stressed the need to identify women of the highest caliber for secretaryships and to provide the necessary training for successful operations. She also stressed the need to train volunteers as an essential complement to the training of the professional staff. Her formula for successful associations included the need to "study the social and religious needs of the women and girls [in the community] and the relation of association work to those needs, and that there the work should be built up on the line to meet those needs."[36] Hunton believed that the National Board should either admit black women to the regular training that was available to white workers or organize special courses for blacks.

During the early years after the formation of the National Board, when no special provisions were made for race, records indicate that from time to time black women attended courses at the YWCA headquarters in New York. Although the National Board provided training and support for local white associations, there were no provisions for blacks, in spite of constant requests from both Hunton and Ross. By 1911, when work with the black associations was clearly expanding, the Board felt compelled to make some decisions on how to deal with this special group. The solution was mixed. When the National Board's headquarters was built in 1911, with classrooms and dormitory facilities, four black women were allowed to attend summer courses. For these women, the Board chose to follow the prevalent segregation pattern and did not allow them to live in the residence. The Board also arranged special practicums in New York's black branch, and their internships were supervised by Hunton. At the time, according to Hunton, "the greatest need of the colored work [in those years] was leaders."[37] After Bowles was hired, she continued the practice of supervising selected black trainees and organized nationally sponsored special conferences for black volunteers and staff members. Occasionally, she included black women who were not employed by or involved with the YWCA but who were considered to be potential YWCA leaders.[38] When the United States entered World War I, the YWCA was the only women's organization invited by the government to develop recreational programs in camps and war centers in the states and oversees. With an unprecedented budget of $1,000,000, the association placed its entire staff and all resources at the disposal of the government for the benefit of women and girls. As part of the War Work Council, in recognition of "the loyalty and needs of the colored girls and women in this country," a minimum of $200,000 was set aside for work with the group. By the end of the war, the organization claimed to have allocated at least $400,000 for "colored work."[39]

With this unprecedented budget, the Colored Work Committee was finally given a clear directive from the national organization to organize throughout the country. The work was arranged in three principal areas. First, the YWCA established "Hostess Houses" inside or near the camps where soldiers in the segregated army could relax and receive visitors under strict supervision. Second, "recreation centers" for women and girls were established to accommodate black women in cities where there were no YWCA facilities available to them. Third, black women who came to work in the nation's industrial centers were organized into "Industrial Clubs" and helped with job placement and employment problems.

At last black club women had institutional support for programs that they had envisioned for years. The large YWCA budget provided an opportunity for race uplift on a scale unlike any other in history. When the war began, there were 16 colored branches in cities and 101 affiliated black YWCA chapters on college campuses. During the war, the YWCA focused on city work as an area for expansion.

With her new authority, Bowles and her staff seized the chance to mobilize the network of middle-class women they had cultivated through the NACW. While the organization had always furnished a reservoir of talent and resources for potential staff and volunteers, the war years offered unprecedented opportunities. In spite of its flawed racial policies, the YWCA provided a structure whereby the women of the talented tenth could finally thrive.

At the outset of the war, Bowles and her staff considered their first priority to be the organization of recreation facilities for soldiers and their families. The segregated camps that were often in southern states confined black soldiers to posts where there were practically no facilities to accommodate them. Also, in many cases, the soldiers faced racial hostility and animosity if they attempted to go into nearby towns. Not surprisingly, black YWCA staff found it extremely difficult to persuade government officials that they were capable of overseeing programs for the soldiers and should be allowed to begin their work.[40] When they were able to proceed, the women most often found that the buildings that they were assigned were woefully inadequate.

In spite of the difficulties, however, Bowles and her staff set up Hostess Houses in sixteen locations, with volunteers and local staff to entertain the soldiers. With the help of NACW-affiliated clubs, they were able to hire forty-six new black secretaries to manage the facilities, all college or normal school graduates or with equivalent experience. The YWCA staff organized special courses at Camp Upton and Camp Dix in New Jersey, where the women spent four weeks of intensive management and program training.

The Hostess Houses provided a refuge from the daily racism that the soldiers faced in the camps. White commanding officers often disregarded the particular problems of their black troops, and racial tensions were inevitable. The YWCA hostesses tried to create a homelike ambiance where the men could relax and feel accepted. In this genteel environment, many of the black men and their families had their first opportunity to come into intimate contact with the black middle class. As a result, upward mobility for members of the race through education, manners, and morals seemed achievable to masses of black people.[41]

Of equal importance was the work that the YWCA accomplished for women war workers. Black women who migrated to cities from rural

Figure 13. Families visiting servicemen at a Hostess House sponsored by the Colored Work Committee of the YWCA during World War I. From Jane Olcott's *The Work of Colored Women, 1919.*

areas were often unskilled, poorly educated, and unprepared for the challenges of city life and industrial employment. Although the women came looking for better opportunities, too often they found low-paying jobs, unsafe living conditions, and literally no wholesome recreation opportunities. To address these problems, the War Work Council subcommittee added an Industrial Secretary for Colored Work.

Once again the association was fortunate in its choice of staff. Mary E. Jackson, an active club woman with great strength and vision who had been working in the Rhode Island Labor Department, was perfectly suited for the job. Right away she began a series of investigations to determine the localities of employment concentration for black women in order to decide which sites would most profit from the services of the YWCA. Under her supervision, field workers in the south Atlantic, south central, northeastern, and southwestern states identified women who could be trained to become industrial secretaries. By the end of the war, her staff had assisted in organizing forty-five Colored Industrial Work Centers in twenty-one states and the District of Columbia, many with locally paid staff.

Jackson's holistic approach to the work was expressed in a report to the National Board when she stated, "Out of twelve years experience, we feel that the organization of colored girls in clubs, without relating them to the whole industrial situation in the community does not develop racial understanding. . . . The responsibility of the Industrial Department is to develop a consciousness in both white and colored groups to know that their interests are independent [sic] upon each other."[42]

Like their coworkers who set up the Hostess Houses, local industrial secretaries found that because of racial restrictions, locating recreation and meeting spaces for the black Industrial Girls Clubs was especially difficult. In some cities, black-owned businesses rented spaces to the YWCA and supported the organization with fundraising activities. In others, the central associations were willing to cooperate with black leaders and occasionally allowed the black workers to use the YWCA facilities at times when they were not in use by whites. In other places, black club women opened their homes for meetings and gave invaluable time to secure schools, church buildings, and other community facilities for the women to use.

Everyplace the YWCA organized, the response was overwhelming. Staff and volunteer leaders sponsored dances, sports activities, and Bible study classes, led numerous clubs for working girls, and performed myriad other duties for women in the communities. The need for association work was obvious, so much so that in many cases, because the national budget relieved the pressure on central boards to assume fiscal responsibility for the work, many associations that had been resistant before eagerly embraced the new organizations and later helped them affiliate as branches. From the perspective of the National Board, this was the most desirable outcome of the war work.

In addition to industrial work, local associations sponsored "Patriotic Leagues" for girls under eighteen during the war. Young girls organized clubs under the leadership of carefully selected women, often teachers in the schools. Camping trips, picnics, sports activities, singing groups, dramatic presentations, and so on helped to cultivate future YWCA members. Besides, the leadership skills that the girls gained in the clubs provided an entrée to summer recreation jobs. By the end of the war, this popular movement in the association among young girls boasted an enrollment of over 4,000 girls in the South Atlantic field alone.

The rapid growth of black associations between 1906 and 1920 set the stage for African American women to reassess their position in the organization. The women were aware that in some ways their very presence as members made the organization unique among women's groups. While other women's organizations struggled to defend race exclusivity, the YWCA could claim leadership in race relations, if only by virtue of its large black membership and the visibility of the association's work in black communities. However, as their numbers grew and as black women invested more of their time and talents in association work, they became more vocal in their insistence that they should be represented on policymaking committees and in the leadership of the organization. The time had come to make the organization more relevant and responsive to the particular needs and concerns of its black members.

In the south, where centers were established through the War Work Council, tensions grew between the National Board and staff and local black club women. Differences in interpretation of policy, for example, and unequal representation at all levels made black women more sensitive to the discrepancies between the stated Christian mission of the association and the racism that they experienced while working within the organization. Although there were many personal stories and examples to indicate that through interaction between the races some racial attitudes were changing, black women were impatient with the YWCA's slow response to their concerns.

By the end of World War I, African American women throughout the country had grown more vocal and active in the association and were determined to press for more control of decisions about the work in their communities. Certainly the black women were encouraged by the victories of the women's suffrage movement and the new freedom women had gained during the war. Also, the war industry had brought unprecedented numbers of white and black women into industrial settings. Although many of these jobs disappeared after the war crisis, African American women's exposure to the industrial workplace forever changed the boundaries that had held them within the domestic sphere. Both the new race militancy resulting from the war and the recent victories of the women's movement helped to mobilize black women to demand changes in the association.

In a statement to the YWCA convention in 1920, Lugenia Burns Hope outlined the major demands that had been drawn up in a meeting of black women YWCA leaders who were active in the association during the war. The meeting, which was called to "discuss and seek a remedy for the troubles existing in the work of the YWCA among the Colored Women of the South," demonstrated the passion and determination of the women to forge a truly egalitarian relationship between blacks and whites.[43]

Black leaders demanded representation on the National Board. Citing the inclusion of two black men on the National Board of the YMCA and black representation on the National Board of the Urban League, the women emphasized their feeling the "no person [could] interpret the

needs and desires of Colored people as well as a Colored person."
Further, Hope asserted, "although a very small group of white women
have taken a forward step . . . the Colored women know that our group
is much more skeptical about white women than the world knows anything about."[44]

Black representatives also demanded a review of the agreement resulting from the 1915 Louisville meeting. Varying interpretations of the
meaning of the statement that there should be "only one Association in
each city" caused much tension between southern associations and those
in other parts of the country and between black National Board staff and
local black members. Women who had attended the Louisville conference
charged that they were misquoted and misrepresented when they
expressed support for this principle as a long-range goal rather than as an
endorsement for a policy to be implemented immediately. As part of this
debate over interpretation, southern black women felt that they needed
to clarify the position of the national organization regarding their right to
form independent organizations whenever the branch arrangement
proved to be undesirable or where no central association existed. The
black women rightfully pointed out that nowhere in the guidelines of the
National Board was race mentioned in reference to who should control a
local central board. However, in practice, there seemed to be an assumption that central associations must be white. This was illustrated in the
case of Jackson, Mississippi, where black women organized and were all
set to open a "Colored Association" when the national YWCA staff ruled
that until white women organized, the black association could not be recognized as a city association.

Hope's committee also demanded direct affiliation and supervision of
colored branches from National Board headquarters rather than from
field headquarters. Citing the success of this model before and during the
war, the women argued that the black staff members at National Board
headquarters were more sensitive to their problems and needs and could
best facilitate their work. An unfortunate experience of a group in
Atlanta, where a black field secretary disregarded the wishes of the local
women and created a rift between the staff and the black women in the
city, was the most often cited case illustrating the need for national staff
involvement. Therefore, the women demanded assurance that the Bureau
of Colored Work would be reconstituted to attend to the particular concerns of black branches, especially since black staff were being assigned
to other departments during the postwar period. Further, on the matter of
staff assignments, African American leaders insisted that black collegiate

MAY B. BELCHER
War Worker
South Central Field

JOSEPHINE
PUIYOU
Special War Worker

EVA DELVAKEA
BOWLES
Executive for
Colored Work

Mrs. MARIA A.
WILDER
War Worker
Southwestern Field

MARY E. JACKSON
Industrial Secretary

Figure 14. Prominent African American YWCA workers who enacted the plans of the Colored Work Committee during World War I. From Jane Olcott's *The Work of Colored Women, 1919.*

work should also be directed from National Board headquarters under the supervision of the National Board's Bureau of Colored Work.

The committee's fourth demand was representation on local boards of directors. Black women were no longer willing to have Committees on Colored Work chaired by white women, and they insisted on having a place on local central boards for the chairs of their branch committees of management. This arrangement would not only assure black representation at policymaking levels, but would also guarantee that the representative was the choice of her peers rather than the choice of a group of white women. In making this demand, black women also wanted assurance that they would have the final say in the hiring and supervision of branch secretaries. This was considered to be a critical step in developing branch staffs who would act in accordance with the desires of their black constituents, rather than have them beholden to the wishes of white board members.

Rather than deal with their demands directly at the convention, the National Board referred the women back to their regional South Atlantic Field Committee, where each point could be discussed in detail. After the convention, the YWCA called a meeting in Richmond, Virginia, which included black and white national staff and volunteers, along with representatives from local associations. During the day-long negotiations the women spoke freely, with Eva Bowles acting as mediator between the interests and position of the National Board and the interests and demands of the local association members.

At the end of the day, it was clear to all participants that there was no agreement on the demands. Representatives of the National Board refused to accept the principle of direct national affiliation for the black associations, and the Board continued to deny charges of racial discrimination in their support for work in local associations. Frustrated by the failure of the National Board to accept their demands, the women took their cause to the NACW, the Southeastern Federation of Colored Women's Clubs, black newspapers, and the black clergy.[45] The outcome was a call for a second Louisville conference on Colored Work to be sponsored by the National Board in February 1921 for southern personnel and executives from the national headquarters. The only concession to result from the Richmond meeting was the appointment of Charlotte Hawkins Brown, founder and head of a school in North Carolina, as member-at-large of the southern regional committee.

Although there were few victories for the black women by 1920, it was apparent that the relationship between the two races had reached a new plateau. Minutes of the Richmond meeting reflect the essence of what was to become the core struggle within the association for much of the remainder of the twentieth century. In summing up the meeting, Lugenia Burns Hope spoke of "the difficulty . . . in the effort the colored women have made and are making to work with the white women of the south—that the white women . . . do not know the colored women in their churches or in their homes or their educational institutions or in any but a very limited way."[46] Mary McCrorey further warned that some "of us [black women] must keep wide awake and remain fearless to stand by the thing we know to be square and helpful to the colored woman . . . without sacrifice of principle."[47]

By 1921, it was clear that the battle lines were drawn. Progressive black women had challenged the movement to live up to its stated mission: to improve the lives of women and girls, and to include in its fellowship women and girls of every kind. If the YWCA was to survive as a multiracial membership organization, neither its leadership nor its members could avoid confronting the critical issues of race and class that would continue to plague the nation. It was this challenge which demanded commitment and dedication from every quarter to respond to the demands of a diverse membership in a changing society. Thus, for the remainder of the century, the association would continue to be an arena in the struggle for black and white Christian women to find common ground.

NOTES

1. Margaret Murray Washington, Tuskeegee, Alabama, to Lugenia Burns Hope, Atlanta, Georgia. February 6, 1920 in YWCA Folder, Neighborhood Union Collection, Atlanta University Woodruff Library, Archives Department, Atlanta, GA (hereafter cited as NUC).

2. Elizabeth Wilson, *Fifty Years of Association Work* (New York: Woman's Press, 1916), 31.

3. "Minutes of the Conference," Mrs. John Hope, Chairman, n.d., YWCA Folder, NUC. Lugenia Burns Hope was the wife of John Hope, president of Atlanta's Morehouse College. Mary McCrorey was the wife of the president of Charlotte, North Carolina's, Johnson C. Smith College. Lucy Laney was founder and principal of the Haines Normal and Industrial Institute in Augusta, Georgia.

4. Wilson, *Association Work*, 32.

5. Mary S. Sims, *The Natural History of a Social Organization* (New York: Woman's Press, 1935), 60. Although Sims discusses the origins of the association, she does not mention the issue of race relations. For a discussion of a more specific case, where black women were very much an issue for the YWCA of

Cleveland, Ohio, see Adrienne Lash Jones, *Jane Edna Hunter: A Case Study of Black Leadership, 1905–1950* (Brooklyn: Carlton, 1992), chapter IV.

6. "Minutes of the Committee of the Women's Christian Association of Philadelphia," January 18, 1973: Annual Reports 1871–1907, and "Highlights of Southwest-Belmont YWCA," n.d., in Philadelphia YWCA Papers, Temple University, Urban Archives, Philadelphia, Pennsylvania.

7. Interview with Anne Garrott, Philadelphia, April 1988. Garrott attributes this story to information found among the papers of Maggie Marcel Griggin (no record of whereabouts). Also, according to "Highlights of Southwest-Belmont YWCA," in "1870, the independent efforts of a group of Negro women formed the Colored Women's Christian Association, with headquarters at 426 S. 16th Street." Official minutes of the Executive Committee of the Women's Christian Association, February 28, 1873 (Philadelphia YWCA Papers), report that the "subject of aiding the colored people was before the meeting and a note read from Mrs. Whaley (colored) asking that this Association should accept the work among their people as an auxiliary to the W.C.A." Mrs. Whaley was probably Caroline Still Wiley (Anderson), daughter of the famous abolitionist William Still. By 1870 Wiley, a graduate of the Ladies Course at Oberlin College and wife of a former classmate, the Rev. Edward Wiley, was a logical choice to lead the movement to secure services for black women. By virtue of her parentage, as well as her associations at the college, Wiley would have been a likely advocate for racial cooperation among women. It seems appropriate that the original group of women organizers might have chosen a woman of Wiley's status in the black community as their leader, especially to advance the idea among the black clergy. Also, through her family connections and as an Oberlin alumna, Wiley had important links with influential whites. Unfortunately, however, neither class similarity nor religious conviction moved the white women to welcome the black women to affiliate with the larger city organization. In spite of numerous appeals, Wiley failed to win their support.

8. "History of Colored Work: Chronological excerpts from reports of secretaries and workers and from minutes showing development of the work among colored women 1907–1920," compiled by Jane Olcott-Walters [for the YWCA National Board], November–December 1920, n.p., NBA. NBA means National Board Archives, YWCA of the U.S.A., New York, New York (hereafter cited as NBA). Olcott-Walters was a staff member of the National Board, and in this capacity is the author of reports and data compilations which are used throughout this essay. She was married sometime between 1918 and 1920. This accounts for the use of the name Olcott on some reports and the names Olcott-Walters on later materials.

9. Cynthia Neverdon-Morton, *Afro-American Women of the South and the Advancement of the Race, 1895–1925* (Knoxville: University of Tennessee Press, 1989), 52.

10. Ibid., 50.

11. "The Rostrum," Wilberforce University, Xenia, Ohio, 1920, NBA.

12. "Minutes of the National Board of the YWCA of the U.S.A.," December, 1907, NBA.

13. "Colored Work, 1907–1920: Preliminary City Work and Foundation of Student Work, 1907–1912," 10. A report prepared for the National Board, YWCA. Records of this period vary according to authors, departments, and so on. For example, in a document entitled "City Work Under A Regular Secretary and A Special Worker Intensive Student Work 1913–1915" (26, NBA), Addie Hunton is quoted as follows: "in 1907 when Miss Dodge first manifested her interest for the extension of Association work to colored women there were but fourteen student Associations. After six years there were 94 student Associations in 19 states." However, on page 29 of the same document, statistics from the report of the Commissioner on Education, 1912, list forty-three student associations, with three additional affiliations pending.

14. The absence of records and information on black association work in many cities makes it impossible to record accurately the names of cities where this work was undertaken. Charleston and Columbia, South Carolina, are mentioned in Jane Olcott, *The Work of Colored Women, 1919* (New York: Woman's Press, 1919). Both of these associations claim organization dates of 1907. However, neither association is consistently listed in National Board records or local association records.

15. "Growth of Southern Work" in "Early Policies Regarding Branches," Report to the National Board, November 19, 1940, Microfilm Reel 107, NBA.

16. Juliet O. Bell and Helen J. Wilkins, *Interracial Practices in Community Y.W.C.A's* (New York: Woman's Press, 1944), 2–10.

17. "Early Policies Regarding Branches (Southern Region), November 11, 1940," Report to the National Board, "Growth of Southern Work," Microfilm Reel 107, NBA.

18. Wilson, *Association Work*, 271.

19. "Colored Work 1907–1920: Preliminary City Work and Foundation of Student Work," Report prepared for the National Board, n.p., 4, NBA.

20. Paula Giddings, *When and Where I Enter: The Impact of Black Women on Race and Sex in America* (New York: William Morrow, 1984), 98.

21. Ibid., 7.

22. Minutes of the Meeting of the National Board, October 5, 1910, NBA.

23. Olcott-Walters, "Colored Work," 16.

24. Ibid., 19.

25. Addie W. Hunton, "Beginnings Among Colored Women," 1913, n.p., Microfilm reel 108, NBA.

26. Olcott-Walters, "Colored Work," 26.

27. Minutes of the National Board Sub-Committee on Colored Work, December 10, 1913, NBA.

28. "Growth of Southern Work." Nowhere do the minutes indicate that the central association must always be the white group, although the report states that "The Central Association may appoint a member of its Board of Directors

to be Chairman of the Colored Work." This was interpreted, in practice, to mean that the traditional white-black relationship should be maintained.

29. "Methods Of Combating Discrimination," National Board YWCA pamphlet, n.p., December 1954, 10.

30. 30. Bell and Wilkins, "Interracial Practices in Community YWCAs," 5.

31. "Forward" by Helen P. Wallace in Olcott, *The Work of Colored Women*, 4.

32. Report of the National Board to the National Convention, Los Angeles, 1915. *Reports of the Biennial Conventions, 1906–1915*, NBA.

33. "Report of the Committee on Colored Work," Microfilm Reel ⁻ ɔ8, NBA.

34. "Suggested By-Laws of the Branch for Colored Women," n.d., Microfilm Reel 107, NBA. The report stated that "Committees on Colored Work shall be composed of an equal number from the Central Board and the Branch for Colored Women. The Chairman of the CCW shall be a member of the Board of Directors, appointed annually by the President of the Association."

35. Olcott-Walters, "Colored Work," 17.

36. Report from Addie W. Hunton, April to May (1911), in Olcott-Walters, "Colored Work," 11–12. Report from Elizabeth Ross Haynes in Olcott-Walters, "Colored Work," 13.

37. Report of Addie Hunton, September 24, 1913, in "City Work," 26.

38. For an example of the accommodation by the National Board to local race policies, see Adrienne Jones, *Jane Edna Hunter*, chapter IV.

39. Olcott, *The Work of Colored Women*, 6–8.

40. Ibid., 13.

41. For a description of the YWCA's Hostess Houses see Nina Mjagkij, "Morals and Morale: The YWCA with Black Troops in World War I," Presented at the Southern Conference on Women's History, Spartanburg, South Carolina, June 10–11, 1988.

42. "Methods of Combating Discrimination," 10.

43. Lugenia Burns Hope, "Minutes of the Conference," n.d., n.p., NUC.

44. Ibid.

45. Jacqueline Anne Rouse, *Lugenia Burns Hope: Black Southern Reformer* (Athens: University of Georgia Press, 1989), 104.

46. "Minutes of the meeting held in offices of the South Atlantic Field Committee, Richmond, Virginia, July 3, 1920, to consider the administration of colored work," YWCA Folder, NUC.

47. Mary McCrorey to Lugenia Burns Hope, May 7, 1920, as cited in Rouse, *Lugenia Burns Hope*, 102.

Chapter Eight

To Be Separate or One
The Issue of Race in the History of the
Pittsburgh and Cleveland YWCAs, 1920–1946

Margaret Spratt

During the period immediately following the Civil War, small groups of white Christian women founded local YWCAs in a number of cities, including two rapidly growing northern industrial centers, Pittsburgh and Cleveland. Intent on aiding women less fortunate than themselves, women who because of family and financial situation were forced to provide their own support, these middle-class Christian missionaries envisioned an organization of women helping other women. They strove to provide a homelike environment that would, they hoped, counteract the cold, impersonal, and immoral city. The early YWCA women attempted to substitute for the traditional family home and Christian values boardinghouses and matrons, supervision of recreational activities, and mandatory religious services. As Sarah Heath discusses in her essay on working women and the Cincinnati YWCA in this volume, the working women who lived in the residences and attended the activities often resented this control over their behavior and sexuality and attempted, often successfully, to influence the policy and philosophy of the local and national associations. Class conflict emerged early in the associations. No doubt, the founders of the YWCA believed that they were extending their Christian charity to young women who, but for financial status, were very much like themselves. These migrants were the white daughters of America's farmers and small town merchants and laborers. That they might be the daughters and granddaughters of former slaves was only an afterthought as the middle-class white women raised funds and built residences to house young white women.

However, rapid industrial growth and the demand for cheap labor in America in the last decades of the nineteenth century guaranteed the rise of the urban population. Not sufficient in numbers, America's native-born daughters were soon joined by those from foreign lands in the factories and on the shop floors. The YWCA adjusted to these changes by offering English and other Americanization classes and by founding the International Institute movement, as discussed in Raymond Mohl's essay. At the same time that immigrants from southern and eastern Europe were streaming into America's cities, African Americans were leaving the rural South with the hope of finding work paying decent wages and freedom from racial hostility.

The YWCA, as a Christian organization, had espoused the mission of providing for the religious welfare and moral protection of young women adrift in the city. To ignore the needs of young African American women was, to the YWCA reformers, a failure to uphold their religious duty. Adrienne Jones has traced the beginnings of African American involvement in the national organization in her essay, showing both the confusion surrounding the founding of African American branches and the dissatisfaction of prominent African American female leaders with YWCA race policy. Whatever its shortcomings, the YWCA provided a forum for the two races to interact. It also acted as a training ground, allowing young African American women to learn leadership skills for future use as social service volunteers and paid workers. All college-educated women had a limited choice of occupations during the late nineteenth and early twentieth centuries. For female African Americans, professions were further restricted because of race as well as gender. YWCA city associations served two functions for educated African American women—as potential places for employment and as acceptable gathering places for young unmarried women enthused by their college YWCA experience.[1]

African American YW city associations began in Philadelphia in 1870, but the early groups struggled in their attempts to secure funding, adequate space, and community recognition. When the National Board of the YWCA was formed in 1906, four African American city associations were accepted as member associations—those located in Washington, D.C., Baltimore, Brooklyn, and New York City. Realizing that the continued migration and resultant housing and recreation needs of African American women in industrialized northern cities in the early decades of the twentieth century would create a problem for local associations, the National

Board of the YWCA called a meeting in Asheville, North Carolina, in 1907 to discuss its race policy. Essentially, the issue was how to placate the white women of southern associations who were afraid that they might be forced to share facilities with African American women at local and national meetings. This meeting did not result in a clear national policy, but in 1910 the National Board issued a statement that a "colored" association could be organized in a city and, if possible, should be a branch of the established white association. Where there was no white association (always referred to as the "central" association) an independent colored association could be established. However, the board stipulated that this was possible only in communities with strong financial support from African Americans and that the local association would affiliate directly with the National Board. Therefore, in cities with an existing central association, the establishment of an African American branch meant that white and African American women were at least nominally united in a common endeavor. However, from the outset, views regarding control of the colored branches, policy, and definitions of the relationship between central and branch differed among the YW members.[2]

This essay examines the struggle of two local associations of the YWCA—in Pittsburgh and Cleveland—to interpret national policy, community attitudes, and a constantly changing racial climate. The YWCA is a very complex organization, composed of varying constituencies with distinct agendas. Nowhere is this more evident than when discussing the organization's history of race relations. However, by studying the histories of two very different associations, we can begin to understand the varied and complex relationships between white and African American women and the place of the YWCA in their lives. Throughout the twentieth century, the YWCA attempted to reconcile its Christian mission of social justice with the realities of the race situation in all sections of the country. The national leadership strove to create an interracial organization that would allow African American and white women to work side by side in their efforts to improve the lives of all women.[3]

In order to analyze the success of race policy in local associations, a number of issues come to the surface. What was the relationship between central and branch organizations? Who provided the funding and leadership? What role did the YWCA play in the community? Who agitated for interracial cooperation and eventual integration, the national organization and/or the local community? Was the YWCA successful in creating an organization where African American and white women could join as sisters in their struggle for social justice?

The YWCA movement came to Pittsburgh as early as 1867, when local church women formed an organization for relief activities. By the 1890s, the city boasted of two separate YWCAs—the East Liberty and the Central Association. The older of the two, the East Liberty YWCA, bought a house that provided rooms for thirty white working women in 1892. The Central YWCA of Pittsburgh and Allegheny County, located downtown, formally organized the preceding year. Like the East Liberty YW, it originally limited its membership to white women. Over the next three decades, the Central YW extended its influence in the city to establish three branches—the International Institute in Oakland, the Lawrenceville branch, and the colored branch in the Hill District, first located on Wylie Avenue and then moved to Centre Avenue in 1924. In 1925, the East Liberty and Central YWCAs merged, forming the Young Women's Christian Association of Pittsburgh, also known as the Metropolitan Association.[4]

The membership of the Central YW decided to open a branch for African American women in the Hill District, a rapidly changing neighborhood which was often the first residential area for new migrants to the city, in response to a request by the National Board. By 1918, Pittsburgh, the center of a heavy manufacturing, steelmaking, and coal region, had attracted thousands of migrants, both European and native born. In the hope of securing steady employment and escaping Jim Crow terrorism, both black individuals and families left the rural South to make new homes in Pittsburgh. Between 1910 and 1920, 10,478 African American migrants moved to Pittsburgh, accounting for 87 percent of the total African American population growth during this period. The new migrants settled in enclaves throughout the city, as well as in surrounding mill towns such as McKeesport and Homestead. Although the Hill District, encompassing the city's Third and Fifth Wards, expanded its African American population throughout the late 1910s and 1920s, Pittsburgh had a relatively low level of segregation. As the historian Peter Gottlieb observed in his study of African American migration to Pittsburgh, "What the immigration of southern blacks brought about in Pittsburgh was not a single, continuous ghetto, but several neighborhoods where the number and percentages of black residences grew sharply." The one common denominator of the African American neighborhoods was inadequate housing. African Americans occupied the worst, most dilapidated structures. A National Board investigator sent to Pittsburgh in 1918 reported that "Poor housing conditions are universal, congestion is very great and the whole situation is critical."[5]

Figure 15. Centre Avenue building (African American branch) of the Pittsburgh YWCA, 1950s. Courtesy of the YWCA of Greater Pittsburgh.

Although employment in manufacturing was plentiful for African American males, albeit in mainly unskilled positions, this was not the case for African American females. From 1910 to 1930, African American women composed about 8 to 10 percent of Pittsburgh's female workforce. Nearly 90 percent of African American female workers were in domestic service. When Elizabeth Butler conducted her famous investigation of working women in 1907 as part of the Pittsburgh Survey, she failed to find a single African American woman working in manufacturing. In 1918, wartime labor shortages resulted in only a handful of African American women being employed by city department stores, and six African American women were hired by the Lockhart Iron and Steel Company. The house-to-house survey conducted in 1918 by Anna Cox Green, Industrial Secretary for Pittsburgh's Central YW, which queried approximately 500 young women, found a number of African American department store workers "who had proved far more satisfactory than white girls in similar positions." However, the great majority of women in Green's survey were domestic workers. Moreover, none of these department store workers kept their jobs after the war ended.[6]

Green's survey, which was sent to the National Board of the YWCA,

Figure 16. Central YWCA Building at 69 Chatham Street, Pittsburgh, 1909.
Photo courtesy of the Carnegie Library of Pittsburgh.

stressed the lack of acceptable recreational facilities for African American women workers. Responding to the survey, the National Board in April 1919 sent Nelsine C. Howard, an African American YWCA recreation worker, to Pittsburgh and instructed her to organize a YWCA center specifically for African American women. After much difficulty because of overcrowded conditions, Howard located a house on Wylie Avenue in the Hill District, and in late 1919 the fledgling group established a committee of management, chaired by Mrs. Sadie Black Hamilton, a "leading black club woman," with Nelsine Howard as the paid general secretary.[7]

Pittsburgh's African American community was experienced at organizing and raising funds for its social service institutions and organizations. By 1900 the African American population exceeded 20,000, a middle class was well established, and a number of community projects were underway. Foremost among the popular causes, the Home for Aged and Infirm Colored Women had been organized in 1880. A local paper viewed it as "an index of a growth of race pride." Numerous women's church groups raised money by holding an annual dinner and a fair, considered to be the charity event of the season. Pittsburgh's African American community also supported the Home for Colored Working Girls, "a place where women can find lodging at very reasonable rates, also those wishing to store their trunks can do so." This last accommodation was made, no doubt, for young women who found employment as live-in domestic servants.[8]

However, the impetus for the establishment of a YWCA branch in the Hill District did not originate from within the community, but rather from the national office in New York City. Following the guidelines established by the National Board in 1910 and reinforced at meetings held in Louisville in 1915 and 1920, the Central YWCA set up a Committee on Colored Work, chaired by Mrs. Samuel B. McCormick, wife of the chancellor of the University of Pittsburgh, to oversee the new branch. Although the branch had its own supervisory committee to manage operations, including a boarding facility since African American working women were not allowed to room at the Central or East Liberty YWCAs, no representative from that committee sat on either the Committee on Colored Work or the board of directors of the Central YWCA for the first few years of its existence. Perhaps because the African American community had no control over its own organization beyond its committee of management, a local newspaper reported that "The Central YWCA has kept its pledge and deserves applause; the race and the community have yet to demonstrate their attitude."[9]

The colored branch attracted young working women in the community who needed a room, as well as women of the African American middle class who desired a social outlet that their families and neighbors would condone. As Lucille Cuthbert, a graduate of Talladega College, former chair of the Centre Avenue Committee of Management, board member and vice president of the Pittsburgh YWCA, and member of the National Board for over twenty years, observed of her first encounter with the YW in Pittsburgh in 1926: "I had a Sunday school class [and] I said, 'Let's go down to the Y and have a club.'" Cuthbert had belonged to the YW while a student at Talladega and realized that because of its reputation as a Christian organization, the local YW was an acceptable place for her to go on Sundays. Besides, her father, a local Methodist minister, was acquainted with the minister father of the branch's executive secretary. Even so, Cuthbert's father visited the branch and reported to his daughter that "It's alright. You girls can go." Thus began Lucille Cuthbert's seventy-year commitment to the YWCA in Pittsburgh.[10]

When Lucille Cuthbert first became active in what was to be known as the Centre Avenue YWCA, no African American members had a vote on the Pittsburgh board. This lack of representation was "a source of dissatisfaction," and after intense lobbying on the part of African American church women and YW members, the situation was rectified by a vote of the Central YWCA board in 1927. However, only the chair of the branch committee of management was made a board member, thus maintaining white majority control. Most likely, local pressure as well as reminders from the national staff as to national race policy and YW philosophy influenced white board members. Nevertheless, this hard-won victory was at least partially a result of the persuasive abilities of African American club women in Pittsburgh, who no doubt had the support of others like themselves around the country. After all, just a few years before, the National Board had been forced to contend with women such as Lugenia Burns Hope and Margaret Murray Washington, who demanded equal representation. Membership on the local board, even if it consisted of only one woman, was the first step toward this goal.[11]

During the early years of the branch, relations between the African American and white women of the central association were very strained. As one of the early chairs of the committee of management observed: "The Centre Avenue branch, while it was considered a part of the Pittsburgh Association, was really an organization unto itself. On the board were some of the outstanding community leaders among the black women of this community." Official YWCA reports characterized the Centre Avenue Branch as being quite successful. One even stated that "The branch was a center for the Negro people of the entire city and much of the county." Activities at the Centre Avenue YW mirrored those at other associations—a room registry, a Girl Reserve club for teenagers, social activities, vocational classes, and an Industrial Girls Club. But because African American women were unable to break into industrial work until the World War II era, the Industrial Girls Club was composed solely of household workers throughout the 1920s and 1930s. Accordingly, Centre Avenue's employment bureau had only mixed success. As one historian of the Pittsburgh Metropolitan YWCA observed: "The girls from Centre Avenue felt the full brunt of the depression. Low pay, long hours, discrimination and the ever present formula 'last to be hired, first to be fired.'" A branch report in 1931 noted that 300 women applied through the YWCA employment service for three available jobs. The Centre Avenue YWCA consistently failed to secure employment for its African American membership outside the traditional occupation of domestic service.[12]

Historical evidence also highlights personnel conflicts within the branch. Cordella A. Winn, National Secretary for Colored Work—Cities, wrote in January 1929 that "Pittsburgh for so long has been an experimental point with wonderful possibilities for development and yet many problems to face. The early history [of the branch]," added Winn, "demonstrates that we need to have close touch with what is going on."[13]

When Lucille Cuthbert attended her first meeting of the Metropolitan Board as the chair of the committee of management of the Centre Avenue YWCA, not a single white woman in the room acknowledged her presence. Uncomfortable with being on an equal footing with their employers, members of the branch who worked as domestic servants often refused to attend citywide activities. But Cuthbert, as well as other Centre Avenue members, cajoled and persevered, attending annual meetings and social events open to the full membership. By the 1930s, the Centre Avenue Branch had made some progress toward achieving equal standing in the Metropolitan Association. Writing to National Secretary Eva Bowles in 1932, Esther Hawes, Pittsburgh's Metropolitan General Secretary, stated: "We feel now that our Centre Avenue Branch has exactly the same prestige as every other Branch. It makes its own budget and spends its own money after the budget is approved; chooses its own staff; has representation on each one of the sixteen city-wide committees; is included in all discussions and conferences that affect the work in the city in just the same way as is every other Branch." However, Hawes also admitted that the secretary of the Centre Avenue Branch was paid less than directors at the other branches and that other staff members were "not receiving what they should."[14]

Adequate financial support of the Centre Avenue Branch was a chronic problem throughout the depression years. Although it appears that the branch had a small but active core of community supporters, they were unable to attract the community funding necessary to make the branch self-supporting. According to a 1940 financial statement, the Centre Avenue Branch spent $22,080 but received only $6,233 in income. The difference came from a citywide campaign fund which was supported primarily by white donors. However, the Metropolitan Association was influenced by the African American women of Centre Avenue in a number of ways. During the 1930s, the public affairs committee of the Metropolitan Association launched a lengthy education campaign to inform and elicit support from members on the issue of federal antilynching legislation. Holding a series of programs, including one in 1937 entitled "Problems of Minority Groups," the local YW leadership sought to carry out national YWCA mandates at the local level. Both African American and white members sent letters and telegrams to elected officials lobbying for such legislation as the Costigan-Wagner Anti-Lynching Bill. No doubt, the presence of African American women in their association helped to remind white women of the philosophy of the organization and of their Christian responsibilities. White and African American women also met in separate and mixed groups to discuss how the Pittsburgh Association could become a truly interracial organization, desegregating their summer camp for girls in 1941 and launching an interracial program for African American and white women employees of the Westinghouse Corporation. In 1944 the Metropolitan Association reported that all citywide events were interracial, and that all program staff members were assigned to committees and activities without regard to race.[15]

The racial situation was very different in Cleveland, however. This industrial city's YWCA was founded only a year after Pittsburgh's, in 1868. Originally known as the Women's Christian Association, it combined with the city's Educational and Industrial Union to form what became known as the YWCA in 1893. Interested in providing a wholesome environment for working women, the association bought a house to use as a boarding facility in 1894 on the city's main thoroughfare, Euclid Avenue, and a few years later constructed a large (over 200 rooms), modern building for the central association. During the first two decades of the twentieth century, the Cleveland Association expanded its work in traveler's aid, established an Industrial Department primarily for factory workers, and opened a "rest cottage" for department store and industrial workers and a summer camp. However, it never established a branch for African American women similar to Pittsburgh's branch in the Hill District. The primary reason for this was a leader in the African American community named Jane Edna Hunter.[16]

When Hunter arrived in Cleveland from the rural South in 1905, she became part of a community which was undergoing a profound change in population, neighborhood composition, and racial attitudes. During most of the nineteenth century, Cleveland's citizens had enjoyed a relatively liberal atmosphere of racial cooperation and integration. The city's African American population scattered throughout its neighborhoods took an active role in the political, social, and economic life of Cleveland. However, as the African American population began to increase, particularly between 1910 and 1920, residential and employment patterns changed. During this decade, the African American population of Cleveland increased from 8,448 to 34,451 (308 percent), making up 4.3 percent of the city's total population. Whereas Cleveland's African American citizens had once lived in every ward of the city, after 1910 the majority resided in an area bounded by Euclid Avenue on the north and Woodland Avenue on the south. Employment patterns also shifted; traditional service sector jobs declined as an increasingly foreign-born population moved in, and unskilled jobs in the steel and manufacturing industries became the only opportunities left to African American men. As was the case in Pittsburgh, industrial expansion due to wartime demand in the late 1910s attracted thousands of southern African American migrants. They arrived in a city with inadequate housing, recreation facilities, and social services.[17]

The Cleveland YWCA, although involved in work with foreign-born laborers, did nothing to meet the needs of southern migrant African American women. Jane Edna Hunter's experience of being unable to room in the Central YWCA when she first arrived in 1905 was echoed by countless others in the following years. Realizing that the situation had not been ameliorated, she met with eight other women with similar experiences and pledged to open a home for African American working women in 1911. That meeting eventually resulted in the establishment of the Working Girls' Home Association, later to be known as the Phillis Wheatley Association, and the rise of Hunter as the city's foremost African American female leader.[18]

Hunter solicited financial aid for the association from the leaders and membership of the white YWCA; however, she believed in Booker T. Washington's philosophy of self-help and separation of the races. She intended that the Phillis Wheatley Association be a comprehensive institution for African American working women within a segregated community. Interestingly, Hunter's vision provoked much controversy, particularly among Cleveland's African American elite. Accustomed to an integrated educational system and business opportunities, many of the community's African American leaders felt that the YWCA should provide these services in an integrated fashion. In fact, the national leadership of the YWCA also wanted Hunter's Phillis Wheatley Association to be incorporated into the Cleveland YWCA. Just eighteen months after the Phillis Wheatley Home opened, National Secretary Eva Bowles predicted that it would become a branch of the city's central association by the summer of 1915.[19]

However, the Phillis Wheatley Association did *not* become a branch of the Cleveland YWCA. Despite the fact that a number of the white board members of the Phillis Wheatley Association, most of whom also sat on the board of the Cleveland YWCA, and the national leadership of the YWCA pushed for a merger, Hunter prevailed and avoided becoming part of the larger organization. According to Hunter, a merger "raised a very serious question as to the rights of colored women to exercise their membership in the Young Women's Christian Association." No doubt, the phenomenal success of the Phillis Wheatley Association gave Hunter confidence in her ability to attract and maintain white financial support for her project. The existence of an organization to meet the needs of young African American women also solved the peculiar dilemma faced by the central association of the Cleveland YWCA. As a result of the 1915 YWCA National Convention, the National Board began to emphasize the need for local associations to provide facilities and programs for African American women and "to develop black leadership." The existence and success of the Phillis Wheatley Association was continually cited by the Cleveland YW as the reason why it did not join in the national trend of establishing separate branches for an African American membership. However, the national leadership was not convinced by Cleveland's explanation, and as late as 1931, Eva Bowles continued to be concerned about the interracial situation in the city when she wrote, "the Y.W.C.A. of Cleveland has not been willing to face the inclusion organizationally and administratively of the Negro woman and girl of Cleveland. It has evaded its responsibility by placing at the disposal of

Miss Hunter all of the facilities necessary to build up an establishment that has been so successfully promoted by her and which could not have been done without the Y.W.C.A."[20]

Because of the untiring efforts of a group of African American reformers including Eva Bowles, the National Board of the YWCA became more and more concerned about its race policy during the 1930s and 1940s. It conducted numerous surveys, published reports, and, through its public affairs committee, sent materials on such issues as civil rights, segregated housing, employment patterns, and lynching to not only the African American branches, but the metropolitan associations as well. The Pittsburgh and Cleveland YWCAs participated in studies concerning the degree of interracial cooperation within the local associations. Unlike Pittsburgh, the Cleveland YWCA had very little to report. Through the years, several African American women had joined Industrial and Girl Reserve clubs of the Cleveland YWCA. However, these women were not allowed to use the central association's swimming pool. Use of the pool was often a measuring stick for the degree of integration in the organization. Bowing to pressure from the national leadership, the association board appointed a committee on race relations, and in 1944 the first African American woman was appointed to the board of the Cleveland YWCA. The white leadership explained that its new board member was not a representative of the African American population but would function in the same way as the other members.[21]

Instrumental to the progress of interracial work and integration of the YWCA was the *Interracial Charter*, passed at the Seventeenth National YWCA Convention in 1946, and the culmination of decades of work and negotiation spearheaded by a dedicated group of African American volunteer and staff members. The document articulated a philosophy that instructed members to "be alert to opportunities to demonstrate the richness of life inherent in an organization unhampered by artificial barriers, in which all members have full status and all persons equal honor and respect as the children of one Father." Among the charter's recommendations was one which suggested that a separate branch for African Americans was not always effective in "integrating those members into the main stream of Association life." When "community patterns" did not necessitate segregation, thus bowing to pressure from southern members, the report suggested eliminating the African American branch.[22]

Following this recommendation, the Pittsburgh YWCA eventually sold its Centre Avenue building in 1957, eliminating the African American branch. The Metropolitan Association of Pittsburgh reorganized, establishing new branches whose locations were based not on group constituencies but on the city's geography. The situation was very different in Cleveland, however. Because the city's central association had never established an African American branch, there was no need to eliminate one.[23]

The YWCAs of Cleveland and Pittsburgh approached the issue of race within their organizations very differently. The Pittsburgh YW, persuaded by the national leadership, made an attempt to meet the needs of new southern migrants and college-educated, middle-class black women by supporting a separate branch in a predominantly African American neighborhood. It essentially created a biracial organization, but through the gradual interaction of African Americans and whites and the influence of a progressive national staff, the local association attempted to create an interracial program in the 1940s and 1950s. Following the recommendations of the *Interracial Charter*, the Pittsburgh YWCA dissolved its African American branch. However, in its quest to become integrated, the Pittsburgh Association destroyed an important institution in the African American community and decreased leadership opportunities for African American women.

On the other hand, the Cleveland YWCA's encouragement of Jane Edna Hunter's venture not only relieved it of a responsibility but also eliminated the possibility of extensive interaction among various groups of white and African American women. By supporting the Phillis Wheatley Association as a parallel institution to the YWCA in the African American community, the Cleveland leadership conveniently avoided the sticky problem of race relations. At least until 1944, the Cleveland YWCA was neither a biracial nor an interracial organization, but rather a racially homogeneous group. It did not reflect the reality or experience of the female working population of the city. The Phillis Wheatley Association was dependent on the leadership of one woman, who, as time passed, was less and less able to meet the demands of a growing black population and increasingly complex community relationships. When the Cleveland YWCA contemplated interracial work in the 1940s, it had no base on which to build.

The Centre Avenue YWCA, as well as the Urban League, the YMCA, and the Irene Kaufmann Settlement House, were important social service institutions in the vital Hill District of Pittsburgh in the pre–urban renewal years. The YWCA served not only as a meeting place but also as a conduit for African American women to become race leaders and converse in the open forum of the YWCA. A commitment to interracial work required faith in the goodness of a Christian sisterhood, and although they experienced disappointments, the African American YW women of the Centre Avenue Branch viewed the demise of their separate association as a victory.

The Phillis Wheatley Association in Cleveland was also a fixture in the community and, for a time, a monument to the self-help philosophy of Booker T. Washington. Many African Americans viewed Hunter's ability to maintain autonomous control over her organization as a remarkable achievement. However, Hunter's refusal of YWCA help and organizational membership also deprived her and the Phillis Wheatley Association of professional training in social work techniques and management pioneered by the national YWCA staff. More important, complete separation of the races deprived both African American and white working-class and middle-class women of opportunities to learn about each other and to practice racial understanding, as espoused by the YWCA. For both associations, the passage of the *Interracial Charter* in 1946 would prove to be crucial in determining the future of African American–white relationships in the YWCA and the communities they served.

NOTES

The author extends her appreciation to the Louisville Institute for the Study of Protestantism and American Culture, the Faculty Development Council of the Pennsylvania State System of Higher Education, and California University of Pennsylvania for their research support. She also wishes to thank the archival staffs of the Sophia Smith Collection at Smith College and the Western Reserve Historical Society, Dr. Carolyn Schumacher and her staff at the Historical Society of Western Pennsylvania, Elizabeth Norris, archivist of the YWCA of the U.S.A., and finally, Henry Wyatt for his support and expertise.

1. Cynthia Neverdon-Morton, *Afro-American Women of the South and the Advancement of the Race, 1895–1925* (Knoxville: University of Tennessee Press, 1989), 52; Jane Olcott, *The Work of Colored Women* (New York: National Board of the YWCA, 1919), 10.

2. Mary Sims, *The Natural History of a Social Institution—the Young Women's Christian Association* (New York: The Woman's Press, 1936), 173–174; Anne Firor Scott, *Natural Allies: Women's Associations in American History* (Urbana: University of Illinois Press, 1991), 109; Addie W. Hunton, "Beginnings Among Colored Women," 1913, Records Files Collection, National YWCA Papers, Archives of the National Board, New York City (hereafter cited as National YWCA Papers); Records of Regular City and Student Work and

Work under Continuation Committee, 1920, National YWCA Papers, 85; Juliet O. Bell and Helen J. Wilkins, *Interracial Practices in Community Y.W.C.A.s* (New York: The Woman's Press, 1944), 2–10.

3. The term "interracial" was first adopted by Will Alexander and his group of southern white progressives when they organized the Commission on Interracial Cooperation (CIC) in 1919. Although the term is used occasionally in reports and speeches of the 1920s, "interracial" is used more frequently by the YWCA in the 1930s. By the 1940s, the YWCA's Race Relations Committee was renamed the Interracial Work Committee. Also, YWCA representatives attended meetings held by the Commission on Interracial Cooperation in the 1930s and 1940s. For more on the CIC, see John Egerton, *Speak Now Against the Day: The Generation Before the Civil Rights Movement in the South* (New York: Alfred A. Knopf, 1994); Minutes of CIC meetings are in the National YWCA Board Archives, New York, Records File Collection, Sophia Smith Collection at Smith College, Northampton, Massachusetts.

4. "History of the Pittsburgh Y.W.C.A.," n.p., Pittsburgh YWCA Papers, Historical Society of Western Pennsylvania, Pittsburgh, Pennsylvania (hereafter cited as HSWP).

5. Peter Gottlieb, *Making Their Own Way: Southern Blacks' Migration to Pittsburgh, 1916–1930* (Urbana: University of Illinois Press, 1987), 63–70; Olcott, *Work of Colored Women*, 95.

6. Gottlieb, *Making Their Own Way*, 104–110; John Bodnar, Roger Simon, and Michael P. Weber, *Lives of Their Own: Blacks, Italians, and Poles in Pittsburgh, 1900–1960* (Urbana: University of Illinois Press, 1982), 98–99; Maurine Greenwald, "Women and Class in Pittsburgh, 1850–1920," in *City at the Point: Essays on the Social History of Pittsburgh*, Samuel P. Hays, ed. (Pittsburgh: University of Pittsburgh Press, 1989), 40; Elizabeth Butler, *Women and the Trades: Pittsburgh, 1907–1908* (1909; rpt. Pittsburgh: University of Pittsburgh Press, 1984); A 1918 photo showing black and white women working side by side in the wrapping department of Horne's Department Store is in the collection of the National YWCA Papers; Olcott, *Work of Colored Women*, 96.

7. Olcott, *Work of Colored Women*, 96; "YWCA, Pittsburgh, Pennsylvania, 1875–1950," Local Association Records, National YWCA Papers.

8. Lawrence A. Glasco, "So Much With So Little So Early: Pittsburgh's Black Community Before the Great Migration," unpublished paper presented at the conference "The Pittsburgh Survey Reconsidered," held at the University of Pittsburgh on November 20–21, 1993, 10–11, 58–64; Glasco, "Blacks in Pittsburgh," in *A Legacy in Bricks and Mortar: African-American Landmarks in Allegheny County* (Pittsburgh: Pittsburgh History and Landmarks Foundation, 1995), 8–23.

9. "YWCA, Pittsburgh, Pennsylvania, 1875–1950," National YWCA Papers, 9–10; Glasco, "So Much With So Little So Early," 64.

10. "Working Together for Community," *Pittsburgh Post-Gazette*, September 19, 1968; Lucille Cuthbert, interview with author, August 7, 1992, Pittsburgh; a transcript of this interview can be found at HSWP.

11. "YWCA, Pittsburgh, Pennsylvania, 1875–1950," National YWCA Papers, 9–10. See Adrienne Jones' essay in this volume for a more extensive discussion of this controversy.

12. Cuthbert interview, August 11, 1992; "YWCA, Pittsburgh, Pennsylvania, 1875–1950," 10, 14–15; "Observations and Recommendations Regarding Industrial Work in Pittsburgh, PA after visit by Miss Lucy Carner, National Industrial Secretary," February 10–15, 1927, National YWCA Papers, 2; Letter from Esther M. Hawes to Eva D. Bowles, March 17, 1932, National YWCA Papers.

13. Letter from Cordella A. Winn to Rachel I. Taylor, January 10, 1929, Pittsburgh YWCA Papers, HSWP; telegram from Eva D. Bowles to Rachel I. Taylor, January 30, 1931, Pittsburgh YWCA Papers, HSWP; letter from Eva D. Bowles to Esther M. Hawes, January 30, 1931, Pittsburgh YWCA Papers, HSWP.

14. Letter from Esther M. Hawes to Eva D. Bowles, March 17, 1932, Pittsburgh YWCA Papers, HSWP.

15. Minutes of the Metropolitan Public Affairs Committee, April 21, 1937, Pittsburgh YWCA Papers, HSWP; Records of the National Public Affairs Committee, including a Report to the Presidents and General Secretaries of Local Associations and Chairmen of Interracial Committees on Lynching, January 25, 1934, National YWCA Papers; "Program of the 1940 Annual Meeting," Pittsburgh YWCA Papers, HSWP, 10–11; "Picture of Present Interracial Practices in the Pittsburgh Y.W.C.A.," September 1944, National YWCA Papers. The National Board of the YWCA joined with other women's organizations, such as the Association of Southern Women for the Prevention of Lynching (ASWPL), in an extensive lobbying attempt to convince Congress to pass federal antilynching legislation; see Jacquelyn Dowd Hall, *Revolt Against Chivalry: Jessie Daniel Ames and the Women's Campaign Against Lynching* (New York: Columbia University Press, 1979), for a detailed account of this effort. Limited correspondence between the ASWPL and the YWCA can be found in the YWCA National Board Archives, New York, Records File Collection, Sophia Smith Collection.

16. "The Y.W.C.A. in Cleveland," 8–9, Western Reserve Historical Society; "Cleveland, Ohio [Y.W.C.A.]," undated report in Cleveland Local Association Records, National YWCA Papers.

17. Adrienne Lash Jones, *Jane Edna Hunter: A Case Study of Black Leadership, 1910–1950* (New York: Carlson, 1990), 1–19; Kenneth Kusmer, *A Ghetto Takes Shape: Black Cleveland, 1870–1930* (Urbana: University of Illinois Press, 1978), 41, 70–73, 160.

18. Jones, *Jane Edna Hunter*, 39–58; Jane Edna Hunter, unpublished manuscript, Section VI, Jane Edna Hunter Papers, Western Reserve Historical Society, Cleveland, Ohio (hereafter cited as WRHS).

19. Letter from Mrs. Charles W. Chase, January 2, 1914, Cleveland Local Association Records, National YWCA Papers; letter from Miss Rathburn to Miss Kinney, August 29, 1914, National YWCA Papers; report of Eva Bowles,

February 20, 1915, National YWCA; Jones, *Jane Edna Hunter*, 36–39.

20. Jane Edna Hunter, unpublished manuscript, Section VI, Jane Edna Hunter Papers, WRHS; letter from Eva Bowles to Grace Mayette, May 2, 1931, Cleveland Local Association Records, National YWCA Papers.

21. Annual reports from Eva Bowles and her successors in the National Services Division were sent to all of the associations and branches during the 1930s and 1940s. Bowles also compiled a study of interracial practices in the YWCA in 1932. Pittsburgh YWCA Papers, HSWP; Executive Staff Minutes, October 9, 1942, December 9, 1942, March 11, 1943, March 10, 1944, May 12, 1944, June 9, 1944, August 22, 1944, and October 13, 1944; Metropolitan Public Affairs Committee Minutes, April 21, 1937, March 15, 1939, April 19, 1939, January 20, 1943, November 1, 1944; letter from Margaret G. Owen to Emily Hickman, November 2, 1944, Pittsburgh YWCA Papers, HSWP; "Seek to Understand Negro," *Y.W.C.A. News* (January 1930), 3, Cleveland YWCA Papers, WRHS.

22. Frances Williams, *Interracial Education as it Affects Negro and White Relationship from the Point of View of Administrative Groups* (New York: The Womans Press, 1941); Bell and Wilkins, *Interracial Practices*, 2–5; Dorothy Sabiston and Margaret Hiller, *Toward Better Race Relations*, (New York: The Womans Press, 1949), 179–187.

23. Centre Avenue Branch scrapbooks, covering events in the late 1940s and early 1950s, contain newspaper clippings from the *Pittsburgh Courier*, Pittsburgh YWCA Papers, HSWP; Jones, *Jane Edna Hunter*, 131–133.

Chapter Nine

"The Price of Integration"
The Story of the Charlotte YWCA
in the 1960s

Michelle Busby

On February 7, 1967, members of the Charlotte, North Carolina, Young Women's Christian Association came together for the dedication ceremony of their handsome Park Road facility, a new headquarters situated in a quiet, tree-lined suburban neighborhood southeast of the city. The ceremony marked the end of an unprecedented, $2 million building campaign which had begun in earnest at the beginning of the decade. The opening of the facility's doors that wintry day assumed historical importance for this local association. Black faces peppered the largely white audience as testimony to a recently integrated YWCA—what was optimistically touted as "the dawn of a new era."

The portrait is one of social promise, but on closer scrutiny, one discovers that the picture does not fit the frame. The racial integration of the Charlotte YW had entailed the merging of the all-white central association and the all-black Phyllis Wheatley branch, a process that had begun in 1960. The National YWCA, with its emphasis on social justice, strongly supported integration of its local associations, but the white membership in Charlotte gave up hallowed ground slowly. The issue of integration in Charlotte became intertwined with a major building campaign and was largely subsumed by it. Through their control of the campaign, white leaders determined the outcome of integration and effectively maintained their long-standing race and class prerogatives. They were able to do this by channeling campaign funds into one fairly elaborate facility that supported a building-centered program which catered to those women who had the means and the time to enjoy the recreational and social opportunities it provided. In addition, white women decided on the site of the new YWCA headquarters. The resulting locale was within a white, middle-class, suburban neighborhood bordering the Queens and Myers Park neighborhoods—Charlotte's most stately and affluent section of town.[1]

Integration of the Charlotte YWCA becomes even more problematic on consideration of the Phyllis Wheatley side of the equation. In contrast to the central association's penchant for class as well as racial exclusivity, the history of the former black branch is marked by class inclusivity. As part of the black women's club movement, branch organizations represented a "race-conscious mission" rather than a "mere imitation of White values"—to quote historian Paula Giddings. As a practical matter, black middle-class women needed to include their working-class sisters in their clubs and associations in order to have a membership large enough to influence the organization and the community. The leadership of the Wheatley branch in Charlotte demonstrated that desire throughout its organizational history.[2]

In short, racial integration within the Charlotte Association not only took place on an unlevel playing field, but also involved a clash of fundamental values between the white members of the central association and the black members of the Phyllis Wheatley branch. The disparate value systems held by supporters of the central and Phillis Wheatley branches, grounded on exclusivity and inclusivity, respectively, marked the historical development of each organization. The following is an examination of their parallel course of development and the inevitable difficulties members of the Charlotte Association faced when convergence of the two groups through racial integration formally took place.

By the turn of this century, Charlotte was well on its way to achieving the status of a New South city. Traveling through the South on a presidential tour, Theodore Roosevelt told a gathering of Charlotteans that "I rejoice in the symptoms of your abounding prosperity . . . here in a great center of cotton manufacture." Indeed, within a 100 mile radius there were 3 million spindles and 85,000 looms, representing $100 million in capital. To the great benefit of the city, manufacturers redirected profits toward commerce, real estate development, culture, and education.[3]

Industrialization had another side as well, one which cast a dark shadow over those who toiled for their daily bread. As a leading textile manufacturer, Charlotte drew men and women from the surrounding

Piedmont countryside into the textile economy. Many of these migrants were initially attracted by the prospect of cash earnings but soon found themselves engulfed by a seventy-hour work week of arduous labor under harsh conditions. Wages often lagged behind the new cost of living, and indebtedness to the "company store" made continued mill employment imperative. Employers preferred the cheap labor of young white female mill hands. These women garnered roughly 60 percent of men's wages, making them especially vulnerable to the vagaries of the cotton economy.[4]

Out of concern for these working women, members of the Charlotte Woman's Club organized a local YWCA in 1902. Club women sought to provide affordable housing, wholesome meals, and other "good influences" to women "from other sections" of town. The formation of the Charlotte Association thus took place along clearly demarcated lines. Affluent white club women determined and ministered to what they perceived as the needs of their working-class constituency. Moreover, the YWCA leadership reflected the predominant spirit of Charlotte, a prototype for the New South. Fully embracing the primacy of business over labor and evangelism over collective action, the YWCA leadership sought to ameliorate the effect of mill working conditions rather than directly challenge the underlying economic structure. Thus, Bible classes, noon prayer, literary courses, and recreational activities tended to mark the association's program during its early years.[5]

For financial support, the Charlotte Association relied on the men who owned and operated local businesses, not those who worked in them. Mill owners on the outskirts of town, who had already devised an elaborate patriarchal system to keep employees under control, welcomed YWCA activity "as instruments of accommodation to factory life." "Organized club . . . at request of the company" is a familiar comment appearing in the board of directors' minutes during the interwar period.[6]

Working-class women comprised only a part of Charlotte YW's constituency, however. In 1914, the association opened the doors of its newly constructed East Trade Street building in downtown Charlotte. Within a month, 1,100 new members joined the association, with a perceptible shift toward *middle-class* program activity. A needle work exchange, a young married women's chapter, and a day nursery for mothers' meetings reflected the new agenda. Along the same lines, the YWCA began a series of lectures in 1915 on law, banking, city government, nursing, and salesmanship. The Charlotte Association engaged in grooming young women from ostensibly middle-class backgrounds for white-collar jobs.[7]

By the end of the First World War, the Charlotte Association's lack of interest in working-class causes was evidenced by its failure to capitalize on wartime opportunities for working women. In 1918, only 1.4 percent of the nation's workforce remained unemployed, empowering the worker, if only temporarily. In this context, the YWCA rose in prominence throughout the war years. On the national level, the YWCA took this opportunity to press for industrial health and safety regulations for workers. In Charlotte, this emphasis took a different turn. Instead of focusing on working conditions in local factories and mills, the association adopted the slogan "Help Win the War by Keeping Strong and Well" and launched a $50,000 fundraising campaign in order to build a swimming pool. Later, the leadership responded to the Second World War in a similar fashion with the establishment of a health club program, "streamlined for streamlining" Charlotte women.[8]

Overriding loyalty to the business community, an emphasis on evangelism, and inaction in the face of wartime economic opportunities undermined any prospect this local YWCA may have had for cross-class cooperation. The Charlotte Association's concern for working-class women was limited to the latter's immediate welfare needs. Developed within a framework of *noblesse oblige*, this particular local YWCA agenda failed to resonate among working-class women. Instead, many working women turned to the labor unions that had established a foothold in the Piedmont region during the interwar period for political and social expression.[9]

A diminished working-class presence coincided with the incorporation of the Phyllis Wheatley branch for black Charlotteans around 1916. Impetus for a YWCA clearly came from the black community. Local institutions such as Biddle University, Good Samaritan Hospital, and a black Chamber of Commerce, as well as a plethora of churches, spoke to the activism of the community and its willingness to support a branch organization. Twelve women from a cross section of churches served on the original branch board of management. Married to prominent men, including two Biddle University presidents, two physicians, one bishop of the A. M. E. Zion Church, and one Episcopal priest—and presumably well educated themselves—these women represented Charlotte's black bourgeoisie.[10]

Middle-class women filled the leadership ranks at Phyllis Wheatley, but unlike their white counterparts, black women never enjoyed the resources that invariably led to sharp class divisions. They offered their personal resources—time and energy, education, and learned skills— which meant, in essence, themselves. Moreover, their small number left middle-class leaders no alternative but to work with a broad-based membership to ensure a viable community presence.[11]

Branch members relied on the central association for material resources, an aspect of the central–branch relationship that mirrored the city of Charlotte's own reputation for civil race relations. In particular, white community leaders demonstrated unusual generosity by their contributions to the material well-being of black Charlotteans. Bishop George W. Clinton, husband of one of the original members of the Phyllis Wheatley board of management, wrote in 1917 that Charlotte had more black homeowners per capita than any other southern city, thanks to "[t]he good white people ready to lend them a helping hand in their endeavor to acquire homes and other property."[12]

Physical structure has always assumed great importance in Charlotte, and the local YWCA endorsed that value, using it as a yardstick by which to measure organizational success. White women projected the value of a building-centered program on a receptive Phyllis Wheatley branch. "Brick and mortar" thus provided some common ground between the races while ameliorating one of the most tangible signs of segregation— inferior facilities within the black community. At the outset of its branch relationship, the central association raised enough funds to provide the Phyllis Wheatley branch with the down payment on a furnished building on South Brevard Street. Similarly, white leaders conducted several financial drives throughout the 1940s and 1950s for the building of a recreational room off the Brevard facility in 1944 and then for a new branch building on Davidson Street in 1955.[13]

For many white women in the Charlotte YWCA, such campaigns became synonymous with "interracial cooperation." This circumscribed definition of interracial cooperation not only satisfied the humanitarian impulses of the white membership, but also contributed to an atmosphere in which the central association viewed the Phyllis Wheatley branch as a service project rather than a junior partner. The white leadership continued in their earlier role of "ladies bountiful." Just as they had failed to address the economic inequities that characterized industrialization, white leaders left the racist structure of the YWCA unchallenged. Unlike their white working-class counterparts, however, black women tolerated their own role as beneficiaries. Given a lack of viable options, black women accepted ameliorative gestures—and the semblance of racial harmony ensued.

In contrast, the National YWCA had taken a more progressive stance on racial issues. During the 1920s, the National Association felt the influence of the Commission on Interracial Cooperation (CIC), brainchild of Will Alexander, southern social activist. Although many historians now regard the CIC as a conservative force, it nevertheless introduced the notion of interracial committees. Such committees were established in local YWCA chapters for the purpose of promoting a dialogue between central and branch members. By the 1940s the National Board had broadened its goals, protesting, for example, the poll tax and the failure of war industries to hire minorities. In 1946, at the Atlantic City Convention, an assemblage of local delegates unanimously passed the *Interracial Charter* and thus affirmed the ideal of a fellowship "without barriers of race." Before the convention's closing, delegates pledged themselves to "continue to pioneer in an interracial experience that shall be increasingly democratic and Christian."[14]

Assertive rhetoric and the adoption of the *Interracial Charter* have led some historians to conclude that the YWCA served as a catalyst for social change. The Charlotte Association, however, illustrates that progressive national policies did not necessarily penetrate at the local level, where they would have had the greatest impact. Indeed, Charlotte's Central Association established its all-white "interracial" committee not during the 1920s, but in 1942. Even then, the local interracial committee received scant attention within the written record until 1944, when it spearheaded a campaign for a "negro recreational center." The minutes of the central association's meetings were likewise silent on larger racial and interracial issues. One finds no mention of the poll tax, minority employment, or even the *Interracial Charter*.[15]

In the week following passage of the *Interracial Charter*, however, the white chairwoman of the interracial committee announced a new building campaign for a future—and segregated—Davidson Street branch building. One local member had already summed up central's aloofness to racial integration when she stated that "the best thinkers and social workers come from the [National] YWCA and *they* are doing the best work with the interracial problem."[16]

Although the white leadership of the Charlotte YWCA continued to address the most glaring discrepancies that existed between central and branch facilities, segregation fell far short of the fictitious "separate but equal" standard. The branch facility on Davidson Street, invariably referred to in the official record as a "new, modern building," developed a rash of maintenance problems within a short time. Throughout 1959 alone, maintenance reports refer to waterproofing the building, repairing broken steps, draining the back lot, repairing the furnace, and paving the parking lot "in order to provide out-door sports."[17]

The financial difficulties of the branch association are evident in the association's financial statements. Taking the 1958 fiscal year as an illustration, the central association generated a total income of $121,035, which was 333 percent higher than the Phyllis Wheatley branch's figure of $27,979. The gap between central and branch resources widens when one considers the membership rolls. The central association claimed a membership of 3,541 by 1958, but the Wheatley branch figure had climbed to 2,518. Similarly, the Y-Teen program at central counted 850 white teenagers, while the branch program contained 736 black teens.[18]

The discrepancy between central and branch annual incomes resulted in a mismatch of professional staff salaries as well. On average, the central association's executive director, teenage program director, and young adult director in 1958 earned salaries 130 percent higher than those of their black counterparts. Moreover, these same three directors at central were supported by five other professionals and six clerical employees, while the three Phyllis Wheatley directors were supported by a clerical staff of two.[19]

How did members of the Phyllis Wheatley branch respond to the inequities that inevitably marked a racially segregated association? Were black members merely on the receiving end of the central-branch relationship? Dr. Elizabeth Mills, a former branch executive director, would answer no. "[T]hrough all of my adult life," she reflected, "I have listened to women who had this extra sense of 'We can get through this; we don't have to underscore the hard part. We can just highlight the positive stuff here.' And that is what the [black] YWCA, I believe, did."[20]

Mills came of age in the YWCA during the postwar era, when the Wheatley branch underwent rapid expansion. Many Americans were poised for an active community life after two decades of depression and war, and the Phyllis Wheatley branch reflected that renewed spirit. Between 1949 and 1955, its adult membership quadrupled from 353 to 1,423 and almost doubled again during the next five years. By 1955, there was a Y-Teen program in every black school in Mecklenburg County; in some cases, there were several programs in one school. More important than numbers was the organization's apparent activism. One indication was attendance at board of management or annual meetings. In 1960, for example, 490 women attended branch meetings compared to central's 135. By 1961, central's attendance had jumped to 546, but Wheatley's attendance had likewise grown—to 666.[21]

Black women demonstrated keen interest in YWCA affairs in other areas as well. The Charlotte Association's affiliation with the National

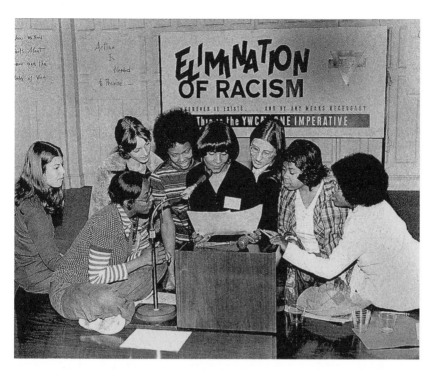

Figure 17. "Attention Is Needed" teen consultation, 1974. Courtesy of the YWCA of the U.S.A. National Board Archives.

YWCA entailed certain responsibilities, including the collection of dues that were designated in part for the World Fellowship Fund, which supported missionaries abroad. The association continually contributed far less in dues than its assigned quota, perhaps further indicating that it did not share National's priorities. The Wheatley branch, however, appears to have supported YW goals more ardently than its white counterpart, as evidenced by Y-Teen fundraising efforts throughout the 1950s and early 1960s. In 1961, black Y-Teens generated $1,410 for world fellowship in comparison to the $552 raised by white Y-Teens.[22]

Historian Anne Firor Scott contends that outstanding leaders were essential to the viability of organizations within segregated communities. Oral history accounts suggest that strong leadership ability propelled Charlotte's Phyllis Wheatley branch. Celesta Shropshire-Miller, whose affiliation with the YWCA began at an early age and continued throughout her term as a YWCA associate executive director, recounts that the attainment of leadership skills topped the Phyllis Wheatley agenda. Former Executive Director Marjorie Belton personified the able leadership that marked this organization's pride, according to the local branch history that refers to her and the women who followed in Belton's footsteps. At the helm from 1949 until 1957, Belton is credited with the expansion of the branch program following the Second World War. Her ability to motivate and recruit like-minded women to Phyllis Wheatley was perhaps her greatest contribution. Elizabeth Randolph, retired teacher and prominent community activist in Charlotte, attributes her first leadership position to Belton. Recruitment of volunteers was particularly heavy among school teachers, who in many cases were already Y-Teen advisors. Soon a leadership cadre made up largely of teachers emerged, which ran parallel to the rapid growth of the Y-Teen program.[23]

The leadership thus maintained its middle-class character during the postwar period, but from the available evidence, it was one that stood for inclusivity along class lines. By 1960, 2,518 women had joined the branch, and given the demographics, a substantial proportion of that number must have belonged to the black working class. Women were attracted not only to standard YWCA fare—dances, card tournaments, sewing and cooking classes—but also to the day nursery available to working mothers. What might have been deemed a middle-class program took on an added dimension with the participation of working-class women. For instance, in 1952 the Mecklenburg Kiwanis Club began sponsoring a sewing project at the branch. Over a six-year period, 1,047 women and girls received sewing certificates. "It is a thrill to know that because of this project," wrote the author of the institutional history, *Phyllis Wheatley Branch Y.W.C.A.*, "mothers can now utilize the scraps of materials from their dresses and make delightful clothes for their children. And several of our former students are now making extra money for their families by sewing for others."[24]

Because the branch leadership directed a large proportion of its organizational energy toward younger members, class differences may have been downplayed. By 1960, the majority of branch members were under the age of thirty-five; the reverse was true for the central association. Illustrative of what Giddings refers to as a "race conscious mission," Elizabeth Randolph remembers the Phyllis Wheatley branch as a place where black women "intent on seeing that black kids got everything that they could give them" came together.[25]

Former teenage director Christine Bowser recalls that the YW leadership and the advisors of Y-Teen clubs saw to it that the membership came from diverse backgrounds, producing "a kind of melting pot for kids no matter where they lived." Matilda Samuda, chairwoman of the board of management from 1959 to 1962, spoke of teachers and principals alike volunteering their time on Saturdays "as part of their weekly chore." Often the children encountered the same women the next day at Sunday school. Such interchangeable roles left its mark on the young people in the community. "You couldn't escape them," Mills laughed. "Once they caught hold of you, there was nowhere to go." Transcending material inequality, black leaders developed a program-centered organization that met the wants and needs of girls and women from varying backgrounds. Rather than a detriment, an inclusive membership proved to be an organizational asset. The viability of the Wheatley branch is evidenced by the expansion of its program up to the point of YWCA racial integration in 1966.[26]

In contrast, the central association developed a comparatively exclusive organization, serving middle-class interests that may only loosely be defined as "needs." Aside from the residency on East Trade Street that housed young working women, the association catered to housewives seeking a social outlet or the central's recreational facilities, which by the mid-1950s housed a professional masseuse. Most telling was a written comment by a national staff person making a study of the central association during this period: "Records are too inadequate to describe the ways by which the Charlotte YWCA has endeavored to keep pace with community needs."[27]

Clearly, the Phyllis Wheatley branch was not simply a watered-down version of the central association. The two had never been parallel organizations; indeed, they were on opposite courses. This had been no problem when branch and central were divided by racial segregation. Their differences would become increasingly problematic, however, as the YWCA entered the tumultuous 1960s, and integration replaced cooperation as an organizational goal.

By the end of the 1950s National YWCA pressure for integration had mounted, and local associations came to grapple with the means of achieving this end. Formal integration of the Charlotte YWCA, a step-by-step procedure, began in 1960 and culminated in 1966 with the merging of central and branch professional staffs. Integrative efforts coincided with the central association's ambitious $2 million building campaign, which quickly became the focus of integration. White leaders directed their energies toward erecting a handsome facility in a white, middle-class enclave on the southeast side of town. Black leaders, on the other hand, wanted an accessible, centrally located YWCA as a requisite for inclusivity and a sign of genuine integration.

White women had begun planning for what they considered a new *central* association headquarters during the mid-1950s. The elements for a successful campaign quickly fell into place. United Community Services, whose president and five other board members were husbands of YWCA board members, approved the central association's raising funds in excess of $1 million. The local board created a steering committee in 1959 with former YWCA Board President Mrs. James Harris, daughter of a former governor of North Carolina, Cameron Morrison, as chairwoman. Nine other women sat on the committee, joined by seven prominent men of Charlotte's business elite, including Thomas Belk and C. D. Spangler.[28]

As a first step, the steering committee recommended bringing in an experienced consultant from National YWCA headquarters to map out specific future development plans. Mildred Esgar arrived in Charlotte in February 1960 with much more in mind than simply a new facility for an all-white central association. As a member of the national staff, Esgar represented the progressive racial policy that had accumulated steam since the Second World War. During the postwar years, the YWCA had broadly supported civil rights activity on a federal level and had adopted its own *Interracial Charter*, but it was not until the 1955 convention that the National YWCA pressed for the accountability of its local associations. Meeting in New York, convention delegates adopted "Recommendations on Inclusiveness" which committed each local association to review its progress since the adoption of the *Interracial Charter* and to outline definite steps to be taken before the next convention in 1958. In a demonstration of leadership, the National Board increased its own black membership from 4 percent in 1946 to 10 percent by 1958.[29]

The minutes of the Charlotte Board of Directors's meetings are characteristically silent regarding the "Recommendations on Inclusiveness." The 1955 national convention coincided with the dedication of the new branch facility on Davidson Street, which the white women at central viewed as their own contribution toward improved race relations. Had they not received so much "manifestation of appreciation and gratitude from so many colored people?" Now it was time to build their own modern facility, white women in the YW reasoned. Therefore, by the time the 1958 convention rolled around, plans for an upcoming building campaign dominated the minutes of leadership meetings, not questions concerning racial inclusiveness.

Esgar, however, brought the issue of racial equality to the fore as she consulted with Wheatley leaders as well as white community leaders in and out of the YW. These consultations resulted in the *Esgar Report on*

YWCA Future Development of 1960, in which the author walked a fine line. As a national staff person, she represented the liberal racial policies the YWCA embraced. On the other hand, she had to be sensitive to the fact that the Charlotte Association accommodated southern community mores. "Because the National YWCA does not hand down a 'fixed' program," she wrote in her report, "there is much freedom for development in relation to needs and consequently the local manifestations of program vary in relation to existing conditions."[30]

Esgar went on, however, to express her concern that the Charlotte Association would follow the white southeasterly population growth away from the city, thus effectively cutting itself off from the minority population, which lived primarily in the downtown or northwest section of town. While acknowledging that women preferred to participate in nearby programs, Esgar nevertheless argued that "residential segregation is one of the characteristics of suburban life and that if the YWCA is to be true to its philosophy of 'inclusiveness' . . . it must provide opportunity for them to meet and communicate." Esgar therefore recommended a new downtown facility to replace the one at East Trade as "a symbol of the YWCA as a whole, a place where members may meet and discuss common problems and even conflict situations in a friendly atmosphere because of what the YWCA is." As a practical matter, she added, the downtown area drew the largest percentage of the 40,455 female employees in Mecklenburg County.[31]

In addition to broaching the issue of an integrated downtown YW, Esgar challenged the Charlotte Association's time-honored notion of a building-centered program. Pointing out that a decentralized program was already the general trend among other social service agencies in Charlotte, she suggested that the YWCA building program include two branch buildings as well as a downtown center. Based on population trends, Esgar recommended building Branch "A" to service the periphery between Providence and Albemarle Roads and Branch "B" to serve the wedge-shaped area between Rozzelle Ferry and Beattie's Ford Roads, the south and north sides of town, respectively.[32]

Esgar called for "slight additions" to the branch building on Davidson Street but recommended postponing any firm decision due to impending urban renewal. The Phyllis Wheatley branch building was near the Brooklyn section, where an estimated 80 percent of black-owned homes and businesses were located. Nevertheless, Charlotte's Redevelopment Plan designated Brooklyn a slum area and the first target of urban renewal. Since the Urban Renewal Commission had rezoned this area for commercial and light industry use, with no provision for new housing, Esgar deemed it an unlikely location for a future YWCA program.[33]

In redesigning the Charlotte YWCA building plan, Esgar addressed the pending issue of racial subordination within the branch structure. If the YWCA built a branch on the south side of Charlotte, by definition it would no longer be a racial entity, but rather an organization designed to serve a group of members living in a defined geographical area. In this federated system, each member would have an equal vote in electing a citywide board of directors, whose meeting place would be the centrally located downtown center. Because black women constituted a substantial proportion of the membership, they would not necessarily be excluded from the decision-making process or YWCA resources. At the same time, the plan allowed white women to carry on a traditionally middle-class program, and as such, they remained within their own comfort zone.

Thus, the Esgar Plan endorsed an inclusive downtown YWCA center that opened up the decision-making process to both white and black women but fell short of complete integration. The plan acknowledged de facto segregation and the integrity of a diverse membership. While this plan followed a racially segregated course, it was predicated on racial equality. The possibility of this new interracial equation undermined a long-standing relationship based on the subordination of black women, softened by white women's notions of *noblesse oblige*.

Esgar presented her report to a joint meeting of the Board of Directors' executive committee and two study committees, which tentatively approved her proposals in February 1960. Ten days later, the board agreed to send Esgar a letter of appreciation and a camera as a gift for her services. Nevertheless, over the following months, the white leadership effectively dismantled Esgar's building program. In the soft-spoken words of former board president Marjorie Speir, the board "did not try to keep up with her recommendations."[34]

Although the central association refused to implement the Esgar building plan, it could not and did not ignore what the consultant represented—pressure for integration. For the first time, someone had articulated directly to the Charlotte Association tangible steps toward desegregation as part of the larger YWCA purpose—not from national headquarters in New York or from a distant national convention, but in Charlotte. During this period of rapid social change, white leaders responded with the pragmatism of Charlotte's business elite, with whom they had enjoyed a strong historical connection. The leadership stepped up to dictate the terms of change before change was thrust on them.

Leaders took the first step in the summer of 1960, when the chairwoman of the food service committee recommended integrating the YWCA dining room. Citing the "Recommendations for Inclusiveness" adopted by the National YWCA in 1955, the committee resolved the following: "Realizing that the YWCA is a voluntary membership organization with a Christian Purpose, we recommend that the dining room be opened without restriction." Central leaders applied Christian purpose and an inclusive standard discriminately, however, and integration of the YWCA food service was a logical starting place. Church-affiliated integrated groups already dined at the YWCA, although they were served outside of the main dining room. Furthermore, the food service department had operated in the red for over a decade, and as recently as February 1959, the board had appointed a committee to study ways to overcome this deficit. By opening its dining room to all YWCA members, the white leadership addressed pressing financial concerns while demonstrating compliance with the national YWCA social policy.[35]

The board proceeded in an equally discriminate fashion in following Esgar's recommendations for integrated future development committees. For example, the board selected a black woman to serve on the building committee but not on the site committee. Moreover, the board president had the power of appointment, allowing her to select agreeable black women, or what former Board President Speir referred to as women with "a strong point of tension." Even then, committees were only partially integrated, typically by one branch representative. Later, in 1962, when the central association opened up positions on the board to black YW members, white leaders were able to monitor black representation in a similar fashion through white-controlled nominating committees.[36]

Despite having only nominal participation in future development plans, black members appear to have been encouraged by what must have seemed to be forward-looking change in the interracial relationship. Throughout 1960 and early 1961, the Esgar building plan was still officially in place and branch members had much to gain from this new spin on future development. Black women demonstrated their enthusiasm in a February 1961 membership drive, recruiting nearly three times more members than the white women, who even added male "associates" to their number.[37]

Nevertheless, the attention that white women on the future development committee paid to floor plans for a single building checked the optimism of some black women. Before 1960 came to a close, the board engaged the services of an architect and a designer with the YMCA

Building and Furnishings Service who charged what must have seemed an exorbitant sum to black leaders used to operating on a shoestring budget.[38] Elizabeth Mills articulated her own unease with the direction development plans were taking and wrote to the central association: "We must realize that buildings are liabilities unless they become places where determined people set into motion their dreams and ideals. The relationship between purpose and program must be clearly defined—so that program is an extension of purpose . . . not a busy scheduling of activities that politely avoids our real concerns about people."[39]

Mills's fear that white women would sacrifice program for brick and mortar was fully realized by the spring of 1961. Reporting to the board of directors, the building chairwoman estimated that the cost of the new building ($1,619,730), as well as projected campaign expenses ($500,000), would exceed the $2 million the YWCA hoped to raise in the upcoming capital accounts campaign. Refusing to scale back on the new YWCA center, the board agreed that plans for new branch buildings would have to be shelved. Revision of the Esgar Plan, wrote acting Board President Lebby Rogers, "was received quietly by Branch members but their cooperative, understanding attitude was typical of [the] YWCA relationship."[40]

Having decided on one elaborate building, the board was ready to hear from the site committee, which had recommended acquisition of the Bevis property on Park Road, three miles southeast of the downtown area. The men who served as advisors on the steering committee protested that while this locale was ideally suited for a branch facility, it was an inappropriate site for a YWCA center. Stating the obvious, W. B. McGuire argued that a center on Park Road would serve only the south, while leaving out the northern and eastern sections of the city. Responding to the concerns of its male associates, the site committee spent another year considering alternatives, including its current downtown location on East Trade Street. Anxious to leave East Trade behind, however, and citing the expense of other downtown properties, committee women found themselves once again eyeing a Park Road property—this time the Nathanson-Snook property, which was located even farther south than the Bevis property.[41]

Calling a special meeting of the board of directors in July 1962, the site committee chairwoman formally proposed the acquisition of the Nathanson-Snook property. At this point, three black women sat on the board, and the branch executive director served as an ex-officio, or advisory, member. Since the spring of 1961, when the board had voted to build a single new facility, the white and black women had reached an understanding that this new YWCA center would be fully integrated. Therefore, the four black board members responded with some alarm to the proposed acquisition of the Nathanson-Snook property on Park Road.[42]

Matilda Samuda was the first to speak, "discussing frankly the feelings of the Negro people who [had] come to her with questions about the new location." Black women considered Park Road too remote from most of the black members who lived downtown but were moving in increasing numbers to the northwest side of town as casualties of urban renewal. Another black board member fused the anger she felt regarding the destruction of inner-city neighborhoods with anger about the Charlotte Association's refusal to work fairly with black women. "It was the same old story," she protested, "of the Negro[es] being pushed out of their own areas to make room for progress, highways, developments by white leaders . . . with no representation from their own people to plead their cause."[43]

Board President Rogers wondered if black members would not be happier with the Davidson Street property or a location on the northwest side of town. However, the branch board of administration had already voted against remaining at the Davidson location in light of urban renewal. C. D. Spangler had donated property around Johnson C. Smith University, located just north of downtown, as a possible site for a black branch. But given the fact that white leaders had gravitated away from the Esgar Plan, black women feared that an all-black branch in an outlying area would doom further integration efforts and erode the small gains they had made toward racial equality. "[T]he real question the Negro members wished to have answered was not location but integration," said Branch Executive Director Christine Claytor.[44]

Samuda challenged the board to take a stand on integration, regardless of consequences, and in a conciliatory gesture, Rogers urged "mutual faith on the part of board members in each other." Given their minority status on the board and their lack of leverage, perhaps that was the best black women could hope for, or possibly they tacitly agreed to assimilation as opposed to genuine integration. At any rate, the motion to purchase property on Park Road passed unanimously.[45]

Once again, it was a male associate who protested a Park Road location for the YWCA center. Thomas Belk, who served as chairman of the YWCA capital accounts campaign, challenged Rogers at a meeting of the Social Planning Council to find a more central location—to invest the money in the "right spot." But this time the board overrode objections to a Park Road center, defending their decision in a follow-up report to the Social Planning Council. Revealing a propensity for an exclusive YWCA center, the report cited the most attractive features of a Park Road location, including the fact that "the largest portion of our [white] membership is in this Southeast quadrant" and the existence of "beautiful surroundings with no slum or low grade housing in the area." The board argued, rather weakly, that potentially 800–1,000 women would be employed in the surrounding area—1 to 2 percent of the female workforce in Mecklenburg County. In conclusion: "People have moved out from the heart of the city; why shouldn't the YWCA?"[46]

A male-dominated Downtown Charlotte Association articulated a response to that question in a resolution adopted at its December 1962 meeting. The downtown area would provide "optimum accessibility to all Charlotteans who use the services of the YWCA, no matter in which section of Charlotte they may reside," read the resolution. The Charlotte City Council expressed similar concerns, and Mayor Stanford Brookshire noted "an undercurrent of dissatisfaction with the decision [to build on Park Road]."[47]

The Downtown Charlotte Association's implied interest in black YWCA members was disingenuous. Its larger concern apparently stemmed from the fact that the city was failing to attract new businesses to the downtown area in the wake of urban renewal. "I'd like to see something go up when the area gets vacant" admitted one councilman to the Charlotte Observer. Another councilman lamented the fact that a trend toward the suburbs was detrimental to a vital downtown area.[48]

Regardless of their pecuniary motives, the negative response of Charlotte's business elite had some effect on white YWCA leaders. White women did not suddenly embrace the notion of a fully integrated YWCA, but board minutes during this period reveal that they felt increasingly marginalized as community leaders. As a result, board members turned to male community leaders for guidance and invited several prominent men to the YWCA during the spring of 1963 to discuss steps toward full integration of the Charlotte Association.[49]

In April, Dr. John Cunningham, chairman of the mayor's Community Relations Committee, spoke to the board, reminding his audience that "[i]ntegration is essential for any one who would give a Christian witness." As a key strategist for Charlotte's integrative approach, Cunningham laid out a blueprint that was remarkably familiar. First, he portrayed white women as "good samaritans" who could assist "[black] others in achieving dignity in the economic field, in education and politically." In a passage of his speech that underscored his own perception of racial inequality, Cunningham spoke to the responsibility that accompanied (civil) rights: "This we have not gotten across to the Negroes."[50]

Articulating the classist overtones in what historians increasingly refer to as the "first wave of integration," Cunningham depicted the white women of the YWCA as bearers of "middle-class values." By contrast, Cunningham relegated all black women, by virtue of their blackness, to the lower classes in need of guidance. The notion that blacks could learn middle-class values through their exposure to white institutions became the cornerstone of integrative policy.

Framed in such familiar terms, integration not only eased white fears but appears to have had a catalytic effect on the Charlotte Association. The year 1963 marked the revitalization of its community service program. Most notably, the program planning committee conducted a communitywide census to determine women's needs and how the YWCA might meet them. Out of this inquiry came a high school dropout prevention program stationed in the [black] Johnson C. Smith University area. And reminiscent of early-twentieth-century YWCA activity in textile mill villages and urban factory districts, the YW developed a modern extension program directed to predominantly black neighborhoods, in which clubs were formed by adults to stress family life, self-improvement, and community improvement.[51]

In this context, a divided Board of Directors voted for a centrally located, downtown center on Davidson Street. The board's decision reflected in part the changes in urban renewal plans. Rather than zoning the area for a light manufacturing and distribution center, the urban renewal commission decided to build a civic center, the board of education administration building, as well as the United Community Services building, in the former Brooklyn neighborhood. As part of the central business district, this rezoned area would contain an estimated 27 percent (45,000–50,000) of all metropolitan employees.[52]

Mildred Esgar returned to Charlotte in June 1963 at the request of the Charlotte Association and applauded the board's decision to renovate the Davidson Street building, setting aside approximately $300,000 for the purchase of adjacent property. In her 1963 report, however, Esgar revealed the "disappointment [of] some of the committee when the question was raised about the possibility of cutting back [for the Park Road facility] and reconsidering ways by which some program might be continued in the 'downtown' area." This disappointment of key committee members, reflected in the board's unusually divided stance, represented the competing priorities of building and program—and foreshadowed the eventual demise of a downtown center.[53]

On the surface, however, it appeared that the Esgar Plan was back on track. In addition to voting for a downtown center, the board appointed a committee to plan programs and services for a cross-class membership. This committee emphasized leadership development and special work with low-income groups, including basic literacy courses and job training at the Davidson Street site. For the Park Road location, given its swimming pool, gymnasium, exercise rooms, and tennis courts, the committee emphasized health and recreation. The committee predicted a membership of middle-aged housewives, as well as young, stay-at-home mothers who resided in the surrounding area.[54]

The "new" program failed to fulfill Mildred Esgar's vision of an integrated YWCA based on racial equality. The Charlotte Association program plan nearly replicated the basic unfairness that had persisted during segregation. The committee insisted that each program was "practically the same . . . with the exception of the Swimming Pool and Residence facilities." Rather than being notable exceptions, however, the swimming pool and residence not only consumed a disproportionate share of YWCA resources, but also served as symbols of racial and class division within the YW.[55]

Dubbed "the business girls' college dormitory," the central association residence housed employed white, middle-class young women. Board members were determined that these charges would relocate to Park Road, regardless of its residential surroundings. The swimming pool likewise represented one of the last vestiges of de jure segregation within the Charlotte Association. The notion of integrated swimming created particular anxiety among white members, who feared they might "catch something" from black swimmers. The board finally integrated the swimming pool in 1963, but only after the city integrated municipal pools.[56]

Indeed, the proposed YWCA program was more than a warmed-over version of the former central–branch program, marked by inequality. In a formally integrated structure, black women no longer served as stewards of a black organization. Instead, they were assimilated into the white power structure, one with privileged middle-class interests. Black women like Matilda Samuda realized the implications of this during a discussion of child care at a program planning committee meeting. The committee rejected a proposal to continue the Davidson Street nursery school for the children of working mothers. Conversely, the committee concluded that child care for Park Road participants was "absolutely necessary," prompting Samuda to pencil in question marks on her own copy of the meeting's agenda.[57]

The double standard that existed within the dual program plan quickly became a moot point, however. In the margins of another program planning committee memorandum, Samuda scribbled numbers that did not add up. At an October 1963 meeting, she told those present that "in thinking in terms of re-allocating the money we do not have enough to carry out the plans that we are considering for both sites." Samuda's declaration drew no response in the official record, but the inability of the Charlotte Association to build both a downtown center and a "branch" building on Park Road was soon evident. Rogers foreshadowed a reversal of YWCA development plans in her president's annual report. Speaking to an audience in January 1964, she stated that "[i]f the YWCA serves the total community, one building, no matter how large or expensively equipped, can contain the program."[58]

The resurrection of YWCA extension work—this time to a predominantly black constituency—represented a consolation prize for the dismantlement of the Esgar Plan. Rogers informed an apparently enthusiastic audience that the YWCA was now ready to begin building its headquarters on Park Road.

Following the January 1964 meeting, events surrounding YWCA development proceeded at a rapid pace. While the building committee directed its attention to the Park Road facility, the executive committee haggled with the Urban Redevelopment Commission regarding the Davidson Street site. The updated renewal plans dictated the acquisition of 6,954 square feet of this YW property in order to widen Second Street. After engaging an attorney, the YWCA ultimately received $7,850 from the commission. Dissatisfied with the deal they had struck, YWCA leaders later attributed their abandonment of a downtown center to the difficulties of working with the Urban Redevelopment Commission and thus obscured their own lack of commitment.[59]

Ultimately, the $300,000 the board set aside for the expansion of the Davidson Street facility proved to be inadequate. In March 1965, the First Baptist Church purchased the surrounding 8.5-acre site for $450,000. With no room to expand, the YWCA sold to First Baptist the former Phyllis Wheatley branch facility for $75,000 in December 1965. Having forfeited the option of a Davidson Street Center, the executive committee reconsidered the East Trade Street locale, but decided that it would need to be "completely rebuilt to become a downtown center that would attract a cross-sectional membership and not become identified as the center for the minority group in our population."[60]

The YWCA could not afford to renovate the East Trade facility any more than they could expand the Davidson Street site, given the paltry sum they had set aside for a downtown YW. Furthermore, by November 1966, they were $375,000 short for the building project on Park Road. Once again the YWCA leaders enlisted the help of the Charlotte business elite, many of whom sat on its advisory board. Businessmen recommended, and the board agreed to, borrowing against the money set aside for what was by then designated a downtown branch.[61]

In February 1967, the YWCA finally celebrated the dedication of the Park Road Center. Having emerged from the Park Road building campaign in debt and with the goodwill of community supporters largely expended, the YWCA returned to the task of creating a presence downtown. Members of the executive, finance, and campaign steering committees agreed in March to use the Trade Street property as collateral so that the YW could borrow $100,000 from its own reserve funds for a second building. The following year, Mrs. E. C. Giles, chairwoman of the center planning committee, surveyed the city to determine the logical site for a new building, asking questions such as: How accessible is the area? Is public and private transportation available? Does the area already have parks and recreational facilities? "By answering these questions," Giles told the *Charlotte Observer*, "[w]e concluded that the logical course of action was to build on the same site"—the East Trade Street location that white leaders had found unacceptable for their own use.[62]

In the face of Giles's positive spin and the board's enthusiasm, YWCA Executive Director Charlis Clarke frankly expressed the limitations of the proposed East Trade facility. "The property we have on East Trade Street isn't large enough, but it's the best we can do under the circumstances," Clarke told the *Observer*. "We're building every square inch with the amount of money we have. . . . It's just a program center, that's all."[63]

Partial renovation of the East Trade Street facility closed the chapter on the Charlotte YWCA's development plans, which had been first laid out at the beginning of the decade. Mildred Esgar's vision of a downtown center surrounded by neighborhood branches never materialized. Instead, the YWCA established its headquarters in a predominantly white, middle-class suburb on the opposite side of town from most former Wheatley members. Rather than serving as a symbol of integration, the remaining downtown facility on East Trade Street became a child development center, which is still in existence today.[64]

The Park Road program closely resembled its predecessor at East Trade, but following the formal integration of the YWCA, the Wheatley-style program faded into a distant memory. Middle-class black women assimilated into the YWCA, most visibly as professionals on staff, but the new YW structure inhibited the cross-class camaraderie that had marked the Phyllis Wheatley branch and touched the hearts of its most active participants. To its credit, the Charlotte Association has continued an extension program that benefits many black Charlotteans. Nevertheless, an "integrated program" generally targeted black women and children as recipients of social welfare work without promoting the agency of black women within a social service organization.

"Go over there [on Park Road] and see how many black folks you got working," mused Samuda nearly thirty years after integration. "It was just like bees at Phyllis Wheatley. . . . You don't find people as busy as bees on Saturdays today." Her observation is mirrored in the composition of the YWCA membership. In 1960, black women made up 41.6 percent of the total membership. In 1993, that figure had fallen to 14 percent. Reflecting similar dissatisfaction with the results of the so-called first wave of integration, Elizabeth Mills sadly concluded that blacks paid a tremendous price for integration. "And I do not think the product we got back was worth much of that giving up."[65]

NOTES

1. Anne Firor Scott, *Natural Allies: Women's Associations in American History* (Chicago: University of Illinois Press, 1991), 5. Scott has discovered that often a gulf existed between what the National Board thought the local units were doing and what they were actually doing.

2. Paula Giddings, *When and Where I Enter* (New York: Bantam Books, 1984), 99; Cynthia Neverdon-Morton, *Afro-American Women of the South and the Advancement of the Race, 1895–1925* (Knoxville: University of Tennessee Press, 1989), 7.

3. Mary Norton Kratt, *Charlotte: Spirit of the New South* (Winston-Salem: John F. Blair, Publisher, 1992), 135.

4. Jacquelyn Dowd Hall et al., *Like a Family* (Chapel Hill: University of North Carolina Press, 1987).

5. *The Charlotte Observer*, 12 May 1935; 28 February 1950; Marion Roydhouse, "Bridging Chasms: Community and the Southern YWCA," in *Visible Women: New Essays on American Activism*, eds. Nancy A. Hewitt and

Suzanne Lebsock (Chicago: University of Illinois Press, 1993), 282. Roydhouse argues that southern YW leaders made valiant efforts to "bridge the chasm" between middle- and working-class women. However, they faced great difficulties in promoting industrial reform. Leaders were often intimately linked to the mill principals. They were silenced by other means as well. The industrial secretary in Charlotte lost her job when she publicly supported a proposal to survey women's working conditions in North Carolina.

6. Hall, *Family*, 136; "The Charlotte YWCA: 1902–1960," Charlotte, North Carolina, YWCA in-house publication, author unknown.

7. *Observer*, 12 May 1935; "A Brief History [of the Charlotte YWCA]," Charlotte, North Carolina, YWCA in-house publication, author unknown. Roydhouse, "Bridging," 277. Roydhouse found that in the social and economic hierarchy of southern urban communities, white-collar workers moved more easily into the YWCA.

8. James Green, *The World of the Worker* (New York: Hill and Wang, 1980), 92; Mary S. Sims, *The YWCA: An Unfolding Purpose* (New York: National Board of the YWCA of the USA, 1950), 12–16; Mary Frederickson, "Citizens for Democracy: The Industrial Programs of the YWCA," in *Sisterhood and Solidarity*, eds. Joyce Kornbluh and Mary Frederickson (Philadelphia: Temple University Press, 1984), 78; "Charlotte YWCA, 1902–1960."

9. Frederickson, "Citizens."

10. Accounts regarding the origin of the Phyllis Wheatley branch vary somewhat. The *Observer* attributed the formation of the branch to the "good [white] women" of Charlotte; historian Glenda Gilmore writes that Mary McCrorey, wife of Biddle University President Henry McCrorey, presented plans for a branch to the YWCA Board in 1915; and "The History of the Phyllis Wheatley Branch of the Y.W.C.A.," an in-house publication, credits Mrs. Elizabeth Preston Allen, a black Sunday school teacher, with winning approval for a branch organization.

11. Scott, *Allies*, 14.

12. C. H. Watson, ed., *Colored Charlotte* (Charlotte: A. M. E. Zion Publishing, 1915), 12.

13. "The Charlotte YWCA, 1902–1960"; Mary Frederickson, "'Each One Is Dependent on the Other': Southern Churchwomen, Racial Reform, and the Process of Transformation, 1880–1940," in *Visible Women*, 308. Typically, white women possessed material resources that black women did not, and thus the latter were designated beneficiaries of those resources. Frederickson argues that black women guided white beneficence, and thus a symbiotic relationship, or mutual dependence, ensued. I have difficulty applying Frederickson's argument here or accepting her definition of mutual dependence.

14. Jacquelyn Dowd Hall, *Revolt Against Chivalry: Jessie Daniel Ames and the Women's Campaign Against Lynching* (New York: Columbia University Press, 1979), 62; Susan Lynn, *Progressive Women in Conservative Times* (New Brunswick, NJ: Rutgers University Press, 1992), 62; Gladys Calkins, "The Negro in the Young Women's Christian Association: A Study of the

Development of YWCA Interracial Policies and Practices in their Historical Setting," master's thesis, George Washington University (1960), 77–85.

15. Central Association Board of Directors Minutes, 11 March 1942; 8 March 1944; 13 March 1944.

16. Central Board Minutes, 20 May 1942 (italics added).

17. Finance and Property Committee Report: 18 March 1959; Central Board Minutes, 20 May 1959, Central Board Minutes, 16 September 1959.

18. "Esgar Report on Future Development," February 1960.

19. 1958–1959 Salaries Report.

20. Interview with Dr. Elizabeth Mills, 14 November 1992.

21. *The Carolina* (clipping), ca. 1955. The existence of dual Y-Teen programs was confirmed by a former teenage program director, Christine Bowser. Membership Report, 1960–1961.

22. World Fellowship Report, 1961.

23. Anne Firor Scott, "Most Invisible of All: Black Women's Voluntary Associations," *Journal of Southern History* LVI, 1 (February 1990): 5; interview with Celesta Shropshire-Miller, 10 November 1992; "History of Phyllis Wheatley"; interview with Elizabeth Randolph, 24 October 1992.

24. "History of Phyllis Wheatley."

25. "Esgar Report"; Elizabeth Randolph, 24 October 1992.

26. Interview with Christine Bowser, 1 December 1992; interview with Matilda Spears Samuda, 3 November 1992; Elizabeth Mills, 14 November 1992.

27. "Esgar Report."

28. Letter to YWCA Board President Mrs. E. L. Hicks from C. R. Harris, chairman of the United Community Services Capital Funds Board, 17 March 1959; Central Board Minutes, 18 November 1959.

29. Central Board Minutes, 18 November 1959; Lynn, *Progressive Women,* 9; Calkins, "The Negro in the YWCA," 99–101.

30. "Esgar Report."

31. Ibid.

32. Ibid.

33. Ibid.; Rev. DeGrandval Burke, ed., *The Brooklyn Story* (Charlotte: Afro-American Cultural and Service Center, 1978), 4.

34. "Esgar Report"; called meeting of the Board of Directors Minutes, 29 February 1960; interview with Marjorie Speir, 22 January 1994.

35. Central Board Minutes, 21 September 1960; 18 February 1959.

36. Marjorie Speir, 22 January 1994.

37. Central Board Minutes, 15 February 1961; 15 March 1961.

38. Ibid., 16 November 1960.

39. "Implications for the Charlotte Association," Elizabeth Mills, 14 December 1960.

40. Building Committee Minutes, 17 April 1961; 17 May 1961.

41. Central Board Minutes, 17 May 1961; called Board of Directors Meeting Minutes, 21 July 1961.

42. Called Meeting Minutes, 20 July 1962.

43. Ibid.

44. Ibid.

45. Ibid.

46. Minutes of the Study Committee of the Social Planning Council to study YWCA site, 2 August 1962; Report to Social Planning Council Sub-committee.

47. *Observer*, 29 December 1962.

48. Ibid., 1 January 1963.

49. Central Board Minutes, 20 February 1963.

50. Ibid., 17 April 1963.

51. Ibid., 18 September 1963; annual report of the local YWCA board president, 14 January 1964.

52. Report of Esgar's visit to the Charlotte YWCA, 25–29 June 1963.

53. Ibid.

54. Building Committee Minutes, 29 October 1963; Memorandum to Building Committee from the Program Planning Committee, 13 November 1963.

55. Building Committee Minutes, 29 October 1963.

56. Executive Committee Minutes, 17 July 1963; "A Brief History."

57. Program Planning Committee Memorandum to Building Committee, 13 November 1963.

58. Building Committee Minutes, 29 October 1963; annual report of the local board president, 14 January 1964.

59. Executive Committee Minutes, 20 October 1964.

60. *Charlotte News*, 23 December 1964; Executive Committee Minutes, 18 May 1965.

61. Called Meeting of Executive, Building, and Advisory Board Minutes, 21 November 1966.

62. Executive, Finance, and Campaign Steering Committee Minutes, 7 March 1967; *Observer*, 12 February 1969.

63. *Observer*, 3 November 1968.

64. Executive Committee Minutes, 9 January 1968.

65. Matilda Samuda, 3 November 1992; Membership Report, 1993; Elizabeth Mills, 14 November 1992.

Chapter Ten

From Character to Body Building
The YMCA and the Suburban Metropolis,
1950–1980

Clifford Putney

In the 1880s, Luther H. Gulick, an instructor at Springfield College, flag-ship school for the YMCA, coined the phrase "body, mind, spirit" to convey his belief that the association should adopt, as its purpose, the for-mation of "all-around Christian manhood."[1] All-around men, averred Gulick, possessed not merely souls demanding salvation; they also had bodies in need of development. In 1891, the YMCA responded to Gulick's ideas and adopted the inverted Red Triangle, symbolizing "body, mind, and spirit," as its official emblem. This marked the point at which physical recreation finally gained legitimacy within the half-century-old YMCA movement. Prior to Gulick, the association kept gymnastics subordinate to evangelism; after him, it viewed physical fitness, no less than religious con-viction, as productive of Christian character.[2]

The YMCA's desire to maintain a balance between athletics, educa-tion, and Christianity held strong throughout the early twentieth century. But in the years following World War II, the association's Red Triangle ideals were thoroughly reinterpreted, and athletics came to overshadow older aspects of YMCA programming. This shift in emphasis was caused by a number of factors, including the postwar suburbanization of America, demographic changes in the YMCA's membership, the secular-ization of the association, and America's increasing perception of physical fitness as an end in itself rather than a means of building char-acter. The YMCA's post–World War II retreat from character building was reflected in the association's cold war campaign for "World Citizenship" during the 1950s, its push for domestic reform in the 1960s, and its increasing involvement in the "personal wellness" movement of the 1970s and 1980s.

Two important factors responsible for weakening the YMCA's traditional emphasis on "all-around Christian manhood" were America's post–World War II suburban growth and the attendant baby boom. These phenomena not only led to YMCA expansion in the suburbs but also changed the association's demographic makeup, a fact most strikingly illustrated by the YMCA's increasing appeal to women. Women had won admittance to the YMCA in 1933, and by 1934 they constituted 5.9 percent of the association's membership. But it was not until the postwar period that female membership in the YMCA skyrocketed from 13.5 percent in 1950 to 21.9 percent in 1959.[3]

Women's attraction to the postwar YMCA had much to do with the fact that the new suburban associations were family-serving YMCAs. These family YMCAs, whose numbers increased from 17 in 1931 to 338 in 1956, included not only more women but also more married men and boys than traditional associations. As a result, the YMCA as a whole diversified its focus. Instead of catering exclusively to young single men, the YMCA's traditional constituency, the association began increasingly to adopt programs and services of relevance to families.[4]

Of special interest to the postwar YMCA was family survival in the nuclear age. The nation's rearmament program and the mobilization for the Korean War "raise perplexing problems for the young people of our country," explained the YMCA *National Council Bulletin* in 1951. Many youths, the association concluded, displayed feelings of "futility, that there is little use in planning for education, vocation or marriage, because of the uncertainties and risks of the future, [or] fatalism, that they are in the grip of forces beyond their control."[5]

Foremost among such menacing forces was the threat of worldwide communist domination. "The youth of today is disturbed," argued one YMCA official, "by a conflict of ideologies—the Communist world against the free world." The free world, for its part, promoted "justice, tranquility, the general welfare, the blessings of liberty." But communism threatened to destroy these boons, replacing liberty with "dictatorship," tranquility with "revolution," and justice with godless exploitation.[6] To fight communism and promote a democratic world order, many in the YMCA advocated producing "world citizens"—people who would represent "Americanism at its best."[7] Others suggested that the association

Figure 18. Following World War II, the YMCA launched a campaign for World Citizenship which transformed the association's traditional Christian character-building program into a cold war weapon in the fight against worldwide communist domination. This is a 1949 or 1950 meeting of the Sacramento YMCA. Annual meeting of the Sacramento (CA) YMCA. Reprinted with permission from the YMCA of the USA Archives, University of Minnesota Libraries.

might expand its presence on the overseas religious front, where foreigners allegedly were seeking "to purge their religion of the non-essentials and to revitalize its basic truths."[8]

But could the YMCA preach democracy and ecumenism overseas if these were not first implemented at home? William Overholt, an association spokesman writing in the *National Council Bulletin*, thought not. In particular, he believed "the disunity of the Christian churches of our time" to be "one of the major factors limiting [the acceptance of Christianity] as an alternative to the idolatries of the modern world." It was not so much the YMCA which Overholt held responsible for Christian division; rather, he blamed the Protestant churches. Years before the YMCA had come into being, he wrote, Christianity's "fragmentation and division continued apace, reaching a kind of ultimate frustration in the hundreds of sects and denominations in the United States."[9]

Overholt's implication that the moral high ground belonged not to the churches, but rather to more inclusive organizations like the YMCA, marked the beginning of a new era in YMCA–church relations. Whereas the association had once viewed itself as a conduit through which unaffiliated young men passed before joining "the church of their choice," many YMCA officials now felt that the pilgrimage need progress no further than the association itself, an agency far better equipped than the churches for promoting worldwide Christian unity. The YMCA's distancing itself from the churches was largely the result of its need to become reconciled to the growing religious diversity of its membership. Protestants may have remained in the majority, but by 1951 nearly two-fifths of the association was made up of Catholics and Jews. Such a large and growing number of non-Protestants convinced many that if the YMCA were to remain a religious institution, its Protestant Christianity would somehow have to be broadened until it became nonobjectionable to the preponderance of its membership.

Throughout the 1950s, numerous YMCA authors debated this issue. Some wished to know where the "C" was in YMCA, others what it meant, and still others whether it was possible for the association to be a Christian organization accepting of those with alternative religious faiths. One YMCA official concluded that the association ought to remain strictly Protestant, since otherwise it might "be diluted by its desire to serve young men of all confessions and faiths."[10] But the majority of YMCA officials believed that for the association to be religious, it need not support a particular creed.[11] In the end, all sides agreed that however they defined religion, theirs was certainly a religious era characterized by "a spiritual seeking and hunger." Indeed, noted the *National Council Bulletin* in 1954, "the heritage of our Christian faith becomes even more precious, and more Americans are turning to their churches for communion with God and the renewal of their religious faith."[12]

The 1950s revival of organized religion manifested itself in new church buildings and increased church membership. But some YMCA leaders wondered if this boom was fueled more by secular impulses than by religious ones. One student of the YMCA speculated that among rank-and-file association members, postwar religiosity was but a gloss. While the YMCA continued "to use the words and phrases of traditional Christian thought," he wrote, the association's objectives had become "predominately [sic] secular in nature."[13]

One likely contributor to the evanescence of the 1950s religious revival was what historian Gordon Dahl calls the postwar "leisure revolution." As job benefits increased and as the standard work week shortened from sixty hours in 1900 to forty hours in 1950, Americans' commitment to such traditional, self-denying values as the Protestant work ethic declined. This decline did not sit well with YMCA traditionalists, many of whom believed that "leisure was still something to be earned by work and to be spent in constructive activities."[14] The challenge, as these men saw it, was for the YMCA to take hold of people's "newfound leisure time" and to prevent it from being "squandered thoughtlessly."[15]

The YMCA's attempt to ensure that people spent their leisure hours constructively was no easy task. After all, most Americans had by 1950 "moved to a new moral equilibrium—an equilibrium which allowed more pleasure for less pain."[16] As a result, associations that had once labored to show how recreation *could* build character now had to demonstrate why it *should* do so. In particular, argued Dr. Ellis H. Champlin of the YMCA's Springfield College, the association needed to underscore the importance of recreation to democracy. Physical education, he explained, was the foundation of democracy because it encouraged "the practice of fair play, cooperation, courtesy and other wholesome and constructive relationships."[17]

But while Champlin took the highest aim of physical education to be "personal and social development in terms of all-round fitness to live the good life in our democracy," other YMCA men still preferred to laud fitness for its spiritual benefits. "When body physique, pleasure, stimulation of the mind and other aspects become an end in themselves," warned one minister, "the spiritual purpose of the YMCA is lost."[18]

Ensuring that YMCA gymnasia remained either "laboratories for democratic experience" or places for "developing Christian character" was not easy.[19] It took real effort to resist what recreation specialist E. O. Harbin called "uncivilized" and "woefully inadequate" leisure-time interests. To counteract such interests and to cut down on such "stereotyped, tinseled, and hollow activities" as "bridge, dancing, auto-riding, and the movies," Harbin had created the Church Recreation Movement (CRM) in 1935. He also did much to promote the use of nature study, bead and leather craft, skits, games, stunts, folk singing and folk dancing in the YMCA, which like the CRM tried to put excess leisure time to good use.[20]

By the mid-1950s, however, folk dancing and leather craft had failed as counterweights to Hollywood and Madison Avenue, whose emphasis on instant gratification convinced many in the YMCA that recreation could be prized for its own sake, not for its socially uplifting qualities. As a result, noted the YMCA in 1958, confusion over association goals was widespread. "[P]articipation and enrollment in programs of YMCA physical education have greatly increased over the last fifteen years," the association acknowledged. Yet, YMCA leaders admitted that 35 percent of those who used association facilities "indicated they didn't know, weren't sure, or didn't feel qualified to comment about the purpose of their YMCA."[21]

YMCA members' uncertainty concerning their association's overarching purpose intensified during the 1960s. Even the YMCA's postwar "world citizenship" ideal came into question as Khrushchev's notorious shoe-pounding tantrum in the United Nations, the Cuban missile crisis, and the country's growing involvement in Vietnam combined to convince many YMCA members that the world was a larger and scarier place than they had hitherto thought.

In addition to concerns about the viability of the YMCA's mission in a changing cold war world, the association faced new challenges as a result of domestic developments such as middle-class emigration to the suburbs and the disappearance of city-bound Protestant farm boys. Both of these developments gravely affected urban associations and helped to transform many inner-city YMCA residences into flophouses and same-sex trysting places. As a result, many in the YMCA concluded that the association had to put dreams for world unity on hold. With pockets of cities resembling "spreading sores which threaten to become killing cancers," it was time, wrote one association official, for the YMCA to realize that the "new frontier of American democracy is in the great cities of America."[22]

In its push to save democracy in the 1960s, the YMCA took on more than just urban poverty; it faced a whole phalanx of difficult social issues ranging from homosexuality to the need for more and better-paid female association employees. "We are living in a revolution," summed up a Boston judge, "and the YMCA is involved."[23] But while all agreed that social involvement was necessary, debates over the degree to which the YMCA should become involved caused a rift between the association's old-style liberals and its more radical visionaries. "Basically our boards have been Protestant, white, and Republican—sort of WASP nests," admitted Chicago YMCA Secretary Bruce Cole in 1966. "Basketball and swimming won't disappear from the 'Y' schedule," promised another association secretary, "but we won't ignore the social questions. God, it's late enough but we're really moving now."[24]

An early casualty in the rush to make the YMCA more relevant was that longtime association staple, character building. Already eclipsed by the 1950s' World Citizenship campaign, character building finally succumbed to the 1960s' penchant for placing society's health above personal morality. As one YMCA reformer put it, action had now passed from "the home or street corner gang or the Y gym" to "city hall, the welfare office, or precinct station," leaving the association's new breed of employees hostile "to the seemingly stagnant and irrelevant activities which pass as program in too many YMCAs."[25]

Scarcely less imperilled than character building was that other YMCA fixture, Christianity. According to a 1966 *Newsweek* article, "local officers now generously admit Jews and even atheists," with only "a wink at the traditional pledge of Christian faith."[26] A few YMCA leaders opposed secularization, arguing that the very word "Christian" "has been so broadly interpreted by our Associations that it now means anyone of good will."[27] But most association secretaries eschewed religious exclusivity, and in 1966 800 of them called for a new definition of Jesus.[28] Jesus, the secretaries proclaimed, "was not popular with the ruling class in government and religion." Instead he was a "rebel," a figure to be respected, not for his divine parentage, but for the intensity of his social commitment.[29]

A 1969 study of the YMCA's Camp Becket in the Berkshires found that "in membership, in ritual, and in symbolism [the camp] was largely non-Protestant and even non-Christian—linked to the broader Protestant tradition only by the concept of man's duty to build the kingdom of heaven here on earth." The muscular, blue-eyed, character-building Jesus who had once played such a large role in the camp's religious life was gone, and nothing, not even Jesus the "rebel," had arrived to take his place. The old "Chumship Service," wherein boys had taken Jesus to be their personal chum, had also vanished. In its place was an evening candlelight service, at the height of which boys rose to pledge their commitment to building a just society.[30]

To achieve this just society, the YMCA advocated an "extension of civil rights."[31] Some association leaders had first taken an interest in racial justice in the early twentieth century. It was, however, not until 1946 that the desegregation of association facilities became a YMCA goal. Twenty-one years later, the YMCA's National Board voted, 294 to 11, to require its member associations to certify annually that their programs operated "without any discrimination on the basis of race, color or national origin."[32]

As the YMCA's attitude concerning segregated facilities changed, so did its perspective on the individual's place in society. Traditionally, the association had maintained that the young man who worked hard would enjoy endless opportunities. But by the 1960s, many in the association had concluded that it was not the individual but society which had to prove itself worthy. As one YMCA official put it, having "reached the level of civilization in this country at which we are unwilling to let people starve," it was time to "move up the scale a step or two to that level at which we are unwilling to let people fail to achieve decent self realization."[33]

When association leaders started to view individual happiness as a byproduct of social justice, the campaign to make society capable of fulfilling individual needs took on added urgency. As a result, President Johnson's "War on Poverty" enjoyed considerable support in the YMCA, which worked hard to improve the lives of the poor and physically handicapped. In the process, observed one historian, "the YMCA might well have achieved its finest hour."[34]

Social activism required money, however, and in the process of procuring funds, the YMCA violated long-standing tradition by going beyond its members to seek government grants. "There have always been camperships for boys who could not pay, free membership and clubs and even YMCA branches for children, teenagers and adults in neighborhoods where residents can pay only token membership fees," explained YMCA National Board President Wilbur M. McFeely in 1968. "But now the need is so great, the problems of our inner cities so critical and the costs of remedying them so high, that no independent, voluntary agency can 'go it alone' and do effective work."[35]

McFeely's decision to seek government aid was a revolutionary step for the YMCA. But there were other, equally significant departures from tradition in the 1960s, including a decision by youth recruiters to relax customary restrictions against smoking, drinking, and profanity.[36] As for the association's long-standing reticence with regard to political matters, the National Council urged that it be set aside. "[I]n order to relate maximally to the human disruptions of our time," association leaders explained, the YMCA had to "be prepared to share in the development of public opinion and policy by taking positions on the issues that have deep bearing on the lives of persons."[37]

That the Council meant what it said is clear from its 1971 repudiation of the war in Vietnam. But such stands, while courageous, often engendered intense controversy that reflected significant disagreement within the YMCA as to where the Great Society should be heading. "Our present programs no longer seem to function adequately in terms of societal needs," conceded one YMCA official, "and are under attack from young and old, radical and conservative members and citizens."[38]

Especially discouraging to YMCA reformers was the fact that association efforts on behalf of the young and disadvantaged were gaining so little approbation. In the past, the YMCA had considered itself a social problem solver; now people were calling it "part of the problem." In Westfield, New Jersey, for example, a black awareness group heavily criticized its local YMCA sponsor. According to the group, the association not only withheld scholarship money from African Americans, it also designed its programs with the intention of excluding minorities. The YMCA, one group spokesperson proclaimed, "has 'white' written all over it."[39]

Some linked the YMCA's social failures, together with the acrimony they engendered, to a breakdown in moral values among America's youth. Designating this perceived breakdown "the fraudulent new morality," one YMCA youth leader blasted young people's modern-day "lack of self-control" and "lack of self-discipline."[40] More conciliatory was the National Board's handling of a fiery anti–law-and-order resolution proposed by youth delegates in 1968. Although the Board rejected the resolution, it did agree to a compromise which, while not calling incarceration itself unjust, did at least concede that "law and order is too often a manifestation of racism." After the compromise, there was a debate among delegates over "the rigidity of the Board's agenda" which "left each age group somewhat baffled."[41]

No matter how "baffling" the 1960s generation gap, YMCA leaders maintained that though "differences are real . . . a new generation can learn to live together and accept each other truly."[42] Thus, association leader James Stooke vehemently disagreed when he heard people saying that the YMCA's youth group "Hi-Y is dead!"—that it was irrelevant to contemporary teenagers and that its programs no longer worked. "The position of our YMCA branch laymen, staff, and this paper is that Hi-Y is not dead, nor absent, nor silent," he explained. "Instead it is a program with as much dynamic potential in today's complex teenage society as it had with its Chapman, Kansas, beginning in 1889."[43]

As it turned out, Stooke was largely wrong. For one thing, Hi-Y, whose name was unfortunately reminiscent of pot smoking, did in fact die out everywhere but the Midwest. More importantly, events seemed to gainsay Stooke's pledge of frictionless intergenerational relations. At the YMCA's 1969 convention, for example, "militant" students, "disenchanted with the prospect of a Saturday spent in what they regarded as fun and frolic when it could be devoted to 'serious' topics," attempted forcibly to effect a program change and had to be turned back by guards and "a squad of hard-nosed riot police."[44]

Considering the 1960s' race and generational tensions, it is little wonder that YMCA physical education programs remained outside the limelight. Except for the early 1960s, when YMCA leaders expressed concerns regarding young America's "softness" vis-à-vis Soviet children, the association focused not on hard-core athletics but instead on comparatively "relevant" programs such as "interracial, intercultural day camp" and "coed high school camp for the disadvantaged." Some association leaders found this plethora of new programs confusing, and one man joked about how hard it had become to do basic exercise at the YMCA. Simply getting into the gym, he quipped, required first turning down dancing lessons, cooking classes, language instruction, and a host of other nonathletic programs.[45]

YMCA directors may never have actually discouraged people from exercising in the 1960s, but it is likely that they considered athletics less central than formerly to the association's overall purpose. This view was confirmed in a 1971 YMCA survey of "19 Noted Americans." The association deserved praise, the notables agreed, for having become "more active in major societal frontiers." Yet, the majority of those surveyed "felt a disproportionate amount of YMCA resources is still being invested in recreational activities for middle-class members." As a result, they urged the YMCA to "quit being what it has been and devote its resources to major community and societal problems," thereby becoming an organization "that is relevant to the major changes and social issues of our time."[46]

Social activism in the YMCA crested in 1972, when the National Board proposed dropping the association's foundational 1855 pledge to convert young men to evangelical Christianity. "Changing conditions of the world and changing language have given rise in recent years to the feeling that the time had come to reconsider this statement," the Board explained. Particularly objectionable in the eyes of American association leaders was the narrowness of the evangelical pledge. Christianity and the conversion of young men, the Board maintained, were no longer the association's chief concerns. Instead, the YMCA stressed inclusivity and social reform. As a result, the Board advocated adopting a new covenant, which promised "to welcome into its fellowship and service men and women of all ages, of all races, of all nations, and of all religious points of view," and "to strive for societies founded upon social justice, peace, and the recognition of the dignity, freedom, and equal worth of all persons."[47]

In addition to readjusting the association's overall vision, the Board proposed a "5-year plan" calling for the implementation of various

Great Society programs. In particular, the plan called for eliminating "personal and institutional racism; changing the conditions that foster alienation, delinquency, and crime; reducing health problems by strengthening physical and mental health; strengthening family structures; and joining people from other countries in building international understanding and world peace."[48] These were all admirable aims, but the association's inability to realize them in the 1970s signaled that the 5-year plan was not the beginning but the end of an era.

The American association's 5-year plan encountered its first setback in 1973. That year the World YMCA meeting in Uganda soundly defeated the National Board's alternative to the evangelical pledge. Concerned that rejecting the pledge would be tantamount to abandoning Christ, the world association expressed its wish "to retain the Christian identity and purpose of this world movement."[49] Another setback to the 5-year plan, YMCA leaders complained, resulted from flagging moral energies. Americans "are in a less buoyant mood than Americans are popularly supposed to be in," explained association leader Elise Brett, "because of the Vietnam War, the ghetto problem, violence used as a means of civic or political protest, crime in the streets and the assassinations of the Kennedys and Martin Luther King."[50] Such troubles struck Brett as reasons to redouble attempts at social reform, but other YMCA leaders appeared tired of endlessly being asked to give of themselves while never being congratulated for their efforts. Many also tacitly acknowledged that post-1960s America was entering a new era of emotional and material limits.[51]

A 1973 *YMCA Today* article written by evangelist Billy Graham reflected the association's declining faith in Great Society liberalism. Graham conceded "that there are many problems facing America today: the Middle East war; fuel shortages; inflation; balance of payments; disillusionment in government," but he concluded that "the main problem—and I know this sounds simplistic, but it's true—the main problem is in the hearts of men." Those who insisted "that the fulfillment of the Gospel message is exclusively to be found in the act of physically binding up a sick world" were wrong, Graham asserted, since healing came not only through social justice but also through an acceptance of Christ.[52]

Graham's plea for Christian renewal in the YMCA brought mixed results. It did not end the association's commitment to ecumenicalism and religious diversity, but it did incline some YMCA leaders to view events such as Watergate as evidence that the nation's moral worth resided not in government but rather in the hearts of its citizens. As a result, the YMCA's perception of itself and its role in society changed. In 1970, for example,

Figure 19. Manly Christian character building appears to have yielded to relaxed coeducational camaraderie. Instead of developing masculine bodies capable of strenuous reform, a hirsute camp counsellor plays for the weenie-roasting day campers on his guitar. Minneapolis YMCA (Southdale Branch) day camp, 1972. Reprinted with permission from YMCA of the USA Archives, University of Minnesota Libraries.

YMCA leaders had praised the Great Society while chastising themselves for failing to live up to its precepts. By 1980, in contrast, association leaders were judging the Great Society bankrupt while finding solace in their own moral integrity. "In an era of chaos, confusion and pessimism," summed up a 1979 publication, "the Y is still to be trusted."[53]

Another factor contributing to the YMCA's embattled image of itself during the 1970s was the eclipse of its erstwhile allies, the mainline Protestant churches. Communitarian in an age of privatism, unable supposedly to distinguish the topical from the eternal, and in general suffering from what Robert Bellah calls "quasi-therapeutic blandness," the mainline churches were in dire straits.[54] Since the 1960s, the churches' impact on society had been receding, both in numerical terms and in terms of cultural influence. Moreover, as one YMCA official pointed out, the "religious scene in America today is confusing if not chaotic. While mainline churches struggle to keep deficits down and membership up fringe groups are booming."[55]

But it was not only churches; families, too, were in trouble. Indeed, noted one YMCA publication, at a time when "the church is facing lessened influence; family life is openly ridiculed in the mass media; [and] education has abandoned character building . . . the Y may be the only values-oriented, human care organization serving all religions, races, ages, and communities which is still strong enough to make a difference."[56]

The YMCA's attempt to satisfy all segments of society had its drawbacks, especially when association leaders tried to instill in people very definite notions of right and wrong. Maintaining values such as "basic beliefs about what is good or what ought to be," YMCA leaders insisted, was essential and the very fact that there appeared to be such a dearth of them made the association's task even more imperative.[57] As a result, an article in *YMCA Today* noted that a "recent accent on values has developed in response to the turmoil in America in the last few years. Corruption in every layer of government, increasing crime in the streets—and elsewhere, drug addiction among school youths, the whole horde of all-too-familiar modern problems has raised community to the immediacy of front page news."[58]

Hoping to preserve values, the YMCA moved to strengthen the individual conscience and the family. For this purpose, the association established the National YMCA Family Communications Skills Center in Palo Alto, California, in 1970 and the National YMCA Values Education Center in Akron, Ohio, in 1974. Both institutions were entrusted with disseminating values by means of then-current models of "values clarification."

Although somewhat reminiscent of the YMCA's old character-building days, values clarification differed profoundly from the association's past goal. Whereas the character builders knew what kind of product they wished to turn out, values clarificationists did not consciously attempt to impose their values on others. Values clarificationists, while acknowledging the importance of values, refused to label one set of values better than another. "*[T]here are no right or wrong answers,*" explained a YMCA clarificationist, because you "are dealing with feelings, opinions and personal concerns. Whatever the individual wants to share is appropriate for him. Whatever he says is 'real.'"[59]

While cultivating respect for individual values remained an important YMCA goal throughout the 1970s and 1980s, the association spent much of its material wealth on fulfilling bodily needs. Although seemingly unrelated, the YMCA's push toward fitness and its fixation on values were linked. Both catered to the individual—values clarificationists ensuring that individuals felt good about where they stood on things and physical therapists seeing to it that they simply felt good. Moreover, the YMCA's growing interest in fitness and values clarification reflected the association's retreat from the idea that the individual's well-being is dependent on the well-being of society.

Although not everyone in the YMCA lost the taste for social reform, the association's reforming spirit was definitely on the wane by 1975. That year a key speaker at a conference of YMCA physical education directors observed that during the 1960s "we were inundated by a tremendous amount of stuff—a lot of challenge . . . we have had an overload and we have almost pushed it away. We do not know much about riots and poor folks and a lot of other things anymore. We have sort of pushed it away. There is what Peter Marin said in *Harpers*: a triumph of narcissism—we are only concerned about ourselves."[60]

Narcissistic concern for oneself and one's physical well-being differed from the rugged individualism of yesteryear. In the past, YMCA members strove to remake the world in their own image, to impose their values on the common herd, and finally to wrest salvation itself from the hands of God. But the attainment of such far-off goals as personal salvation had lost much of its attraction by the late 1970s. "The contemporary climate is therapeutic, not religious," argued Christopher Lasch. "People today hunger not for personal salvation . . . but for the feeling, the momentary illusion of personal well-being, health, and psychic security."[61]

To some extent, this demand for personal security has altered the purpose of the YMCA. In the past, the association prided itself on equipping individuals with the tools necessary to forge ahead in life. Today, however, the emphasis rests more on providing for the individual's personal needs. In the words of National Board Chairman Sam Evans: "Your local Y is committed to your local community and your personal wellness."[62]

In addition to providing its members with a sense of well-being, the YMCA worked to achieve this state as quickly as possible. The "leisure revolution" and its vitiating effect on the old Protestant work ethic had not abated since the 1950s. By the 1970s, people appeared doubly inclined to store up their treasure neither in heaven nor in personal savings accounts. Instead, many Americans lobbied for immediate fulfillment of their desires. As one YMCA guide warned in 1978, "participants and parents want immediate payoff and will easily drop out of a program if this is not the case."[63]

In the 1950s, the YMCA had responded to like demands for an "immediate payoff" with an old-fashioned array of "wholesome" activities which were fun but at the same time character building. By the 1970s, the YMCA appeared less eager to elevate the public's leisure time and more ready to admit that recreation could be good in itself. Once this change in attitude was finalized, physical educators could cease justifying their product on the grounds that it built character or team spirit. Instead, they merely had to announce that "done right, exercise feels incredibly good."[64]

Another factor that contributed to the post-1960s fitness boom was the growing importance of looks in a service economy. "[I]t is for profoundly *social* reasons that we've directed so much attention to our bodies in the 1970s and 1980s," explains psychologist Barry Glassner. Television especially is making appearances more important than ever before, and "increasingly, the ideal images are also the standards against which our employers judge us."[65]

An indication of the perceived link between employability and physical fitness is the YMCA's burgeoning involvement in corporate training programs. Designed to improve the health of white collar workers, corporate training programs gained popularity during the 1980s, and by 1986 68 percent of all YMCAs offered fitness programs for corporate employees.[66] This collaboration between the YMCA and corporate America also helped to improve the material prosperity of the association, which according to *Time* magazine "is shedding its image of serviceable shabbiness and putting up gleaming facilities that rival the ritziest of private clubs."[67]

The spectacle of the YMCA going upscale did not please a Washington, D.C., association member, who observed that his posh new downtown facility offered neither low fees nor much access to children. "What I found was not a Y at all," he complained, "at least not the Y [I] had known in the past, but something else entirely: a fancy new health club for the rich, disguised in the tax-exempt, non-profit wrappings of the YMCA."[68]

Other YMCA members, however, saw nothing wrong in making the association "every bit as viable as its commercial competitors." The YMCA ought not to go back to being "an outfit that did a lot of good— but didn't do very well," argued one modernist. Instead, it ought to be known less for its "$1-a-year teenagers" than for its state-of-the-art exercise equipment.[69]

Such sentiments reflect the fact that for many Americans the YMCA has come to symbolize nothing but sport. This was certainly not the outcome envisioned by Luther Gulick, whose Red Triangle was meant to symbolize the association's tripartite commitment to body, mind, and spirit. But Gulick's version of manly Christian athleticism lost currency in the post–World War II YMCA, as suburbanization, secularization, and changing membership demographics combined to make the association more inclusive of women, families, and non-Christians. These individuals had little reason to preserve the YMCA's traditional focus on the religious and intellectual concerns of young, Protestant, city-dwelling men. But they did stand to benefit from YMCA athletics, which in the postwar years came to serve as the association's chief means of appeal.

NOTES

This essay is reprinted by permission of the author and the *Journal of Sports History* © 1993 by Clifford Putney.

1. Luther H. Gulick, "The Legitimate Place of Athletics in the YMCA," paper delivered before the 1894 Massachusetts State Convention of the YMCA, Archives, Springfield College, Massachusetts.

2. The most comprehensive study of YMCA involvement in physical education is Elmer Johnson, *The History of YMCA Physical Education* (Chicago: Association Press, 1979). Other studies on the subject include C. Howard Hopkins, *History of the YMCA in North America* (New York: Association Press, 1951); Clifford Putney, "Character Building in the YMCA, 1880–1930," *Mid-America* 73:1 (1991): 49–70; and Putney, "Muscular Christianity: The Strenuous Mood in American Protestantism, 1880–1920" (Ph.D. diss., Brandeis University, 1995).

3. See Johnson, *The History of YMCA Physical Education*, 317; and Jodi Vandenberg Daves, "The Manly Pursuit of a Partnership Between the Sexes: The Debate over YMCA Programs for Women and Girls, 1914–1933," *Journal of American History* 78:4 (March 1992): 1324–1346.

4. See Louis E. Nelson, *A Study of Services for the Family in Family-Serving YMCAs* (New York: Association Press, 1956), 85, 8; and "Characteristics of YMCA Members," *National Council Bulletin* (January 1959): 1.

5. "Young People and the Present World Situation," *National Council Bulletin* (January 1951): 1.

6. Clifford C. Gregg, "The Spiritual Challenge of the Centennial Year," *National Council Bulletin* (June 1951): 1.

7. Glen Heathers, *Young People and World Citizenship* (New York: Association Press, 1950), v, 14.

8. George C. McGhee, "The Y.M.C.A. in Today's World," *Y Work with Youth* (May 1951): 3.

9. William Overholt, "The Ecumenical Opportunities of the YMCA," *National Council Bulletin* (March 1958): 1.

10. R. H. Espy, "The Y.M.C.A. Reaffirms Its Mission," *Christianity and Crisis* 15 (October 17, 1955): 132.

11. "Membership Inclusiveness and Religious Effectiveness?" *National Council Bulletin* (March 1950): 6.

12. "The Power and Unity of Our Faith," *National Council Bulletin* (January 1955): 4.

13. Alan Eddy Hugg, "Informal Adult Education in the Y.M.C.A.: A Historical Study" (Ph.D. diss., Columbia University, 1950), 189.

14. Gordon J. Dahl, "Protestant Responses to a Leisure Revolution, 1945–1970" (Ph.D. diss., University of Minnesota, 1974), prefatory abstract, 121.

15. James M. Hardy, *Focus on the Family* (New York: Association Press 1966), introduction.

16. Dahl, "Protestant Responses to a Leisure Revolution," 121.

17. Ellis H. Champlin, "Physical Education and the Good Life," *National Council Bulletin* (January 1956): 5.

18. Ray M. Snyder, "Christian Discipline in YMCA Physical Education," typewritten manuscript, 1965, Archives, Springfield College, Massachusetts, 5. Quotation from the Rev. O. C. Sappenfield.

19. See Champlin, "Physical Education and the Good Life," 4; and Snyder, "Christian Discipline in YMCA Physical Education," 5.

20. Dahl, "Protestant Responses to a Leisure Revolution," 107, 115.

21. "The YMCA's Place in Health and Physical Education," *National Council Bulletin* (June/July 1958), 8–9.

22. Mark C. Shinnerer, "The YMCA on the Big City Frontier," *National Council Bulletin* (March 1962): 1.

23. Leon A. Higginbotham, "We Are Living in a Revolution and the YMCA Is Involved," *National Council Bulletin* (October 1968): 3.

24. "New Shape of the YMCA," *Newsweek* 111 (July 11, 1966): 86.

25. YMCA Office of Urban Development, *The YMCA in the Streets* (New York: YMCA Office of Urban Development, 1969): 1–3.

26. "New Shape," 86.

27. Snyder, "Christian Discipline in YMCA Physical Education," 1.

28. John Burkhart, "The Changing Image of the YMCA," *National Council Bulletin* (March/April 1963): 4.

29. "New Shape," 86.

30. Mickey K. Clampit, "Religious Subculture of a YMCA Camp" (Ph.D. diss., Harvard University, 1969), 241, 232.

31. "Plan Now for Inter-Racial Progress," *Y Work with Youth* (April 1964): 2.

32. "Y Takes Positions on Public Issues," *YMCA Bulletin* (October 1971): 13. For an account of race relations within the YMCA, see Nina Mjagkij, *Light in the Darkness: African Americans and the YMCA, 1852–1946* (Lexington: University Press of Kentucky, 1994).

33. Shinnerer, "The YMCA on the Big City Frontier," 1.

34. Johnson, *The History of YMCA Physical Education*, 351.

35. Wilbur M. McFeely, "Urban Action Offers YMCA Chance to Work with New Program, People," *National Council Bulletin* (October 1968): 2.

36. Johnson, *The History of YMCA Physical Education*, 351.

37. "Council Suggests Six Steps for Tackling Urban Problems," *National Council Bulletin* (June/July 1968): 3.

38. "45th Council Asks End to War; Drops Age of 'Youth' Members from 36 to 30 Years of Age," *YMCA Bulletin* (June/July 1971): 2–3.

39. "Black Awareness Group Declares White All Over Y," *YMCA Bulletin* (March 1970): 9.

40. Paul Popenoe, "The Fraudulent New Morality," *Y Work with Youth* (January 1968): 2–4.

41. "Youth and Adults Debate Law and Order at Fall National Board Meeting in Chicago," *National Council Bulletin* (November 1968): 2.

42. "Barriers Between the Generations," *Y Work with Youth* (March 1968): 1.

43. James G. Stooke, "Is Hi-Y Dead?," *Y Work with Youth* (October/November 1968): 1.

44. "Convention '69," *YMCA Bulletin* (August/September 1969): 2–5. At issue were student demands that the YMCA hire more minorities, oppose the Vietnam War, and fight the draft—all of which the Board agreed to discuss but not under threat of force.

45. See Clarence G. Moser, "Fitness for Living," *Y Work with Youth* (October 1962): 1; and Gary Lautens, "Sure, You Can Still Exercise at Y—Just Don't Tell Anybody About It!," *National Council Bulletin* (October 1965): 9.

46. John Burkhart, "19 Noted Americans Talk on the YMCA," *YMCA Bulletin* (December 1971): 8–9. Despite the move among YMCA leaders toward social activism, most rank and file association members continued throughout the 1960s to label physical education as their "major area of interest." See Johnson, *The History of YMCA Physical Education*, 345.

47. "Paris Basis: Replace, Modify, or Reaffirm?," *YMCA Today* (June/July, 1972): 10–11.

48. "National Board Approves 5-Year Goals," *YMCA Today* (May 1972): 6.

49. "World YMCA Meets in Uganda, Reaffirms Its Christocentric Character," *Christian Century* 90 (September 5, 1973): 860.

50. Elise M. Brett, "Got Enough to Worry About Now?" *National Council Bulletin* (November 1968): 5.

51. Robert N. Bellah et al., *Habits of the Heart* (Berkeley: University of California Press, 1985), 266.

52. Billy Graham, "Rising to Opportunity," *YMCA Today* (Winter 1973): 4–5.

53. Russ Kohl and Win Colton, eds., *Enriching Parenting and Family Life Through YMCA Program: A Resource Manual for YMCA Professional Directors* (Foster City, CA: The National YMCA Family Communications Skills Center, 1979), 4.

54. See Steven Tipton and Mary Douglas, *Religion and America: Spirituality in a Secular Age* (Boston: Beacon Press, 1983).

55. Paul M. Limbert, "How Open and Still Christian?" *YMCA Today* (Fall 1974): 16–17.

56. *Y into the 80s*, misc. pamphlet, n.d., Archives, Springfield College, Massachusetts, 10.

57. National YMCA Values Education Center, *Values Education and the YMCA* (LaGrange, IL: National YMCA Values Education Center, 1979), 10.

58. Jerry Glashagel, "The Values Element—What Is It?" *YMCA Today* (Winter 1976): 7.

59. Ibid., 13. In addition to promoting values, the YMCA worked hard in the 1970s to promote self-esteem because in the words of one association official "[w]e believe that the strongest people in our families, neighborhoods, communities, and nation are those who believe in themselves and have a healthy self-image." See James F. Bunting et al., "The YMCA from 1939 to 1979," *Journal of Ecumenical Studies* 16 (Winter 1979): 93–94.

60. YMCA Physical Education Society, "YMCA Health and Physical Education: A Plan for the '80s," report of a conference held at the Sheraton O'Hara Motor Hotel [city unknown] on October 16–17, 1975, Archives, Springfield College, Massachusetts, 15. The speaker was Leonard Duhl.

61. Christopher Lasch, *The Culture of Narcissism* (New York: W. W. Norton & Co., Inc., 1978), 7.

62. Sam Evans, "A Few Words," *Discovery YMCA* 6:1 (Spring 1988): 4.

63. YMCA of Metropolitan Los Angeles et al., *YMCA Staff Notebook* (Los Angeles: YMCA of Metropolitan Los Angeles, 1978), I-1.

64. Bob Kleinmann, "Why Exercise? It Is Virtue Rewarded," *Discovery YMCA* 1:4 (May/June 1983): 19.

65. Barry Glassner, *BODIES: Why We Look the Way We Do (and How We Feel about It)* (New York: G. P. Putnam's Sons, 1988), 13, 173.

66. Syma Jelen, "Employee Health: Working Out?" *Discovery YMCA* 5:3 (Winter 1987): 7.

67. "Putting on the Ritz at the 'Y,'" *Time* [127] (July 21, 1986): 65.

68. Arthur Levine, "Serving the Rich: The Washington Y," *Washington Monthly* 10 (December 1978): 13.

69. Bob Kleinmann, "The YMCA: The Times, They Are A-Changin'!" *Discovery YMCA* 1:2 (January 1983): 11.

Chapter Eleven

Taking the Young Stranger by the Hand
Homosexual Cruising at the YMCA, 1890–1980

John D. Wrathall

In November 1912, in response to concerns expressed by juvenile court officers, Oregon police raided the Portland YMCA and arrested more than twenty men on charges of "indecent and degenerate conduct." As the men confessed to juvenile court authorities and the police, they implicated others, and law enforcement agents began a hunt to track down the remaining members of this "ring" of "perverts." Eventually, more than fifty men were indicted, and many others who were accused fled town when they learned of warrants for their arrest. One man left in such a hurry that he forgot his packed bags in his room, and at least one of the men implicated, a member of the YMCA and a resident of the association's dormitory, attempted suicide. Most of the apprehended men were so devastated that they immediately confessed, perhaps hoping for leniency. A juvenile court officer confidently assured the public that during the interrogations the men were "coming through like little children. Not a man has balked [in his testimony]."[1]

Perhaps the men were willing to confess quickly because most were members of Portland's respectable Protestant middle class and profoundly humiliated by their public exposure. Following the initial questioning, a *Portland News* reporter described the accused as "well dressed, above the average in apparent intelligence, and with no outward signs of degeneracy. It was not a collection of bums or sots or street scourings. It was an orderly, solemn, quite respectable appearing aggregation." The investigation revealed that the men implicated in the sex scandal included clerks, doctors, lawyers, and "some of the most prominent" businessmen of the city, many of whom had either resided in the YMCA dormitories or were members of the Portland association.[2]

YMCA leaders and supporters professed shock and outrage over the incident and insisted that the men's activities were an aberration. Certainly, the Portland incident did not epitomize the typical behavior of association members; however, it was also not an isolated case. In 1919, for example, the association in Newport, Rhode Island, was rocked by a homosexual scandal when Navy decoys entrapped two YMCA ministers. Association leaders vehemently denied and the public generally refused to believe that the YMCA or affiliated ministers could possibly be implicated in this kind of activity.[3] Yet, court testimony and studies of sex researchers suggest that the use of YMCA facilities to find sexual partners was widespread and dated back to the late nineteenth century.[4]

Beginning in the 1890s, YMCA leaders, staff, and members, as well as young men in transit who had little, if any, interest in the association's Christian agenda, started to use the organization's facilities as sexual testing grounds.[5] After all, the YMCA's single-sex environment offered an ideal setting for men interested in experimenting with new relationships. The YMCA, founded to provide young men adrift in the city with "a home away from home," had inadvertently created safe, accessible, public spaces for young men to explore their sexual identities. Throughout the twentieth century the association came to play a crucial role in the creation of a new sexual subculture, and by midcentury in cities such as San Francisco, New York, Los Angeles, and Chicago, the YMCA had become "gay turf, almost as much as the [gay] bars."[6] Gay guidebooks like Francis Hunter's *The Gay Insider* not only listed YMCAs but also offered readers specific advice, providing information on the various sexual activities that men could expect to find in individual branches and advocating use of caution in those associations that required more discretion. The YMCA, Hunter assured his readers, "is invariably a place where you will find other gays—though perhaps with difficulty, depending on the political climate."[7]

The gay community had been aware of the sexual activities at the YMCA since the turn of the century. Indeed, the YMCA assumed such an important role in modern American gay life that jokes and anecdotes about sexual encounters at the association have become an integral part of the gay community's oral tradition.[8] Moreover, gay artists have celebrated and popularized male-male sex at the YMCA in songs, paintings, and literature. Gay erotic writers and pornographers, for example, have often set their stories in YMCAs, and gay artist Paul Cadmus immortalized cruising at the association in his 1930 painting the "YMCA Locker Room." In addition to literary and visual arts, songs such as Rae Bourbon's "Queen of the YMCA" and the Village People's chart-topping "YMCA" have capitalized on the connection between the YMCA and gay sex.[9]

The existence of homosexual cruising on YMCA premises presents a particular irony. After all, YMCAs were originally founded largely for the purpose of sheltering young Protestant men from debauchery and sexual immorality. The New York YMCA, for example, played a seminal role in the American sexual purity movement and gave the notorious censor Anthony Comstock his start in the New York Society For the Suppression of Vice.[10] Moreover, the YMCA assumed a pioneering role in American sex education and invested an increasing amount of its resources in programs that advocated self-restraint and celibacy outside of marriage. Given the YMCA's commitment to chastity and sexual purity, it seems ironic that the association acquired a reputation in America's urban sexual subculture as the most reliable source of public gay sex in the United States. Perhaps YMCA leaders' participation in the sexual purity movement simply reflected what sociologist and sex researcher Laud Humphries has called the "Shield of Righteousness" syndrome, a clinging to moral self-righteousness as a denial of cruising.[11] Yet, the historical record suggests that many YMCA employees, leaders, and members were aware of and participated in the cruising scene, and that despite the organization's knowledge, association officials did little to curb gay sexual activities until public pressure mounted in the 1960s and 1970s.

Evidence about the nature of cruising at the YMCA also indicates that many, perhaps most, participants were men who did not identify themselves as gay. Gay men knew about and participated in the cruising scene, but they were not solely responsible for creating it. While public cruising provided a necessary prerequisite for the emergence of a self-conscious gay subculture, it was not synonymous with it. Public cruising could be a first step toward learning about the existence of a gay subculture and internalizing a homosexual identity. Yet, many men who participated never internalized a gay identity or attended any of the other institutions which became the matrix of gay culture. George Chauncy, for example, demonstrates in his study of early-twentieth-century cruising that participants differentiated between "normal" men who played the active role in the sex act and "queers" who were effeminized by their willingness to play the passive role.[12] Similarly, Humphries' investigation of 1970s tearoom cruising suggests that perhaps as many as half of those who participated considered themselves to be straight and did not take part in gay community institutions.[13]

Sexual interaction between straight and gay men was also a standard feature of the same-sex cruising scene at the YMCA throughout much of the twentieth century. For obvious reasons, sources on the history of YMCA cruising are scarce. Not only has the YMCA had an interest in denying the existence of cruising, but the phenomenon under study is by its nature furtive and ephemeral. In addition to artistic and literary sources which document the YMCA cruising scene since the 1920s, this study relies on scattered references in newspapers and YMCA publications dating back to the early 1900s. It also makes use of oral histories of nineteen gay men who participated in the cruising scene at YMCAs as early as the 1920s or knew through acquaintances in the urban gay subculture of sexual activities at associations. Moreover, newspaper reports and court proceedings from the trials of the men involved in the Portland and Newport scandals offer valuable insight into the phenomenon of YMCA cruising.[14]

Evidence documenting public, anonymous, male-male sex in American cities dates back to the late nineteenth century. During the 1880s and 1890s, doctors, psychiatrists, law enforcement officials, and social workers began to comment on "cliques" or "networks" of "inverts" gathering at certain clubs, theaters, cafés, parks, particular streets, bathhouses, gymnasiums, cheap hotels, and YMCAs. The existence of male brothels and the staging of grand cross-dressing spectacles known as "drag balls" were other manifestations of early gay male subcultures. Reflecting prevalent attitudes of mainstream American society, these urban subcultures were divided along racial lines. Black gay men developed their own social networks, and socialized in private settings and at elaborate drag balls more commonly than their white counterparts. Nevertheless, there were contexts in which men of all classes, races, and ethnicities interacted.

Many of the popular gathering spots of men in search of same-sex sexual activity were also patronized by prostitutes and their clients, as well as the more bohemian and artistic elements of the urban population. These sites provided a common ground for the convergence of the gay and straight sexual underworlds, and many men moved freely between same-sex and mixed-sex sexual settings. By the first decade of the twentieth century, gay subcultures had emerged in virtually every major American city and in every region of the country.[15]

The emergence of these same-sex sexual communities was stimulated in part by the massive migration and immigration that occurred at the turn of the century. Attracted by the growth in industrial opportunities, a large young, single, male workforce from the American countryside as well as from abroad moved to America's cities. Urban areas offered these newcomers not only employment but also public spaces where they could meet and interact anonymously, and where church and family no longer imposed moral guidelines or restraints. The growing number of young men adrift in the cities and the existence of public gathering spaces, as well as an increased level of anonymity and personal freedom, were prerequisites for the emergence of urban gay subcultures.

Ironically, the same conditions that gave rise to gay sexual communities were also responsible for the tremendous growth of the YMCA at the turn of the century. Members of the Protestant urban middle class who dominated the YMCA's leadership ranks were concerned about the anonymity and personal freedom the young men encountered on their arrival in the cities. Hoping to provide a wholesome and proper Christian environment for the newcomers, the association positioned itself at the city's points of entry to

> meet the young stranger as he enters our city, take him by the hand, direct him to a boarding house where he may find a quiet home pervaded by Christian influence, introduce him to the rooms of the Association, and in every way throw around him good influences, so that he may not feel that he is a stranger, but that noble and Christian spirits care for his soul.[16]

As the number of young men adrift in the cities grew, YMCA leaders increasingly advocated the construction of buildings specifically designed for association use.[17] The emergence of a building-oriented program had several implications for the YMCA. It required a long-term commitment to the YMCA's "fourfold" plan designed to nurture "the whole man" by providing physical, social, and intellectual as well as spiritual programs. Moreover, the construction of buildings forced the YMCA to rely increasingly on vast fundraising efforts to pay for the structures and their maintenance and to raise salaries for the employment of full-time, professional staff. Financial concerns compelled the association to "sell" membership privileges to a broad constituency, bringing an ever-growing number of men to the YMCA. Aside from creating a financial burden, the association buildings established a permanent and recognizable place for the YMCA in America's urban landscape. Yet, the buildings also helped to create safe spaces where erotic interaction between males became easier and more accessible, allowing men to negotiate new kinds of sexual relationships. For the first half of the twentieth century YMCA buildings remained male-only domains, physically oriented, largely free of supervision, relatively safe from police surveillance, and thus an ideal setting for same-sex sexual activities.[18]

Many young men who came to the cities from rural areas made the YMCA their first stop because it was a cheap and safe place to stay while seeking permanent housing. Martin Block, a gay man who lived in New York in the 1920s and 1930s, recalled that "a lot of country boys" stayed at the YMCA because "people from small towns had no place else to go." The YMCA, he remembered, was known as a "nice, religious place" where "they'll take care of you."[19] Aware of the YMCA's reputation as a respectable institution, parents, ministers, and teachers who were concerned about the young men's moral welfare often sent them to the association. Harry Hay, a founder of the early gay rights movement, recalled that most of the men he encountered at the Reno and San Francisco YMCAs in the late 1920s were "lower middle-class farming men, sent to the 'Y' by Sunday School teachers or ministers."[20]

Once the men arrived at the YMCA, they not only found a "home away from home" but also discovered the existence of sexual activities which they had likely never encountered prior to their arrival. Fay Etrange, the main character of the 1920s gay novel *Scarlet Pansy*, for example, came to Baltimore from rural Maryland. On his arrival a friendly police officer at the train station directed him to the YMCA, where he was subsequently introduced to the gay sexual underworld. Though a fictional account, Etrange's first encounter with same-sex sexuality illustrated the experience of many men who came to the YMCA in search of accommodation and companionship at the turn of the century. Larry Littlejohn, who had his first sexual experience at New York's Sloane House YMCA, claimed that joining the association marked for many "the beginning of a gay lifestyle."[21]

While the YMCA was for rural migrants a convenient stop in the transition from country to city life, the association's physical culture movement and its single-sex emphasis also attracted those men who were interested in experimenting with male eroticism. Many of these men did not consciously identify themselves as gay, nor did they visit the YMCA for the express purpose of having sex with men. They felt, however, strongly attracted to other men and may have been drawn to the YMCA because it was a place where they could enjoy male companionship in a physical setting. Paul Hardman, a gay man living in Los Angeles, admitted that he was attracted to the YMCA by "all the muscular trappings—the sports."[22] The biographer of Charles T. Griffes claimed that the gay musician's "need to be with boys" was so great "that though his home contained two pianos, he chose to practice on a public instrument at the Y, and his favorite hour was the time when players were coming and going from their games."[23] Dorr Legg, a gay man from Los Angeles, was convinced that homosexuals were drawn to the association because the YMCA was a "one-sex thing" and "a safe refuge to single, homosexual men." Legg knew of many bachelors who "opted out of two-sex society" and preferred to live in the YMCA's residence halls.[24] The association dormitories were especially appealing to homosexual men because at the YMCA, unlike many hotels, "young men could share a room without suspicion."[25]

While many men happened on same-sex sexual activities at the YMCA by chance, others came for the specific purpose of finding sexual partners. Information about where male sex could be found was easily available in the emerging gay subculture, but it was by no means the only source of information. Even condemnation of purported cruising activity was an effective means of spreading the word to the sexually curious. By the early twentieth century the YMCA had acquired a reputation as a sexual meeting place, and homosexual networks existed in associations in every major city in America.[26]

Although YMCA leaders were often aware of these early cruising activities, they usually chose to ignore them and did not confront those who participated, preferring denial and toleration to the public humiliation which might ensue in the wake of determined efforts to root out cruising. While official records are largely silent about same-sex sexual activities, oral history sources indicate that cruising became popular at the YMCA precisely because the association denied its existence. The YMCA's refusal to concede that cruising occurred on association premises permitted the flourishing of a sexually ambiguous environment which enabled men to test new sexual identities. Only rarely did association leaders acknowledge or express concern about homosexual activities in the YMCA. A 1906 editorial in *Association Men*, the YMCA's national publication, for example, warned YMCA officials of a "danger, more serious than is understood," and cautioned them "that effeminate, moral degenerates, men who may move in the higher circles, cultured, refined and devilish, often musical and affecting spirituality, may come and bring their unmentionable immoralities."[27] Yet, despite occasional expressions of concern, YMCA officials did nothing to curtail or end cruising.

Even after the 1912 Portland sex scandal resulted in the indictment of more than fifty men, and despite court testimony showing that the YMCA had long been a sexual meeting place for men, the association's primary response was denial. Portland's YMCA leaders, as well as supporters in the business community and churches, made stirring public statements asserting the moral rectitude of the association and condemning those who "dredge the sewers of society and spread the dredge out before us to study their horrible content."[28] Similarly, *Association Men* avoided any serious discussion of the issue and instead commended the Portland association for its efforts in the areas of sex education and "social purity" work.[29]

Despite the initial surge of publicity the YMCA took no further steps, and within a year after the scandal, a George Williams College student, preparing for association leadership, pronounced that "immorality has been a comparatively small problem in our dormitories." To address the problem, he recommended greater efforts at recruiting the "right kind" of residents. YMCA publications concurred and suggested that visual inspection of association patrons entering the buildings was sufficient to screen out the "wrong kind" of men. The association's screening efforts, however, proved to be inadequate, and the wrong kind of men continued to flock to the YMCA.[30]

The association's cruising scene particularly expanded during World War I as a result of the YMCA's Army and Navy work, which brought a huge influx of soldiers and sailors to the dormitories. Prior to World War I the number of men who resided at the YMCA had been relatively small. In 1910, 335 associations operated dormitories housing 55,000 nightly visitors. By 1920 the number of YMCAs with dormitories had nearly doubled to 716, reporting close to 10 million nightly visitors. And whereas pre–World War I dormitories had often been small, consisting of a few rooms on one floor of the building, postwar residence halls were much larger, designed to accommodate hundreds, perhaps thousands, of men at a time. This influx of men had a dramatic effect on the YMCA cruising scene.[31]

As a result of World War I, more men had become aware of the YMCA's reputation for cruising, and in the aftermath of the war a growing number of men started to seek out the association in search of sex.[32] By the 1930s, there were two places to go for public sex, "the Y or the park," and as Harry Hay recalled, sex at the YMCA was more leisurely since one did not have to fear police intervention. Although association leaders and "most of the clerks knew what was going on," the organization continued its policy of denial, and only occasionally did YMCA secretaries expel individuals who were too flagrant.[33]

While the YMCA's World War I work with the Army and Navy had brought record numbers of men to the association, "World War II opened the floodgates," ushering in the "Golden Age" of YMCA cruising.[34] The concentration of men and women in training camps and adjacent cities provided gay individuals with the opportunity "to meet persons like themselves" and connect with already existing gay communities, "while others were able to act on erotic desires they might otherwise have denied." Moreover, as Alan Bérubé has demonstrated in *Coming Out Under Fire*, the Army's psychological screening of homosexuals forced many gay men and women to begin their coming-out process.[35]

As a result of the wartime changes, the cruising scene at the YMCA reached a new peak of activity and flagrancy. In part this was due to a surge in gay male participation in the years following World War II. Sparked by the wartime mobilization, more individuals than ever became aware of and embraced a gay identity, yet relatively few gay community institutions provided social outlets.[36] Moreover, the military's psychological screening, which had made many homosexuals aware of their sexual identity, had also generated increasing public homophobic paranoia. Thus, in the aftermath of the war, cruising in bars and parks became more dangerous than ever as individuals risked becoming the victims of crime as well as police harassment.[37] Not surprisingly, the YMCA enjoyed much popularity as a cruising ground. Protected by its middle-class, Christian aura, the YMCA offered all the advantages of other public spaces for male-male erotic interaction, and "men could feel relatively safe."[38] Indeed, Martin Block recalled that a "police friend" admitted going to the association for sex because it was the one place he assumed his fellow officers would never raid.[39]

Despite the surge in cruising, YMCA officials largely continued to ignore or tolerate its existence throughout the 1940s and 1950s. This may have been due in part to the fact that homosexuals had joined the desk staffs of many YMCAs.[40] Martin Block recalled that the managers of New York's Sloane House and 63rd Street YMCAs "had an attitude of pretending it didn't exist, except [the] clerks [who] were flaming queens."[41] When interviewees characterized YMCA desk staff as "flaming queens," perhaps they were referring to behavior like that observed by Donald Vining, a gay clerk at the Sloane House YMCA. Vining recorded in his diary that Andy, one of his gay coworkers, "really embarrasses me when he does things like yelling, when a plain soldier turns away from the window, 'Oh, Christ, why don't we get some attractive customers?'"[42] Gay desk clerks not only tolerated cruising but often provided a conducive environment for it. George Mendenhall's buddy, a gay YMCA clerk, for example, helped friends by assigning them to desirable dormitory rooms.[43] Jim Kepner, a gay activist and archivist living in West Hollywood, remembered that some desk clerks even funneled potential cruisers to select rooms. They "would sort of size people up, and suggest that they go either upstairs or downstairs to the locker room." Sometimes they gave "knowing advice," warning men to "close the door if you're having fun."[44]

Gay clerks, however, were not the only ones who tolerated and sometimes supported cruising at the YMCA. Straight association managers often knew that members of their staff were gay and were aware of cruising activities but looked the other way. When Bob, a desk clerk at New York's Sloane House, tried to turn in a resident who had passed a note soliciting sex, a straight coworker threw the message "away without getting the house man to check on the guy who wrote it." Another incident suggests that even if he had turned the man in, nothing might have come of it. Vining chronicled in his diary a World War II episode involving a sailor who complained to the YMCA staff that "the guy with whom he had taken a room made a pass at him and would somebody go up for his clothes, as he was leaving." The staff, however, "did nothing about it and made the sailor go get his own clothes."[45]

Apparently, the only antihomosexual witch hunt which occurred at New York's Sloane House was initiated by a closeted gay staff member in 1946. However, Vining observed that straight employees denounced and opposed his endeavors and were "even more furious than I." Mr. Henry, the straight supervisor, "whose language is ordinarily quite decorous," Vining commented, "kept spitting 'The son-of-a-bitch, trying to make trouble for other people. We've never in the history of the house had anyone who hounded people that way.'" Mae, another supportive straight employee, denounced closeted gay men who launched witch hunts, explaining to Vining that they "don't even have the guts to speak out and go ahead like you and Andy do." Vining was "delighted" with her comment, which was "the closest she's ever come to putting her cards on the table in admitting she understands tho [sic] we've each known she really did for some time." Although Vining's straight coworkers knew that he and a number of other desk clerks were gay, it did not seem to bother them and occasionally they even discussed their social lives with gay employees. Vining noticed that when Mr. Henry introduced him to a new gay colleague he was "trying to sound us out," musing, "I better arrange for you two to have the same nite [sic] off together."[46]

Although most straight YMCA employees tolerated, and a few even supported, gay coworkers, some members of the staff made occasional attempts to curtail cruising. James Dawson, a gay man who had experienced the YMCA cruising scene in New York and Chicago, recalled that in one association "some segment of the management" periodically locked the doors in the stairwell to prevent easy passage between floors, though YMCA patrons responded by propping them open.[47] Despite the rampant sex going on at New York's 63rd Street YMCA, Wayne Flottman, a gay man from rural Kansas, who cruised at associations in Kansas City, New York, and Chicago, recalled that "no great efforts were made . . . to stop [it]." YMCA management occasionally asked him to show his dorm key to prove that he was staying at the association, but that was apparently the only precaution.[48]

Despite some local and fairly ineffective efforts to limit cruising at the YMCA, association officials largely continued to ignore the matter until 1964. That year, the cruising scene at the YMCA was brought with embarrassing force to the public's attention when police arrested Walter Jenkins, a high-ranking Johnson administration official, for soliciting sex at the Lafayette YMCA near the White House.[49] Jenkins had a long history of cruising at the association, including a 1959 arrest for the same offense. Reactions to the 1964 incident were similar to those involving the 1912 Portland scandal, indicating that the general public still found it difficult to accept the connection between homosexuality and the YMCA. A letter to the editor of the Los Angeles Times, for example, suggested that the incident had somehow been rigged by Goldwater Republicans because such unspeakable acts could not possibly occur at the YMCA.[50]

The public's persistent refusal to acknowledge the existence of homosexual cruising at the YMCA may have been due in part to a shift in the association's constituency. After World War II, as a growing number of Americans left the inner cities for the suburbs, the YMCAs followed them and established branches that catered to families rather than single young men. Although cruising persisted in many of the downtown and central YMCAs, which continued to attract a disproportionately large number of men, it was virtually nonexistent in the newer suburban YMCAs.[51]

In 1964, perhaps in response to pressure from its new family constituents as well as the publicity generated by the Jenkins incident, the YMCA's National Council established a committee on homosexuality. The committee consulted liberal and conservative scholars of sexuality, including Wardell Pomeroy of the Kinsey Institute and psychologist Irving Bieber, as well as the writings of Alfred Kinsey and Evelyn Hooker. In 1966, after completing its deliberations, the committee made several recommendations to the YMCA's National Council. Noting that the YMCA's "family-oriented" activities had been a deterrent to cruising, the committee suggested the promotion of more mixed-gender programs, hoping to increase the association's "heterogeneity." Yet, the committee also called on the YMCA to help develop more positive attitudes toward homosexuals in American society. Although the report tended to characterize homosexuality as a misfortune, the committee encouraged compassionate, nonpunitive responses to cruising on YMCA premises. The report's relatively progressive recommendations alarmed some YMCA executives at the national headquarters. Afraid that too lenient a posture toward homosexuality would offend many association members, the National Council disbanded the committee and tabled its recommendations.[52]

As the YMCA returned to its traditional policy of denial and toleration, the association's cruising scene reached new heights in the wake of the sexual revolution of the late 1960s. Wayne Flottman made regular business trips to New York City and stayed at the 63rd Street YMCA, where "there was always something happening—a continuous sexual scene. If I went to the Y I might not make it to the village [because there was so much sex going on]. . . . It was almost like the bathhouses of the '70s."[53] Similarly, San Francisco's Embarcadero YMCA was "like a sex place." Paul McGuinness, who lived in San Francisco at the time, remembered "people masturbating naked, people tied up, people in uniforms, cowboys, a man wearing a leash like a dog," while some men "just lived on the toilet seats." It was hard to sleep in the dorms at night, he recalled, because of the noises of men having sex coming from adjoining rooms.[54]

While the 1960s sexual revolution generated years of the wildest sexual activities at the YMCA, it also gave rise to the emergence of a militant gay rights movement which signaled the beginning of the end of the golden era of YMCA cruising. As early successes of the gay rights movement made coming out less dangerous, participation in gay community institutions became more attractive to those who had accepted a gay identity, and a growing number of men resorted to bars in search of relationships. Many of the gay men who had cruised the YMCA in earlier years stopped going to the association, either because they had entered into committed relationships or because they felt it was no longer "necessary to go to the Y now—so much more [is] available." Fear of the AIDS epidemic also appears to have had a dampening effect on the public cruising scene. McGuinness returned to the Embarcadero YMCA in the 1980s, only to learn that the scene "had totally changed . . . the whole [cruising] thing died out."[55]

The successes of the gay rights movement also made the YMCA less safe as public awareness of and opposition to cruising at the association increased. Beginning in the early 1970s, YMCAs made more heavy-handed and often successful efforts to curtail cruising as their public image began to suffer under accusations that they were soft on homosexuality.[56] By the 1970s the cruising scene at Sloane House, which gay men had once jokingly dubbed "the French Embassy," practically ceased to exist as a result of heightened security.[57] Some associations even began to consider the use of closed-circuit television monitoring to put an end to cruising.[58] At times these efforts led to clashes between gay rights activists and the association. In the early 1970s, for example, when YMCAs began to end the practice of nude bathing, presumably for purposes of hygiene, members of the gay community accused the association of homophobia. The 1991 closing of the steam room at the downtown Minneapolis YMCA provided the basis for similar charges and resulted in a meeting between association administrators and the local Gay and Lesbian Community Action Council.[59]

Regardless of the recent controversy between YMCA officials and the gay community, homosexual cruising had been a ubiquitous feature of the association throughout much of the twentieth century. The existence of homosexual cruising in an institution that stood for moral rectitude suggests that cruising thrived in an environment that allowed men to maintain sexual ambiguity. Indeed, the YMCA was an ideal place for public cruising not in spite of its Christian reputation but because of it. The association not only supplied homosexuals with a convenient and relatively safe cover, but also exposed many other men to a disturbing and possibly desirable option. By creating an environment in which intentions could remain ambiguous, the YMCA provided men with the possibility of sexual experimentation while permitting them to avoid embracing a homosexual identity. Unlike going to a gay bar, a notorious park, or a house of male prostitution, which clearly signaled sexual intentions, visiting the YMCA indicated a desire for self-improvement. Yet, the association also provided men who sought sexual encounters with ample opportunities, while it allowed those who did not accept a gay identity or feared to come out to dismiss same-sex experiences as "blowing off steam" or as a "slipup." Thus, the YMCA cruising scene permitted men to slip into whichever role or denial strategy they deemed appropriate, enabling them to explore their relationship to their own bodies and to experiment sexually without having to surrender their masculinity.

Perhaps the clearest example of this "role slippage" appears in Donald Vining's diary. Vining had a crush on Bob, a fellow YMCA desk clerk, who was presumably straight. At one point, Bob invited Vining to shower with him, and although nothing sexual came of it, Bob invited him to "do this every morning." Yet, when a YMCA resident was told to leave the premises after "going from room to room with open door and [having sex with] the fellows," Bob "vehemently declared himself disgusted by such behavior and said he'd have poked [hit] him." Up to this point, Vining assumed that Bob was straight, though he was intrigued by Bob's interest in showering with him. Two years later, however, during a chance encounter at the YMCA swimming pool, Vining and Bob started to "horse around" and then went to a dorm room to have sex. Following the incident, Bob became so actively involved in the YMCA cruising scene that he risked being caught on several occasions.[60]

The eroticization of relations between gay and straight men was a way of ritualizing and acknowledging the reality of role slippage, and many gay men were attracted to the association because of the relative ease with which they could connect with "real" men. Bob Basker, an older gay man living in San Francisco, remembered getting presumably "straight trade" in YMCA shower rooms in the late 1930s and early 1940s. "Most of the men I had sex with," he claimed, "considered themselves completely straight." Paul McGuinness who had a preference for "men who were really men, not just a bunch of faggots running around," maintained that it was easy to meet and have sex with "straight" men, particularly "soldiers, marines on leave, truck drivers, [and] construction-worker types." George Mendenhall, who "was very much into straight guys," went to San Francisco's Embarcadero YMCA because that was where people went if they were looking for "straight trade." "Everybody hoped they would connect with servicemen," Mendenhall recalled, though he professed an interest in "construction workers." "Thank God for young married husbands who've gone to the Y," reminisced Hal Call, a gay man living in San Francisco.[61]

YMCA executives and ordained ministers also participated in the YMCA cruising scene. Despite the greater risks run by men in these positions, and thus the need for extreme discretion and secrecy, gay men were aware of such individuals, who cruised just like everybody else.[62] Dorr Legg remembered one particular high-level YMCA executive who had sex with men but "used [his] wife and family as a front."[63] Many YMCA officials were aware of the involvement of association leaders in the cruising scene. A 1962 YMCA study of men preparing for association leadership at George Williams College, for example, claimed that there was considerable evidence of "latent homosexuality" among YMCA leaders and employees.[64] "Michael James," an ordained Christian minister who became acquainted with the YMCA through its student chapter, recalled hearing about the association's reputation for cruising at McCormick Seminary.[65] For some gay men, the involvement of ministers and other devout Christians in the YMCA cruising scene was particularly attractive. Jim Kepner related that he enjoyed cruising at the YMCA because the men he could pick up there were more "religious."[66]

It seems unlikely that a majority of association members were involved in the YMCA cruising scene. However, association cruising was an important field of erotic interaction between straight and gay men, and far more men participated than most were or are willing to admit. For those who participated, whether they later denied it or celebrated it, as many gay men have, cruising played a crucial role in the redefinition of gender and sexual relations in urban America in the twentieth century. An awareness of the possibility of male-male sex, which cruising had created, required men to reflect on their sexual identities. The tendency to dismiss cruising as a marginal activity of a minuscule, perverse minority says more about the American imagination than it says about cruising or its relationship to the YMCA.

NOTES

1. "Rotten Scandal Reaches Into the Y.M.C.A.," *Portland News*, November 15, 1912, vol. XIII, no. 45; and "40 Men and Boys in Big Y.M.C.A. Scandal," *Portland News*, November 16, 1912, vol. XIII, no. 46, Oregon Historical Society, Portland, Oregon, hereinafter cited as OHS.

2. "Mayor Puts Police On Job For Decency," *Portland News*, November 21, 1912, vol. XIII, no. 50, OHS.

3. See George Chauncey, Jr., "Christian Brotherhood or Sexual Perversion? Homosexual Identities and the Construction of Sexual Boundaries in the World War I Era," *Journal of Social History* 19 (Winter 1985): 189–212.

4. I use the term "homosexual" rather than "gay" because the word "gay"

connotes a self-conscious identity, while "homosexual" connotes any same-sex sexual activity. See Chauncey, "Christian Brotherhood or Sexual Perversion?" Studies of sex researchers include Magnus Hirschfeld, *Die Homosexualität des Mannes und des Weibes* (Berlin: Louis Marcus, 1914), 550–554, cited in Jonathan Katz, *Gay American History* (New York: Thomas Y. Crowell Company, 1976), 51; Alfred C. Kinsey, *Sexual Behavior in the Human Male* (Philadelphia: W. B. Saunders Company, 1948), 617; Evelyn Hooker, "Male Homosexuals and Their 'Worlds,'" in Judd Marmor, ed., *Sexual Inversion* (New York: Basic Books, 1965); and Laud Humphries, *Tearoom Trade: Impersonal Sex in Public Places* (New York: Aldine Publishing Co., 1975), 3, 85.

5. Prior to this study, historians have largely ignored the social history of homosexual cruising at the YMCA because of cultural blind spots, denial, and silence surrounding sexuality. This study has been made possible by the growth in the last twenty years of new fields of scholarly research such as lesbian, gay, bisexual, transgender, and sexuality studies. I am particularly indebted to scholarship in the field of lesbian and gay history. Some of the more important works on the development of urban lesbian and gay subcultures in America include John D'Emilio, *Sexual Politics, Sexual Communities: The Making of a Homosexual Minority in the United States, 1940–1970* (Chicago: University of Chicago Press, 1983); Elizabeth Lapovsky Kennedy and Madeline D. Davis, *Boots of Leather, Slippers of Gold: The History of a Lesbian Community* (New York: Routledge, 1993); Jonathan Ned Katz, *Gay American History: Lesbian and Gay Men in the U.S.A.* (New York: Meridian, 1992); Jonathan Ned Katz, *Gay/Lesbian Almanac: A New Documentary* (New York: Harper & Row, 1983); and George Chauncey, *Gay New York: Gender, Urban Culture, and the Making of the Gay Male World, 1890–1940* (New York: Basic Books, 1994). Historians have only recently begun to examine the phenomenon of cruising in North American cities. See Steven Maynard, "Through a Hole in the Lavatory Wall: Homosexual Subcultures, Police Surveillance, and the Dialectics of Discovery, Toronto, 1890–1930," *Journal of the History of Sexuality* 5, 2 (1994): 207–242; and John Howard, "The Library, the Park, and the Pervert: Public Space and Homosexual Encounter in Post–World War II Atlanta," *Radical History Review* 62 (Spring 1995): 166–187.

6. Interview with Jim Kepner, West Hollywood, CA, August 20, 1992; all interviews in the possession of the author.

7. John Francis Hunter, *The Gay Insider USA* (New York: Stonehill Pub., 1972), 218.

8. Interview with Paul McGuinness, West Hollywood, CA, September 11, 1992. McGuinness recalled that some gay men even collected and framed YMCA memorabilia such as towels.

9. YMCA references in gay erotic literature and films are numerous. A recent anthology of gay erotic literature edited by John Preston, *The Flesh and the Word* (New York: Penguin Books, 1992), for example, includes several short stories set in the YMCA. Clay Caldwell's "From Cruising Horny

Corners" provides an extended account of how an honored association executive died of a heart attack, yet "with a smile on his lips," while having sex with
a young man in a YMCA steam room. Another short story in the anthology is
Sam Steward's autobiographical "Correspondence with George Platt Lynes,"
which includes a description of a sexual encounter at the Embarcadero YMCA
in San Francisco. One producer of gay erotic videos, not so subtly called
"YMAC Video" [sic], specializes in all-male pornography films like Camp
YMAC (1988), which capitalizes on the link in gay male culture between sex
and the YMCA. Robert Scully, The Scarlet Pansy (New York: Royal Publishers,
n. d. [ca. 1925]).

10. For a brief discussion of Comstock's early participation in the YMCA
and the association's involvement in campaigns to suppress vice, see C. Howard
Hopkins, History of the Y.M.C.A. in North America (New York: Association
Press, 1951), 383–386.

11. See Humphries, Tearoom Trade, 136–147.

12. See Chauncey, "Christian Brotherhood or Sexual Perversion?"

13. Humphries noted that only a minority of tearoom customers belonged to
the gay subculture. The majority of the men he studied were married, and "a
large group of them have no homosexual self-identity." Humphries, Tearoom
Trade, 11, and 41.

14. In evaluating the reliability of oral history data gathered for this
research, I have taken into consideration whether information was offered in
response to a question or volunteered, the amount of detail provided, and how
the information compared with other narrations. Thus, I have considered
detailed information which was freely volunteered by more than three narrators
as more trustworthy. It was usually easy for me to establish a relationship of
trust with the narrators, since I identified myself as an openly gay researcher. In
at least one case, a man refused to answer any of my questions until I identified
myself as gay. Because of the fairly sensitive, personal nature of the material I
was gathering, I was sometimes shocked by the candidness with which some of
the narrators told their stories. I found that my willingness to tell stories about
my own sexual experiences and coming-out process created a more relaxed
interviewing situation and let the narrators know that I would not judge their
experiences, but simply interpret them as a part of the history of the gay community. One interviewee initially denied ever having cruised at the YMCA, but
as we continued to converse, he gradually opened up and started to relate his
experiences. Usually the narrators were delighted that I, as a younger gay man,
was interested in their experiences and that I felt their stories were worth historical preservation. Often narrators were as interested in recounting other
aspects of gay community life before and after Stonewall as they were in
describing YMCA cruising, which provided a better context within which to
judge the reliability of their accounts and helped place association cruising in
the broader context of gay community formation. The oral histories represent a
rich source of information providing insights into early sexual identity forma-

tion which would have been impossible to gather from the handful of available manuscripts or published sources. I was able to supplement oral accounts with written materials, and together these sources provide a varied and fairly detailed picture of a phenomenon which otherwise might seem too ephemeral to document. It would have been interesting to interview men who did not identify themselves as gay but still participated in the YMCA cruising scene. For reasons which should be obvious, these interviewees would have been extremely difficult, if not impossible, to find.

15. See Katz, *Gay American History*; Chauncey, *Gay New York*; and D'Emilio, *Sexual Politics, Sexual Communities*. For a brief description of African American gay male communities in the early twentieth century and their relationship to white gay male communities, see Eric Garber, "A Spectacle in Color: The Lesbian and Gay Subculture of Jazz Age Harlem," in Martin Bauml Duberman, Martha Vicinus, and George Chauncey, Jr., eds., *Hidden From History: Reclaiming the Gay and Lesbian Past* (New York: New American Library, 1989), 318–331.

16. From the original Boston YMCA Constitution and By-Laws, quoted in L. L. Doggett, *History of the Boston Young Men's Christian Association* (Boston: The YMCA, 1901), 12–13.

17. Hopkins, *History of the Y.M.C.A.*, 457, 560.

18. For a detailed account of the role of YMCA buildings in the cruising phenomenon, see John D. Wrathall, *Take the Young Stranger By the Hand: Male Homoeroticism and the YMCA in North America* (Chicago: University of Chicago Press, forthcoming).

19. Phone interview with Martin Block, West Hollywood, CA, August 27, 1992.

20. Interview with Harry Hay, Los Angeles, CA, August 29, 1992.

21. Phone interview with Larry Littlejohn, West Hollywood, CA, August 31, 1992; Scully, *Scarlet Pansy*, 11–13, 18–20, 24–33; and phone interview with Martin Block.

22. Interview with Paul Hardman, West Hollywood, CA, August 31, 1992.

23. Pierre Foreau, "The White Peacock," *One* VIII, 1 (January 1960): 13, drawing on Edward H. Maisel's, *Charles T. Griffes: The Life of an American Composer* (New York: A. A. Knopf, 1943).

24. Legg's uncle, a lifelong bachelor, lived in a YMCA residence hall between 1900 and the 1930s. Legg, though, had no idea whether his uncle ever had sex with men. Phone interview with Dorr Legg, San Francisco, CA, August 21, 1992.

25. Interview with Paul Hardman.

26. See the *Portland News*, 1912–1913; *Oregon Reports*, 1912, OHS. William Billings, a gay man presently living in Los Angeles, believed that YMCAs, like the one in Oklahoma City which he frequented, were particularly important as sexual meeting grounds because in the rural midwest few other options existed. Phone interview with William Billings, West Hollywood, CA, August 31, 1992.

27. *Association Men* (March 1906): 259.

268 JOHN D. WRATHALL

28. Dr. Winfield S. Hall, M.D., "Slumming," *Association Men* (December 1912): 122.

29. *Association Men* (November 1912): 10–12.

30. Dexter A. Rau, *The Dormitory Question* (graduating thesis, George Williams College, July 24, 1913), 34–37, YMCA of the USA Archives, Minneapolis, Minnesota, hereinafter cited as YMCA Archives. See *Suggestions Regarding A Young Men's Christian Association Building* (New York: International Committee, 1891); and Louis E. Jallade, *The Association Building: Supervision and Circulation* (New York: Association Press, 1913). For a more detailed discussion, see Wrathall, *Take the Young Stranger By the Hand.*

31. See YMCA *Yearbooks*, 1905, 1910, 1915, 1920, 1925, 1930, 1935, 1940, and 1945; see also Richard C. Lancaster, *Serving the U.S. Armed Forces, 1861–1986: The Story of the YMCA's Ministry to Military Personnel for 125 Years* (Schaumburg, IL: Armed Services YMCA of the U.S.A., 1987).

32. Paul Hardman first went to the YMCA in search of sex "as a kid" in the late 1920s, when he had heard about association cruising from friends; interview with Paul Hardman, West Hollywood, CA, August 31, 1992. Martin Block knew that the 63rd Street YMCA in New York was "notorious," though he found sex easier to obtain at Sloane House and made a conscious decision to stay at the association during a trip to Washington, DC, in the 1930s. Phone interview with Martin Block, West Hollywood, CA, August 27, 1992.

33. Interview with Harry Hay, Los Angeles, CA, August 29, 1992.

34. Interview with Paul Hardman.

35. Allan Bérubé, *Coming Out Under Fire: The History of Gay Men and Women in World War Two* (New York: Free Press, 1990); and John D'Emilio, "The Homosexual Menace: The Politics of Sexuality in Cold War America," in Kathy Peiss and Christina Simmons, (eds.), *Passion and Power: Sexuality in History* (Philadelphia: Temple University Press, 1989), 234.

36. Phone interview with William Billings. For a discussion of the postwar emergence of homosexual rights organizations such as the Mattachine Society, the Daughters of Bilitis, and One Magazine, Inc., see D'Emilio, *Sexual Politics, Sexual Communities.*

37. D'Emilio, "The Homosexual Menace," 226–240.

38. Phone interview with William Billings.

39. Phone interview with Martin Block.

40. Phone interview with Larry Littlejohn; and interview with Sam Steward, San Francisco, CA, September 2, 1992.

41. Phone interview with Martin Block.

42. Donald Vining, *A Gay Diary, 1933–1946*, Vol. 1 (New York: Pepys Press, 1979), 395.

43. Interview with George Mendenhall, West Hollywood, CA, September 2, 1992.

44. Interview with Jim Kepner.

45. Vining, *Gay Diary*, 274, 372.

46. Ibid., 436, 434, 381.

47. Interview with Jim Dawson, West Hollywood, CA, August 25, 1992.

48. Interview with Wayne Flottman, West Hollywood, CA, August 25, 1992.

49. The events surrounding the Walter Jenkins scandal are a matter of public record. Every major newspaper in the country covered the circumstances leading to his arrest on October 7, 1964. In particular, members of the Republican Party tried to capitalize on the scandal to discredit the Johnson administration, arguing that Jenkins represented a national security risk. For a brief account of the scandal and its effect on the Johnson administration, see George C. Kohn, *Encyclopedia of American Scandal* (New York: Facts on File, 1989), 174–175; see also Humphries, *Tearoom Trade*, 49.

50. Letter to the editor, Pearl M. Campbell, *Los Angeles Times*, October 24, 1964, International Gay and Lesbian Archives, West Hollywood, California, hereinafter cited as IGLA.

51. For a more detailed discussion of the growing emphasis on families and "family values" see Wrathall, *Take the Young Stranger By the Hand*; and Mayer N. Zald, *Organizational Changes: The Political Economy of the YMCA* (Chicago: University of Chicago Press, 1970).

52. "Statement by the Committee on Counseling of the Program Services Department Concerning the Homosexual and the YMCA," National Council of Y.M.C.A., New York, January 1966, and Memo. Charlotte Himber to Bob Harlan, May 11, 1971, Bob Harlan File, YMCA Archives; see also magazine and newspaper articles in the same file documenting gay dissatisfaction with the YMCA and a speech Harlan gave to the National Council urging implementation of the 1966 report.

53. Interview with Wayne Flottman.

54. Interview with Paul McGuinness.

55. Interviews with Paul Hardman, Paul McGuinness, Jim Dawson, and William Billings.

56. Bob Harlan collected a number of newspaper clippings documenting charges leveled against YMCA leaders for allowing homosexuality on association premises through negligence; see Bob Harlan File, YMCA Archives.

57. Phone interview with Dorr Legg.

58. Humphries mentions in a footnote a "confidential" report by the Central YMCA of Philadelphia entitled "The Use of Closed Circuit TV for the Study and Elimination of Homosexual Activity in the YMCA," Humphries, *Tearoom Trade*, 83.

59. Friends of mine were involved in some of the protests, and I discussed the consultations between YMCA administrators and gay activists with friends who worked for the Minneapolis Gay and Lesbian Community Action Council.

60. Vining, *Gay Diary*, 274, 404, 424, 433.

61. Phone interview with Bob Basker, San Francisco, CA, September 3, 1993; interviews with Paul McGuinness and George Mendenhall; and interview with Hal Call, San Francisco, CA, September 2, 1992.

62. Phone interview with Martin Block.

63. Interview with Dorr Legg, San Francisco, CA, August 21, 1992. James Dawson recalled that some association managers "were less strait-laced than others" and suspected them to be gay, interview with Jim Dawson.

64. *Counseling* 20, 2 (March–April 1962): 3, YMCA Archives.

65. Phone interview with anonymous source, West Hollywood, CA, August 21, 1992. The individual requested that I not use his real name in print.

66. Interview with Jim Kepner.

Chapter Twelve

"Without Documents No History"
Sources and Strategies for Researching the YWCA

Nancy Robertson with Elizabeth Norris

> Papers. Records. These we must have. Without docu-
> ments no history. Without history no memory. Without
> memory no greatness. Without greatness no develop-
> ment among women.[1]

Many scholars have been interested in the YWCA because of the vast
quantities of material saved and made available to researchers, although
there are frustrating gaps in documentation. These materials also reveal
a number of far-ranging issues. Even a cursory look suggests the merits of
Anne Firor Scott's observation that women's voluntary associations, the
YWCA among them, "lay at the very heart of American social and political development."[2] The operative word is, perhaps, "development." The
YWCA did not remain static in its definition of the women it would serve
or of their needs. The changes say as much about the history of the
United States as they do about this specific organization. "Development"
should not be taken to imply only progressive activities. It is not contradictory to say that the YWCA is an important organization, worthy of
study, yet point out the racist, condescending, or repressive attitudes
which have characterized it in some times and in some places.

A historian can approach the YWCA in at least two ways. One is to
focus on the history of the institution, a specific program, a leader, a

member, or a constituent group. The other is to see the YWCA as a case study that permits insights into matters of broader significance. The essays in this volume demonstrate the wide range of issues that the YWCA can illuminate. The discussion of sources for the YWCA below opens by listing some of the themes raised in its history, many of which are highlighted in this collection, although others are only suggested. Identifying these issues not only strengthens the argument about the significance of the YWCA but reveals less likely sources for a given topic. For instance, the YWCA's commitment to its overseas programs (particularly during the years between the world wars) influenced its interest not only in internationalism but also in promoting improved race relations at home. After identifying some of the pertinent themes in YWCA history, this essay discusses the structure of the YWCA as background before identifying possible research strategies for studying the YWCA.

The notes of the essays in this book point to useful starting places to look for YWCA records. The repositories suggested in this essay can be divided into four categories: those with material on the National Board and its two predecessors; those with files of local associations, whether community or student; those with biographical information; and those of organizations with strong ties to the YWCA. The collections mentioned here are intended only as examples to lead the researcher to new sources.

When the YWCA of the U.S.A. was formed in the early twentieth century, members stated that its purpose was "to advance the physical, social, intellectual, moral and spiritual interests of young women."[3] Some ninety years later, the YWCA states its mission as creating "opportunities for women's growth, leadership and power in order to attain a common vision: peace, justice, freedom and dignity for all people. The association will thrust its collective power toward the elimination of racism wherever it exists and by any means necessary."[4] The following paragraphs elaborate on some of the less obvious meanings of these goals.

The role of the YWCA in promoting physical education, sports, and athletics and providing access to gymnasiums, pools, and camps was based on its stated purpose: to improve the health of young women and girls. Besides requiring health exams for members, the YWCA offered employment to female physicians and housing and training facilities for nurses. Over the years, the YWCA interpreted physical needs to include sexuality, hygiene, sex education, and, eventually, access to birth control and abortion rights. Recently, some local associations have become key players in combating domestic violence. When *Ms.* magazine selected Prema Mathai-Davis, the current national executive director of the YWCA of the U.S.A., as one of its "Women of the Year" for 1995, it recounted her surprise on discovering that "the YWCA is the nation's largest not-for-profit provider of shelter services for women and their families."[5]

Attention to the issues of employment and unemployment resulted in vocational training programs, employment bureaus, and in-depth studies and conferences on the concerns of working women. The YWCA itself offered work opportunities for women. Board members gained experience by working as volunteers developing their leadership skills. Paid staff positions represented an important profession open to middle-class women from the late nineteenth century on. For several years, the YWCA used the term "secretaries" for these college-trained professional workers, but changed to "directors" in the years following the Second World War as secretaries were increasingly identified with clerical workers. The YWCA also employed women in clerical and manual labor.

As women migrated to the cities from the country, associations offered residence accommodations and room registry alternatives which were regularly inspected by association staff. Some local associations opened cafeterias. While often implemented as revenue-generating projects, they were also intended to provide affordable eating spaces in downtown areas for women. Cafeterias, residences, and gymnasiums represented public or quasi-public spaces under the control of women and present an opportunity to raise questions about women and the public. Some of these spaces—pools, residences, and cafeterias—became arenas for struggle over racial integration during the civil rights movement.

Residences and cafeterias also served the social interests of the constituencies. There was a wide array of recreational activities and classes in addition to those in physical education departments, ranging from dramatics and pageants to music, arts, and crafts. YWCAs fostered clubs as a key organizational and educational tool to promote self-development in a group setting. Influenced by John Dewey's emphasis on experiential learning, the YWCA staff discussed their efforts at group work not only as a form of social work but also as a means of governance to train citizens for democracy.[6] They stressed the goal of training women for leadership. Another social aspect appears in the networks of women active in the YWCA. Bonds forged at meetings helped them to become regional, national, and international leaders. As an autonomous women's organization, the YWCA continued to create a homosocial environment for women of different ages long after other groups had become coeducational or dissolved.

Staff and board members saw these group work efforts as meeting an intellectual need, but they also favored more conventional educational

Figure 20. Early photo of a typewriting class, about 1916. Dayton, Ohio YWCA. Courtesy of the YWCA of the U.S.A. National Board Archives.

efforts. YWCAs offered courses in vocational or occupational training which they deemed appropriate for different groups of women. They provided some of the earliest courses in typing and other skills necessary for the growing opportunities in business for white (usually native-born) women as clerical workers. They taught courses in household management, practical nursing, and beauty culture for African American women. Such vocational programs present an opportunity to discuss how much YWCAs reinforced or promoted occupational segregation and how much they accurately reflected the employment possibilities open to different women. There are examples of women like the African American staff member Anna Arnold Hedgeman, who deliberately used the YWCA in a campaign by the Urban League and the NAACP to gain new jobs for African American women in retail stores in Brooklyn, New York, in the 1930s.[7] Sometimes YWCAs implemented innovative programs in less traditional occupations for women of any race in fields such as photography. They offered classes in English and other languages along with beauty courses, flower arranging, and charm classes. Over the years, some of these functions were taken over by other institutions; much of the vocational and English programs were absorbed by public night schools, and free public libraries answered a need initially met by YWCAs.

Because women and men active in the YWCA saw many of the problems of their times through the lens of morality, many of the organization's programs had moral components. This is apparent in the physical issues of hygiene and sexuality, but it is also true for recreation and education. Recreational activity and leisure time became terrains for intense debates about morality. The YWCA's work in providing "acceptable" housing, referrals to "suitable" employers, and Travelers' Aid had a moral component. The images of migrating and transient women threatened the conceptions of women's proper roles. The YWCA was active in social purity efforts and programs designed to encourage the film industry to promote "better" motion pictures. A largely unstudied effort is its long-standing involvement in the Hollywood Studio Club, a residence for aspiring actresses, in Los Angeles.

Given the presence of "Christian" in its name, the emphasis on spiritual interests is not surprising. Yet the connection between the YWCA and religion was apparent in more than its prayer circles and Bible study classes. The YWCA represented an arena in which conservative Protestants struggled with those influenced by the social gospel over programs, policies, and theology.[8] The YWCA offered employment opportunities to unmarried Protestant women unable to be ministers or overseas missionaries.

Just as programs and goals changed over time and varied from place to place, so did the perceptions change of which young women the YWCA was to serve. The essays in this volume give a sense of how and when some of these changes took place and remind us that they were often the result of heated struggles as well as transformations in the larger society rather than a simple or inevitable evolution. It may be helpful to indicate the terms used to refer to different groups of women because those terms will be used in the following discussion of the structure of the YWCA.

In the early years, "student associations" referred to those found in high schools and colleges. By the 1920s, "students" most commonly meant those in colleges, normal and professional schools, and universities. In 1918, high school girls became exclusively referred to as the "Girl Reserves," superseding "school girls" or "adolescent girls." In 1946, the girls voted to rename themselves "Y-teens."

YWCAs met the needs of different groups of working women and girls. "Industrial" referred not only to workers in factories but also to those in other occupations such as domestic service. "Business and professional" indicated those we now think of as clerical workers, as well as those in middle management or professions such as medicine or teaching.

Beginning in the 1920s, members discussed the needs of homemakers or "home women," who frequently attended programs like Y-wives. Some local YWCAs had experimented earlier with day care and nursery services. In the nineteenth century, some associations had attempted to aid unwed mothers, but for the most part, the YWCA stressed its role as a "formative" rather than a "reformative" body and referred those women and girls who had crossed the moral line to other organizations.

Facing competition from the YMCA and community centers in the late 1920s, YWCAs expanded their programs to include work with boys or the whole family. Some programs, like the International Institutes or branches for African Americans, may have always extended their efforts to males.

For most of its existence, when the YWCA used terms like "minority" or "race," it usually referred to programs for African Americans or, in the lexicon of the early twentieth century, "colored" work, later "Negro," and then "black." Programs for Native Americans were ordinarily conducted in boarding schools for them; they were phased out by the Second World War. There was, however, some mention of "Oriental" women and girls, and there were "Oriental" branches in at least two cities, San Francisco and Los Angeles. During World War II, the YWCA had programs in some relocation camps for Japanese Americans. By the 1930s and 1940s, there were occasional references to Mexican Americans in YWCA materials. In part, the emphasis on African Americans reflected their position as the largest racial minority in the United States and in the association itself. It was also indicative of the fact that many African Americans were already Protestant (unlike other racial groups). Non-Protestants may not have been as interested in the YWCA, with its Protestant-dominated culture and theology. However, with the official adoption of the *Interracial Charter* in 1946 and the changing demography of urban areas, as well as the YWCA's loosening of its religious requirements, YWCAs expanded their constituency after World War II.

Work in the United States with immigrant groups through YWCA foreign-born departments and the International Institutes is discussed in this volume. It may be useful to mention links between the institutes and the YWCA's foreign division. At points in their careers, some institute staff members served overseas in YWCA missions. Such personal connections, combined with the YWCA's commitment to internationalism, linked work with immigrants in this country with programs in their homelands.

Like much Protestant mission work, overseas programs were as much about cultural evangelizing and social welfare programs as they were about religious evangelizing.[9] While the YWCA of the U.S.A. sent women all over the world, it made its largest effort in China. The British YWCA, on the other hand, reserved its most intense work for India. The American YWCA sent women throughout Asia, the Mideast, Latin America, and, to a lesser extent, Africa. The YWCA of the U.S.A. also played a role in Europe during the world wars and in postwar reconstruction. Work at home and abroad often focused on the needs of refugees, whether their condition resulted from war or from political or religious persecution. Involvement in war relief efforts and international programs contributed to the YWCA's emphasis on peace and internationalism.

YWCAs were initially organized in urban areas, and an overlooked area of YWCA history has been its services to "women stranded in the cultural poverty of small towns and rural areas."[10] The YWCA organized and supervised various types of rural associations in villages, towns, and counties in new kinds of structures such as District Associations and Registered Clubs. The work was overseen by bodies like the Town and Country Department. The public affairs agenda for the 1946 National Convention carried a resolution "to remove rural inequalities in education, health and housing." An Agricultural Assembly was held at the Twentieth National Convention in 1955. Research possibilities are suggested by a bibliography of some thirty titles on rural work, published and unpublished, plus scrapbooks, personal papers, newsletters, and program suggestions.

Distinguishing between activities, policies, and personnel of the national body and local associations is an important step in understanding the various players at a given moment. It is not the purpose of this essay to analyze the relative power of local associations versus the national body, or the authority of volunteer boards versus that of paid staff, but rather to remind the researcher that the distinctions may be important. When discussing the leadership of an association, it may be critical to distinguish the middle-class, paid staff from the more wealthy volunteer board members. Locals and the national body had different funding sources, organizational structures, constituencies, and goals. As both Sarah Heath's and Michelle Busby's work indicates, the tensions within an association could entail disagreements between the leadership of an association and the constituency it felt it was serving.

The current national organization, the YWCA of the U.S.A., had two predecessor umbrella groups: the International Board of Women's and

Young Women's Christian Associations (1893–1906)[11] and the American Committee of Young Women's Christian Associations (1899–1906).[12] The International Board focused on urban YWCAs, while the American Committee concentrated on student YWCAs. In the years before 1906 when they merged, they competed to gain local affiliates and the American Committee did have member YWCAs in urban areas. In some cities, such as New York, Washington, DC, and St. Louis, there were separate YWCAs affiliated with each national organization.

The Young Women's Christian Associations of the United States of America was founded in 1906 as the result of a merger between these two organizations. It was essentially an affiliation of autonomous local associations. YWCAs establish policy at national conventions held every two or three years, although there were no conventions during the war years of 1916–1919 and 1941–1945. Delegates at the convention establish priorities for the next biennial or triennial period, amend the Constitution, and elect women from various geographic regions to serve as National Board members. One of the more critical policies that changed over the years concerns the requirements that locals must fulfill in order to remain affiliated with the national association, thus retaining the legal right to use the name "Young Women's Christian Association of the U.S.A."

The YWCA of the U.S.A. remains an unincorporated association formed by autonomous member associations and operated by the National Board. The autonomy of local associations precludes generalizations about local activities as being true for *all* associations. Between the conventions, the National Board, with its paid staff, acts as the executive body of the organization. The National Board was incorporated in 1907 by New York State, where it remains. It is composed of women who are members of local associations. Over the years, the National Board has reflected the programs and activities of the local associations. Historically, the national staff was identified as working for the National Board of the YWCA, but more recently, it has been identified as working for the YWCA of the U.S.A.

In addition to providing services to local associations, the National Board represents the interests of the organization as a whole, both in maintaining connections with other organizations and in promoting the social action agenda adopted by the convention. These roles entail testifying before Congress, assessing the impact of proposed federal and state legislation on women, disseminating information to locals on how to lobby governmental groups, and working with other organizations on common goals. The public affairs program has addressed issues ranging from child labor to peace to fair employment practices. For several years (1908–1930), the National Board maintained the National Training School in New York City to train secretaries for the local associations.

The association walked a thin line, and not always successfully, between saying that all women were sisters and trying to recognize that different women and girls had different interests. At national conventions, there were separate assemblies for students, industrial women, and business and professional women. After World War II, the working women's assemblies were reorganized into the National Employed Women's Coordination Assembly before being discontinued altogether. This structural change reflected the decreasing interest of working women in the YWCA and vice versa as industrial women moved into trade unions and professional women increased their activity in their own organizations. Students have remained an active subgroup within the YWCA through the National Student Assembly and the National Student Council. As indicated in the essay by Raymond Mohl in this volume, much of the work for foreign-born women and girls was done in the somewhat autonomous International Institutes, which eventually split off from YWCAs. Work for and with African Americans was done, as Margaret Spratt and Michelle Busby show, through the structure of the "branch." Neither institutes nor branches were permitted to have the structure of assemblies at national conventions, although each had conferences and meetings for their workers.

While the national conventions occurred only every two to three years, there were other meetings throughout the year. These usually were regionally based for a particular constituent group, but sometimes they were national meetings held on a specific topic. These meetings were referred to as "conferences," "retreats," "workshops," and "training sessions." Unfortunately, documentation of these meetings is often sketchy. It is useful, when coming across a reference to a YWCA convention, to verify whether it is one of the official national conventions or one of the smaller meetings.

The YWCA has continued to restrict active membership, defined as who can vote or hold office, in local associations to women and girls. Men and boys may join as auxiliary members. At both the local and national levels, there is one body of men whose participation remains to be studied: those on boards of advisors or trustees. Male members of these boards, with occasional token women, were responsible for legal, financial, and property transactions. As in any corporation, the actions of the trustees are considered confidential unless released by them. A male presence may have been a necessary strategy as women tried to raise money and conduct business transactions. At the same time, forming an incorporated organization allowed women to manage buildings and real estate and handle finances even before individual (married) women could legally own property. For the first time in some nineteenth-century communities, women were allowed to buy property and negotiate with city hall. They hired personnel for the residences, dining halls, and classes; they supervised carpenters and repair crews; and they consulted with lawyers and bankers.

A critical difference between the national body and local associations may well be their differing sources of income. Local associations, like other community groups, were dependent on community support through membership dues and local donations. The national organization received money from foundations and philanthropists in addition to contributions from member associations, determined on a quota basis. This combination of financial resources could shelter the national body from criticism of its programs by local funding sources. There are cases, however, of wealthy women, such as Helen Gould (Mrs. Finley J.) Shepard, who left the national YWCA in disagreement over the liberalization of its religious requirement, or Alice Vanderbilt (Mrs. Dave H.) Morris, who opposed its increasingly progressive policies.[13]

Just as it is important to differentiate between the volunteer members of the National Board and its paid staff members, it is useful to look at the parallel differences in the local associations. It is in the locals that one finds the membership of the organization. The YWCA did experiment, with some women in isolated areas having direct membership with the national organization, but for the most part, membership was through a local group. Members joined the YWCAs through classes and activities. Clubs and councils were supposed to be self-governing experiences in group development as well as conducive to individual growth. There was also a larger constituency of people who participated in individual activities but who did not sign up for membership.

At different points in the YWCA's history, there were intermediary structures known as "field" or "regional" or "state organizations" which varied in terms of how much they were controlled by the locals or the national body. Regional divisions at the present time still govern the election of National Board members.

Before turning to suggestions of repositories that have collections of interest to those researching the YWCA, a few tips may be offered.

Andrea Hinding's guide to collections, though dated, is an excellent place to start.[14] She lists more than 170 collections that have material on the YWCA; there are even more collections when one looks for individuals active in the YWCA or affiliated groups that had a YWCA connection. References to articles in smaller journals and unpublished theses can be found in Karen J. Blair, *The History of American Women's Voluntary Associations*, and Janet Sims, *The Progress of Afro-American Women*.[15]

Before going to a repository, be sure to check on the access policy for the collection. In some cases, permission from the local association is required. Be aware that even computerized finding aids are not always up-to-date and that collections move. Grace Towns Hamilton's papers, for instance, are no longer at Atlanta University; they are at the *Atlanta Historical Society*.

Other scholars researching the YWCA are a good source for suggestions of possible collections or resources like unpublished theses; while Ph.D. dissertations are relatively easy to find, the YWCA has served as the basis for a vast number of M.A. theses that are frequently inaccessible through standard reference tools. Increasing help is available through the Internet. A number of collections now make finding aids accessible through Web sites. There are a growing number of "bulletin boards" or "list servs" that periodically post queries and references for the YWCA. Check out ones for women's history, women's studies, American studies, American religion, and the welfare state, to suggest just a few.

There is an increasing number of automated tools to use when researching the YWCA, not the least of which is the Research Libraries Information Network (RLIN), which contains information on books and periodicals as well as archival holdings.[16] A reminder of the literal nature of computerized searches may be necessary here. While there was always some variations in the old-fashioned card catalogs, those variations have a greater impact in a reference tool that looks only for what you precisely ask for. It is necessary to check under both author and subject. It is essential to keep in mind that material may be listed under *any* of the following and *not* cross-referenced:

Young Women's Christian Association[17]

Women's and Young Women's Christian Association

Y.W.C.A.

Y W C A

YWCA

YW

Y

National Board of the YWCA

Women's Christian Association

Local associations may be indexed as City X YWCA, not the YWCA of City X.

World YWCA has a number of references to the YWCA of the U.S.A. in RLIN misfiled under the world body.

World's YWCA

Check under organizations mentioned in this essay such as affiliated organizations, predecessors, or subdivisions, such as the National Student Council of the YWCA, Girl Reserves, and so on.

It is essential, when looking for information on the YWCA, to look under "YMCA," "Y.M.," "Young Men's Christian Associations," and so on. Items are misfiled or there are typos where material that is clearly for the YWCA has been filed or listed under the YMCA. Because many assume the two organizations to be the same group, namely, the YMCA, material for both organizations is sometimes placed with the YMCA entry. If someone skimped on indexing, they usually noted only the YMCA.

Even properly filed material may include information about the YWCA. Historically, as parallel organizations, the YWCA and YMCA sent representatives to each other's conventions and frequently tracked what the other was doing. Some constituent groups, such as college students or high school Tri-Y and Hi-Y clubs, worked closely together. In some larger community associations, the YMCA and YWCA worked jointly on major projects, fundraising, and war-relief efforts. In areas with limited resources, such as rural locations and smaller cities, YMCAs and YWCAs sometimes shared facilities and staff. And, in the extreme case, some YWCAs merged with YMCAs, even though this led to their disaffiliation from the National YWCA. The YMCA permits women as members, so its records will have information on women in the YMCA, a separate but related issue. There have been a number of periods, especially in the late 1920s and early 1960s, when the two organizations discussed merging.

It may be useful to distinguish between the structure of the YWCA and the YMCA. In spite of the similar names, there were critical structural differences between the two organizations within the national bodies and with the national vis-à-vis the locals.

The National Association

The *Archives of the National Board of the YWCA of the U.S.A.* (hereafter called the National YWCA Archives) is in New York City. It is open to advanced researchers, but limited referencing is possible by mail.[18] Although the archives has concentrated on the records of the national organization, it has supplemented them with the personal papers of board and staff members; these include diaries, speeches, news clippings, snapshots, scrapbooks, unpublished manuscripts, and memorabilia related to YWCA experiences. The archives also has some correspondence and reports from local associations submitted for accreditation. Visitation reports of the national staff discuss local performance in meeting national requirements and assess the implementation of specific policies or programs.

Beginning in 1964, many National Board official records for the time period 1876–1960 were microfilmed. The guide, with an index, to the almost 300 reels of microfilm, *Inventory to the Records Files Collection of the National Board of the Young Women's Christian Association*, was prepared by Louisa Bowen in 1978.[19] The 300+-page finding aid is available at scattered libraries around the country. The guide includes a seven-page history that assists researchers in positioning their subjects within the total time frame and organizational structure of the YWCA. The reel headings contains useful information about the history and structure of the YWCA and are well worth scanning. After the original microfilming, a schedule was developed to film newly generated material at ten-year intervals, but with less detailed subject indexing. There are additional indexes, inventories, and card catalogs at the National YWCA Archives.

It is important to note that not all materials were filmed; some remain in hard copy only and are not indexed in Bowen's *Inventory to the Records Files Collection*. These include some periodicals and departmental, committee, and subject files, as well as materials collected after 1960. Of particular interest are the public affairs files that document the YWCA's involvement in social and political issues. Some of this material is available only on a restricted basis. Copies of M.A. and Ph.D. theses on the YWCA have sometimes been sent to the National YWCA Archives.

The YWCA of the U.S.A. holds a photograph collection of over 23,000 images. These illustrate the YWCA's activities both in the United States and abroad. Images document YWCA buildings, war work efforts, YWCA members socializing at conferences, women engaging in nontraditional occupations, people being trained in other countries, and scenes revealing social problems. There is a subject index for the collection.

Beginning in 1993, the YWCA sponsored a touring exhibit on its history utilizing these visual documents. The exhibit opened at the National Museum for Women in the Arts in Washington, DC, and has continued to be shown in communities throughout the country. There is a catalog with vivid images and historical information on the association.[20] One can contact the YWCA of the U.S.A. for the exhibit schedule.

The complete holdings of one of the first publishing houses owned and operated by women, The Womans Press, form an integral part of the National YWCA Archives. Its catalogs cite hundreds of titles dealing primarily with women's issues, ranging from small pamphlets to hardcover books. The press was organized in 1918, when trade publishers told the YWCA that they were not interested in publishing books about women. It was sold to a subsidiary of Doubleday in 1954.

The YWCA conducted studies and surveys of issues that were sometimes formally published either by the YWCA itself or by other houses. The 1932 *International Survey of the Young Men's and Young Women's Christian Associations* was published by the International Survey Committee,[21] while Annie Marion MacLean's 1910 study *Wage-Earning Women* was published by a mainstream press.[22] The latter was the result of a study commissioned by the National Board of the YWCA that went well beyond analyzing what the YWCA was doing in the field.

Other holdings include the complete files of the national house organ from 1907 to the present, with the title changing about every twenty years: *Association Monthly* (1907–1922) (be careful not to confuse it with the YMCA publication of the same name), *Womans Press* (1922–1945), *Woman's Press* (1945–1950), *The YWCA Magazine* (1951–1973), and *YWCA Interchange* (1974–present).[23] Since the first recorded announcement of a YWCA magazine in June 1874, "leaders have pinned extravagant hopes on four or five slim pages of printed propaganda."[24] By 1996, the slim pages had mushroomed into 137 different serials, each intended to facilitate communication between the disparate associations. Locals had their own periodicals, as did some of the constituent groups, such as the Girl Reserve national newsletter, *Bookshelf*.

Publications generated for the national conventions, although frequently condensed, represent a useful source of information. Each convention usually included a *Report of the National Board* for the preceding time period, *Guiding Principles and Emphases*, with suggestions for the ensuing time period, *Proceedings of the Convention* (sometimes broken down into "Business Sessions" and "Services and Addresses"), and *Actions of the Convention*. More complete transcripts of some conventions are available on microfilm. Advance materials, issued to prepare delegates for the decision-making operations of the convention, are similarly available.

In 1984, the National Board of the YWCA of the U.S.A. built a Leadership Training Center in Phoenix, Arizona. The expressed purpose of the center was to provide state-of-the-art technological capabilities for training YWCA personnel: a television studio, simultaneous language translation, an electronic audience response system, an on-site satellite uplink, editing equipment, and professional staffing. In storage were hundreds of outdated films and audiotapes, reels of untranscribed oral interviews, large radio station discs of YWCA commercials from the 1950s and 1960s, phonograph records used in training programs, and slide presentations of conventions and other meetings. When technological updating is completed, the historical content may be evaluated. A video lending library is already in operation in Phoenix.

Some originals for the National Board's microfilmed material were donated to the *Sophia Smith Collection at Smith College*, Northampton, Massachusetts. The twenty-six linear feet of correspondence, minutes, reports, conference proceedings, publications, case studies, speeches, and other records are divided into subject series, including Business and Professional, Industrial, World War I (primarily War Work Council), Health, Immigration, International Institutes, Employment and Unemployment, Interracial Work, Household Employment, and World War II (mainly Japanese relocation). An inventory is available from the Sophia Smith Collection, and material donated to Smith has been so indicated in Bowen's *Inventory to the Records Files Collection*.[25] It is worth consulting the originals at Smith; the microfilm copy is often hard to read, and in some cases, the back sides of documents do not appear to have been microfilmed.

A number of repositories have materials for the National YWCA. Published materials, including periodicals, convention materials, and publications printed by the Womans Press, can be found in public and research libraries or those at women's colleges and divinity schools. It is helpful to think of the different ways the YWCA might be categorized to identify logical collections. It is a women's organization, an urban institution, a religiously affiliated body, and a social welfare group. Not surprisingly, repositories concentrating on those topics have YWCA collections. The *Schlesinger Library, Radcliffe College* and the Sophia Smith Collection, as women's archives, are logical places to start. So are those archives that concentrate on urban topics: including the *Urban Archives* at *Temple University*, Philadelphia, or the *Urban Archives Center at the California State University*, Northridge. Various libraries at *Yale University*, especially the one for the *Divinity School*, have collections dealing with religious issues and the YWCA's mission work overseas. Material at Yale can also be found in the China Records Project and the World Student Christian Federation. The *Social Welfare History Archives, University Libraries, University of Minnesota* has the records of the National Board's participation in the United Service Organizations, Inc. (USO), beginning in World War II, as well as materials for the Minneapolis YWCA and the Mount Vernon (NY) YWCA; it also contains evidence of YWCA involvement with other groups like the National Social Welfare Assembly (earlier, the National Social Work Council), the National Association of Social Workers and its predecessors, and the National Association of Travelers Aid Societies.

For information on immigrants, check the *Immigration History Research Center at the University of Minnesota*. Information on African American women's involvement with the YWCA can be found in collections at the *Woodruff Library, Atlanta University Center*, which holds papers for the Neighborhood Union, Lugenia Burns Hope, and the Commission on Interracial Cooperation. There are a significant number of M.A. theses done at Atlanta University on the YWCA.

Funders of the YWCA are also a useful place to look for materials. The Dodge family, the Russell Sage Foundation, and Rockefeller-affiliated foundations, especially the Rockefeller Foundation, the Davison Fund, and the Laura Spelman Rockefeller Memorial, have all been major contributors to the YWCA. Abby Aldrich Rockefeller was a longtime National Board member, an authority on wartime housing for women, and chairwoman of the Grace Dodge Hotel in Washington, DC. Records for Abby Rockefeller, the Rockefeller-affiliated foundations, and the Russell Sage Foundation can be found at the *Rockefeller Archive Center* in North Tarrytown, NY. Other female philanthropists who supported the YWCA were Grace Dodge, Helen Gould Shepard, Olivia Phelps Stokes, Jessie Woodrow Wilson Sayre, and Elisabeth Luce Moore. There was some money from Julius Rosenwald, but most of his emphasis was on the YMCA.

There is an interplay to be found between the national body and local associations; studying locals allows one to examine how programs or policies mandated by the national body were actually implemented.[26] There is a similar interplay in the records. Local associations contain materials disseminated by the national, while some information on local associations can be found in repositories with national sources. Most material generated by the locals stayed with them, often to be lost or destroyed over the years. Other locals have carefully preserved their papers, arranging them for access to users. The YWCAs in *New York City* and *Elizabeth, NJ*, have finding aids. In other cases, the records have been donated to repositories. Schlesinger Library has the collections for the Boston and Cambridge, MA, YWCAs. Some collections have been placed in local historical societies or libraries; the files for the La Crosse, WI, YWCA can be found in the *La Crosse Public Library*, and the metropolitan St. Louis YWCA records are in the *Western Historical Manuscript Collection at the University of Missouri–St. Louis*. Local schools may document campus and/or urban YWCAs, known as "city" or "community YWCAs." The Durham YWCA records are in the *Women's Studies Archives at Duke University*, and the campus YWCA (and YMCA) records are available in the *Duke University Archives*. While records most often stay locally, there are exceptions, such as the presence of the Mt. Vernon, *New York*, YWCA files in the Social Welfare History Archives in Minnesota or various local records found in the *Tennessee State Archives*, Nashville.

Even when libraries or historical associations are not the repositories for associations' papers, they frequently have invaluable information. Check their vertical files and newspaper morgues, if they exist, for material that may include annual reports, brochures, and clippings. Before the Second World War, YWCAs were recognized community organizations. Local papers reported on their social activities, public affairs programs, and classes. The *Brooklyn Public Library*, Brooklyn, NY, has the clipping files for the *Brooklyn Daily Eagle*, which saved material from the *Eagle* and nearby newspapers, including small papers no longer in existence. The activities of African American YWCAs were covered by African American newspapers such as the *Pittsburgh Courier*, available at the *Historical Society of Western Pennsylvania*, Pittsburgh. In addition to looking at individual newspapers, see the papers of Claude A. Barnett and the Associated Negro Press at the *Chicago Historical Society*. The *State Historical Society of Wisconsin* in Madison is working on a project, "African-American Newspapers and Periodicals: A National Bibliography and Union List," that will permit researchers to identify the locations for over 5,000 periodicals. Local and regional history and oral history projects may include information on various aspects of the YWCA.

Predecessor associations bore different names. The YWCA of New York City was an offshoot of the Ladies Christian Association. "Women's" or "Woman's Christian Association" were common names. In looking for the records of local associations, keep in mind that while the documentation for board of director meetings for a local association may be retained by the association, information kept by board members themselves may be more likely found in personal papers. The office files generated by the staff may well be retained by the association.

Before 1950, with the encouragement and occasional guidance of the National Board, local associations conducted surveys or studies of the communities in which they were based. Topics included demographics and statistics, working conditions, the situation of specialized groups, and so on. These surveys or studies may have been done in conjunction with other social welfare organizations. Their findings may be available in local libraries and historical societies. They give insight into how the YWCA saw the community in which it operated, sometimes analyzing its own role. As early as the 1880s, local YWCAs joined with other social welfare groups in umbrella organizations intended to coordinate their activities and make them more efficient.[27] The YWCA in Chicago was a member of the Welfare Council of Metropolitan Chicago, whose records are in the Chicago Historical Society.

While the emphasis on physical buildings seems to have been more of a priority of the YMCA, local YWCAs were proud of their facilities as well. The files of architects and builders contain material on YWCAs. The renowned architect Julia Morgan designed fifteen YWCA buildings in California. She planned the spectacular conference grounds for the YWCA, Asilomar, on 105 acres on the Monterey Peninsula. Buildings required a major fundraising campaign. For these efforts, associations usually turned to professional fund raisers. The *Ruth Lilly Special Collections and Archives at Indiana University–Purdue University* in Indianapolis has the papers of a number of prominent fundraising firms that have worked with YMCAs and YWCAs since the early twentieth century.

For ongoing funding, YWCAs relied on dues and local donors. After World War I, they increasingly relied on local funding agencies. During the Progressive Era, many charities and philanthropies had federated together in umbrella bodies.[28] The YWCA worked with the Community Chest/Council and the United Way and their predecessors. The history of the YWCA indicates a sometimes troubled relationship with the Community Chest, either because the Community Chest did not understand their role or because the Chest felt that YWCAs were too progressive. Collections for these organizations may consist not only of applications with valuable financial information but also of annual reports or periodicals intended for the public. The records for the Community Fund of Chicago, a predecessor of the United Way, are at the *University of Illinois at Chicago Circle Library, Manuscript Collections* and offer information on the Chicago YWCA and the Phyllis Wheatley Association. These umbrella funding agencies sometimes had connections to the groups intended to coordinate social welfare agencies' programs; the Community Fund of Chicago merged with the Welfare Council of Metropolitan Chicago to form the United Way for Chicago.

Work done by, with, and for African American women and girls at the local level was frequently carried out by branches. Sometimes simply referred to as the "colored branch," they often bore the name of their street or of an individual. When an individual's name was used, it was usually that of an African American woman deemed to be of historical or political importance. While Phyllis, occasionally spelled "Phillis," Wheatley was the most common choice, it was by no means the only one; other women include Sojourner Truth (Newark, NJ), Mary McCleod Bethune (Sumter, SC), and Susie B. Dudley (Greensboro, NC). Some groups started in the First World War were known as "Blue Triangle Centers" or "Branches," but not all Blue Triangles were race-based.

In some cities, including Chicago, Cleveland, and St. Paul, the organization bearing the name "Phyllis Wheatley" was not directly linked to the YWCA, although there were informal connections. Jane Edna Hunter of the Phyllis Wheatley Association in Cleveland was in contact with the African American leadership of the YWCA in New York City; see records in the *Western Reserve Historical Society* in Cleveland.

While the focus of this book on the urban setting might suggest not bothering with campus YWCAs, this would be a mistake. Student associations in the first part of the twentieth century were involved in settlement or settlement-like activities. Someone researching industrial women, for instance, may want to look for information on the "Students-in-Industry" program that sent students into factories as workers from the 1920s to the 1940s. In the 1950s and 1960s, some campus Ys were able to raise controversial community issues, such as integration, because they were less bound by the constraints of local funding.[29] The diversity of their programs may be reflected in how the records are kept. The Christian Associations[30] of the University of Pennsylvania sent their settlement work projects to the Urban Archives at Temple, but the rest of their materials stayed at the *University of Pennsylvania Archives*. Since they have more recently become involved with programs for the homeless, even these later records have information on urban America. Likewise, the Duke campus association records reflect involvement with local churches in disadvantaged areas of Durham.

In the early twentieth century, YWCAs were one of the most popular student organizations on campus, as witnessed by accounts in student newspapers and yearbooks. Some of their services were later taken over by the colleges themselves. It was not unusual for the Dean of Girls/Women to have been the YWCA secretary. Participation in YWCAs declined as denominationally based religious groups gained popularity on campus, as did nonreligious groups. Prior to this decline, campus YWCAs were one source of training for women who would go into community YWCA work. This seems especially true for students at the traditionally African American schools.

For information on student associations, check for records of the National Student Council YMCA and YWCA, the National Intercollegiate Christian Council, and the National Student Assembly YMCA and YWCA, as well as the World Student Christian Federation and the Student Volunteer Movement. These groups had their own publications, like *The Intercollegian*, a YMCA magazine with an occasional mention of the YWCA.

The papers for individual women are an invaluable source of material about the YWCA; they may include information not found in official organization reports. A reference librarian can point one to the tools that make searches more efficient. Many guides, including the *Biography and Genealogy Master Index*, published by Gale, are now available on CD-ROM or on-line, greatly enhancing search capabilities. In the case of wealthy funders and board members, it is worthwhile to check their male relatives' involvement in the YMCA. Men of a family were active with the YMCA, while women were active with the YWCA. This is true of both the Dodge and Rockefeller families. In many cases, women's papers are often filed with their husbands' papers and are not always cataloged.

The women's history archives are a good source for papers of women who were active in the YWCA. The Sophia Smith Collection holds the papers of influential local, national, and international secretaries like Ruth Woodsmall, World YWCA Chief Executive from 1935 to 1947; Eleanor Coit, an expert on workers' education; and foreign secretaries Ruth Hill (Liberia), Virginia Heim George (Latin America), and Bessie Bois Cotton (Russia). Schlesinger has additional papers for Eleanor Coit, as well as the recently accessioned collection for Winnifred Wygal, who was active in student work and social action projects.

For those women whose documents have not always been retained, a number of oral history projects include information on the YWCA. One of the more notable efforts has been the Black Women Oral History Project of the Schlesinger Library. A published index, as well as the transcripts, are available in libraries.[31] Another such project, the "Regional Oral History" series, has been conducted by the *Bancroft Library of the University of California at Berkeley*. The section on volunteer leadership contains interviews with YWCA people, both employed and volunteer leaders. Check the library for a list of participants and to purchase transcripts.

The female networks found in the YWCA have provided a challenge for researchers interested in women's private lives and the history of sexuality. Many of the women on the staffs remained single their whole lives while creating lifetime commitments to other women, who themselves may have been active with the YWCA. Only recently have catalogers been willing to identify some of the relationships as "lesbian" rather than identifying them under more innocuous categories such as "friendships."

A final challenge for those researching individual women involves studying the membership. Studies to date have creatively used the records generated by staff or board members to determine the interests and activities of women and girls who usually did not leave their own records or, at least, did not leave them at the YWCA. Some members became sufficiently active with the YWCA so that one can find their views in comments at meetings or in articles in YWCA periodicals; how representative they were of the larger membership is a question that must be asked. Finding the voices of average members, or of those women and girls who tried an activity but never joined, is more difficult. Some of the items retained by the YWCAs, such as club records, yearbooks, or scrapbooks, may be useful. There are a few autobiographical or fictional accounts that offer some perspective: see Nella Larsen's *Quicksand* or Dorothy Richardson's *The Long Day*.[32] On the whole, however, this area requires both creative research and informed speculation.

It is worthwhile to check groups with which the YWCA worked. In the case of the United States government, these included the National Youth Administration and the Women's Bureau. The YWCA contributed to war work during both world wars through governmental and private agencies. During World War I, the YWCA was an official affiliate of the Commission on Training Camp Activities (a federal agency) and provided Hostess Houses which developed recreational opportunities for male soldiers and sailors and established centers to meet the needs of female workers.[33] It was a member of the United War Work Campaign, an umbrella group of voluntary organizations which raised money during the First World War. In 1941, the YWCA joined other voluntary associations to help found the USO, another umbrella group. The YWCA was the only women's organization in both the United War Work Campaign and the USO.

The network of women active in supporting the Women's Bureau also worked with groups such as the Committee on the Cause and Cure of War, the Women's Joint Congressional Committee, and the National Council of Women. Business clubs in the YWCA were instrumental in founding the National Federation of Business and Professional Women in 1919. YWCA activities with industrial women declined after World War II. Up to then, the YWCA played a role with working women. An important part of this effort was the YWCA's support for the educational programs of the Bryn Mawr Summer School for Women Workers in Industry and the Southern Summer School for Women Workers, as well as other labor schools like Brookwood, WI, and Barnard College, NY. Such programs were coordinated through the American Labor Education Service, whose long-time director was Eleanor Coit, a former YWCA secretary. The National YWCA worked with the Women's Trade Union League, although some member associations working closely with local industrialists were hostile to union efforts.

YWCAs were involved with social purity groups. At the national level, women helped to found the American Social Hygiene (later Health) Association in 1912 and the National Association of Travelers Aid Societies in 1917; records for both are at the Social Welfare History Archives. As suggested in the essays in this book, support of the "physical, social, intellectual, moral and spiritual interests of young women" could lead in repressive directions. Historians studying some local associations have found overlaps between YWCA membership and groups like the women's auxiliary of the Ku Klux Klan.[34] On the other hand, research on the campaigns against lynching indicate an overlap in membership between organizations like the Association of Southern Women for the Prevention of Lynching and local YWCAs.[35] The diversity and autonomy of local associations make characterization—either positive or negative— of the politics and attitudes of *all* members or associations impossible.

Women from the YWCA had ties to other religious bodies, including the Federal Council of Churches. The FCC was reorganized in 1950 as the National Council of the Churches of Christ, and the YWCA held an affiliate position with it. The YWCA joined umbrella groups of women's missionary societies conducting work domestically and/or overseas. While the YWCA was strongest among Protestant women, Jewish and Catholic women were involved as participants in programs, if not as members.[36] One may find some documentation on this in the records of local Catholic and Jewish organizations resisting involvement of their young people in the YWCA and YMCA, but also check the records for the International Institutes.

As noted in Raymond Mohl's essay in this volume, beginning in 1910, Edith Terry Bremer oversaw the YWCA's work in immigrant communities through its settlement-like International Institutes. In 1933, Bremer created the National Institute of Immigrant Welfare, a forerunner of today's American Council for Nationalities Service; most Institutes split away from the YWCA. Records for International Institutes can be found in collections of immigrant history such as the one in Minnesota, rather than at the YWCA. In 1978, Nicholas Montalto prepared a guide to these records entitled *The International Institute Movement*.[37] The professional papers of Ludmila Kuchar Foxlee, a second-generation national YWCA secretary assigned to Ellis Island for seventeen years, are now in the *Ellis Island–Statue of Liberty Archives*, New York City. An eighteen-page finding aid is available in the National YWCA Archives. References to YWCA work may be found in collections indexed under International Institutes. *Be careful not to confuse them with a different organization— the International Institute for Industrial Relations.*

Over the years, the YWCA worked with a number of organizations focusing on African Americans. Information on the YWCA can be found in the records of the National Association for the Advancement of Colored People at the *Library of Congress, Manuscript Division* and at the Urban League.[38] One of the founders of the National Urban League was George Haynes. His wife, Elizabeth Ross Haynes, was one of the early African American national staff members and the first African American to serve on the National Board of the YWCA. The papers of Lugenia Burns Hope reveal interactions between the YWCA and the National Association of Colored Women, as the latter tried to pressure the YWCA to improve its racial policies. Dorothy Height, longtime President of the National Council of Negro Women (NCNW), was a professional staff member of the National Board of the YWCA for twenty-nine years until her retirement in 1976 as Director of the Center for Racial Justice. The bulk of her papers have been deposited at the *Bethune Museum and Archives* in Washington, DC. The NCNW was, in fact, founded at the African American branch of the New York City YWCA in 1935.

In 1894, representatives of the national YWCAs from Great Britain, Norway, Sweden, and the United States founded the World's (as of 1955, the World) YWCA.[39] Now incorporating work in over ninety countries, it has records of and reports on and by many national associations. These provide an international context for the YWCA of the U.S.A. In addition, women from the United States played important roles in the operation of the world body. The *World YWCA Archives* in Geneva is open to researchers, but the staff is too small to fill research requests from individuals.[40]

A final suggestion is to research YWCAs in other countries. Many national YWCAs were supported by the YWCA of the U.S.A. Women from those countries visited the United States and spoke to local associations. For their part, local associations sent staff and money to countries around the world. Addresses for YWCAs outside the United States may be found in the current directory of the World YWCA. A growing number of scholars are researching the YWCAs in countries other than the United States, especially Canada, England, Denmark, Germany, China, Australia, and New Zealand; their bibliographies indicate the locations for materials. The records for the YWCA of Great Britain are in the *Modern Records Centre, University Library, University of Warwick* in Coventry, England.

Conclusion

Mary Beard's recognition of the importance of papers and records in writing history, along with the importance of history to social progress, resonates in the scores of articles, theses, and books written about the YWCA. Many have chosen to examine the YWCA as a way to engage the issues of class, race, religion, age, sexuality, and gender, reflecting the concerns of their own day along with those of their historical subjects. The essays in this volume suggest the range of issues that can be illuminated by the YWCA. As scholars in the future come to this material, they will raise new issues and questions and reexamine old ones. And the records of the YWCA will be there to be used. Enjoy delving into them!

NOTES

1. Mary Ritter Beard, letter to Dorothy Porter (March 31, 1940), quoted in Nancy F. Cott, "'Enlightenment Respecting Half the Human Race': Mary Beard and Women's History," in *Revealing Women's Life Stories: Papers From the 50th Anniversary Celebration of the Sophia Smith Collection, Smith College, Northampton, Massachusetts* (Northampton: Smith College, 1995), 37.

2. Anne Firor Scott, *Natural Allies: Women's Associations in American History* (Urbana: University of Illinois Press, 1991), 2.

3. *Report of the First Biennial Convention of the Young Women's Christian Associations of the United States of America* (New York City, 1906), 13.

4. *Women First for 135 Years, 1858–1993: An Exhibition of YWCA Historic Photographs and Memorabilia* (New York: YWCA of the U.S.A., 1993), inside cover.

5. Kristen Golden, "Prema Mathai-Davis," *Ms.*, v.6, #4 (January/February 1996): 61.

6. Grace H. Wilson, *The Religious and Educational Philosophy of the Young Women's Christian Association: A Historical Study of the Changing Religious and Social Emphases of the Association as They Relate to Changes in its Educational Philosophy and to Observable Trends in Current Religious Thought, Educational Philosophy, and Social Situations* (New York City: Teachers College, Columbia University, Bureau of Publications, 1933), 38, 77–78, 113, 115; Mary Frederickson, "The Southern Summer School for Women Workers," *Southern Exposure*, v.4, #4 (Winter 1977): 71–72; and Frances Sanders Taylor, "'On the Edge of Tomorrow': Southern Women, the Student YWCA, and Race, 1920–1944" (Ph.D. dissertation, Stanford University, 1984), 83–84.

7. Anna Arnold Hedgeman, *The Trumpet Sounds: A Memoir of Negro Leadership* (New York: Holt, Rinehart, and Winston, 1963), esp. 74–78.

8. Early membership rules restricted voting membership to members of evangelical Protestant churches. This was at a time when "evangelical" had a broader meaning than it does now. The most commonly represented denominations were those regarded as mainline Protestant: Baptist, Congregationalist, Methodist, Presbyterian, and Episcopalian.

9. William R. Hutchinson has suggested that overseas Protestant missionary work ended up resembling the kinds of programs that today we expect from the Peace Corps; see his *Errand to the World: American Protestant Thought and Foreign Missions* (Chicago: University of Chicago Press, 1987).

10. Martha Foote Crow, *The American Country Girl* (New York: Frederick Stokes, 1915).

11. The International Board was known earlier as the International Conference of Women's Christian Associations (1877–1891) and then as the International Board of Women's Christian Associations (1891–1893).

12. The American Committee was initially known as the National Association of the Young Women's Christian Associations of the United States

(1886–1889) and then as the International Committee of Young Women's Christian Associations (1889–1899).

13. "Mrs. Shepard Quits Board of the Y.W.C.A.—Disapproved of Progressive Platform of the National Convention at Cleveland," *New York Times*, April 18, 1920, 9.

14. Andrea Hinding, ed., *Women's History Sources: A Guide to Archives and Manuscript Collections in the United States* (New York: R. R. Bowker, 1979), two volumes.

15. Karen J. Blair, *The History of American Women's Voluntary Associations, 1810–1960: A Guide to Sources* (Boston: G. K. Hall, 1989), and Janet Sims, *The Progress of Afro-American Women: A Selected Bibliography and Resource Guide* (Westport, CT: Greenwood Press, 1980).

16. Note that a number of RLIN records for the YWCA include as the location "NYHV" (Cornell University New York Historical Resource Center). This does not represent a location, but rather a records survey project that located records throughout New York State. If the actual location is not clear from the body of the entry, a researcher can consult the project's guides, available in libraries throughout the state.

17. YWCAs were not always consistent or uniform about whether they used "Woman" or "Women" and, in the case of umbrella organizations, whether "Association" was used or "Associations."

18. Archives of the National Board of the YWCA of the U.S.A., 726 Broadway, New York, NY 10003 USA.

19. Louisa Bowen, *Inventory to the Records Files Collection of the National Board of the Young Women's Christian Association* (New York: National Board, YWCA, 1978).

20. *Women First for 135 Years.*

21. *International Survey of the Young Men's and Young Women's Christian Associations* (New York: International Survey Committee, 1932).

22. Annie Marion MacLean, *Wage-Earning Women* (New York: Macmillan, 1910).

23. There is a card catalog at the YWCA of the U.S.A. Archives that has some indexing for the periodicals.

24. Elizabeth D. Norris, "Putting It All Between Covers: A Short History of YWCA Magazines," *YWCA Magazine* (December 1973): 4–7.

25. The material at Smith has since been rearranged, so it does not necessarily follow the order indicated in Bowen's guide.

26. This point is made by Anne Firor Scott, about women's organizations in general, in her review of Theda Skocpol's *Protecting Soldiers and Mothers*; see Anne Firor Scott, "Discovering Women," *Contemporary Sociology*, v.22, #6 (November 1993): 778.

27. Associated Charities or Charity Organization Societies were founded in many cities to make charities more efficient and to prevent duplication, and especially to ensure that recipients did not collect from more than one organization.

28. "Federated" or "Federations" commonly appeared in the names of these organizations.

29. For example, see Doug Rossinow, "'The Break-through to New Life': Christianity and the Emergence of the New Left in Austin, Texas, 1956–1964," *American Quarterly*, v.46, #3 (September 1994): 309–340, esp. 314–315.

30. Student associations were often more likely than community YWCAs to work closely with male counterparts; their work is sometimes filed under "Christian Associations."

31. Ruth Edmonds Hill, ed., *The Black Women Oral History Project* (Westport, CT: Meckler, 1990), 10 volumes, and Ruth Edmonds Hill and Patricia Miller King, *Guide to the Black Women Oral History Project* (Westport, CT: Meckler, 1990).

32. Nella Larsen, *Quicksand* (New York: Knopf, 1928), chapter 5, and Dorothy Richardson, *The Long Day: The Story of a New York Working Girl, as written by herself* (New York: Century Co., 1905; reprinted in William L. O'Neill, ed., *Women at Work* [New York: Times Books, 1972]), chapter 11.

33. See Nancy K. Bristow, *Making Men Moral: Social Engineering during the Great War* (New York: New York University Press, 1996).

34. See, for instance, Kathleen M. Blee, *Women of the Klan: Racism and Gender in the 1920s* (Berkeley: University of California Press, 1991), 106, 143.

35. Jacquelyn Dowd Hall, *Revolt Against Chivalry: Jessie Daniel Ames and the Women's Campaign Against Lynching* (New York: Columbia University Press, 1979), 178.

36. The YWCA has moderated its initial membership requirements to permit Catholic and Jewish women to be eligible for all levels of membership and office.

37. Nicholas V. Montalto, comp., *The International Institute Movement: A Guide to Records of Immigrant Service Agencies in the United States* (St. Paul: Immigration History Research Center, University of Minnesota, 1978).

38. The NAACP records are also available on microfilm.

39. Anna V. Rice, *A History of the World's Young Women's Christian Association* (New York: The Woman's Press, 1947), and Carole Seymour-Jones, *Journey of Faith: The History of the World YWCA 1945–1994* (London: Allison and Busby, 1994).

40. World YWCA, 16, ancienne route, 1218 Grand Saconne, Geneva, Switzerland; telephone: 41-22-929-6040.

Index

Abbott, Edith, 114
Abbott, Grace, 114
Adair, Ward, 76
Adamic, Louis, 116, 117
Addams, Jane, 114
African American YMCA: and accommodationism, 141, 149, 152; athletic work of, 145, 146; in Atlanta, 147; branches, 162; in Brooklyn, 145; and character building, 139, 140, 146, 149; in Chicago, 151; and churches, 143, 144, 149; on college campuses, 140, 164; desegregation of, 152, 237; educational work of, 145, 147, 148, 167; growth of, 142; impact of migration on, 142–44; impact of urbanization on, 11, 142; interracial work of, 152, 239; leadership of, 11, 140, 141–45; manhood ideal of, 11, 12, 138, 139, 141, 142, 145–52; number of associations, 142; number of members, 142, 144; origins of, 11, 139–40; and racial advancement, xvi, 11, 12, 138, 139, 141, 148–52; religious work of, 145, 149; as safe haven, xvi, 11, 151; segregation of, xvi, 18, 139, 140, 147, 150, 151, 152; social work of, 148; and Talented Tenth, 141–45, 150; in Washington, D.C., 148. *See also* African American YWCA; Association for the Study of Negro Life and History; Du Bois, W. E. B.; Hunton, William A.; Moorland, Jesse E.; National Association for the Advancement of Colored People; racism; segregation; Urban League; Washington, Booker T.; Woodson, Carter G.
African American YWCA: affiliation of

branches, 172, 179, 189; in Baltimore,165, 166, 189; in Brooklyn, 165, 169, 189; in Charleston, S.C., 186 n. 14; city associations, 161, 165, 167–69, 171, 189; on college campuses, 161, 163–66, 181; in Columbia, S.C., 186 n. 14; committees on colored work, 172, 173, 183; Conference of Volunteer and Employed Workers in Colored YWCAs, 170; growth of, 13; Hostess Houses, 176–77; impact of migration on, 13; impact of World War I on, 13, 161, 176, 179–80; industrial clubs, 176, 179; leadership of, 168, 174–75, 177, 189; membership of domestic and factory workers, 162, 170; in New York City, 165, 169, 171, 189; origins of, 12, 161, 189; racial autonomy of, 12, 167; recreation work, 177; in Philadelphia, 170, 189; in St. Louis, 170; secretaries of, 12, 170, 175; segregation of, 18; services of, 12, 18; conducted southern industrial survey, 170; Talented Tenth, 177; volunteers of, 175; in Washington, D.C., 165–66, 189; white central boards, 175, 183; and women war workers, 177, 180. *See also* African American YMCA; Bowles, Eva del Vakia; Charlotte YWCA; Cleveland, African American YWCA; Hunton, Addie W.; National Association of Colored Women; Pittsburgh African American YWCA; Young Women's Christian Association
Agricultural and Mechanical College at Normal, Ala., 165
AIDS. *See* homosexual cruising at the YMCA; YMCA, gay subculture